DACHAU REVIEW

History of Nazi Concentration Camps: Studies, Reports, Documents

Edited by

Wolfgang Benz and Barbara Distel

published for the Comité International de Dachau, Brüssels

VOLUME I	1988

Contents

Editorial   1

Barbara Distel
29 April 1945   3
The Liberation of the Concentration Camp at Dachau

Hermann Weiss
Dachau and International Public Opinion   12
Reactions to the Liberation of the Camp

Wolfgang Benz
Between Liberation and the Return Home   32
The Dachau International Prisoners' Committee and the Administration of the Camp in May and June 1945

Max Mannheimer
Theresienstadt – Auschwitz – Warsaw – Dachau   55
Recollections

Eli A. Bohnen
The Shoe on the other Foot   93
An US Military Rabbi remembers the Liberation of Dachau Concentration Camp

David Max Eichhorn
Sabbath Service in Dachau Concentration Camp   96
Report on the First Week in May 1945 by an US Military Rabbi

Hermann Langbein
Work in the Concentration Camp System   106

Ladislaus Ervin-Deutsch
About Those who Survived and Those who Died 116
Auschwitz - Arrival and Departure ... Kaufering Labor Camp III

Constantin Goschler
Controversy about a Pittance 157
The Compensation of Forced Laborers from Concentration Camps by
Germany's Post-War Industry

Barbara Distel
In the Shadow of Heroes 177
The Struggle and Survival of Centa Beimler-Herker and Lina Haag

Anise Postel-Vinay
A Young Frenchwoman's Wartime Experiences 211

The Odyssey of the Women from Rhodes 234

© Verlag Dachauer Hefte, Alte Römerstrasse 75, 8060 Dachau
set and printed by Appl, Wemding (Federal Republic of Germany)
Price DM 25.- US $ 16.- UK £ 8.-

Contributors

Wolfgang Benz, historian, Institut für Zeitgeschichte (Institute for Contemporary History), Munich

Eli A Bohnen, rabbi, Providence, Rhode Island, USA

Ladislaus Ervin-Deutsch, Hungarian writer, formerly lived in Bucharest, now in Hamburg

Barbara Distel, director of the concentration camp memorial site at Dachau

David Max Eichhorn, rabbi, Satellite Beach, Florida, USA

Constantin Goschler, Munich

Hermann Langbein, publicist, secretary of the Comité International des Camps, Vienna

Max Mannheimer (ben jakov), artist, now living near Munich

Anise Postel-Vinay, member of the French resistance who was imprisoned in Ravensbrueck, lives in Paris

Hermann Weiss, historian, Institut für Zeitgeschichte (Institute for Contemporary History), Munich

Mary Ellen Bass (Frankfurt) translated the article by Hermann Weiss and the one by Barbara Distel on Centa Beimler-Herker and Lina Haag

Eva Kochen (Munich) corrected the proofs

Grace Mannheimer (Haar near Munich) translated Max Mannheimer's Memories

John Ormrod (Munich) translated the article by Anise Postel-Vinay

Herbert Otter (Heidelberg) and Susan Arase translated the article by Constantin Goschler, the one by Barbara Distel on 29 April 1945 and the report about the odyssey of the women from Rhodes

Wendy Philipson (Munich) co-ordinated the English manuscripts

Olaf Reinhardt (Sidney, Australia) translated the articles by Wolfgang Benz and Hermann Langbein and Ladislaus Ervin-Deutsch's Memoirs

Bruno Schachtner (Dachau) designed the cover

Acknowledgements

We wish to thank Jonathan David Publishers, INC, Middle Village, N.Y., USA for permission to reprint the articles by Rabbi Eichhorn and Rabbi Bohnen

Editorial

In spring 1933, immediately after Hitler's assumption of power, the first concentration camp was established at Dachau. Here the political opponents of the new regime were imprisoned and abused, here the terror system of the concentration camps was tried out and developed: Dachau was a testing ground for the SS and became the model for all the other concentration camps throughout the area controlled by Germany. And when from autumn 1944 the territory commanded by the NS state began to dwindle, it was to Dachau that the inmates of the other camps were evacuated – from Natzweiler, from Buchenwald, from Auschwitz and from almost all the other sites of terror convoys of prisoners came to Dachau. This was where the trail finally ended: the oldest concentration camp survived longer than almost all the others and was one of the last to be liberated by the Allies. And throughout the world the concentration camp at Dachau was seen as the epitome of the concentration camp system in the state created by Hitler.

Every year almost a million people from all over the world come to the memorial site at Dachau. There is clearly an interest in what happened here and in other camps, in the causes and background, and above all there is a desire for explanation, for elucidation, especially among younger visitors to Dachau and to other sites of persecution and extermination. Many people expressed the need to see in the Federal Republic a forum for information and documentation – comparable to the *Hefte* of Auschwitz or of Buchenwald – which would be available to all those able to make a serious, objective and important contribution to clarifying the historical background and thus also to preventing any repetition of National Socialist injustice.

Thus in 1985 the first volume of the yearly *Dachauer Hefte* appeared. The contents, which are organized thematically, are not restricted to the camp at Dachau and its immediate environment. The subtitle, "Studies and documents in the history of National Socialist concentration camps" indicates the character and range of the *Hefte*. It is intended to provide space for the publication of academic *studies* and for *documents* – reports, diaries and other authentic records describing the experience and fate of those persecuted under National Socialism.

The *Dachauer Hefte* are published under the moral authority of the Comité International de Dachau. The *Hefte* are intended both as an academic publication and as the mouthpiece of those who were persecuted and of those who offered resistance to the NS regime. The editors, who have no conflicting interests either in their function as editors or as the initiators of the *Dachauer Hefte,* vouch both for academic standards and for the authenticity of records published.

Many people have expressed regret that the *Dachauer Hefte* have so far appeared only in German. The *Dachau Review* is the first volume of a new periodical which contains in unabridged form in English the most important contributions of the previous three issues of the *Dachauer Hefte*. This first volume focusses on three main areas: the liberation in 1945 (concerned principally with Dachau itself), slave labor in the concentration camps in German territory, and the resistance and persecution of women in the National Socialist state.

The description of the liberation in 1945 (Barbara Distel), of international reactions to conditions in the camp (Hermann Weiss) and of problems after the liberation (Wolfgang Benz) are followed by the accounts of two eye witnesses, Rabbi Eli A Bohnen and Rabbi David Max Eichhorn, who both came to Dachau with the US army in April 1945. This section is completed with Max Mannheimer's account of the final stage of his period as a prisoner.

The part that slave labour played in the National Socialist ideology and in economic policies forms the second subject of this volume. The dual function of work – as a form of occupation and as a means of destruction – is examined by Hermann Langbein. Ladislaus Ervin-Deutsch recalls his nightly labours in construction in the underground factories at Dachau's subsidiary camp at Kaufering. In his article on the issue of compensation Constantin Goschler shows that the struggle for charity is still going on. Women as the victims of National Socialist persecution or as active participants in the struggle against a regime that tortured and killed opponents to it in the concentration camps form a subject that has been sadly neglected. Most of these women remained in the background, overshadowed by the heroes, and their suffering seems to have been more quickly forgotten than the men's. The general public has never become fully aware just how many women were victimized under the NS regime: imprisoned in the women's concentration camp at Ravensbrueck, in the earlier camps at Lichtenburg and Moringen, in the extermination camp Auschwitz-Birkenau, in ghettos, labor camps, in jails and penitentiaries and other sites of terror. But the persecution of women and the resistance they put up is a wide subject. Two articles here are devoted to three women active in resistance work. Centa Beimler-Herker and Lina Haag, who live in Munich, who were themselves active in resistance, were persecuted and who are both the widows of men who were in Dachau, put up a long struggle without gaining any recognition. They stand here for all those women who did not live according to the cliché of feminine passivity. So too, Anise Postel-Vinay, who as a young woman joined the French resistance and was as a result put into a German concentration camp. And finally four Jewish women, who were deported from Rhodes to Auschwitz in the summer of 1944, describe the journey that finally brought them to Dachau.

Wolfgang Benz   Barbara Distel

Barbara Distel
29 April 1945
The Liberation of the Concentration Camp at Dachau

The liberation of the concentration camp at Dachau by units of the US Army was a tremendously moving event for everyone involved. It marked the end of the camp's twelve-year history, a history of oppression and suffering, of misery and death, but also of resistance and survival, of tenacity and mutual support.
Attempting to approach the matter forty years later is not easy. At first glance it seems as though time had simply passed it by, as though the problems of 1985 had hardly anything in common with issues topical in 1945. Has the drama of those days retained its significance only for those few survivors celebrating the 40th anniversary of their liberation?
Dachau is the place where the 'SS State' began, which was to lead to the mass extermination of Auschwitz. But here too it fell, when on 29 April 1945, as the last but one of the concentration camps, it was liberated.
Today, as we inquire into the causes and conditions which made 'Dachau' and finally 'Auschwitz' possible, we must also tackle the problems of the disastrous end – that was at the same time a deliverance – which was the result of the twelve preceding years.
In attempting to reconstruct the course of events, the most important source of information is found in the reports of surviving prisoners written largely in the initial years after the liberation. Many of them are now out of print; others were never even published.[1] Through the liberators of the camp films and pictures were made available, illustrating that in the end the camp in Dachau looked just like all the other sites of the holocaust. The SS bureaucracy broke down in the spring of 1945. Although the camp files were kept up to the last day, in many instances incriminating evidence was destroyed at the last minute, so that documents which would have answered many as yet unresolved questions are no longer available.
In the last phase of the Second World War, when it became clear that the military defeat of the German army could no longer be avoided, the prisoners' situation and living conditions at Dachau concentration camp also changed drastically.

---

[1] On the territory of the former concentration camp at Dachau a memorial was erected in 1965. Affiliated to it are a library and an archive where all documents at all related to the history of Dachau concentration camp are collected.

By 1944, as an increasing number of concentration camp inmates were put to work in the factories of Germany's war industry, the number of work commandos and subsidiary camps had grown to over 120. In the winter of 1944/45 another 44 were added. At that time many of the 'old Dachauers', i.e. the German political prisoners, who had been imprisoned for a number of years, were kept in one of those subsidiary camps. Moreover, in November 1944, several hundreds of them were recruited for so-called 'probation units' and sent to the front, so that only very few prisoners lived to see the final months and the liberation of Dachau. In the end Polish and Soviet inmates accounted for the largest national groups.

The beginning of the last act of the Dachau drama, with its final toll of far beyond 15,000 lives, is marked by the outbreak of the typhus epidemic in December 1944, from which 3,000 prisoners had died by January 1945.

There was not enough room for the numerous patients, and conditions of hygiene were disastrous. There was no nutritious food, no dressings, and medication neither to prevent nor to treat the disease. Prisoner nurses and doctors fell victim to the epidemic, as did the inmates of other work commandos. The Dutch writer, Nico Rost, wrote in his secret diary, "... I have asked almost all doctors about the mortality rate in the case of typhus fever: under the age of 35 it hovers around 40%, over the age of 45 – and especially under the prevailing conditions – it is 80%. Moreover, in most cases other diseases, such as thrombosis, ear infections and paralysis complicate the situation even more ...".[2]

In the course of the winter of 1944/45 the situation continued to deteriorate through transports of prisoners arriving from other camps, which had been evacuated on account of approaching Allied troops. In January the first to be moved off westward – in an attempt to avoid the approaching Red Army – were the Auschwitz inmates. In March the inmates of the subsidiary camps situated around the Natzweiler camp in Alsace were evacuated and moved off eastward in an attempt to keep them from the Western Allies. Between January and March and until the end of April, when Dachau was the only concentration camp, except Mauthausen, that had not yet been liberated, thousands of prisoners arrived there. The conditions under which they arrived were always the same: totally exhausted human beings, who had marched for days and sometimes for weeks or who had been jammed in railroad cars, exposed to cold, hunger and disease, dragged themselves into the camp. But in Dachau there was neither adequate accomodation nor sufficient food; on the contrary, these arrivals only added to the devastating circumstances that already existed, and the number of deaths continued to grow. "The death lists are becoming longer and longer. At least four times a day I have to go and see the clerk of Block 30 – the sick block, which is

---

[2] Nico Rost, Goethe in Dachau, Berlin 1948. New Edition Hamburg 1981, p. 201.

nearly finished – to pick up a list of the most recent deaths ...", Nico Rost wrote in his diary on 4 March 1945.[3]

By that time the prisoners knew – as did their SS guards – that the fall of the SS empire was imminent, and that the days of Dachau concentration camp were also numbered. The Czechoslovakian clergyman Bedrich Hoffmann, who also secretly kept a diary, characterized the atmosphere in February 1945 as follows: "... The SS men who used to come up to the blocks to check on us made an effort to point out to the inmates that they always meant well with them and that in actuality they were their best friends ...".[4]

As far as the prisoners were concerned, these final weeks were a race against time, a race which thousands of them ended up losing. And apart from the question as to whether they would succeed in holding out until the liberators arrived – with food and medical treatment – they increasingly feared that there were plans to liquidate all prisoners. Rumors and conjectures circulated in the camp, and the fear that the SS would not even shy away from mass murder in order to eliminate the witnesses of their crimes grew stronger.

That an evacuation of the more than thirty thousand inmates would itself be a death sentence was something they had been made clear to them by the transports of evacuees from other camps all winter long. Of course they also asked themselves where the Dachau camp should be evacuated to anyway, after units of the Western Allies had already crossed the Rhine and finally the Danube as well. The representatives of the national prisoners' groups began to meet in secret in order to discuss how a possibly planned mass murder of the inmates could be prevented. At the time they could do nothing but wait, compile information and keep an eye on the SS.

Suddenly, at the end of March 1945, several hundred German clergymen were released. The reason why 170 others had to stay behind was not clear. On 4 April the Danish and Norwegian prisoners were handed over to the Swedish Red Cross. But in contrast to these hopeful events, was the fact that the executions continued and, above all, that the epidemic continued to spread, and that each additional day lowered the prospects of survival for the ill and weak.

For in Dachau, as in other concentration camps, there was a class system which spread the prospects of survival unevenly among the prisoners, in particular during the final phase. There was a small group of prisoners in privileged positions who did not suffer from hunger and therefore were not as prone to disease as others. On the one hand, the majority of the prisoners who worked in the various commandos were underfed, but in many cases they had held out until then by helping each other, for example, by sharing packages from the Red Cross. On the other hand, there was a steadily grow-

---

[3] Ibid, p. 194.
[4] Bedrich Hoffmann, A Kdo vás Zabije ..., Prerov 1946, unpublished translation by Ernest Bornefeld (Dachau Archive No. A.O. 031).

ing number of the so-called 'unassigned', who received smaller rations of food; these included the sick and those who, though they were not assigned to work, had to spend the day outdoors because they were not allowed to stay in the barracks.

As of mid-April, the cannon fire of the approaching front could be heard at Dachau camp. The SS had discontinued handing out the Red Cross's packages to the prisoners. At the camp's headquarters, documents were burned. SS squads on guard searched the inmates' huts. From Flossenbuerg and other camps the so-called special inmates were brought in to Dachau. They were prominent German opponents to the NS regime, above all from circles such as the resistance group '20 July 1944' and its supporters, who were taken into so-called 'Sippenhaft' custody (liability of all members of a family for the crimes of one member), high-ranking individuals of both the military and the Church from various countries and foreign politicians like Leon Blum and Kurt Schuschnigg and their wives. These prisoners – a group of special prisoners also existed at the Dachau camp – were kept separate and accomodated under much better conditions than the ordinary prisoners. Now they were just as uncertain about their fate and were fearful of falling victim to a fanatic 'Durchhalteideologie' (ideology of persistance) so shortly before the end. As late as 9 April some of the leading resistance fighters of the '20 July 1944' group were executed in Flossenbuerg.

On 23 April 1945 for the first time the work commandos no longer left the camp at Dachau. Towards noon the more than two thousand Jewish prisoners were ordered to stand formation on the parade ground and to get ready for march-off. "This means evacuation and they are going to start with the Jews...", Nico Rost wrote.[5] On that day the Jewish inmates did not leave the camp. They had to wait at the parade ground until the following day, when they were loaded into railroad cars, which by 26 April had still not left the site.

On 24 and 25 April, no evacuation marches left Dachau camp, but more than 2,000 survivors of a 'death march' from Hersbruck, a Flossenbuerg subsidiary camp, arrived. Now the prisoners impatiently waited for the almost daily air-raid warning, which would make a march-off impossible and with which they hoped to be able to delay the evacuation of the camp until the arrival of the liberators.

On 26 April, in spite of ever clearer indications that they were about to break up, by applying force the SS once again succeeded in maintaining their control over the camp at Dachau. Although the representatives of the national groups were determined to sabotage the evacuation of the camp in any way possible, and although those responsible for the various work commandos were taking advantage of the increasingly chaotic situation to delay the carrying out of orders by the SS and gain time, they had to follow the order issued

---

[5] Nico Rost, loc. cit., p. 227.

on the morning of 26, according to which the 'Reichsdeutschen' and Soviet prisoners, as well as the Jewish prisoners, also had to stand formation on the parade ground and get ready for march-off. By prolonging the distribution of the food rations, the departure could be delayed by hours; some of the prisoners even managed to hide, mainly in those huts the SS avoided for fear of contracting a disease. However, as becomes evident from statistics on the camp, 6,887 prisoners in groups of 1,500 had left the camp, with "Oetztal" as their destination. The prisoners themselves did not know to where they were going. It can no longer be ascertained how many of the prisoners died on this march. The survivors were not rescued by American soldiers until 2 May. "Joy and hope have vanished in the camp", a Belgian prisoner wrote after their departure.[6] A total of 137 of the prominent special prisoners were transported in buses and trucks. Their first stop was a camp of war prisoners near Innsbruck and, with the help of members of the German *Wehrmacht*, they were finally able to convince the SS men accompanying them that it would be best to hand over the well-known prisoners to the Allies unharmed.

At last, on 4 May, they were able to be taken over unharmed by units of the US Army at a hotel near Niederndorf in South Tyrol.[7] The last commander at Dachau also left the camp on 26 April. He drove to the castle at 'Itter', a Dachau subsidiary camp in the Tyrol, where he shot himself in the head on 27 April. Although additional evacuations were ordered on 27 and 28 April, the prisoners, ready for march-off, did not leave the camp. Again there was an airraid warning and most of the members of the SS began to leave Dachau quickly after having removed prisoners' valuables and undistributed Red Cross packages from the special storage room.

At the same time, several thousand prisoners arrived who were being evacuated from Dachau's subsidiary camps, and from Flossenbuerg and Buchenwald. Many of them died immediately upon arrival at the camp, others were so weakened that they simply collapsed on the parade ground. Once again, the situation regarding provisions deteriorated rapidly.

The representatives of the national prisoners' groups, who continued to meet in secret and discuss developments, at that point realized that the main goal was no longer to prevent the evacuation of the camp, but to survive on the remaining food until the arrival of the liberators, and to avoid panic. From then on, a group of prisoners guarded and patrolled the prisoners' huts. Yet the prisoners' fear of falling victim to a massacre by the SS persisted until the end. Almost all the reports written about the final days and the liberation of

---

[6] Arthur Haulot/Ali Kuci, Dachau, Brussels 1945. New Edition, Brussels 1985; unpublished translation by Gustav Görsch (Dachau Archive No. 10083), p. 18.

[7] Cf. Memories of this transport: 'Reise durch den letzten Akt', Isa Vermehren; Hamburg 1946. New edition Hamburg 1979, pp. 140; 'Von Preußen nach Europa, Lebenserinnerungen', Stuttgart 1968, pp. 174; 'The Venlo Incident', London 1950, pp. 221.

the concentration camp at Dachau mention that the prisoners gained knowledge of an order issued by Heinrich Himmler on 14 April 1945 to evacuate the camp immediately and to prevent any prisoner from falling into the hands of the enemy alive. It was not until after the end of the war that it became known that, apart from this order, at least two different plans for the extermination of the prisoners before the arrival of the Allies had existed.

On 27 April a representative of the International Red Cross was sent from the town of Uffing in Upper Bavaria to Dachau, on a mission personally to distribute food packages directly among the prisoners and to see to it that the camp be handed over to the Americans. However, the assistant to the camp's commander, who was still present, did not grant him permission to enter the protective custody camp.

On 28 April the noise of tanks coming from the city of Dachau could be heard at the camp. At the same time, by means of hidden radio sets, the prisoners were informed through repeated announcements on the radio that day about the 'liberation of Bavaria' (Freiheitsaktion Bayern),[8] calling for a peaceful handover of Munich to the US Army. It was not until after their liberation that the prisoners found out that those calls had actually caused the 'Dachau rebellion': here, too, a group of opponents to the regime had prepared for peaceful transition. Among them were prisoners from the concentration camps who had escaped work commandos located outside the camp and who had hidden in the city of Dachau. After a group of twenty to thirty men had occupied the city hall for a few hours they were surrounded by SS units. Most of the rebels were able to escape, six of them – among them three prisoners from concentration camps – were executed on City Hall Square.[9]

In the morning of 29 April, the prisoners found that the entire SS had apparently left. On one of the buildings in the vicinity of the neighboring SS camp a white flag could be seen. "The SS have put up a white flag! At the entrance of the camp. The excitement among us is indescribable. Anybody who can is running to 'the parade ground' from where the flag can be seen ...", Nico Rost wrote in his diary that morning.[10] However, the machine guns up on the watch towers were still manned and the feeling of being threatened had not yet disappeared.

The representatives of the national prisoners' groups, who in the meantime had formed the International Dachau Committee, no longer had to hide. "We are in permanent session. The first proclamation has been drafted. It calls on the comrades to remain calm. It appeals to them to stay in their blocks and wait for further instructions ...", the French prisoners' represen-

---

[8] 'Aufstand in Dachau', Adolf Maislinger, unpublished (Dachau Archive No. 7676).
[9] 'Die Sechs vom Rathausplatz', Hans Holzhaider, Dachau 1982.
[10] Nico Rost, loc. sit., p. 242.

tative, Edmont Michelet, reported.[11] In the course of the morning, the noise of approaching and departing tanks could be heard. At the same time, the prisoner Karl Riemer of Augsburg was attempting to make his way to the American commander of the small town of Pfaffenhofen approximately thirty kilometers away in order to direct his attention to the prisoners' desperate situation at Dachau concentration camp. On 26 April, along with a group of seventeen prisoners, he had escaped from the camp with the help of a squad in charge of emptying trash cans. Their mission was to go and get the Americans to come to the camp as quickly as possible. The group was separated on the way and when Karl Riemer finally reached Pfaffenhofen he was alone. In a report from 11 May 1945 he describes his encounter with the American commander at Pfaffenhofen: "He had me describe the situation from the moment the abduction in the mountains took place. I urged him to rescue the remaining prisoners in the camp and described the circumstances to him. Every moment was important and not a moment was to be lost ... After questioning me on a few matters concerning the reason why I had been sent to the camp, etc., he dismissed me, promising immediate help ...".[12]

Colonel Felix Sparks of the Third Battalion of the 157th Infantry Association of the 45th Infantry Division reported that he and his soldiers had been on their way to Munich when they were ordered via radio to first liberate the concentration camp at Dachau. Upon arrival, the first thing they found in the vicinity of the SS camp was a parked train of forty cars,[13] but not until they had approached did they realize that it was full of dead prisoners. Most likely it was the last evacuation transport from Buchenwald. The German prisoner Walter Leitner reported that among the approximately two thousand bodies, seventeen survivors were found,[14] but that the best medical treatment could not keep them alive. This atrocious discovery, even before reaching the prisoners' camp, most deeply shocked the American soldiers. Colonel L. Sparks reported that many of them broke out in tears or vomited, although they belonged to a battle-tried unit. Whether Colonel Sparks and his men were the first to climb over the walls of and arrive at the camp to liberate it, or General Linden, who came driving through the entrance gate with a vanguard of the 42nd Rainbow Division, among whom was also an American war correspondent, will be impossible now to prove with ultimate certainty.[15]

[11] 'Die Freiheitsstraße', Edmont Michelet, Stuttgart, no year (1960), p. 249.
[12] 'Amerikaner helfen', Karl Riemer, unpublished report from 11 May 1945 (Dachau Archive No. 7560).
[13] Felix L. Sparks 'Dachau and its Liberation', unpublished (Dachau Archive No. 20202). The figures on the number of train cars given in the various reports and publications vary considerably.
[14] 'Die letzten Tage im Konzentrationslager Dachau', Walter Leitner, unpublished (Dachau Archive No. 7675).
[15] Arthur Haulot/Ali Kuci, loc. sit.; Hermann Langbein: '... Nicht wie die Schafe zur Schlachtbank', Frankfurt 1980. In numerous reports written by prisoners, General Linden's arrival coincides with that of the American reporter.

Nico Rost depicted the arrival of the liberators as follows: "It started at three o'clock! The tormenting silence was suddenly broken by the noise of machine gunfire and the rattle of handguns, vigorously answered by firing from the SS watchtowers. The shooting was coming closer and closer and became increasingly fierce. I went to the death chamber and climbed onto the flat roof with the help of a ladder. Dr van D. already stood up there and even Steensma, despite having only one leg, came climbing up. The Americans were approaching! We could clearly see them in the distance in the bushes! They were approaching extremely slowly and carefully, their machine guns in firing position, every now and then aiming at the SS watchtowers, from which they were fiercely fired at, despite the white flags and rags ... It was 5.28 sharp – according to the headquarters clock – when the big gate opened ...".[16] All reports written by prisoners describe that at the same time soldiers were firing from the towers, in the process of which a Polish prisoner was hit fatally. According to all reports SS soldiers were also taken down from the towers by American soldiers and shot immediately. It was found that they were not the former guards of the camp, but that they had either been transferred to this unit only shortly before or brought in from the SS disciplinary camp located near the protective custody camp. Colonel Sparks wrote that a total of approximately two hundred SS soldiers had been detained, and some of them shot on the spot.[17] As soon as the prisoners had grasped the fact that the liberators were present in the camp, anybody who could manage to stand on his own two feet rushed to the parade ground in order to see the soldiers with his own eyes, salute them, thank them or simply to cheer them from a distance. "Oh, this overwhelming and unforgettable moment", the Belgian Arthur Haulot wrote,[18] and the German prisoner Edgar Kupfer-Koberwitz, whose diary notes are among the most impressive documents about the camp at Dachau, depicts the moment of liberation as follows: "The Americans are here! The Americans are in the camp! Hurrah, hurrah, they are at the parade ground!" Everybody is in motion. The sick are leaving their beds, those who are almost well, and the block personnel are running out into the block road, jumping out of the windows, climbing over wooden fences, rushing to the parade ground. From the distance, all the way to here, you can hear the shouting and cheering. They are shouts of joy. Everyone is continuing to run around. Everybody has expressions of excitement on their transfigured faces. "They are here, we are free, free!" We all can hardly believe it, but we hear the cheering outside. Comrades are coming back, out of breath, telling us: "The Americans are at the parade ground.

---

[16] Nico Rost, loc. sit., p. 243.
[17] Felix L. Sparks, loc. sit. There are varying and contradictory accounts on the execution of SS guards by members of the US Army. It is unlikely to be determined exactly how many people died during the battles for the liberation of the concentration camp at Dachau.
[18] Arthur Haulot/Ali Kuci, loc. sit., p. 29.

They are shooting the SS. The camp has been taken over, we are free." Even the severely ill are getting out of their beds, stumbling towards the windows. Comrades are coming towards me: Frenchmen, Russians, Jews, Italians. We are kissing each other like brothers and congratulating each other. Many have tears in their eyes. We tightly grab each others' hands: Free, free!".[19]
They had survived, they had been rescued.
Only slowly did the immense problems of taking care of 32,000 malnourished prisoners, of providing medical treatment for thousands, and checking the typhus epidemic come to the fore again. For in Dachau too as the prisoner Jorge Semprun, liberated at Buchenwald, had put it, "the end of the camp by no means meant the end of the dying".[20] Thus, in May 1945 alone, over 2,000 prisoners died at Dachau.
Yet many of them who had survived the camp soon felt the urge to make sure that what happened at this place would not fall into oblivion. After all, it was thanks to their efforts that the former concentration camp with its diverse history (after the last prisoners had left the camp, war crime trials were held there by US military authorities for three years, and in 1948 the grounds served as a refugee camp) was turned into a memorial on the 20th anniversary of its liberation.

---

[19] Edgar Kupfer-Koberwitz, 'Die Mächtigen und die Hilflosen', Vol. 2, Stuttgart 1957, p. 254.
[20] Jorge Semprun, 'Die große Reise', Hamburg 1964, p. 75.

Hermann Weiss

Dachau and International Public Opinion
Reactions to the Liberation of the Camp.

*"I've always
thought they
exaggerated to make
us hate the Krauts."*

Shortly after the National Socialist seizure of power, the foreign press had already made the National Socialist concentration camps a subject of their reports. The foreign press based their description of the conditions in German concentration camps to some considerable extent on the testimony of released prisoners who had escaped from Germany and published reports about their experiences.

In order to counteract negative foreign propaganda concerning concentration camps, the SS soon proceeded to have German journalists write faked positive reports about the camps.[1]

Common to all reports about German concentration camps in both the German press and the foreign press was the fact that their accuracy was not verifiable for foreigners and that Allied propaganda about atrocities during World War I actually proved positive for the Germans in the formation of public opinion in western countries. Reports such as the one published by the London *Times* on 16 December 1939, about the alleged plan of the Germans to establish a type of Jewish state in occupied Poland in a "concentration zone" around Lublin, to which all German, Austrian, Czech and most Polish Jews were to be deported – altogether around 2.27 million people – in order to be gradually exterminated there, were so far beyond the power of

---

[1] Especially typical is a five-page "Special Report" of the *Illustrierter Beobachter* of 3 December 1936 about the camp at Dachau. An assortment of photographs of stubbly-bearded, shorn heads held in unfavorable poses with corresponding captions under the pictures, as well as downright idyllic photographs of camp life were to suggest to the observer that in reality disreputable "sub-humans", meaning Communists, loafers and professional criminals, were to be rehabilitated through work in this place, which was a model of order and cleanliness. In the two-page illustrated report "about a concentration camp" in the *Münchner Illustrierte Presse* of 3 August 1939, which consists entirely of pictures of the work of prisoners in the concentration camp Dachau, particular attention is drawn to this in order to counteract the "most hair-raising things" in the descriptions in the foreign press.

human imagination, at least in the western democracies, that the *Times* made the attenuating remark that although such a massacre of European Jews might well firm with the Nazis' imaginary world, even they would not be able fully to carry it out.[2]

The British government also took into consideration that certain things were just inconceivable to its citizens and, in a directive from the Ministry of Information of 25 July 1941, warned political journalists not to risk their credibility with too drastic reporting.

In this evaluation of the effect that the reports of atrocities would have the fact that ideological opponents had with the outbreak of the Second World War become declared enemies, who were no longer to be treated according to standards of fairness but rather according to criteria of psychological warfare, clearly also played a part. But even though one could assume that in the Allied countries people were in principle aware of the system followed in the National Socialist concentration camps, the treatment in the Allied and nonpartisan press of the first eye-witness accounts from the death camp at Auschwitz shows how little credence was given to details of National Socialist persecution and extermination measures which exceeded the power of human imagination. It was, for example, not until the summer of 1944, eleven months before the end of the war, that a report launched to an international public through all possible channels, received a widespread response in the press.[3]

For this reason the first reports from Allied correspondents to appear in western newspapers since April 1945, were a shock to the international public. After the capture of the death camp at Auschwitz the world was given its first foretaste of the cold-bloodedly executed, criminally inhumane world the system of the National Socialist "death mills" concealed. On 28 January 1945, one day after the capture, the Soviet *Pravda* drew attention to what had happened. On 1 February, as a supplement to a report from the front, *Pravda* printed a report of thirty lines about the size of the camp, the number of inmates and the nutritional condition of the liberated prisoners. This was followed the next day by a two-column report in which the numbers of victims were made public. On 14 February, in a report about the work of the Polish commission for disclosure of the NS crimes in Auschwitz, *Pravda* published details of the extermination machinery, the gas chambers and crematoria, and also of the reuse of the hair, the gold fillings and the clothes of the dead prisoners.

Finally, on 7 May, when detailed reports on the German concentration

---

[2] See: Martin Gilbert, Auschwitz and the Allies, New York 1981, p. 14.
[3] The so-called Wetzler-Vrba-Report, which contains the accounts of three prisoners who escaped from Auschwitz, appeared in extracts in June and July 1944, in the Swiss press in 383 articles and reprints. (See: John S. Conway, Frühe Augenzeugenberichte aus Auschwitz, in: Vierteljahrshefte für Zeitgeschichte 27 (1979), p. 278, footnote 35; see also Gilbert, op. cit., p. 10 and 272-281).

camps captured by western Allied troops were already appearing in the press of the western Allied countries, *Pravda* followed once more with a two-page article about Auschwitz, which was rather sparsely illustrated with two photographs; here for the first time the number of 4 million prisoners killed there was quoted.[4]

In Great Britain the first reports about concentration camps appeared on 12 April 1945. They were written by correspondents of the western Allies who were eye-witnesses after the liberation of the concentration camp at Buchenwald, which was close to Weimar. Three days later, the German army surrendered the concentration camp Bergen-Belsen, which was situated between Celle and Soltau south of the Lüneburger Heide. Bergen-Belsen was for months so overcrowded with transports from other camps, among them Auschwitz and Buchenwald, that the conditions which the Allied troops encountered there surpassed everything they had seen until then or were still to see. In March 1945 more than 18,000 prisoners died there; in the first two weeks of April before the liberation more than 9,300 died, among them many women.[5]

In the reporting, however, Buchenwald remained in first place not only because it had been liberated earlier, but also because it was dangerous to enter Bergen-Belsen due to the typhus epidemic which was raging through the camp. After several smaller news items and photographs concerning Buchenwald, Bergen-Belsen and subsidiary camps such as Nordhausen and Ohrdruf,[6] there appeared in the London *Times* of 28 April 1945, a two-column report on the visit of a delegation of British members of Parliament and American congressmen to Buchenwald. In this article the story already surfaced about lamp shades made of human skin which had allegedly been found there.[7] The delegation of congressmen and members of Parliament had

---

[4] Although the lack of adequate sources makes it impossible to state exact figures, the computation from camp files and transport lists existing for certain periods and from the use of all other relevant sources and statistical material show the number of killed to be between one and two million. See Ino Arndt/Wolfgang Scheffler, Organisierter Massenmord an Juden in nationalsozialistischen Vernichtungslagern, in: Vierteljahrshefte für Zeitgeschichte 24 (1976), p. 134.

[5] See: Eberhard Kolb, Bergen-Belsen, in: Studien zur Geschichte der Konzentrationslager, Stuttgart 1979, p. 151.

[6] Concerning Buchenwald see the "Times" of 18 and 19 April (photographs) and 23 April 1945. A report about the filming for newsreels in Buchenwald appeared in the "Times" of 1 May 1945. Concerning Bergen-Belsen see the "Times" of April 19, 1945.

[7] Conclusive evidence of this has still not been put forward. The allegations in connection with treated human skin, which played a particularly important part in the trial of Ilse Koch, the wife of the notorious camp commander of Buchenwald, Karl Koch, are in our context not so much to be seen as a problem of the sensationalist press, but more as an example of how much the image of the Germans suffered in the eyes of the international public after the reality of the concentration camps became known. A fair, scholarly discussion of the problem of human skin preparations from concentration camps can be found in: Arthur L. Smith jr., Die Hexe von Buchenwald. Der Fall Ilse Koch, Cologne 1983, especially pages 102-105 and 123-137.

come to Germany at the explicit request of the Allied supreme commander, General Eisenhower. According to a report in the *New York Herald Tribune* of 21 April, he was of the opinion that information about the living conditions in these German camps should be circulated as widely as possible in the USA. The same issue of the newspaper also carried a report on conditions in Bergen-Belsen, which was illustrated with photographs. A few days later, on 29 April, the *Herald Tribune* published a first summary of Buchenwald. It stated that the function of Buchenwald was primarily of a political nature, that is to eliminate Europe's political elite. To that end opponents of National Socialism were killed by a combination of underfeeding and heavy labor, by abuse, beatings and torture, unbelievably overcrowded sleeping quarters and by diseases like typhus and tuberculosis. Reports on the visits of various delegations of congressional representatives and leading members of the press also take up substantial space in the American press. On 7 May 1945 the magazine *Life* published a pictorial report including some particularly shocking photographs from Bergen-Belsen and Buchenwald. This report certainly did not fail to have an effect on the American public.

Information about the SS prison camps in Germany was by no means as extensive on the Continent of Europe as it was in the Anglo-Saxon countries. Relatively detailed reports about Buchenwald were followed, mostly, by only short notices about the liberation of the other camps. One example is from the *Neue Zürcher Zeitung* which printed a full report of the Swiss News Agency on 26 April 1945. On the next day this was supplemented with a two-column article by its own correspondent. It followed on 1 May with a short dispatch from United Press about the liberation of the concentration camp at Dachau:

A first view of the extensive installation of the concentration camp Dachau, which was liberated yesterday, and the SS community lying beside it, provides essentially the same picture as in Buchenwald. Around 32,000 prisoners were freed, many of them in a pitiful condition and practically starved to death. The prisoners had been treated according to the same barbarian methods as in the other concentration camps already captured. The usual gas chambers, crematoria, torture chambers, whipping posts, and gallows were to be found. In addition there was found in Dachau a train of 50 cars, all of which were packed with corpses ... The survivors, insofar as they are able to travel, will now be transferred with American ambulances to improvised hospitals near the Czechoslovakian border. An honorable burial is to be given to the dead.

In the English press, too, the reportage on Buchenwald was far more detailed than on Dachau, although neither camp was liberated by British troops. On 23 April, already before the liberation of Dachau, the *Manchester Guardian* published a letter that reads almost like an introduction to what was later to be demanded of the public in understanding and self-examination; it was written by a German emigrant who knew the camp at Dachau from personal experience.

Before I was so lucky as to come to this country as a refugee in the summer of 1939, the Gestapo had sent me from one concentration camp to another for several years. I will recall one incident which was significant not only when it occurred, in 1938, but up to a few months ago in this very country, Great Britain.
In May 1938, a batch of prisoners arrived at Dachau (near Munich). Amongst them was the editor of a well-known Viennese Socialist paper (I cannot give the names, as I have simply forgotten them). We asked him:
'You have been visited by our comrades who have been released previously, you have even printed and published their reports. Why did you not act accordingly?'
His reply was:
'I have to admit that we received numerous reports about the conditions in these concentration camps. Some of them we even published. But, to tell you the truth, we did not believe them!'
That is the point. Not only in Vienna but all over the world nobody believed us. The cruel realities were unimaginable. Now the world is bound to believe. Why not earlier? How many lives could have been saved!

O. Winter, Huddersfield

The capture of Dachau and the liberation of the prisoners on 29 April was followed on 1 May by the first press information which was based entirely on news agency reports. While the London *Times,* using a Reuter dispatch, added nothing new to the information in the *Neue Zürcher Zeitung,* the report in the *Manchester Guardian* on the same day, published under the headline "32,000 Freed at Dachau – SS Guards Attacked", contained some additional information:

The capture of the notorious concentration camp near Dachau, where approximately 32,000 persons were liberated, was announced in yesterday's S.H.A.E.F. communiqué. Three hundred SS guards at the camp were quickly overcome, it said.
A whole battalion of Allied troops was needed to restrain the prisoners from excesses. Fifty railway trucks crammed with bodies and the discovery of gas chambers, torture rooms, whipping posts, and crematoria strongly support reports which had leaked out of the camp.
An Associated Press correspondent with the Seventh Army says that many of the prisoners seized the guards' weapons and revenged themselves on the SS men. Many of the well-known prisoners, it was said, had been recently removed to a new hide-out in the Tyrol.
Prisoners with access to the records said that 9,000 died of hunger and disease, or were shot in the past three months, and 4,000 more perished last winter.

As well as this notice, in the same issue the *Manchester Guardian* dedicated an editorial to the camp at Dachau:

Dachau has the infamous distinction of being the first Nazi concentration camp. Hitler came to power on 30 January 1933. Within six weeks the president of the Munich police announced that Dachau was being prepared for political prisoners – Communists and 'Marxists' – for whom it was impossible to find room in the State prisons. Dachau was to hold 5,000. From that time onwards Dachau was a name at which to tremble. Into it went a steady stream of political prisoners of all sorts, from Communists to Nazis who had fallen foul of all their authorities, and Jews. It was one of the show places of the Nazi system, in which, under proper guidance, visitors were permitted to see the 'educational work' by which the politically backward were converted into good German citizens. But the visitors never saw the whole nor did they see what happened in those dark detention cells and overcrowded dormitories or on the work parties. The details of what Dachau was like before 1939 are well known. We published several accounts at the time and they were confirmed by the evidence in the Government's White Paper of October 1939. What has happened in the five and a half long years since we are now hearing from the American liberators.

The most thorough coverage of Dachau appeared understandably in the American press. After all, American soldiers had liberated the camp; additionally, as in Great Britain, Dachau was in the US a synonym for the coercion and persecution of National Socialist Germany. The American public and the American soldiers at the fronts which were still being desperately held, above all by SS troops, were very greatly agitated by the reports so far published about the atrocities in the concentration camps which had already been liberated.

The first press reports about the liberation appeared in the issues of 1 May, two days after the liberation – Dachau was taken on a Sunday. The individual articles agreed with one another on many details; but they deviated from each other in strikingly many points which could easily have been verified. Concurrence appeared to be greater with information which apparently came from prisoners' accounts and which could be based on the prisoners' internal camp information system, for example, statements about the numbers of evacuation transports in the last days or of deaths in the final months before the liberation.

There are more contradictory statements in the events directly observed by American war correspondents, for example, in the number of railroad cars on the sidings of the camp filled with people who had starved,[8] in the descriptions of combat actions in the camp itself, in the number of SS guards killed or taken prisoner, the reactions of the prisoners and the GIs toward the SS men. The drama of events which have just taken place and the portrayal dominated by the narrow field of personal observation necessarily produces a different relation to objectivity than the epic report focusing an events lying farther in the past and based on a series of similar or identical testimonies.

Before all the US press reports, which are available to everyone, the information service of the 42nd US Infantry Division, the Rainbow Division, deserves to be reprinted here. It was intended only for the officers and a small group of specialists in the Division. The report was produced as a one-

---

[8] Nico Rost. Goethe in Dachau. Literatur und Wirklichkeit, München, n. d. The transport train of Jewish prisoners, which was to have left Dachau on 24 April, could at first not leave the camp for days because of a lack of locomotives and because of low-flying aircraft. At the liberation on 29 April the train with cattle cars, which the US troops found, was however an evacuation transport from Buchenwald.

page hectographed leaflet. On the back it carries the headline "42nd Infantry Division - World News - Tuesday, 1 May 1945":

Dachau is no longer a name of terror for hunted men. 32,000 of them have been freed by the 42d Rainbow Division. The crimes done behind the walls of this worst of Nazi concentration camps now live only to haunt the memories of the Rainbow men who tore open its gates and first saw its misery, and to accuse its SS keepers of one of the worst crimes in all history.
When Infantrymen of the 42d Division fought their way into Dachau against fanatical SS troops who met deserved violent deaths along the moats, behind the high fences and in the railyards littered with the bodies of fifty carloads of their starved victims, these hardened soldiers expected to see horrible sights. But no human imagination ... could have been prepared for what they did see there ...
Seasoned as they were by long acquaintanceship with stark reality, these trained observers gazed at freightcars full of piled cadavers ... and they could not believe what they saw with their own eyes.
Riflemen accustomed to witnessing death had no stomach for rooms stacked almost ceiling-high with tangled human bodies adjoining the cremation furnaces, looking like some maniac's woodpile ...
Ten days before the arrival of the Rainbow Division fifty carloads of prisoners arrived at Dachau from the Buchenwald concentration camp in a starving condition after 27 days without food. When Buchenwald was threatened by advancing American troops the Nazis hurriedly crowded about 4,000 of their prisoners into open flatcars unfit even for cattle. 27 days later - days of exposure to freezing weather without anything to eat, a trainload of human suffering arrived at Dachau ...
In these stinking cars were seen the bodies of these prisoners too weak even to get out. A few tried, and they made a bloody heap in the door of one of the cars. They had been machine gunned by the SS ...
Some of the cars had been emptied and the bodies carted to the crematory. In one room adjoining the furnace-room on the left they were neatly stacked. The stripped corpses were very straight. But in the room on the right side they were piled in complete disorder, still clothed.
These on the right were just as they were dumped out of the freight cars where they had died of starvation.
It was incredible that such things could happen today, but there was the visible proof.
It was unbelievable that human beings were capable of perpetrating such unspeakable atrocities, but there were the men who did it. The SS.
At least 25 and perhaps 50 were beaten to death by inmates who struck with all the fury of men who suddenly release years of pent-up hate.
Someone said there were 14 in the canal.
One in a railroad car had no face left.
Now the SS Guards were dead. But their deaths could not avenge the thousands dead and dying there in Dachau.
Those tortured dead can only be avenged when our world is aroused so much by what the 42d uncovered at Dachau and by what others have found at the other Dachaus scattered throughout Germany, that never again will any party, any government, any people be allowed to mar the face of the earth with such inhumanity.

In the *Rainbow Reveille,* obviously the Division newspaper of the 42nd US Division, there appeared ten days later, on 11 May, an article about the concentration camp whose title "This Was Dachau" already suggested a more distant view. The author attempted to link the still fresh experiences of the days of the liberation with the historical development in National Socialist Germany, with the expansion of the concentration camp Dachau and with the simultaneous disintegration of moral norms to produce an historical overview of the phenomenon of the concentration camp:

In the year 1933, near the pleasant, conventional suburb of Munich called Dachau, a prison was established. It began in the form of wooden barracks in a barbed wire enclosure, and was called a 'concentration camp'.
It was the beginning of the New Order in Europe. As the power of the new Chancellor, Adolf Hitler, grew, the camp at Dachau grew with it. Grim, grey-black walls rose around it, closing it in from the rest of the world. Horrible sounds, babbling, animal-like screams of pain, sometimes came to the ears of the citizens of the suburb from the direction of the sinister camp ... As the years passed, more and more thousands were herded into the vast torture-chamber. Few ever left it alive. Similar open sores erupted elsewhere on the face of Germany, at Buchenwald and Landsberg and a dozen other places, but Dachau was the oldest, and the biggest.
On 30 April 1945, American soldiers ended Dachau's 12-year reign of terror, and men of the 42d Division saw for themselves, when they overran the camp, what was probably the greatest concentration of human misery in the history of the world ...
All the prisoners were political prisoners, but not all were foreign. Many were Germans. Many were Germans who had been there from the first, for twelve years. They had survived only because they could work. Those who became too weak to work, who broke an ankle or an arm, perhaps, got no food. Either they starved to death, or went to the crematory.
Why was Dachau established? What had these men done to cause the Germans to send them to such a place? There is not one but various answers to this question. Some were there because they had dared to stand up for their convictions, as opposed to the vile theories of Hitler's New Order. Others were there because they were Jews ...
Others in Dachau had been sent there simply because they had been denounced by some enemy with political connections, perhaps merely a disgruntled neighbor or some business competitor ...
Unnatural as were the horrible crimes committed at Dachau, they were the natural outcome of the Germans' belief in themselves as a master race, a natural outcome of their contempt for the political and religious beliefs of all who differed with them. What was violated at Dachau was not only the bodies of countless victims of the master-race bullies. The spirit of democracy, of decency and tolerance was also consumed in the flames of its hideous crematories ...

Although an extensive textual criticism is not intended, it does seem important here to draw attention to some points which are either typical of the articles compiled here or which need supplementary explanation. What, in comparison to memoirs, is rather disagreeably noticeable is the attempt, understandable in the medium of the newspaper, of the journalists to put together some hastily gathered information, without precise background knowledge, to make an interesting article. Language difficulties alone meant that it was often not possible for the reporters to assess the reliability of their informants. And this explains reports about mass gassing in the one gas chamber of the camp. Since the prisoners, apart from certain squads, could

not go into the crematorium structures – at least as long as they lived – it is understandable that they took the numerous executions carried out in the crematorium to be in part gassings and after the liberation gave testimony to this effect. In fact, the gas chamber in the crematorium at the camp Dachau was never put to use. In Dachau no gassing took place.[9]
Of course, one could not expect an exhaustive study of the concentration camp Dachau from the reporters "of the first hour". The details reported often have a very random character; in some articles one clearly sees, for example with the repetition of facts which had already been described, that the authors were under time pressure. This explains the frequent contradictions in details. In the *Rainbow World News* of 1 May, it is, for example, reported that the train with the Buchenwald prisoners arrived in Dachau already ten days before the liberation of the camp. But in a later report of the *Rainbow Reveille* of 11 May, they say only four days. In addition to this, of course, is the widespread lack of knowledge about Germany in general and about the concentration camps in particular, which leads to the consequence that the camp Landsberg, one of the many subsidiary camps of Dachau, is called an independent camp like Dachau itself or Buchenwald.
In this matter, the daily newspapers differ in no way from the military bulletins and newspapers – aside from literary style, where the professional papers clearly have the advantage. The first newspaper reporters and news correspondents came to the camp directly with the fighting troops; because it was Sunday, however, their reports did not appear until two days later. On 1 May, the *New York Times* simply brought a shortened report from the Associated Press:

Dachau, Germany's most dreaded extermination camp, has been captured and its surviving 32,000 tortured inmates have been freed by outraged American troops who killed or captured its brutal garrison in a furious battle ...
The troops were joined by trusty prisoners working outside the barbed-wire enclosures. Frenchmen and Russians, grabbing weapons dropped by slain guards, acted swiftly on their own to exact full revenge from their tormentors.
The sorting of the liberated prisoners was still under way today but the Americans learned from camp officials that some of the more important captives had been transferred recently to a new hideout, probably in the Tyrol ...
Prisoners with access to records said that 9,000 captives had died of hunger and disease or been shot in the past three months and 14,000 more had perished during the winter. Typhus was prevalent in the camp and the city's water supply was reported to have been contaminated by drainage from 6,000 graves near the prison.
A short time after the battle there was a train of thirty-nine coal cars on a siding. The

---

[9] Concerning crematoria and gas chambers, see the contribution of Barbara Distel in: Nationalsozialistische Massentötung durch Giftgas. Eine Dokumentation hrsg. v. Eugen Kogon, Hermann Langbein, Adalbert Rückerl u. a. Frankfurt/M. 1983, p. 277–280; also a contribution by Günther Kimmel, Das Konzentrationslager Dachau. Eine Studie zu den nationalsozialistischen Gewaltverbrechen, in: Bayern in der NS-Zeit, Bd. 2, hrsg. v. Martin Broszat u. Elke Fröhlich, München-Wien 1979, p. 391 f., 407.

cars were loaded with hundreds of bodies and from them was removed at least one pitiful human wreck that still clung to life. These victims were mostly Poles and most of them had starved to death as the train stood there idle for several days. Lying alongside a busy road nearby were the murdered bodies of those who had tried to escape. Bavarian peasants – who traveled this road daily – ignored both the bodies and the horrors inside the camp to turn the American seizure of their city into an orgy of looting. Even German children rode by the bodies without a glance, carrying stolen clothing ...
The camp held 32,000 emaciated, unshaven men and 350 women jammed in the wooden barracks. Prisoners said that 7,000 others had been marched away on foot during the past few days. The survivors went wild with joy as the Americans broke open their pens ...
Bodies were found in many places. Here also were the gas chambers – camouflaged as "showers" into which prisoners were herded under the pretext of bathing – and the cremation ovens. Huge stacks of clothing bore mute testimony to the fate of their owners ...
The Americans stormed through the camp with tornadic fury. Not a stone's throw from a trainload of corpses lay the bleeding bodies of sixteen guards shot down as they fled.
In the mess hall of the guards' barracks, food was still cooking in the kitchen. One officer was slumped over a plate of beans, a bullet through his head. Nearby was a telephone with the receiver down and the busy signal still buzzing. Outside the power house were the bodies of two Germans slain by a Czech and a Pole working in the engine room.
The main part of the camp is surrounded by a fifteen foot wide moat through which a torrent of water circulates. Atop a ten foot fence is charged barbed wire. When Lieut. Col. Will Cowling of Leavenworth, Kan., slipped the lock in the main gate, there was still no sign of life inside this area. He looked around for a few seconds and then a tremendous human cry roared forth. A flood of humanity poured across the flat yard – which would hold a half dozen baseball diamonds – and Colonel Cowling was all but mobbed. He was hoisted to the shoulders of the seething, swaying crowd of Russians, Poles, Frenchmen, Czechs, and Austrians, cheering the Americans in their native tongues ...
The joyous crowd pressed the weight of thousands of frail bodies against the wire, and it gave way at one point. Like a break in a dam, the prisoners rushed out, although still penned in by the moat. Three tried to climb over the fence, but were burned to death on the top wire, for the current still was on. Two guards fired into the mass from a tower, betraying their presence. American infantrymen instantly riddled the Germans.

The *Chicago Daily Tribune* printed a more complete impression of the Associated Press report in its edition of the same day; here the reactions of the German population are also reported:

Correspondents and infantry men found 39 open type railroad cars on a siding that ran thru the walls of the camp.
At first glance the cars seemed loaded with dirty clothing. Then one saw feet, heads and bony fingers. More than half the cars were full of bodies, hundreds of bodies ...
The best information available was that this trainload of prisoners, mostly Poles, had stood on the tracks several days and most of the prisoners had been starved. Others had been shot thru the head. Clothing had been torn from some and their wasted bodies bore livid bruises. Some had tried to escape; their bodies lay along the tracks five or six steps way. One, shot thru the head, was astride a bicycle.

This spectacle was outside the walls of the camp, along a widely traveled road inside the city of Dachau where Bavarians passed daily.
The civilians were looting an SS warehouse nearby, passing the death train with no more than curious glances at the American soldiers.

One woman, the correspondent of the *New York Herald Tribune*, Marguerite Higgins, produced the most impressive report about conditions in the camp.[10] Of all the articles of the daily press which have been reviewed here, hers is not only the most vivid, but also the most reliable. More precisely than any of her colleagues she described the special features of the crematorium, its hidden, inaccessible location, the executions through shooting in the neck, the torture of hanging by the hands; indicatively, she did not report about gassing. The details in her article serve an informative purpose and are not to the same extent as with many of her colleagues filled with striking embellishments; her accounts have been confirmed by memoirs and results of research:

Troops of the United States 7th Army liberated 33,000 prisoners this afternoon at this first and largest of the Nazi concentration camps ...
This correspondent and Peter Furst, of the army newspaper "Stars and Stripes", were the first two Americans to enter the inclosure at Dachau, where persons possessing some of the best brains in Europe were held during what might have been the most fruitful years of their lives.
While a United States 45th Infantry Division patrol was still fighting a way down through SS barracks to the north, our jeep and two others from the 42d Infantry drove into the camp inclosure through the southern entrance. As men of the patrol with us busied themselves accepting an SS man's surrender, we impressed a soldier into service and drove with him to the prisoners' barracks. There he opened the gate after pushing the body of a prisoner shot last night while attempting to get out to meet the Americans.
There was not a soul in the yard when the gate was opened. As we learned later, the prisoners themselves had taken over control of their inclosure the night before, refusing to obey any further orders from the German guards ... The prisoners maintained strict discipline among themselves, remaining close to their barracks so as not to give the SS men an excuse for mass murder.
But the minute the two of us entered a jangled barrage of "Are you Americans?" in about sixteen languages came from the barracks 200 yards from the gate. An affirmative nod caused pandemonium.
Tattered, emaciated men, weeping, yelling and shouting "Long live America!" swept toward the gate in a mob. Those who could not walk limped or crawled. In the confusion, they were so hysterically happy that they took the SS man for an American. During a wild five minutes he was patted on the back, paraded on shoulders and embraced enthusiastically by prisoners. The arrival of the American soldier soon straightened out the situation.

---

[10] Her entrance into the enclosed camp area while the fighting was still going on is also mentioned in printed memoirs; see Edgar Kupfer-Koberwitz, Die Mächtigen und die Hilflosen. Als Häftling in Dachau, Bd. 2: Wie es endete, Stuttgart 1960. p. 257; Johann Steinbock, Das Ende von Dachau, Salzburg 1948, p. 28; Yéfime, Die letzten Tage in Dachau, in: Wort und Tat, September 1947, p. 103.

I happened to be the first through the gate, and the first person to rush up to me turned out to be a Polish Catholic priest, a deputy of August Cardinal Hlond, Primate of Poland ...
In the excitement ... some of the prisoners died trying to pass through electrically charged barbed wire. Some got out after the wires were decharged joined in the battle when some ill-advised SS men holding out in a tower fired upon them. The prisoners charged the tower and threw all six SS men out the window. After an hour and a half of cheering, the crowd was calmed down enough to make possible a tour of the camp.
The only American prisoner, a flyer, with the rank of major, took some of the soldiers through.
According to prisoners, the most famous individuals who had been at the camp had been removed by SS men to Innsbruck ...
The barracks at Dachau, like those at Buchenwald, had the stench of death and sickness. But at Dachau there were six barracks like the infamous No. 61 at Buchenwald, where the starving and dying lay virtually on top of each other in quarters where 1,200 men occupied a space intended for 200. The dead – 300 died of sickness yesterday – lay on concrete walks outside the quarters and others were being carried out as the reporters went through ...
The crematorium and torture chambers lay outside the prisoner inclosures. Situated in a wood close by, a new building had been built by prisoners under Nazi guards. Inside, in the two rooms used as torture chambers, an estimated 1,200 bodies were piled.
In the crematorium itself were hooks on which the SS men hung their victims when they wished to flog them or tu use any of the other torture instruments. Symbolic of the SS was a mural the SS men themselves had painted on the wall. It showed a headless man in uniform with the SS insigne on the collar. The man was astride a huge inflated pig, into which he was digging his spurs.
The prisoners also showed reporters the grounds where men knelt and were shot in the back of the neck ...
Just beyond the crematorium was a ditch containing some 2,000 more bodies, which had been hastily tossed there in the last few days by the SS men, who were so busy preparing their escape they did not have time to burn the bodies.
Below the camp were cattle cars in which prisoners from Buchenwald had been transported to Dachau. Hundreds of dead were still in the cars due to the fact that prisoners in the camp had rejected SS orders to remove them.

Even after the liberation American newspapers still published articles about living conditions in the former concentration camp Dachau, which were only slowly getting back to normal. Of chief interest was everyday life in the camp with all its torments. But in the reports the revenge of the prisoners on their torturers also found a sympathetic response. A good example for this is the report which the *New York Times* published on 2 May, under the headline, "Dachau Inmates Get Revenge on Nazi Torturers. SS Men Are Found Slain. Beaten to a Pulp. Their Middle Fingers Cut Off":

A terrible vengeance met SS (Elite Guard) tormentors guarding the Dachau concentration camp when they fell into the hands of some of the infuriated inmates.
Bodies in SS uniforms were found in a half-dozen places, beaten to a pulp, the middle fingers cut from their hands before or after death.
Many inmates displayed their own mutilated hands from which fingers had been severed, and swore their Nazi guards did this to them to add to their torment.
The incongruous sight in this stinking den of sadistic Nazi torture and extermination of

helpless prisoners is a variety of signs admonishing inmates and others how to behave and be sanitary. In the filthy crematory where the bodies of the slain were destroyed, for instance, was a big sign reading: 'Cleanliness is a special obligation here. Therefore don't forget to wash your hands.'
At the entrance gate ... prisoners faced a huge sign on the administration building roof informing them: 'there is only one way to freedom. Its milestones are obedience, industry, cleanliness and love for one's people.'
The inmates were marked with letters indicating their nationality and with colored triangles indicating the nature of the offenses with which they were charged. For instance, 'P' meant they were Poles. A green triangle meant they were accused of a criminal offense, pink meant homosexual, red stood for political, black for so-called social or anti-social prisoners.
Their food consisted of a slice of bread and a bowl of watery soup daily ... The barracks were overcrowded, with two prisoners to a narrow bunk. The death rate normally was 112 to 135 a day.[11]
Buildings for the SS guards and administrative staffs occupied at least four times as much space as the narrow inner compound for prisoners ...
Electrically charged barbed wire and a water-filled ditch surrounded the inmates' compound. Guard turrets and concrete bunkers were placed along the ditches, from which SS guards safely could fire upon the prisoners in event of a wholesale escape attempt. Hangings, they said, were done publicly. But when prisoners were beaten to death, this was done secretly."

The prominent figures from all over Europe, some of whom had lived for years in the concentration camp Dachau and who were evacuated in the last hours before the liberation, filled the newspaper columns for some days still. With the title, "Odor of Death Still Pervades Dachau Camp", the *Chicago Daily Tribune* published an A. P. report on 3 May:

The stench of corpses, filth, and pollution, the perils of typhus and the horrible spectacle of the 'living dead' still pervaded the Nazis' Dachau prison camp today. But American troops and military government officials have moved in and started to cleanse it of the filth. There is food for the hungry, and those who smoke receive cigarets.
The Americans learned that many more of the notables ... were spirited from the camp to a stronghold in the Tyrol, Austria, just before the advancing Americans liberated Dachau. Among these was Nicholas Kallay, former Hungarian premier who had been believed dead.
A niece of Russian Foreign Minister Molotov, listed as Aleksel Hokorin; a son of Italian Marshal Pietro Badoglio; a German General von Falkenhausen, and at least one member of the Krupp industrial family were among those also reported removed from Dachau.

A further A. P. report from the headquarters of the 6th US Army, which the *New York Times* published on 7 May, was concerned in as much detail as was possible at the time with the contradictory behavior of the SS in the clearance

---

[11] The number of over 100 dying daily certainly is correct for the months after January 1945. The prison camp recorder Domagala registered a total of 27,839 dead for the years 1940-1945 alone, not including those executed, who were not listed in the camp books. The International Trace Service Arolsen registered a total of 31,951 dead. See: Kimmel, op. cit. p. 385, footnote 167.

of the camp, which had not been completed, and cited once again the evacuation order[12] of Himmler, which is also often mentioned in memoirs, but is no longer available today:

Gestapo Chief Heinrich Himmler ordered the evacuation of the notorious Dachau concentration camp on 14 April and the extermination of all its inmates to prevent any witnesses to German inhumanity falling into Allied hands, the Sixth Army Group said in an official statement tonight.
The commander at Dachau suggested to Himmler that the camp be turned over to the Allies, the announcement said it was learned through documents seized by the United States Seventh Army. Himmler replied with an order prohibiting such a move and concluded, over his own signature:
'No prisoner shall be allowed to fall into the hands of the enemy alive. Prisoners have behaved barbarously to the civilian population at Buchenwald' (The Buchenwald camp was liberated by the Americans the week before the Himmler order was written).
No explanation was given immediately why the camp was not evacuated as ordered by Himmler and why stacks of dead prisoners and long rows of the barely living victims were left to betray the German brutality.

The effect of the many corpses, marked by hunger and brutality, which still lay in and around the camp, on the soldiers of both Divisions who had captured the camp was graphically described in a report in the US Army newspaper *Stars and Stripes* on 3 May 1945:

Fifty boxcars still stand on a spur track beside the Dachau prison camp. Twenty are filled with human bodies killed during the past week. Some are wrapped in filthy rags, others completely nude.
Many doughboys who took Dachau with the 42d and 45th Divs. surveyed the mournful sight today and talked about it in hushed, shocked tones. Pvt. John Mackisin, of Youngstown, Ohio, in the 232 FA Bn., said:
'I've always thought they exaggerated to make us hate the Krauts. Now I know these things are true. More GIs should see this with their own eyes. It would harden us up a lot.'
Doughboys cast angry glances in the direction of German civilians passing by the freight cars ... They avoided looking in the direction of the trainload of corpses and pretended they did not know they were there.
All along the track lay corpses which had fallen out of the cars. Not one good German had the decency to stop and cover a body with a sheet. They seemed to think it none of their affair.
The Dachau crematorium is a long low brick structure with a tall smokestack from which smoke poured day and night. The gas chamber is 20 feet square and has 18 nozzles across the ceiling which look like shower outlets ...
The guards told the murder-house victims to undress and prepare to shower. They entered the room nude and when the room was full, the door was shut tight and the gas turned on while attendants watched the death throes through a telescopic device in the wall.
Adjoining to the death house is a dog kennel where 122 huge dogs were kept to tor-

---

[12] Published as an appendix in Rost, op. cit. p. 310. See the contribution of Stanislaw Zàmečník in Dachauer Hefte, No. 1.

ment prisoners. The dogs were Great Danes, shepherds, Wolfhounds and boxers. SS men frequently stripped prisoners and hung them up for the dogs to jump at while they tapped the prisoners' testicles with sticks. When the dogs leaped up and tore off a man's organs, SS men howled and patted the dogs and gave them meat. Many dogs now lie dead beside the kennels where doughboys shot them.

Cremating was done by habitual criminals who were fed well while on detail and promised liberty and parole after several months of good service. But the Nazis played a wry joke on their helpers. When parole time came they were pushed into the gas chambers themselves.

The biggest headache of the Dachau camp commander, who ran all camps in Bavaria and Austria[13] was the shortage of fuel for ovens. When coal was lacking, people were taken from the gas chamber and thrown in a great pit within the camp where 8,000 now lie.

It is even more obvious in the article in the army newspaper than in the one already cited from the *New York Herald Tribune* of 2 May that at least some Americans had in the meantime learned to distinguish between the "good" and the "bad" Germans in the camp itself, between those imprisoned for political reasons and the criminals of the camp. For good reasons this was at first true only of the inmates of the prison camp, and even towards them there was some resentment; the "bad" Germans rubbed off on the "good". This can also be seen indirectly in a report from the *New York Herald Tribune* of 12 May, which appeared with the headline, "34 Nations Represented Among the Dachau Inmates. Official Check Sets Total at 31,601 Prisoners":

A reminder of the wholesale enslavement of people of many nations which was practiced by the Germans came today in an announcement at Supreme Headquarters that among the 31,601 prisoners at Dachau, an official check has shown, were persons of thirty-four nationalities.

Those imprisoned at this infamous German camp were Poles, Russians, French, Slovenes, Italians, Czechs, Belgians, Hungarians, Dutch, Austrians, Greeks, Spaniards, Luxemburgers, Iranians, Croats, Norwegians, Serbs, Rumanians, Slovaks, Lithuanians, Albanians, Letts, Estonians, Bulgarians, Portuguese, Sudetans, annexed Germans, Armenians, Swiss, Arabs, Danes, Irakians, Maltese and Finns.

There were also 2,539 Jews whose distinct nationalities were not given.

---

[13] The subsidiary camps or detachments belonging under the authority of the concentration camp Dachau were scattered across wide areas of Bavaria, mainly, south of the Danube and in the western half of Austria. Since subsidiary camps such as Landsberg or Kaufering are repeatedly treated as independent concentration camps in Allied press reports, the attribution of a kind of supervisory function over the Bavarian and Austrian concentration camps is probably based on this fact. A list of all the Dachau subsidiary camps can be found in Kimmel, op. cit. p. 381-383. The former camp commander of Dachau, SS battalion leader (SS-Sturmbannführer) Martin Gottfried Weiss, had become "unemployed" as the commander of the concentration camp Lublin due to the advance of the Red Army. He was ordered to return to Dachau shortly before the end of the war to support the actual camp commander, SS head battalion leader (SS-Obersturmbannführer) Eduard Weiter. Whether he occupied such a position or if Weiter made the practice of such a position possible, cannot be substantiated documentarily. See: Kimmel, op. cit., p. 373 f.

Germans (Reichsdeutsche) do not appear at all in this listing. Nonetheless, the Germans and the Austrians, with together over 6,000 prisoners, made up the fourth largest group among the nations in the camp even in 1945. The largest group was the Poles (almost 15,000), then the Russians (over 13,500) and then the Hungarians (around 12,000). The Germans formed a larger group than the French, the Italians or the Lithuanians.[14]

How difficult, even impossible, it had become for Americans to form an objective judgement about Germany and the Germans, precisely because of the increasing number of publications[15] about what had happened in the concentration camps, is shown by an article about the findings of American publishers and newspaper editors who had returned from viewing Buchenwald, Dachau and other camps. The article was published in the *New York Times* on 9 May:

American editors and publishers who were flown to Europe at the suggestion of Gen. Dwight D. Eisenhower to investigate German atrocities returned here yesterday morning, convinced that peace terms for Germany must be harsh.
Spokesmen for fifteen of the original delegation of eighteen newspaper and magazine executives asserted that published reports of the horrors and tortures perpetrated in German concentration camps at Dachau and Buchenwald were 'all too true.' ...
Joseph Pulitzer, editor and publisher of The St. Louis Post-Dispatch, voiced the sentiment of his colleagues, when ... he said:
'We were asked to go there to verify the conditions reported in the press. We found they were not exaggerated. As a matter of fact, they were understated. I am for a just but very severe peace as far as the Germans are concerned.'
'I'd say it couldn't be too severe,' Norman Chandler, publisher of The Los Angeles Times, added.
Gideon Symour, executive editor of The Minneapolis Star Journal, said: 'We've got to police Germany for the next twenty years, if the American people will stand for it.' ...
Stanley High, associate editor of Reader's Digest, said: 'We found no feeling of remorse among the Germans. If you talk to a German now, you wouldn't think there are any Nazis left – or at least only one, and that would be Hitler or the fellow next door.'
Mr. Pulitzer said he did not see how the average German could help not 'knowing of conditions when they saw thousands of these people being shipped out to work every day.' All Americans should see the atrocity pictures and newsreels, he added, declar-

---

[14] See: Statistik der Nationalitäten im Konzentrationslager Dachau und seiner Außenlager vom 16.–26. April 1945 aus der Lagerschreibstube; original is at the ITS Arolsen, a copy is in the museum of the memorial site at Dachau, No. 845.

[15] Magazine articles illustrated with photographs from the camps deserve mention here, for example, "Army Talks", 4th year of publication, no. 9 from 10 July 1945, issued by ETOUSA, the high command of the American Army in Europe. It placed a photograph of the main entrance of the camp Dachau at the front of a "Report about German Death Mills". See also articles in "Life" from 14 May 1945, in "Collier's" from 15 and 23 June 1945 and the most detailed and vivid one in "Time" from 7 May 1945. – Cf. also the documentary film about the concentration camps with which the US Army confronted the German population. See Brewster S. Chamberlin, Todesmühlen. Ein früher Versuch zur Massen-"Umerziehung" im besetzten Deutschland 1945–1946, in: Vierteljahrshefte für Zeitgeschichte 29 (1981), p. 420–436.

ing: 'The greater the shock to the American people, the better will be the realization of the horrors.'
The group expressed impatience with the theory that such pictures should not be shown in a 'family theatres.' William L. Chenery, publisher of Collier's Magazine, said that 'if some people have to endure these atrocities, certainly other people can look at them.'

As a reaction to the horror of the camp, the occupation powers had begun to draw upon the German guards and in some cases even the male inhabitants of the surrounding communities for cleaning out the concentration camps. The German language New York newspaper *Der Aufbau* reported on a compulsory visit which had been ordered by the Military Government for the German civilian population, including 30 dignitaries of the city of Dachau under the heading "The Jewish Flag Flies above Dachau":

The correspondent of the JTA reports from Dachau: 'The blue-white Zionist flag flies above the watch tower of this feared concentration camp. When I came here to make observations about the life of the Jewish inmates of the camp, it turned out that the American troops were still having to fight serious adversities in order to clean away the terrible conditions which the Germans have created in Dachau. Many things are still crying out for improvement, but nonetheless, 1,000 of the 2,539 Jews are already under hospital care. Dr. Benjamin Zacharin, a very well-known surgeon from Kaunas, who works in the camp hospital, explained to me that, with the appropriate care, most of them would survive.
All the camp inmates, Jews and non-Jews, are terribly impatient to leave the camp. However, that will not be possible yet for some time since 500 cases of typhus have appeared here ... The Jews themselves are not represented in the international camp committee. They have constructed their own Zionist 'center' under the direction of Chaim Kagan, who earlier headed the statistical office of the city Kaunas.
Lt. William Montague, a former film producer from Hollywood, ... has just completed, after ten days' work, filming the Dachau murder factory.
The population of Dachau maintains that it had no idea what was going on behind the electric barbed wire, only a few steps away. The lieutenant was able to bring a group of more than 30 leading citizens of the city of Dachau into the camp and to photograph the reactions reflected in their faces. Some fainted, as is shown in the film; others held handkerchiefs in front of their noses, and those, who were still able to speak as they left the camp, whispered outside again and again, 'unbelievable'.

A document of a special kind is represented by the comprehensive article by the London correspondent of the Polish newspaper *Rzeczpospolita* of 29 May 1945, which he had telegraphed to his editors on 17 May. The report is reprinted here in a shortened form, especially with personal references to relatives of the prisoners in Poland emitted:

I am sending today the first report about my visit to Dachau in the capacity as the accredited correspondent of "Rzeczpospolita" ...
Somewhat less than one kilometer before the gate of the concentration camp, the road divides into two directions. The one to the left goes to the city of Dachau with 15,000

inhabitants. The other one to the right goes to the concentration camp Dachau with twice the number of inmates. The sign with the inscription 'to the concentration camp' points out the way – and above this sign there is a colorful bas-relief which depicts the well-known picture of the German painter Spitzweg, 'The Three Merry Musicians'. The first plays a violin, the next a bass and the third a trumpet – all three frisk merrily about, showing the way to hell – to the concentration camp Dachau. Can one imagine a greater cynicism? ... We drive along a wonderful, magnificent avenue as if we were approaching a palace. On both sides stands a row of modern luxury-houses. These are the dwellings of the SS criminals. Finally, we arrive at the camp gate. We cannot drive farther because of the typhus and the outbreak of lice which prevail in the camp grounds. Therefore, at the entrance we have to undergo a special procedure: inoculation against typhus and spraying with insecticide. While standing in line, I speak in Polish to a camp translator from the group of camp inmates. I had, of course, recognized him as being Polish by the white-red badge in his buttonhole and the letter 'P' on the obligatory red background on his jacket. I have in my life often seen people who are happy and touched, but it is difficult for me to describe the rapture of this Pole when I addressed him in his mother tongue. It turns out that he is a priest ... He tells me that the American troops captured the camp on Sunday, 29 April, at 6:00 pm, three hours before the intended massacre of the prisoners, which had been set for 9:00 pm. In one of the guard houses abandoned by the Germans there was found an order of Himmler from 14 April. In answer to the question of the head squad leader (Obergruppenführer) Pohl, under whom all the concentration camps stood, about the future fate of the camp Dachau, Himmler ordered: 'There is no question of surrender. The camp is to be evacuated immediately. No prisoner shall be allowed to fall into the hands of the enemy alive. Prisoners have behaved barbariously to the civilian population in Buchenwald, signed Himmler.' ...

In this moment the car of the current American commander arrives. It is Colonel Joyce, who gives instructions, in concise military words, about conduct on the camp grounds and about relations with the former prisoners. The colonel has not yet come to an end, when, suddenly, his driver rushes up to me and excitedly shakes my hand. It turns out that he was also a prisoner – the Pole Zenon Tim ...

Finally, we got to the camp. The way leads through a wide avenue to an area surrounded with barbed wire which had formerly been electrified. In the middle a walled double gate with a high watch tower. Behind the gate a wide area, behind that, to the left, a long street with barracks on both sides. The grounds and the street are filled with people. A beautiful, warm day, and thousands of former prisoners are walking, conversing in various languages, sunning themselves and enjoying freedom, still for the time being in an area surrounded with barbed wire because of the epidemics and contagious diseases in the camp. For the time being the former prisoners are not allowed to leave the camp unauthorized ... Their faces are emaciated, their eyes sunken and with many of them, their eyes are glowing with fever. In prisoners' clothing with long white and blue stripes or in ragged suits, the former prisoners give the appearance of being creatures from another world. ... Those inside the barracks, who on the tenth day of their freedom are still not able to enjoy the sun, lie motionless on the plank-beds, barely able to lift their heads. Only now and then do their eyes reveal a certain interest in the new world surrounding them. They are closer to death than to life. Still today, the tenth day of freedom, 125 persons die each day in the camp, as reported to me by the American senior medical officer of the camp. ... On the tenth day of freedom 32,250 of the former prisoners of Dachau are still alive ...

At the end of my visit in the camp I was still the witness of a terrible proceeding, that is, the removal of the dead from the crematorium. In the last weeks of their murderous activities, the Hitler criminals ran out of coal which was necessary for burning the corpses. The corpses had simply been thrown on a pile in the crematorium, where they have lain for three weeks. When the Americans opened the crematorium, a terrible sight was offered to them: five-thousand decomposing bodies, attacked by worms, from which arose a horrible odor. At present the bodies are buried in mass graves – 400 daily. From the city Dachau Germans have been mobilized to clear the bodies out of the crematorium. I was still a witness to the heartless impassivity with which the Germans cleared out those bodies and how with complete detachment, they threw them like wooden blocks on the open wagons – each time, thirty bodies on a wagon drawn by two horses. When twelve wagons were loaded in this way, the train of wagons, driven by the Germans, began to move toward the gate, along the main road, through the streets of the city of Dachau to the cemetery – to the mass grave. On the wagons lay, visible for all, charred corpses and skeletons, covered over only with thin skin, with the stink of decomposing bodies. Witness to the shame and proof of the crimes of the Germans.'

The mass of readers' letters on the themes of tyranny, war and dictatorship are devoted to the conquered Germans and above all to the concentration camps. An exemplary collection of such remarks was published by the *New York Herald Tribune* on 24 April 1945 under the eloquent headline "Hell on Earth", with the sub-title "Shocked and Enraged Reactions of Readers to the Mass Atrocity of the Nazis". "What citizen of the civilized world can hear the names 'Germany' and 'Japan' without a feeling of rejection? Why don't we extinguish these names forever from the family of nations?" asked one indignant reader. And the American delegation of publishers declared in a common resolution on their return from Germany, that the German people could not be released from their part in the responsibility for these crimes. And furthermore, a just punishment was demanded for the leading figures of the Third Reich and the German general staff, for the party functionaries, all members of the Gestapo and the SS. The demand was also made that for sheer reasons of justice and for the future of world peace these people be indicted as war criminals on the basis of their official positions. (*Chicago Daily Tribune*, 6 May 1945.)

The idea of the collective guilt of the German people was once more enormously popularized in the foreign press at the end of the war through the discovery of the concentration camp horror. Almost all peoples of continental Europe had, through a long-term process of habituation, accomodation and the development of counter-reactions, to a degree internalized the "normal" hardships of war and the pecularities of the National Socialist race and minority politics, so that to them the discovery of the SS prison-camp system only represented a gradual intensification of what they already believed the Germans capable of. But the exposure of the net of concentration and death camps shocked the American public in a totally different proportion. Many Americans of German descent felt themselves to be in a situation of collective consternation. America had a high percentage of European emigrants, many of them Jews, who by now formed part of public opinion with their own personal interest in the future fate of the Germans. Moreover at the end of the Second World War America had a position of undisputed moral supremacy in the world. The USA thus not only took a leading part in preparing and conducting of the International Military Tribunal in Nuremberg, but in their twelve subsequent Nuremberg war crimes trials against the leadership elite of the Third Reich they also surpassed all similar trials of other Allied states against former Axis powers, both in the rank of the accused as well as in the political importance of the trials. There is a clear line of development from the reporting about the persecution and extermination measures in the camps of the SS to the Nuremberg trials, the so-called Dachau trials and finally even to the series of trials against Nazi criminals in German courts. In this line of development lies the importance of the reporting about Dachau, Buchenwald and other camps rather than in the historical sources of individual accounts, which often raise as many questions for historians as they answer.

Wolfgang Benz
Between Liberation and the Return Home
The Dachau International Prisoners' Committee and the Administration of the Camp in May and June 1945

When Liberation came, the concentration camp changed from a place of imprisonment, exploitation and annihilation under the control of the SS to the "autonomous Republic of Dachau under American protection".[1] This peculiar social entity existed for about six weeks and ended with the departure of the last exprisoners some time in June 1945.[2]
But as far as externals were concerned, for most of the prisoners the situation after 29 April, the day of the Liberation, did not differ much from before. Even if the threat from the SS had ceased, the danger to life continued, from typhus and typhus fever, from the shocking sanitary conditions and from the corpses that lay about everywhere and the removal of which was still in progress a week after the Liberation. Nor did the Liberation mean liberty, at least not the liberty to leave the camp area.
Under the date of 29 April 1945, a declaration was promulgated, from which the "Comrades" – this was now the official designation and form of address – discovered that "as the supreme representatives of the prisoners of all nations and for the preservation of order, an International Prisoners' Committee has been formed" which decreed, among other things, the following with immediate effect: "The supreme executive organs of the camp are the Camp Elder and the Camp Secretary. All their instructions, which are given with the approval of the International Prisoners' Committee, are to be carried out at once. The entire police force is under the command of the Camp Elder and is to ensure peace and security with all the means at its disposal. Any infringement will be punished immediately in the strictest manner."[3]

---

[1] Edmond Michelet, *Die Freiheitsstraße*. Dachau 1943–1945, Stuttgart, n. d. (1960), p. 252.
[2] The exact point in time cannot be established exactly on account of the bad state of the records; the Italians were still in Dachau at the end of June; it is possible that there were still stateless persons and some people too ill to be moved in the camp area or at the evacuation points much later. As an indication, c.f. the Communique I/45 of 3.7.45, in which Jan Domagala as "Camp Secretary" announced rules of behaviour in the name of the "Camp Office of Dachau" (Collection of the Instructions of the International Prisoners' Committee, Archive of the Dachau Memorial Site).
[3] idem.

And a few days later the Camp Elder made it known that the commander of the American Liberation army had issued this decree.: "Anyone found outside the camp without a pass will be shot" and the Camp Elder added that the "Commandant demanded the strictest discipline, quiet and order within the camp as well".[4]

The situation of this social entity consisting of people of many nations was without precedent. In many ways it no doubt resembled a medieval town in which the plague had raged, but where in contrast to the latter over-population also prevailed. The imprisonment suffered together had, as was soon revealed, by no means resulted in an awareness of equality and fraternity among all the inmates, and not all regarded patience and solidarity as the most important virtues demanded by the situation.

The task faced by the International Prisoners' Committee as legislative and executive organ of self-government at the same time was gigantic. 32,000 former prisoners from nearly all the countries in Europe had not only to be fed and clothed, they had to be issued with a provisional proof of identity, and for many of them a home country had first to be found: for the Spaniards, for example who had fought against Franco, for the Yugoslavs who had become Italian citizens through no action of their own or who, as opponents of Tito, had no wish to return to their homeland. There were Greeks and Albanians in Dachau who were listed as Italians; there were Lithuanians, Estonians, Latvians and Ukrainians who were claimed by the Soviet Union against their will; there were nearly 10,000 Poles and over 2,000 Jews in the camp, the nationality of some of whom was the subject of controversy. To say nothing of those unfortunate young men from Belgium, Norway and Holland who had let the Nazis seduce them into service with the Waffen-SS, then deserted and had finally arrived in Dachau as prisoners. In those cases where their compatriots did not make short work of them on the spot, terrible things awaited them when they arrived home.[5]

Spontaneous vengeance also threatened all those prisoners who had acted as agents of the SS; numerous capos, the overseers, met their fate in the same hour that brought liberation to their victims.

The first meeting of the prisoners' committee after the Liberation, which took place in the presence of the commander of the American troops, Lt. Col. Fellenz, on the evening of 29 April 1945, or perhaps not until the morning of 30 April,[6] was taken up with the problem of preventing the chaos that was

---

[4] Idem, Announcement of the ce, undated.
[5] Michelet, *Die Freiheitsstraße*, p. 258 f.
[6] The "Report on the first meeting of the International Prisoners' Committee in the liberated camp at Dachau" is undated. As stated there, the report was to be "made public in the most important languages in the course of the morning" which makes the early morning of 30 April seem the probable date. All the subsequent reports which have the character of minutes of meetings, are dated. They are in the archive of the Memorial Site of the Concentration Camp, and subsequent quotations refer to these.

threatening for the reasons mentioned. In this meeting, the American commander handed over all authority in the camp to the President of the committee, Patrick O'Leary. The Americans wanted to restrict themselves to providing protection in relation to the outside world, they promised to take over the supply of provisions in a few days' time. The camp Elder, Oskar Müller, a German Communist, an inmate of many years' standing who combined an essential honesty with stubbornness, and the Camp Secretary, Jan Domagala, a Polish priest, were designated as the executive agents of the camp. The camp police was put under the command of Gustav Eberle "until further notice".

The first and most important decrees issued by the Committee were:

1. "Nobody is permitted to leave the camp".
2. "Any weapons in the camp must be handed in to the office immediately".
3. "Arbitrary actions, acts of personal vengeance etc. will be punished at once with the most vigorous measures."

The commandos necessary for supplying the camp (the term "commandos" was retained from the terminology of the time before the Liberation, and officials involved in the internal self-administration also continued to be called "capos") were able to leave the grounds with passes. The Prisoners' Committee established three sub-committees which were to be responsible for food (Jan Marcinkowski), discipline (Oskar Juranic) and disinfection and sanitation (Frantisek Blaha). This was the first organizational framework the International Prisoners' Committee provided for the Camp.

The Committee itself had been formed before the Liberation, indeed it had existed as an underground organization for some time before the arrival of the Americans, and had taken over the internal control of the camp immediately before they appeared. Its activities in the last week of April had consisted of sabotaging the evacuation transports out of Dachau, of offering help to those arriving from other camps until the very end (for instance, the 400 women from Landsberg, who arrived on 23 April, and the 120 women from Auschwitz, who arrived in Dachau on 26 April). Their assistance consisted of organizing food and blankets. The representatives of the national groups had been preparing in particular to resist the expected final annihilation action of the SS against the whole camp. The Committee maintained a well-functioning underground communications network, through which instructions for the ultimate emergency could be spread and through the branches of which news from the SS camp hierarchy could also be gathered.

In the night of 28 to 29 April, when it became clear to the men that the greater part of the guard had vanished, the first "official" meeting of the International Prisoners' Committee took place.[7] The first goal was to organ-

---

[7] Cf. the account in Arthur Haulot and Ali Kuci, Dachau (July 1945, unpublished translation in the archive of the Memorial Site, Dachau) p. 25: "At 11.30 p.m. fifteen men

ize survival until the arrival of the Allied troops. Enormous difficulties would continue after the Liberation or only become apparent then, namely the health of the 32,000 prisoners, two thirds of whom were ill and debilitated, the supply of food, the absence of medicines and medical equipment. Apart from that, the atmosphere in the multi-national community of the camp was characterized by explosive emotions. "What is important now", wrote Haulot and Kuci, the chroniclers of these events, "is to snatch these 32,000 people from the jaws of death so that they may return home alive and recover from their physical and spiritual sufferings in their home countries. That is the task that lies before us, and that we want to try to fulfil. Under the chairmanship of Major O'Leary, we constituted ourselves as the International Prisoners' Committee, and from that moment on regarded ourselves as the only legitimate authority in the camp ..."[8]

There were fourteen members who, as representatives of the individual nations (or of the national committees), constituted the IPC, the generally accepted abbreviation of the International Prisoners' Committee. Its composition soon changed[9] and the body became smaller and smaller in the course of the repatriation of national groups. Until 7 May, Patrick O'Leary, who represented Great Britain, was President. Arthur Haulot (Belgium) and Edmond Michelet (France), both Resistance fighters who made political careers for themselves after their return home, were the Vice-Presidents. The writer Giovanni Melodia represented Italy, Oskar Juranic Yugoslavia; the Soviet Union was represented by Nikolai Michailov, a general, who for some curious reason had escaped the fate of so many high-ranking Russian officers as German prisoners of war. Georg Pallavicini spoke for Hungary, Alfons Kothbauer for Austria, Dr Ali Kuci sat on the committee for Albania (and

---

gathered as quietly as possible in Block 24: the Canadian, Patrick O'Leary; the Englishman, Tom Groome; the American, René Giraud; the Frenchman, Michelet; the Yugoslavs, Jurenic and Popovic; the Poles, Maczewski, Domagala and Kokoszka; the Czech, Blaha; the Dutchman, Boelard; the German, Müller; the Austrian, Kothbauer; the Belgian, Haulot; the Albanian, Kuci. The Russian General Michailov was unable to appear on account of illness." Michelet, *Freiheitsstraße*, p. 258f. on the other hand, dates the first full meeting of the International Prisoners' Committee as being on the morning of 29 April "in the library of the first room of Block 2, on the left avenue, that is, the one nearest to the 'jour house' [the camp gate]". Cf. also Arthur Haulot., "Lagertagebuch" (Camp Diary), in: *Dachauer Hefte*, 1, Introduction and entry of 29. 4. 1945. Haulot there dates the beginning of the Committee at 6th April, 1945. Cf. also Nico Rost, *Goethe in Dachau*, Munich, 1946, p. 296f.

[8] Haulot/Kuci, *Dachau*, p. 26.
[9] The composition of the IPC was made public in the proclamation of 29 April. Fourteen representatives were named; the following information is verified by the minutes of the meetings. Some uncertainties (including in the spelling of some of the names) could not be removed. Thus, for instance, the American and the Englishman mentioned by Haulot/Kuci do not appear; it is also unclear from what date the Greek representative belonged to the IPC, and from when until when the "small groups of Balkan peoples" had their own delegates.

for the small groups of peoples from the Balkans, later for Greece as well) – he achieved remarkable things as the person in charge of the press and cultural matters, having been Minister for Information in his homeland. Josef Kokoszka represented the Poles and the delegate of the Czechs was Frantisek Blaha, a doctor who plays an extremely praiseworthy role in many of the memories of the suffering in Dachau. Norway, Holland, Luxemburg and Spain also had representatives on the IPC at various times. As a result of objections from General Michailov, members of individual nationalities of the USSR such as the Lithuanians were not separately represented. Nor did the more than 2,000 Jews have their own representative at first, since their national status was not easy to clarify. And the 1100 German prisoners were not represented as a nation in the first instance either.

While the Austrians celebrated a national rebirth with red-white-red flags and insignia and demonstrated a new selfconfidence before everybody in the camp,[10] the Germans had become outcasts. Their two-fold identity – as compatriots of the SS and as companions in suffering for in most cases many years of imprisonment in the concentration camp – now sent them to the bottom end of the camp community. They had no flag when the whole camp broke out in a sea of bright national colours (the liberated prisoners had found large quantities of material for them in the stores and workshops of the SS), and the German language, yesterday the only official idiom, retreated entirely into the background. Despite this, of course, German remained an important means of communication in the Babylonian confusion of Dachau, within the new government of the camp as well as in interaction with the outside world.[11]

"The first have become the last", wrote former prisoner No. 16921 Karl Adolf Gross in his diary on 30 April. This was, he wrote, somewhat unfamiliar to the Germans who even as prisoners still belonged to the "master race and noble class". And Gross continued: "Just between ourselves, we have to be glad that they did not bash our skulls in; did not the various kinds of pashas, moguls, pharaohs, capos and those on fatigues do all they could to encourage the mistaken notion that there is no difference among the Germans whether they be SS-Führer or prisoners, that they are all the same block-heads and all belong into the bull family? For our pashas had right up to the end been chosen almost exclusively from among the Germans; and did they do anything to destroy this notion? Certainly, the SS is not in the least

---

[10] Johann Steinbock, *Das Ende von Dachau*, Salzburg 1948, p. 34f.
[11] At the 7th meeting of the IPC on 8 May, the French representative Michelet had declared that French had to be the prevailing language for the negotiations of the Committee. As in the founding conference of the UNO in San Francisco, English, Russian und French were to be the official languages; for practical reasons, German could be retained as a fourth one. The Belgian Haulot, who presided, noted that all previous meetings had been held in French, English and German, he himself always translated from German to French and vice versa.

exonerated by this. On the contrary, it is evidence of the cunning they employed in that they had direct maltreatment replaced more and more by the cruelty of the prisoners to one another, thus building human weakness and malice into their system".[12] For this reason the fact that a German exercised the functions of "Camp Elder" is a more a miracle than an accident. This fact can perhaps be better explained by the personal qualities of the anti-fascist Oskar Müller, who had only been appointed to the office shortly before by the SS, and had then, in close cooperation with the still illegal national committees, made preparations to prevent the catastrophe feared by all – the massacre they expected of the retreating SS in the final hours before the arrival of Allied troops.[13] Oskar Müller, an energetic and political man (later, from October 1945 to December 1946, he was Minister for Labour in the first post-war government in Hesse), succeeded the notorious Armenian Johann Meanssarian, who had been removed from the position as Camp Senior by the SS in the middle of April 1945 and had been executed by firing squad on the orders of the US commander immediately after the Liberation, together with the German Wernicke, capo of the camp police.[14] Even in view of the vengeance that was wreaked everywhere in the concentration camps against the former prisoners who had been given functions by the grace of the SS, it was remarkable that a German Camp Senior was able to retain his authority. Finally, on 6 May, a German committee was also formally constituted[15].

There were several reasons why the gate of the camp remained closed for most prisoners after the Liberation and why for many, it took weeks before they were free. While fighting continued in Southern Germany, there were no means of transport available for the former prisoners and at the very least

---

[12] Karl Adolf Gross, *Fünf Minuten vor zwölf. Des ersten Jahrtausends letzte Tage unter Herrenmenschen und Herdenmenschen. Dachauer Tagebücher des Häftlings Nr. 16921*, Munich n.d. (1947), p. 216.

[13] Cf. "Einer von 'Nacht und Nebel'. Was Arthur Haulot zu Dachau sagt", in: Süddeutsche Zeitung, 18.12.1945. See also Hermann Langbein... *nicht wie die Schafe zur Schlachtbank. Widerstand in den nationalsozialistischen Konzentrationslagern 1938-1945*, Frankfurt 1980, p. 382.

[14] Report of the first meeting of the IPC; Meanssarian, born in Saloniki, stateless spy and Gestapo agent, had not become camp Elder until the beginning of 1945. The police-capo Wernicke was a former member of the SA in the Horst Wessel-Sturm, who had got into the concentration camp as a result of criminal offences. These two had created an atmosphere in the camp in April, "which was supposed to lead to an explosion. 'Our way lies with the SS', they emphasized again and again and tried to gain control of the camp with a group of 500 dark elements. Had this been successful, the consequence would have been a devastating bloodbath." (Oskar Müller, So wurden 33,000 befreit, in: *Mitteilungsblätter der Lagergemeinschaft Dachau*, December 1970.) Meanssarian and Wernicke were the two officials of the camp hierachy who were removed by the illegal prisoners' organization, cf. Haulot, Lagertagebuch, Einführung und Eintragung vom 29.4.1945 Introduction and Diary entry of 29.4.1945.

[15] K.A. Gross, *Fünf Minuten vor zwölf*, p. 242f.

they would have been in danger on their homeward journey. But the population of the area surrounding the camp had to be protected from marauding liberated prisoners wanting to make up for the deprivation they had suffered. (It was not possible to prevent this entirely despite all precautions, but the depredations of plundering camp inmates in the Dachau hinterland did not come anywhere near the grave fears.)

Apart from the difficulties with transport, the state of health of most of the prisoners was a decisive obstacle to their returning home; even the constitution of the apparently healthy proved not to be to the drastic improvement in nourishment after a few days. Typhus and typhus fever had been epidemic for months in any case. This fact, together with the catastrophic hygiene conditions, prompted the Americans to place the entire camp under quarantine. A further reason for maintaining the prison-like conditions lay in the fact that former guards and officials from the ranks of the SS as well as of the prisoners, had disappeared in the camp, hoping to escape justice by wearing prisoners' clothes.

All this, and not least the repatriation question characterized the situation and the problems between Liberation and the return home. There was an absolute contrast between the high spirits of the Liberation and the bureaucratic procedures which the Americans had thought up with the best of intentions and which they implemented in cooperation with the national prisoners' committees.

Reports and chronicles of the concentration camp at Dachau usually end at the latest with the description of the festivities on 1 May 1945, when on the parade ground of the camp in the middle of a forest of flags and banners, the Liberation and imminent end of the war were festively celebrated with speeches in fifteen languages.[16] But the celebrations – many national groups also celebrated the Liberation in their own separate functions – were followed for most inhabitants of the camp by periods of waiting that were hard to bear. In the late afternoon of 1 May, the third meeting of the International Prisoners' Committee took place. On this occasion, the American Captain Martin Agather elaborated (in German) the approaching struggle with redtape in the following words: "The main thing is that you get home as soon as possible. So that we can do this as quickly as possible, we would like you all to give us a little help. We have here a questionnaire. Everyone who is in the Camp has to fill in a questionnaire. So we want you as a group, each from his own nation, to make sure that we get help with these questionnaires. You can choose as many assistants as are necessary. It depends on the size of the group. So that this will happen as quickly as possible, the Major, who is our assistant officer, will check that all questions are correctly answered. I shall show you this evening how this questionnaire is to be filled out. For this rea-

---

[16] *Idem*, p. 217; Michelet, *Die Freiheitsstraße*, p. 253 f.; Steinbock, *Das Ende von Dachau*, p. 36 f.

son, I am now distributing the questionnaire to all those present. These questionnaires are printed in English and German and the answers are to be written in block capitals. Pay attention, there are a few questions here that require some explanation. In the question about profession, we mean profession in civilian life. In the question about the place of arrest, we mean the place where the arrest took place. Under details concerning imprisonment, we mean any cruelty that you personally have suffered. An American court will be set up in the camp. All those who have committed atrocities will appear before this court and receive their punishment. On the second page, line six, there is the question: Have you ever been convicted of a punishable offence? This question must be answered precisely. There are some people in the camp who are here because of crimes; we have to know this. The next question refers to anything that relates to the previous question: date, court, trial, date of release from prison – everything has to be answered precisely on the questionnaire. We need four questionnaires for each person. We have to have the questionnaires filled in as quickly as possible, so only one copy of the questionnaire is filled in. As soon as we have the individual questionnaires we will ask you to have the other three copied on a typewriter and signed by the person filling it in."[17]

A lively discussion developed, in which the representatives of the national groups demonstrated the difficulties faced in filling out of the questionnaires: linguistic problems, since English was one of the rarer languages in the camp, doubtful or no longer valid citizenships, questions of nomenclature. Typical of the requests for further information was that of the Italian Melodia, who wanted to know whether in the case of Italian military prisoners who had been transferred from an Italian military prison to a German concentration camp, the date of the Italian or German arrest was decisive; General Michailov wanted to know which citizenship Russian emigrants had to state, who had emigrated in 1917 and now wished to return to their old homeland.

Despite all this, the American Captain was confident that the clearance of the camp could be accomplished in 30 days. He already had five thousand forms at his disposal, he was expecting a further 100,000 in the next few days. The clerks and interpreters got to work.

The greatest difficulty in the next few days lay in explaining to the inhabitants of the Camp the limits of their liberty and in keeping these limits effective with appeals and threats. On 2 May the Americans drew the reins in more tightly. An order had come from Eisenhower's headquarters that no-one was permitted to leave the Camp who had not been disinfected. Besides this and despite all precautions inhabitants of the camp who were plundering and loafing about in the town of Dachau were a cause for concern. Anyone found outside the camp without permission would be shot, orders to this effect had been issued to the US troops in Dachau, Captain Agather declared

---

[17] Report on the 3rd meeting of the IPC, 1. 5. 1945.

in the meeting of the IPC on the evening of 2 May. Inside the camp as well, conditions were giving cause for concern. Agather implored the men of the International Prisoners' Committee: "There is to be no strife in the camp, rather you ought to live together as good comrades. We do not want to be guards. You are free and you shall live in freedom, only you cannot go out for the time being until the requirements have been met."[18]

In order to restore order and discipline which had started to falter in the camp, the organization of the authority structures responsible for Dachau were tightened on 2 May on the orders of the American commandant. The commander of the US troops installed himself as the "Camp Commandant", the president of the IPC became the "Lagerführer" or Camp Leader, and in this capacity Patrick O'Leary was the executive agent and directly responsible to the US commandant. On the level below this - "Lagerältester" Camp Senior and "Lagerkapos" Camp capos - everything remained as it had been. The "police capo", the chief of the camp's internal police troop, was given the power to arrest any miscreants immediately. The authority in legal matters was vested in the person of the Jugoslav Committee member Juranic as it had been previously, this received complaints, carried out "trials" and reported on these to the IPC. How seriously the Americans took their function in preserving security and order can be gauged from all sorts of complaints and grievances with which the International Prisoners' Committee was obliged to concern itself. For example, the American military police confiscated a truck laden with spare parts for radios which an official unit had obtained outside the Camp on the instructions of the IPC. Radio receivers were vital for the morale in the camp. In another instance, they would not even allow a unit to leave the camp to acquire clothing, even though it was properly equipped with the regulation passes. And the President of the International Prisoners' Committee, Patrick O'Leary, who, as a British officer, was urgently called to London by telegram, was initially refused permission to

---

[18] 4th meeting of the IPC, 2. 5. 1945. Some insight into the life of the camp is given by the circular of the Camp Elder to all blocks of 9. 5. 1945: "During a check by American medical personnel, it was observed that cleanliness and hygiene in the individual blocks leaves extraordinarily much to be desired. I therefore order: The cleaning of the blocks will take place in the usual fashion. That is, after waking and breakfast, the rooms and dormitories must be cleared of all comrades insofar as they are not bedridden or ill. The cleaning/fatigue duty will then clean dormitory, living room, washroom and latrines most thoroughly. Buckets with calcium chloride are to be placed in all latrines. The latrine duty is to strew calcium chloride over the toilet bowl and basin. I remind you once again that, in the interests of the proper distribution of food, the sick must be brought to room 4, and if there are too many, to room 3 of each Block. Only in this way is it possible to hand out normal food for the healthy and semi-solids for the sick. In irresponsible fashion, in isolated dormitories the ceilings have been destroyed with the intention of hiding and concealing organized things in the roof. I am making the Block officials responsible for obtaining new ceiling boards in cooperation with the Camp Capo in order to repair the damage."

make the journey by the Americans who pointed out that no-one was allowed to leave the Camp on account of the quarantine regulations. Nonetheless, O'Leary was able to leave the camp on the evening of 7 May;[19] this brought about another change in the hierarchy. O'Leary's successor as camp leader was the American lieutenant Charles Rosenbloom; this gave the advantage of very close contact with the American authorities. As a member of the liberating army, however, Rosenbloom could not be a member of the IPC. O'Leary's position as President of the International Prisoners' Committee was now taken over by the Russian Michailov. This was actually merely pro forma. In fact, the affairs of the camp government were run by the Belgian Haulot, as they had really been from the start. The composition of the camp government changed a number of times before the disbanding of the Camp. But until 6 June, when the worst was over, Haulot and Rosenbloom provided continuity and efficiency during the concluding work. Haulot, who took over the office of President officially from 26 May after Michailov's departure, does not appear to have had a successor. After this the almost entirely empty Camp was administered solely by the Americans, who tried and sentenced the former masters of Dachau and other concentration camps before military courts there from November 1945 onwards.[20]

The International Committee had shrunk more and more from the end of May. The Czech doctor František Blaha, who had rendered such outstanding services to the medical care in the camp, left for home on 23 May. (He ran a hospital in Prague until 1968, when he fell into disfavour.) His successor as head of the medical service in the camp was a Dr Dortheimer, who represented the Jews on the IPC. Pallavicini, the Hungarian, went to Paris on 26 May to confer about the repatriation of his countrymen. The majority of the French had left the camp on 22 May; on 26 May the Greeks representative also changed; their delegate on the IPC had been arrested on suspicion of having collaborated with the SS. Ali Kuci, who represented the Rumanians and Bulgarians as well as his own Albanian compatriots, now also took over the representation of the Greeks in the IPC. Kuci remained in the camp until the end and, in his capacity as head of the press and in charge of cultural activities, he provided information and entertainment. (He then returned to

---

[19] 5th meeting, 5. 5. 1945 and 6th meeting, 7. 5. 1945. Patrick O'Leary was in reality a Belgian, whose name in civil life was Albert Guérisse. He arrived in September 1944 from the Natzweiler Concentration Camp and was regarded as a Canadian. It was for this reason too that he had become President of the IPC, since the rivalries among the French, Poles and Russians for this office were avoided by the election of the representative of the smallest national group. O'Leary was the only "Canadian" in Dachau. Cf. Langbein, . . . *nicht wie die Schafe*, p. 172.

[20] The last extant minutes of a meeting of the IPC is dated 31. 5. 1945 (18th meeting); the last plenary meeting of the IPC took place on 6 June, and at this Rosenbloom was discharged. His successors were Captain Smith and Lt. Smolen. On 6 June, it was decided that, instead of the IPC, a sub-committee including the two Americans would meet every morning. Cf. Communique of the IPC, NO. 32 of 6. 6. 1945.

Albania and was not heard of again). On 31 May, the Polish representative also changed, because Josef Kokoszka departed. On 2 June the time came for Oskar Müller, the Camp Senior, to return home too; his successor was the Jugoslav Senko Knez who had hept the minutes of the IPC until then and who knew all the languages spoken in the camp. On 5 June Oskar Juranic, the "Minister of Justice" in the camp government also left Dachau.[21]

One aspect that was not only extremely remarkable but also fairly problematic for the camp community was the nationalism which flared up immediately after the Liberation. It was only natural that the individual national groups should conduct ceremonies on the parade ground to celebrate their survival and freedom. In view of the situation, however, national egoism, and worse still, the occasions on which it manifested itself, were strange and difficult to comprehend. The fact that the Norwegian Rasmus Broch complained in the International Prisoners' Committee that the Norwegian flag had not been hoisted during the celebrations on 1 May was harmless. The French, on the other hand, evidently often made the lives of their comrades of other nationalities thoroughly difficult. On 7 May Haulot declared in the meeting of the Committee that there was French agitation in the camp that could no longer be tolerated. Thus for instance, he said, French officers had repeatedly demanded that their compatriots be admitted into the overfilled sick bay, for which there was neither cause nor justification. At first there had been disagreements about insufficient consideration of the French language and about the inappropriate placement of the Tricolour; the French were of the opinion that their flag should fly next to the American Star-Spangled Banner and the flags of Great Britain and the USSR, but in the spring of 1945 China was regarded everywhere as the fourth nation of the "Big Four" instead of France. A donation of food by the French Army immediately after the Liberation, before the Americans could provide supplies, and the utilization of this assistance for propaganda purposes, kept the International Prisoners' Committee in suspense for some time.[22]

The French representative Michelet liked to revert to fundamentals in questions of prestige, and even compared the Prisoners' Committee with the inaugural conference of the UNO in San Francisco to prove, for example, that

---

[21] Cf. especially the 17th meeting of the IPC on 26. 5. 1945, as well as the communiques of the IPC, in which the head of the press section Kuci farewelled the departing national groups and IPC members with cordial words. - At the 15th meeting of the IPC, Dr Schreiber was welcomed as the representative of the Jewish group. Haulot noted that he was invited to all future meetings of the IPC, but did not act "as a delegate of the Jews as a national group", as the Jews hat not been recognized as such a group, "since, in accordance with the current resolutions of the views of the Committee, the Jews belonged to those national groups whose citizens they are. The Jews have established their own information office, of which Dr Schreiber is the head. He takes part in the meetings without the right to a vote."

[22] Michelet, *Die Freiheitsstraße*, p. 252 f. and 256 f.; 7th Meeting of the IPC, 8. 5. 1945 and 12th Meeting 14. 5. 1945.

the French representative really deserved the presidency of the IPC. When Michelet, in the course of such an argument, complained vehemently that no representative of the French National Committee had been invited to meet the US ambassador to Paris, who had paid an inspection visit to the Dachau camp on 8 May, it was the last straw. Kuci pointed that they had only found out about the event the night before: "If Michelet slept while we worked and slaved away to have everything ready, then he has only himself to blame for the consequences." And Haulot added "while we made these preparations in the greatest imaginable haste, we really did not have the time to think about all the possible consequences". And he went on, incidentally, there were more urgent matters to be attended to and people ought not to fritter the time away with this sort of thing.

Michelet justified himself by pointing out that his compatriots had been upset, he as a "disciplined member of the Committee" had tried to pacify them and had been able to prevent a protest demonstration. Apart from this the French were among the poorest inhabitants of the camps; this fact and the particular sufferings of the French were acknowledged by the members of the Committee. Frantisek Blaha did remark, however, that, as long as he had been on the Committee, no one had heard a single word from him that referred to his nation in particular: "We must all consider only the well-being of the camp as a whole".[23] Other members of the Committee expressed similar sentiments.

An appeal to practise solidarity and to desist from political demonstrations, to await the procedures involved in disbanding the Camp patiently in order to avoid chaos and anarchy, was issued in the name of the International Prisoners' Committee by the press chief Ali Kuci to the press sections of the national committees. Under the heading: "Two Duties and one Principle: Friendship, Brotherhood and No Politics..." the article read as follows:[24]

Twelve years have passed since this Dachau Camp was founded. Twelve years have passed since Hitler the beast grasped power in Germany. Only twelve years. Years of suffering and monstrous pain. A very small span in the enormous space of countless centuries, but a very sad and depressing chapter of human history ... A Hitler obsessed with power wanted to subjugate the world, and the soil of Germany became the grave of Europe. This our Dachau was a grave too. The grave of hundreds of thousands. And we survived it. And today, we are alive ...
We have woken from a long sleep and a terrible dream. The darkness of that long uncertainty and of the macabre scenes of the dream are fresh in our memories: we cannot comprehend the reality. Our conscious mind is incapable of grasping the happiness of liberty.
The most important thing is that we have been returned to life, that we are alive today. And the reason we are alive today is thanks to the friendship and brotherhood that existed in the Camp. We shared all the sorrows and sufferings of the difficult times, but

---

[23] 7th Meeting of the IPC, 8. 5. 1945
[24] IPC, Information and Culture, Central Press Bureau, 8. 5. 1945: To all the Press Bureaus Dachau. Two duties and one Principle: Friendship, Brotherhood and No Politics ... Archive of the Dachau Memorial

we never hated one another, never spied on one another. In the Nazi-hell, there were no Germans, no Russians, no Poles, no Jugoslavs: here there lived a community of friends and brothers, a family threatened by death on all sides, a society with the same principles and ideals. All had one and the same aim: the death of Hitler's thugs and their supporters. It was for this that we waged war in the high mountains and the wide plains of our homelands. This was the motto of the emaciated in Dachau.
And now we are free. The glorious armies of the Allies have fatally wounded the beast. It lies dying already . . .
Tomorrow, we shall return to our home and hearth. We shall find our loved ones and above all our homelands free and independent. It is there that we shall begin our social activities. Not here. Here we are in Dachau, the scene of the cruelty and the mass murders. And in this place, our thoughts would always dwell full of horror with the events of the past. Nothing more. Nothing else. We must give our liberators time to help us and for the wounds of the past to heal. We must make it possible for our representatives to carry out their tasks. No chaos, no anarchy! Those who yesterday betrayed our cause will have to answer before the camp court and will be charged. But the lives of thirty three thousand people so run down as to be mere skeletons must not be placed at risk. Anyone who tries to disturb the peace will be punished by all. Nothing will be forgiven him . . . Here there are only two duties and one principle: friendship, brotherhood and no politics . . ."

Naturally, those who had been imprisoned in the Camp for years on account of their political views, as opponents of the Hitler regime or as resistance fighters, could not desist from politics at all or only with difficulty. To demand political abstinence in the situation of the liberated camp was hardly realistic. The French representatives certainly did exaggerate a little when they anticipated on a lower level, as it were, the sort of obstruction carried out by the French military governor in the Allied Control Council in Berlin from the summer of 1945 onwards. They had made themselves unpopular with the Americans in Dachau because of the constant concern about the prestige of their nation while at the same time showing a great lack of concern about the general situation in the camp. The Meeting of 14 May was characteristic. The International Prisoners' Committee was invited to it at the quarters of the American Commandant, Colonel Joyce, who was receiving a visit from General Adams. Lieutenant Rosenbloom introduced the members of the IPC to the General. Michelet, the French representative, was absent. As the items to be discussed included matters of concern to the French, Joyce explicitly stated his regrets at Michelet's absence. When he discovered that the Frenchman had been properly invited, but had declared that he would probably not appear, the American colonel blew a gasket. He complained that Michelet had already failed to comply with a request the previous evening and added that if this were repeated he would have the guards fetch him. Moreover, the situation in the French area was terrible, they disregarded the quarantine regulations, they walked around the hospital with typhus patients and generally behaved as though the kitchen was for them alone.[25]

---

[25] 13th Meeting of the IPC, 14. 5. 1945.

Because the main occupation for most of the inhabitants of the camp was waiting, discipline was soon in a bad way. To the sorrow of the International Prisoners' Committee the force exercised by the SS was not automatically replaced with a feeling of solidarity that might have served as a mechanism for regulating the life in the camp. Thus for instance, the Camp Senior Müller reported that during a check on two work commandos, one had been found in the roof, where the men were lying in the sun, while the other had dispersed completely, in order to "organize". (On the following day, the head of the work services, Malczewski, announced – "as an illustration of work morale" – that the entire kitchen unit, consisting of 60 men, had run away.) If it was not possible to bring about order by means of the national committees, Oskar Müller declared, "then we shall have to do what we would like to avoid: to ask the Americans to have guards accompany the individual commandos".[26] This would have meant that the US Army would have had to take over the functions of the SS.

The Americans, however, had enough to do with guarding the camp to maintain quarantine and with processing the questionnaires, As far as the Prisoners' Committee was concerned, they contented themselves with appeals about establishing discipline somehow or other. The continuing looting and refusals to work would have to stop. It happened regularly, IPC-member Malczewski reported, "that, for example, a unit is delegated to clean a hut. In fact, however, no-one is at work, since everybody is busy looting. The Americans say to themselves: we don't really care how long this work, which is supposed to make camp life tolerable, is dragged out by those involved themselves ..."[27]

The food supplied by the US Army caused unforeseen problems as well. The empty tins increased the mountains of rubbish in the camp, the removal of which was so troublesome, and in addition, the army rations encouraged many to cook in the streets of the camp in front of the huts; this was problematical not only for reasons of hygiene, but also because some used boards from the beds and other fittings as fuel.[28] The authority of those responsible for discipline in the camp was naturally limited; the "Camp Police", consisting of former prisoners, could not, for example, control the numerous visitors who wandered around the sick-bay area and made the quarantine pointless, as Dr Blaha complained. He would have preferred to have his patients guarded by GIs: "It is difficult for a prisoner (member of the Camp Police) to send all visitors away. For that, there has to be authority, since a uniform is a uniform and a rifle is a rifle ..."[29]

---

[26] 7th Meeting of the IPC, 8. 5. 1945.
[27] 8th Meeting of the IPC, 9. 5. 1945.
[28] 6th Meeting of the IPC, 7. 5. 1945.
[29] Idem. On the orders of the newly appointed LF Rosenbloom, the Camp Elder had issued an announcement on 7. 5. 1945 demanding order and discipline: "The sensible comrades in the camp must stand together and support the general order. In the bar-

The "Lagerälteste", Camp Senior Müller, on the other hand, tried to provide authority for his camp police by means of an appeal to common sense and a feeling of community in a circular to the Block Seniors: "The Camp Police is not the old 'Lager Polizei'. The Camp Police is only a voluntary service of your comrades to maintain order and security in the camp. For this reason, people ought not to make difficulties for the Camp Police or to abuse them, but to obey their orders, and, wherever possible, to give them full support. Any justified and true accusations are to be reported in writing to the Camp Senior. The Camp Police will, however, take firm action against undisciplined and malicious elements damaging to the Camp community."[30]

A good leisure activities programme would save half the Camp Police, a member of Kuci's Cultural Section had sighed in the IPC Meeting of 5 May, and Michelet had demanded a resolution of the Committee to solve the question of entertainment and activities during the leisure hours. If the people were to sing and entertain themselves, he said, there would be fewer difficulties with them. This was clear to all the members of the Committee, but the possibilities for doing anything were extremely limited. Above all, there was no space for cultural activities in the overcrowded camp. The problem with making the deer-park established by the SS next to the camp available, for example, was partly that it had to be guarded, since many inhabitants of the camp were only waiting for the opportunity to "escape"; quite a few succeeded too, even though the Americans issued strong warnings against leaving the camp for home without papers and without a copy of their questionnaire.

The death statistics in the camp for the months of May and June show how terrible the conditions in the camp were after the Liberation, and in what areas the activities of the camp's self administration and those of the Americans were most urgently required. Jan Domagala, the Polish priest who kept a tally in his capacity as Camp Secretary until 16 June, records 2226 dead for May and in June there were still 192.[31] The removal of the bodies of the dead, which had been lying in the camp's street since April, had still not been

---

racks, rooms, toilets, wash rooms and on the block streets the most painstaking cleanliness must prevail in the interests of the health of all comrades. Any breaking out of a new illness or epidemic will necessarily result in the extension of quarantine." And as a measure to strengthen discipline in the Camp, a "special list" was announced, in which the LF was to enter the names those who had been insubordinate: "Those comrades reported for lack of order and discipline will be released last from the Camp." Notice dated 7. 5. 1945, Archive of the Concentration Camp Memorial Site, Dachau.

[30] Circular of the ce. dated 9. 5. 1945

[31] Jan Domagala, *Die durch Dachau gingen* (translation of the report which appeared in Warsaw in 1957 in the Archive of the Concentration Camp Memorial Site, Dachau). By way of comparison: the death rate in Bergen-Belsen, which was liberated by British troops on 15. 4. 1945, was even higher. Between 15 April and 20 June 1945, approximately 14,000 people died there. Cf. Eberhard Kolb, *Bergen-Belsen,* Hannover, 1962, p. 314f.

completed a week after the Liberation. According to the information supplied by the Camp Senior in the meeting of the IPC on 5 May, 100 to 300 dead were buried every day. Particular concern was caused by those dead who were lying in drainage ditches or were floating in the narrow River Wuerm. This small river between the concentration camp and the camp of the SS, supplied water to the inhabitants of the camp.[32] The Americans carried out a vaccination campaign against typhus and typhus fever and expended considerable efforts on disinfecting the camp inhabitants and furniture. But in order to improve the sanitary conditions, it was necessary in the first instance to reduce the overcrowding, to separate the sick from the healthy – in so far as it was possible to speak of any "healthy" among the former prisoners – and to create space generally. By including the adjoining SS-grounds, where there were, above all, better facilities for admitting the sick, the situation gradually improved. As far as possible, the relocation took place in closed national groups, which, however, created new problems again.

While the re-quartering into the outer areas of the camp complex did bring some relief, the greatest improvement in the situation occurred when several thousand men were evacuated to the grounds of an SS-huts near the Schleissheim airfield, about 10 km from Dachau. The exodus began in the middle of May; it had been preceded by intense debates and controversies in the International Prisoners' Committee as to which groups should go to Schleissheim. As Lieutenant Rosenbloom announced, they were to stay in the new surroundings for about a fortnight, at the end of which they were to be repatriated. Quarantine was to be complete for everybody on 28 May, as Blaha had already announced in the meeting of the Committee on 10 May. The arguments now broke out as to which groups should be re-located to Schleissheim. According to Domagala's information, the original camp precincts at that time – on 14 May 1945 – held approximately 4,500 Russians, 3,100 Yugoslavs, 9,000 Poles, 2,200 Italians and 1,100 German nationals. Kuci suggested that all the Poles be re-located, that would solve the problem. Haulot objected that there were not enough healthy Poles (the sick could not and would not be moved), the Italians would to be included. Michelet opposed this on the grounds that the Poles were "les doyens du camp", all the functions vital to the operation of the Camp were in their hands and they should remain there so that everything did not get into a mess. Haulot then suggested that the 4,500 Russians, together with the 3,100 Yugoslavs, 1,600 Czechs and 1,100 Germans be moved, but General Michailov protested

---

[32] The supply of drinking water was a frequent topic at the meetings of the IPC. It is characteristic for the isolation of the inhabitants of the Camp that they thought the river next to the camp in which the bodies floated, was the Isar. Cf. 6th Meeting of 7. 5. 1945. Cf. also the circular of the Camp Elder of 9. 5. 1945, which states inter alia: "Drinking the water is highly dangerous. The pumping station has been damaged by sabotage on the part of the SS. The water supply is taken from a stream in which corpses have been found. We warn all comrades against drinking the water."

against this. For the most part, the Russians were hardly fit to be moved, since they had only recently arrived exhausted in Dachau from Buchenwald and Flossenbürg. Apart from this, there were, he maintained, not 4,500, but only 3,500 Russians in the camp, of whom only 2,500 were in a position to be moved. Nor could the Germans be considered for re-location either, because, as Oskar Müller pointed out, they were just being moved to the outer areas of the Dachau Camp. The Czechs were ruled out because their repatriation was imminent.

The suggestion that certain quotas of individual nationalities (Italians, Yugoslavs, Poles and Russians) be moved drew protests first from the Jugoslavian representative; his compatriots had always been badly treated, and now they had got the thin end of the wedge again compared with the French and smaller groups who had gone to the outer precincts of the camp. The Polish representative declared that the Poles had spent the longest time in Dachau and had made the greatest sacrifices. Only the Spaniards and the Italians were prepared to move to Schleissheim. After Lieutenant Rosenbloom had once again emphasized the usefulness of having whole national groups move, and the Polish representative had again expounded why the Poles did not wish to move, the US-Lieutenant consulted his superiors and conveyed the recommendation of the Russian Michailov, that the choice should be left to the American authorities. Rosenbloom was able to inform the Committee at once of the decision of the Commandant, Col. Joyce. The first transport was to leave on 15 May and was to consist of 1,000 Russians, and the first releases home were to be from Schleissheim, even before there were any from Dachau. This enticement had its effect (the accommodation, being former SS-barracks, were said to be better there as well), Oskar Juranic announced that, provided the men there would be released more speedily, he agreed to the re-location of the Jugoslavs to the interim camp, though he would first like to get a better picture of the place for himself.

It was decided to form a commission which would have a Pole, a Jugoslav and an Italian as members representing the national groups who were to move. This commission was to inspect the new camp. The Russians did not appoint a member to the commission; General Michailov had refused with a fine justification: "He said he had no wish to see anything, since he had complete faith in the American autorities. We have voiced our reasons, but if it has been determined that we are to move, then we have complete confidence and it is not up to us to choose or to verify, so an inspection is pointless."[33]

Naturally, the conditions in the Dachau camp did not improve suddenly as a result of the loosening up and of the evacuation to Schleissheim. There were

---

[33] 12th Meeting of the IPC, 14. 5. 1945. Because of the move to Schleissheim, three meetings of the IPC took place in the course of 14 May; in the afternoon and the evening, the Committee met in Colonel Joyce's quarters in the presence of General Adams who personally calculated the quotas of those to be moved.

even opinions to the contrary. In the old camp there was a terrible atmosphere, declared IPC member Malczewski on 17 May; those who had been moved to the outer areas had a host of advantages, those who had remained behind were living in a desert. The suggestion that the deer-park of the SS be opened to these people as a recreation area still remained unanswered by the Americans; the re-location campaign to Schleissheim had been stopped, as not sufficient accomodation had been prepared there as yet. Conditions were no different and no better than at the time of the Liberation, the Pole Kokoszka put on record, the people were still sleeping on the floor, the situation was catastrophic, there could be mutinies.[34] Five days later, there were complaints about insufficient and bad provisions, it was suspected that the German population outside the camp was living much better, which fears Lieutenant Rosenbloom tried to dispel.[35]

In order to improve the atmosphere, the chief of the Press Bureau had taken up his pen again. Under the title "Three Questions and two reasons", Ali Kuci urged perseverance in the name of the International Prisoners' Committee, once again imploring the inmates of the Camp to exercise patience and solidarity:

When are we going home? This is the question everyone is asking the American authorities, the members of the Prisoners' Commitee etc. The people in this Camp are very eager to find out something about the date they will be repatriated. And they are right. For after so many years of suffering and sadness, we all want to go home. To return immediately to our home and hearth and into the circle of our loved ones, to know and see how our countries and our people are faring now that the black clouds have been driven from the sky over Europe, clouds that have darkened the shining past and future of this continent for so many years.

But why are we not going home? There are very few people who can answer this question. Only those who are familiar with the present circumstances and know what is going on here in Dachau. This group of responsible persons knows the true situation. And they are working day and night to help their comrades and to facilitate their way home.

The living conditions in the Camp have greatly improved in the meantime. Our sick are being cared for as well as at all possible in the American evacuation hospitals. The food they are receiving is of a kind that we could not even imagine hitherto. They are content and full. The majority of those whose fate had been sealed in the SS-time now past are saved and are back in the land of the living. The sick, who had been languishing in the misery of quarantine, are now enjoying reasonable health. Their lives have been saved.

How can we go home? Many Camp inmates are suffering from typhus, tuberculosis and other serious epidemic diseases. That is the state of affairs. If the Americans had tried to evacuate us at once, many - about 80 per cent - would have died on the journey. This is one of the reasons why we were unable to return to our home countries immediately. The lives of many thousands were saved by these wise measures of the American authorities.

And the second reason? The epidemics we would have taken home with us would have

---

[34] 15th Meeting of the IPC, 17. 5. 1945.
[35] 16th Meeting of the IPC, 22. 5. 1945.

seriously endangered health in our own countries. We would have caused misery in the beloved places of our homelands. That would have been unfair.
We have lived for many long years in this place as prisoners and deathly shades. We had the courage and the endurance to survive the greatest sufferings known to the history of mankind. We were the victims of the cruellest tyranny in the world.
But now we are free. And we know that we shall be home in a few weeks. Why such haste? All haste, lack of order and insubordination hampers the work of our liberators and postpones our return home. This is why we should stand united together. This is why we should help each other, we among ourselves and all of us the Americans, who are doing so much for us.[36]

When the article appeared, a silver lining was beginning to appear on the camp horizon. Frantisek Blaha, who took part in a committee meeting for the last time on 22 May (this meeting had even been called especially as a farewell to him), announced that the infectious diseases in the camp – except for the sick bay – had ceased and Michelet added that there were no more cases of typhus among the French. Oskar Müller reported that the situation was improving in the camp, which was becoming emptier and emptier. The day before, 2,200 Russians had left the camp, the remaining 1,100 departed on 22 May; of the Czechs, some of a group of 990 had been repatriated, others evacuated already, the rest in the process of departure. The old camp now contained Poles, Jugoslavs, Italians, some smaller national groups, and Jews with unclear nationalities. In all, the population now amounted to only about 10,000 men, who were gradually better distributed. The deer-park was finally made accessible (until 9 p.m.), though the use of the SS swimming pool had to be prohibited again after a short time because the water was contaminated; living conditions altogether had improved,[37] and for many the camp gates had already opened to freedom. The quarantine had been lifted early; and, much to the amazement of those involved, in the bureaucratic procedures too, the Americans had done an about-turn, some details of which anticipated the denazification policy as practised later in the American Occupation Zone.
The 12 May came to be the dramatic climax in the tug-of-war about the release procedures thought up by the office-desk strategists, of the US Army. Captain I.V. Peterson had invited the Prisoners' Committee to his office in order to thank them for their successful work so far in relation to the filling in of the questionnaires; he expressed the hope that the work would be continued at the same rate. It was "the wish of the office concerned with the collection of information on the inmates of the camp who were to be repatriated, as well as the wish of the American Army, that this work be speeded up as much as possible".
This announcement by the American Captain hinted that for many, release

---

[36] IPC, Information and Culture, Central Press Bureau, Communiqué No. 20, Three Questions and two reasons, 21. 5. 1945.
[37] 16th Meeting of the IPC, 22. 5. 1945.

into liberty would not follow immediately upon filling in all the forms: "Those about whom there are no doubts or open questions will be considered for release first. But the questionnaires of those where there are doubts will be retained until everything has been completely resolved." For many, the time when they could enjoy freedom again would depend on the astuteness or the goodwill of the CIC officials, the American secret service investigating the "dubious" cases. In view of the background of so many of the Camp inmates, this was a depressing prospect. The former prisoners thus preferred by the hundred to withdraw from camp life regardless of the bureaucracy requiring the filling in of the questionnaire in quadruplicate before release. Captain Peterson issued a stern warning about such unauthorized behaviour, pointing out that, since the fighting had stopped, there was now plenty of personnel available as military police, who would keep a very strict watch to ensure that no-one would get out without permission. Apart from this, those who went home illegally would have difficulties once they got there. Captain Peterson requested that the following information be made clear to the camp inmates: "For every inmate properly released from the camp, one of these four forms is sent to his destination; but there will be no form for anyone who runs away. This will cause him many troubles and much unpleasantness and can even be dangerous for him."[38]

That was at nine o'clock in the morning.

At six in the evening of the same day, another meeting of the Committee took place with very good reason. Haulot, acting as chairman, informed the Committee that Captain Peterson had received new instructions, according to which the camp was now to be cleared in the shortest time possible. The US military authorities had decided to cancel the questionnaire campaign. Only the Germans and the Austrians now had to fill in the tedious forms before being released. Members of other national groups would merely be registered on lists and then be repatriated. The Americans would not interfere in the "special cases" (any longer), it was up to the authorities in their home countries what happened to these people. Major Goormaghtigh, as representative of the US Army, declared emphatically that as soon as a responsible officer appeared with the necessary means of transport, he could have his compatriots. If any country was not in a position to do this, the Americans would transport the people to the border of the country concerned.

In the meantime, there were evidently rumours circulating to the effect that the camp would be cleared within a week. In any case, Lieutenant Rosenbloom appeared in a meeting of the IPC and declared that the Camp Commandant knew nothing about this. A deputation thereupon made its way to

---

[38] 10th Meeting of the IPC, 12. 5. 1945. One illegal return home from Dachau has been described in Floris B. Bakels, *Nacht und Nebel. Der Bericht eines holländischen Christen aus deutschen Gefängnissen und Konzentrationslagern*, Frankfurt a. M. 1979, p. 345 ff.

ask Colonel Joyce himself. They returned and Major Goormaghtigh assured the Committee that it had been a false alarm. It was certainly true that the Camp was to be cleared swiftly, but not within a week: "Col. Joyce nearly had a stroke when he heard that according to rumours circulating the camp was to be burnt down within a week. He is simply not aware of the false rumours often flying around the camp so vigorously."[39]

The clearance of the camp was now only a transport problem, since the Americans had completely changed their attitude in the quarantine question as well. Only those actually ill came under it, all the others would have to undergo fourteen days' quarantine when they got home – so the Americans affirmed, and they perhaps even believed it. Haulot welcomed the improvement of the general living conditions in the camp and was pleased that they could now look forward to a logical and practical solution to the repatriation question and that there were no further paper problems.

This did not, however, apply to the Germans and Austrians, and their spokesmen did not conceal their indignation at the discrimination they saw in the fact that they were the only ones to fill in the questionnaires. The representative of the Austrians, Anton Kothbauer from Vorarlberg, said furiously "If I have understood correctly, we as Austrians are being treated as second-rate or being classed with the Germans – we who actively fought for the Austrian and the Allied cause against Hitlerism in the concentration camps and prisons, some of us who had been deported to Germany as early as 1938! Only yesterday, Radio London reported that Austrian citizens in Czechoslovakia are not to be regarded as Germans and do not fall under the provisions applicable to Germans. As the representative of the Austrians, I wish to express my displeasure at the fact that we, who had to build this Camp in double quick time with blood and sweat, are to be the last to leave. Like many other comrades, I personally fought against National Socialist Germany under Dollfuß and Schuschnigg. I shall probably no longer be able to attend meetings of the International Committee and I shall ask the national committee whether it still has confidence. You cannot appeal to us for years through Radio Moscow, London and America to take up resistance and then not recognize those who end up in prisons and concentration camps as equals."[40]

Major Goormaghtigh tried to pacify him by pointing out that the questionnaire matter was no more than a formal affair. The main thing he was expecting was a list of suspects – he meant the accomplices of the SS in prisoners' clothing – and assured him that the fact of having been a citizen of the German Reich that had been decisive for the discrimination, and that no sweeping condemnation was intended by it and so there was no reason for indignation.

---
[39] 11th Meeting of the IPC, 12. 5. 1945
[40] Ibid.

But Oskar Müller saw it differently. And one of the things that may well have played a part in his reply was the painful awareness of the difference in status which the well dressed representatives of the well fed US Army without even thinking about it demonstrated at every turn towards the wretched figures of the liberated men: "We German anti-fascists were the first to have borne unspeakable suffering in the prisons and concentration camps for eight and ten years, and it is unjust towards us too that special surveys are made for us."[41]

The representatives of some other national groups had different worries. Thus Pallavicini asked what those who still had no contact with their home countries such as the Hungarians and the Yugoslavs might hope for. (On this and other occasions, the Poles too gave expression to the problem of their unclarified future: which Polish government was to be responsible for them, the government-in-exile in London or the Lublin-Committee, and where should they have themselves repatriated depending on which political direction gained the upper hand?)

Major Goormaghtigh consoled the representatives of those national groups who still had no contact with their governments: "The whole world knows about Dachau. It is a focus of public interest the world over. No-one can maintain that your governments know nothing about Dachau. No doubt they are interested in Dachau. Material difficulties are responsible for their not having made contact. It is extremely difficult to get through a military zone; a long time passes before one can get permission. It is a bureaucratic process. The French have established contact so quickly because their troops are in the vicinity. The fact that the Belgians had contact from the beginning is a result of the coincidence that he himself – not as a Belgian but as an officer of an allied army – had been appointed to deal with repatriation questions here in Dachau."[42]

The imminent return home and the question "What will it be like there?" were also the principal topics in the camp newspaper. From the beginning of May, there existed in Dachau a press scene that was short lived but extremely diverse. The newspapers, which were published by the national committees, mostly consisted of a few hectographed pages of A 4 format. The paper of the Soviet committee was even handwritten on stencils and duplicated, presumably because there was no typewriter with Cyrillic type available. The Spaniards published a "Boletin de Informacion de los Espanoles Internados en Dachau", the Polish "Glos Polski-Biuletyn Komitetu Polskiego w Dachau" began to appear on 3 May; there was a Greek and a Jugoslavian information sheet; the Italians produced 37 issues of "Gli Italiani in Dachau" up to 29 June 1945, while the paper of the Belgians ("L'Union Belge") ceased to appear early in May because of the repatriation, as did the

[41] Ibid.
[42] Ibid.

French "Liberté" in which there was more discussion of great political issues than in other Camp newspapers. The Dutch informed themselves (for the last time in issue 11 on 14 May) by means of "De Stem der Lage Landen - Orgaan der Nederlanders in Dachau" and the Luxemburgers were served by "Ons Zeidong" in their own language.

The Austrians had one of the most extensive papers, which however only appeared rarely, though it did change its title in the third (and last) issue: the "Weg und Ziel der Österreicher" (Path and Goal of the Austrians) with the sub-title "Mitteilungsblatt der Österreicher in Dachau" (Information paper of the Austrians in Dachau). The main topic here was the rebirth of the nation, and there was surprisingly detailed reporting about the situation at home.

The German newspaper was called "Der Antifaschist. Stimme der Deutschen aus Dachau" (The Anti-fascist. The Voice of the Germans from Dachau) and it appeared twenty times beginning on 6 May. The last, undated issue, which had contained mainly announcements, short information items and news, was devoted to looking back ("German Anti-fascists did their duty" from the pen of Oskar Müller), but also to the future. The paper closed with the words: "We leave Dachau with the firm conviction that our lives will continue to be devoted to fighting against any form of fascist tyranny and for a free, democratic and anti-fascist Germany."[43]

The words of farewell written by Ali Kuci as head of the press bureau of the International Prisoners' Committee at the beginning of June as a kind of final proclamation, were directed to all those who had suffered in Dachau. They reminded of the past but they also contained optimistic expectations of the future couched in amical pathos: "The people are going home. Many, many have gone home in the last few days and even now many are setting off. In the next few days, Dachau will be deserted, a deserted monastery, which will bear witness of the greatest martyrdom in history to coming generations. Until now it has been a grave. In the twelve years of its existence about a million Europeans have been tortured behind the walls and behind the electrified barbed wire of this gigantic grave. The surviving men are returning home. Their homelands are free and their flags fly proudly in their countries. The great work of reconstruction has already begun. And we must all cooperate with this reconstruction. Happy and full of joy, we leave this hell: it has finished. No more threats, no more fear: Great life is - as they say - awaiting us!"[44]

---

[43] All the Camp newspapers, insofar as they are extant, are in the Archive of the Concentration Camp Memorial Site, Dachau.
[44] IPC, Information and Culture, Central Press Bureau, Communiqué No. 30, 2. 6. 1945.

Max Mannheimer
Theresienstadt – Auschwitz – Warsaw – Dachau
Recollections

In the Wiener Library (London/Tel Aviv), in the archives of Yad Vashem (Jerusalem) and in the archives of the Concentration Camp Memorial in Dachau are copies of interviews with Max Mannheimer concerning the herein described events and personal experiences. These interviews took place on January 12, 13 and 18, 1956 in Frankfurt-on-Main. The recollections, first published in German in the DACHAUER HEFTE, No. 1, in December 1985 originated, in December 1964, independent of these interviews, on the occasion of a severe illness. Max Mannheimer wrote the manuscript for his daughter, publication was not intended. A few explanatory insertions have been added at the request of the editor, who is responsible for the footnotes.

W. B.

Among my earliest impressions, which were important for my later life, was the giving of Christmas presents in the Neutitschein kindergarten. At that time I had no idea about the difference between Jews and non-Jews. However I felt that the way in which the teacher, disguised as Santa Claus, distributed the gifts, was unjust. Especially the handsome rocking horse, which one of the children received, appealed to me, but I only got two carved wooden figures which rolled on parallel bars from one end to the other. At home I complained to my mother about this injustice and later, when I began to grasp the significance of the Christmas celebrations and the difference between Christians and Jews, I felt more and more, the Christ child doesn't like Jews.

Only after my entrance into primary school did I realize that I was different from the others. Also I felt discriminated against, because I couldn't take part in religion in school like the other children, and for a collection of tin foil that allegedly served the liberation of African Negro slaves, I received no small pictures of saints. I was very sad about this and was only consoled when Mrs Mandl, the widow of the Neutitschein rabbi, explained to me that the Jews had a history of their own that was much older. I always listened intently to the tales from biblical history and was convinced that the priest, whom I greeted like the other children with "Christ be praised," couldn't tell such wonderful stories. Besides, the Christian children got no sweets, which I received during our religion class outside the school, as a reward for good behaviour.

My parents got to know each other in the last year of the war. My mother was a saleswoman in the butcher's shop of my uncle. Uncle Jacob was the oldest of fourteen brothers and sisters; my mother, Margarethe, was the youngest. My parents married on March 25, 1919. The dowry of my mother consisted of old-fashioned furniture with thousands of ornaments. The wedding itself, including the acquisition of a tailcoat for my father, was financed by my uncle.

My father leased a tavern in the Neutitschein Landstrasse, No. 20, that belonged to the Huppert family, and I was born in the room next to the public bar a year later. My brother Erich was born in 1921, in 1923 Ernst, in 1925 Edgar and in 1927 my sister Kate.

My first word was not, for instance, "Papa" or "Mama", but "Auto". This fascination for the vehicle that moves on four wheels was never to leave me.

My father had little time for us children and I therefore valued it highly when he told us stories. His account of the meeting with a good friend, whom he valued above humans because of his faithfulness, especially impressed me. It was in 1915. The second year of the war. The regiment to which my father belonged was at that time stationed in Galicia. It was night. My father was on guard duty. He spoke with another soldier. Suddenly he heard the neighing of a horse that kept getting louder. My father went closer and recognized the horse that had drawn the delivery van of his uncle, who owned a wholesale food business in Witkowitz, with him across country. The story of this encounter pleased me so much that my father had to tell it over and over.

We children were proud of our father's friendship with a Jewish locomotive-engineer named Allerhand. One day we got to know him. Above all a pocket watch that hung on a long, heavy chain stirred our fantasy. Its hands marked the departure of each train reliably and in our imagination it looked as though this watch had the power to set trains in motion.

Of my father's youth I only know that when he was twelve he started a merchant's apprenticeship with his uncle, Adolf Guttmann, and was a passionate dancer – so passionate that he once danced through three successive nights and worked during the day. To be sure, in the third night a pail of cold water was needed to bring the over ardent dancer, who had fainted, back to life.

Like most inhabitants of big towns – Witkowitz belongs to Maehrisch-Ostrau – and although he came from a rural region near Cracow, my father became a genuine café addict. Billiards and card games, of course, were just as much a part of this as reading newspapers.

My paternal grandfather, from whose second marriage my father stemmed, was the owner of a wagon with two horses and made a living by transporting all kinds of wares from Cracow, 18 miles away, for several merchants. An enterprise with two horsepower. Apart from this, he possessed a forest and fields. I'm not sure any more whether it was my grandfather or my great-grandfather who succeeded, in only a few years, in drinking away the above-mentioned forest. This event in the history of my family had the effect that I vowed never to drink and I have stuck to this up to this day. Certainly my upbringing and the example of the Maccabi Sport Club also contributed to this decision.

My grandfather allegedly had tremendous strength. Once, when a horse broke its leg during a lumber transport, he was said to have wrapped it in a sheet and carried it on his shoulders several hundred yards to the stall. However, I must note here that there is a breed of horses in Poland that is only slightly larger than a pony. But for me, a horse was a horse and the deed of my grandfather admirable.

My grandmother, who lived in Myslenice, a small provincial town in Poland, was a warm-hearted woman who seemed very ancient to me, hugged us children tightly when she kissed us and cooked wonderful noodle soup with big beans. I especially enjoyed watching her when she baked bread. It was much better than simply fetching bread from the baker. On Friday evening my grandmother put on a handsome dress, lighted the candles and was proud that I could recite the blessing over bread so well. Uncle Ludwig, the brother-in-law of my father, took me with him to his synagogue on the Sabbath, where it was much louder than in our synagogue at home. A great many men wore long beards and payes (cork screw curls), youths wore only payes, long, black coats and yarmulkas (small round caps.) At ten I couldn't understand that only a few hours east by train the Jews looked so different from those in Neutitschein, that they lived in such isolation, communicated exclusively with each other and that the women in the synagogue were hidden behind a curtain. But there were also men in Myslenice who on the Sabbath secretly sought out a tavern with a bowling alley and violated the Sabbath in this way.

The experiences during vacations at my grandmother's made a deep impression on me. I was especially happy that I could spend a part of my childhood in the same setting where my father had presumably played his pranks and at that time I hoped very much to be able to grow up in such lovely surroundings with woods behind the house. The only thing missing was the soccer field, but that made it easier for me to leave.

My mother was superior to my father intellectually. When one took into account that she only attended school for eight years, her knowledge was astounding. She read a great deal, owned most of the classics and, in spite of the fact that her schooldays were long since over, she could recite a French poem fluently. It delighted me every time anew, although I didn't understand a word. It had something to do with spring, flowers and the song of birds.

My mother was beautiful. At least she seemed so to me. She was a loving mother and she had the gift of giving each of us children the feeling of being her favorite. My mother was very devout. Not only for appearances' sake. To be sure, she went to the synagogue only on holidays, but her cooking was kosher and she was a patient wife. Due to my father's passion for card games, my mother was often alone. On Sundays in the early evening, because I was the oldest, she sent me to Café "Heinrichshof" to pick up my father. The heavy cloth that spanned the lower half of the window, as a protection against draughts, obstructed the view so that only a jump enabled me to spot the splendid bald head of my father. Then I went in. My father greeted me as warmly as if we hadn't seen each other for months and offered me a lemonade, a kind of bribe in order to prolong the card game, that I accepted or declined, according to mood.

My mother was often alone. Although she at no time complained, I resolved never to play cards so as to have more time for the family. And I have always stuck to this.

To vindicate my father, my mother occasionally told us a story that allegedly took place in Uhersky Brod. A prolific father, the owner of a small house, had gambled away the house at cards in a single night. The family had to move out within a few days. When the man died, his widow remarked at his grave: You were right to gamble. That way you had at least one joy in your life.

Despite this weak point my father was a good, if strict father with a strongly developed sense of justice. He was a correct merchant and was highly respected. In 1927 my father purchased a motor bicycle with a sidecar that looked like a tin crate, loaded it with cheese, fish preserves and similar products and visited shops in the vicinity. A year later he bought a delivery van, added chocolate and built up a wholesale business. In 1930 my father gave up the tavern and bought a house. He used to explain to the curious that he borrowed half the money and owed the other half.

Shortly before my 13th birthday I was prepared for the Bar Mitzwah. It's a big event in Jewish life, such a Bar Mitzwah, that transforms a youth into a member of the synagogue community with equal rights. Today I can still feel my mother's agitation as I approached the Torah-Shrine in the synagogue and I, too, was very excited. In the future I could be a minyanman. When Jews want to pray together, there must always be ten men. Through the Bar Mitzwah I became a minyanman. On weekdays, on the anniversary of someone's death, when the prayer for the dead, the Kaddish, is spoken, I would be picked up at home and would take part in the service. Apart from the tefillin (phylacteries) and the taleth (prayer shawl), I received many gifts – a watch, books, money and many other things.

Actually my schooldays weren't very eventful. I was never molested in school because of my faith, although now and then on the street someone shouted "dirty Jew." Whenever I could, I defended myself with my fists. In one case, it concerned an older and stronger boy, I called on my brother Erich for help. My brother took a ball of horsedung and continued to stuff it into the mouth of the abuser until he promised never to say "dirty Jew" again.

In the commercial school that I attended from 1934 to 1936 I noticed the first signs of National Socialism among my 15 to 17-year-old schoolfellows. A pupil named Haas had a picture of Hitler in one of her school books that she looked at often and at length during classes. I was somewhat alarmed because, after all, the Jews were already being persecuted in Germany at that time. From a book of a German emigrant which had appeared in Czechoslovakia, I knew something about this, but the danger, as described in the book, I didn't want to see. Apart from the "Sudentendeutsche Heimatfront" (SHF), later the "Sudetendeutsche Partei" (SDP), which was underestimated by everyone,[1] we detected no signs that pointed to a destruction of the Czechoslovakian Republic. The founder and first president of Czechoslovakia, Thomas Garrigue Masaryk, wanted to create out of the partly highly industrialized and partly agriculturally-developed land, that was populated by Czechs, Slovakians, Germans, Poles, Ruthenians, Hungarians and Jews, a state of many peoples after the Swiss model. To be sure the Czechs, who after many centuries of foreign rule had gained independence, made mistakes that were exploited for propaganda by the German minority. Above all, the selection of personnel for important and unimportant posts was handled very ineptly.

After finishing the commercial school I entered the firm of J. Schoen & Co. in Znaim-Alt-Schallersdorf. The work in the shop and office wasn't difficult for me, as I had been an active assistant in my father's business since I was twelve. I worked very hard. The shop, a kind of warehouse, was open daily from five-thirty a.m. to nine p.m. and even on Sunday mornings from seven to eleven a.m. I used my free time for walks, bicycle excursions, movies or soccer.

The picture that the village inhabitants had of us Jews can be expressed in one sentence: The Jews are good merchants, further their children in learning and stick closely together. In a soccer game they regarded me as something special, since I deviated from their picture. "Look, a Jew is playing too." This news spread quickly and in the intermission I was surrounded by curious crowds like a real star. That I was also quite a good player astonished the spectators even more.

The activity of the Sudetendeutsche Henlein Party increased constantly and when Hitler, on March 13, 1938, invaded Austria, the awareness that his troops were only 6 miles away burdened us Jews especially. In the following nights many illegal Jewish refugees crossed the border and several slept in my bed, while I made myself comfortable on a chair. Early in the morning a

---

[1] The "Sudetendeutsche Heimatfront" was founded on October 1, 1933 by Konrad Henlein and renamed the "Sudetendeutsche Partei" in April, 1935. Thenceforth the party, which functioned as a collective movement of all those of Sudeten German nationality, was financed by the Deutsches Reich. In 1935 it received the most votes (15,2%), subordinated itself in November, 1937 completely to Hitler, served then as an instrument of National Socialist politics toward Czechoslovakia and was incorporated in the NSDAP in December, 1938.

taxi brought them to the station, from where they travelled into the country, mainly to Brno, the capital of Moravia. The police knew, of course, about the illegal immigrants, but they turned a blind eye.

A young woman, who had spent the night with us and was about to be taken to the station, couldn't refrain, although I asked her to hurry (the taxi was waiting before the door), from calmly adorning herself with rouge and lipstick. At the moment I was annoyed by this behavior but later, when I thought back on it, I admired the unobtrusive woman for her attitude. She had been forced to flee, had lost so much – nonetheless she had retained her dignity and self-control.

In the second half of September the political tensions and the uncertainty caused me to return to my parents and brothers and sister in Neutitschein. The constant manoeuvers of the military, the political and diplomatic activity, the aggression of the Nazis and finally the partial mobilization in May 1938 foreshadowed the disaster that was to befall us. We set our only hope in the political and military alliances, that later proved to be merely paper.

When Hitler, Mussolini, Chamberlain and Daladier in September 1938 signed the abdication of the so-called Sudetenland to Hitler in the hotel "Vier Jahreszeiten" in Munich, a new era dawned.[2] Especially the Jews in Czechoslovakia regarded it with anxiety.

October 10, 1938 – Occupation of the "Sudetenland."

A small town is beside itself. Swastika flags and banners with "We thank our Fuehrer!", "We greet our liberator!" are everywhere. The German troops march into Neutitschein. The population shouts with frenzy. No, they don't shout, they roar. "Sieg heil! Sieg heil! Sieg heil!" In every shop window is a picture of Hitler and expressions of thanks. I don't dare go to the main square, the center of the festivities. The enthusiasm is fanatic.

At home we confer. Surely it won't be so bad. One can't run away. The house is there. It can't be so bad. Father is optimistic. He took part in the First World War and paid his taxes on time. He is very popular and has a good reputation. Everyone knows him. Not only the rabbi, the priest, too. He was never anything but a merchant, always unpolitical. God willing, everything will be all right. God willing.

Two days later the driver of the firm Markus and the son of the soap-boiler Piesch confiscate our Chevrolet delivery van for the NS Public Welfare. Their bearing is impudent. It's astonishing how the military tone, a pair of boots and riding-breeches transform people.

After a few days our driver, Albert, having been discharged from the Czech army, is allowed to drive "his" van for the NSV (National Socialist Welfare.)

---

[2] On September 29/30, 1938 the Munich Agreement, a treaty between Germany, Great Britain, France and Italy, that ended the "Sudeten Crisis" fanned by Berlin since the end of 1937, was signed by the heads of government. On the grounds of the Munich Agreement, Czechoslovakia was forced to yield her regions populated in the main by Germans (1/5th of the territory, 1/4th of the population) to the German Reich.

Bread and canned food are distributed to the "starving" population. A grotesque situation. German preserves from a Jewish van! Our firm name on both sides of the van is pasted over with NS-posters. It's that easy.
"Hitler does something for the people," Albert says to me. At that moment he forgets that for this "doing" the van of his old employer Mannheimer was "borrowed." Beyond that, Albert receives his salary from us. "Yes, he does something," I replied.
After October 10, 1938 – Neutitschein.
The general impression of the town has changed greatly since October 10. Overnight the traffic was converted from left to right, the police were given new uniforms, the bilingual posters disappeared. Swastikas were everywhere, people wore NS party badges as big as coat buttons. Our neighbor, Herr Demel, a dealer in groceries who was very short, struck a pose and declared: "Before we were small, but now ...?!" I literally saw him grow. One could clearly feel his self-assurance.
Frau S. in the Muehlgasse replaced the image of the Virgin Mary, under which an oil lamp burned, with a picture of Hitler. Apparently the new god was revered by the aging spinster, a fact which was underlined by fresh flowers.
Most of our German customers declared that they could no longer buy from us. On the other hand, two of them bought more than before and made no secret of their views.
Some of my former schoolfellows wore brown uniforms and when we met they looked away, which was fine with me. I was glad that they only looked away. They might have spoken to me. They didn't.
Several Czechs remembered their German mothers and grandmothers and were suddenly Germans and National Socialists. The children who were born at that time were given forenames in the new style. Adolf, Hermann, Horst and girls' names from the heroic German legends were all the fashion. People with Slavic family names suddenly had German family names. The dirndl and white stockings with plait design, anyway a genuine German symbol in the sense of National Socialism during the last years, were adopted together with the hairstyle of the leaders of the BDM (Bund deutscher Maedel).
Due to the favorable exchange rate of the Reichsmark with the Czechoslovakian Crown (1 RM = 8.33 Kc) it was possible for the new occupants to buy out the stores within a short time. At the beginning the shopkeepers were elated by this boom. Before long, however, they had to recognize that for good wares they were receiving bad money, for which they could no longer replace what had been sold. But they realized it too late. Several small shops closed down. Their owners either put on uniforms or became officials.
When I visited our regular barber, in November 1938, I had to wait. Two other customers were before me. Master Kunz thrust "Der Stuermer" into my hand and advised me to read it. With particular pleasure he pointed to the

caricature of a Jew and asked me how I liked it. I was at no loss for an answer. To be sure, I wasn't aware of the risk. "The master race is of course better looking!" Kunz said nothing. He cut my hair as usual but on this day the customary barber conversation caused him great effort.

The Czech butcher, Tonda Neumann, barely missed going to jail. He had quoted the sign in his shop window at the wrong moment. When a customer wanted to know why the assortment was much smaller than in the past, he replied: "We thank our Fuehrer!"

The former owner of a ready-made clothes shop turned to the provisionally appointed trustee for help. The trustee had been treated like a son by his Jewish employer for more than twenty years. In reply to the cry for help, he advised his former employer to hang himself. The advice was followed two days later.

November 10, 1938 – "Kristallnacht." (So-called because, in addition to other and far greater destruction, the windows of all Jewish shops were smashed.)

Yesterday the synagogues burned. They burned in Germany. They burned in Austria. They burned in Czechoslovakia. If there was danger of the fire spreading, they were blown up. Most of the Jewish shops were demolished. "My" synagogue was plundered. Fire or explosion would have been dangerous, because of the gas tank across the street. Prayer books, Torah scrolls and prayer shawls lay on the street in shreds. The book that for two thousand years had held the Jews in the diaspora together was trampled with boots. The organ will no longer accompany our songs on the Sabbath and on holidays. There will be no more Sabbath, no holidays and no more songs. Only at home, as long as we have a home, Mother will kindle the Sabbath lights on Friday evening and Father will speak the blessings over bread and over wine. "Lechem min Haaretz. Bore B'ri Hagofen." And then my mother, as in the past, will take up the prayer book, printed in German, and will read the chapters "Greeting the Sabbath" and "Prayer of the Jewish Woman" quietly to herself.

The prayer books, Torah scrolls and prayer shawls from the synagogue were thrown on the street. Tomorrow they will probably be thrown out of the houses. For my mother nothing would change. She would have spoken her prayers even without a book.

Officially the destructive action of the Nazis was depicted as a spontaneous act of revenge of the "seething national spirit," in reply to the murder of Embassy Councillor von Rath by Hershl Grynszpan in Paris. That the national spirit seethed so uniformly in three countries at the same time was due to the skillful organization of the responsible Nazis.

An open police car drives up to our house. Jewish men are in the car, guarded by Schupos (Schutzpolizei, protective police) in green uniforms. Two Schupos come up the stairs. My father is told that he will be taken into protective custody so that nothing will happen to him. Presumably because of

the "seething national spirit." I'm standing near the door. "How old is the chap?" asks the Schupo. My heart beats very loudly. If Mother had revealed my age, I would have been taken to prison. The protection came from Mother, not from the Schutzpolizei.
December 1938.
The Jewish men have been released from prison. They had to sign a declaration that they would leave the territory of the German "Reich" within eight days and never set foot on it again. They sign it. My father drives from Neutitschein to Uhersky Brod, the birthplace of my mother. It is in South Moravia and is known because of Comenius. We must present a list of goods to take with us to the Gestapo for approval. The furniture van is packed. The customs officials, who supervise the packing, behave correctly. They are old officials from the "Reich," who presumably had already served during the Weimar Republic. Marie, our Czech housemaid, cries when she takes leave of us. "One doesn't cry over Jews," says Master Carpenter Jirgal, who lives in our house and observes the moving not entirely without malignity. In the past years he was always so friendly to us, his daughters Minna and Hildegard played with us in the yard. Maybe one really doesn't cry over Jews.

On January 27, 1939 we leave our house in Neutitschein in the hope that we can lead a life without fear in the unoccupied part of Czechoslovakia. In the meantime, Father had procured a very old apartment with two rooms and kitchen-parlor in Uhersky Brod, 165 Masaryk Square. It's not exactly spacious for six people, but we're happy to have escaped. In the spice and seed shop of Rudolf Holz I start working again. A few weeks later, I experience the marching in of the German troops for the second time. It is exactly the same picture as four months earlier in Neutitschein. The public buildings are decked with swastika flags. The motorcycles, with and without sidecars, line up in a row on the main square, next to the military cars. Masaryk Square, where we live, becomes over night Adolf Hitler Square. Only the enthusiasm of Neutitschein is missing. In Uhersky Brod there are few German families. Perhaps the troops are disappointed, anyway they notice the difference: whereas the German border areas felt "liberated," the Czech population feels "occupied." With the exception of the sporadic Czech fascists.[3]

Since the Jews are only allowed to perform manual labor, I take a job in road construction in summer, 1939. On September 1 a vast column of military vehicles rolls over "my" road – it is the beginning of the German campaign against Poland and of the Second World War.

---

[3] In violation of the guarantee of the remainder of Czechoslovakia affirmed in the Munich Agreement, Hitler forced upon the Czechoslovakian President Hácha, on March 14/15, 1939, a treaty which deprived the CSR of its sovereignty and annexed the Czech territory as "Protectorate of Bohemia and Moravia" to the German Reich. (Slovakia became, as a satellite state, "independent".)

1940.

In the old Jewish quarter of Uhersky Brod one debates; in the café, at home – seldom on the street. Despite the blitzkrieg against the Poles, the mood is optimistic. An optimism without apparent reason. An optimism with purpose. Jews are not permitted to leave their homes from eight p.m. to early morning. Restrictions on buying are imposed: Jews can only enter shops between three und five p.m. Entering the parks is forbidden to Jews. Now I am working on road construction in the vicinity of the health resort Luhacovice. My lodgings during the week are a shanty behind the tool house. From there I go to the park, despite the eight o'clock curfew and the veto on entering the parks. I count the signs "Forbidden to Jews." There are six in number. Later, towards eleven, I pull all the signs out of the ground and throw some of them in the bushes, some in a stream. My courage was in vain. The next evening every sign is back. A second time I don't muster the courage. I'm just not a hero.

The work in road construction is actually not so bad. It's useful and one sees something. The road leads through a forest. A reservoir is only five minutes away and after work one can refresh oneself. And it's only a twenty minute walk to the park. I simply overlook the signs with the nonchalance of a twenty-year-old. My fellow laborers, exclusively Czechs, are friendly to me and I am fully recognized by them. They even accept me in the piece-work group, which is a special distinction. And when I learn to really swear, I'm "their man."

One day a Mercedes convertible drives past us. Three men and two women are sitting in it. The car comes from my home town. One of the occupants I recognize as the son of the soap-boiler Piesch, another is the son of a lawyer. The two had presumably spent the weekend in the health resort. I gaze after the car until it has disappeared around a bend. I shovel my wheelbarrow full and think: In the sweat of your brow ...

Road construction alone cannot support the family. Our reserves are long since used up. The moving of many Jewish families from Uherske Hradiste provides additional new earning possibilities. Furniture is transported, firewood sawed and chopped.

My brother Edgar learns shoemaking from Master Cingalek. Already, at thirteen, he fits up for himself a cobbler-corner in the woodshed. Karli Langer, aged ten, was his "apprentice." He looked up Jewish families, offered to repair heels and his "master" repaired them. The prices were of course lower than at Bata's since he certainly couldn't compete with this world-wide firm.

April 20, the birthday of Adolf Hitler, has in 1939 a different meaning for me than for the Nazis. On this day I meet my first love. Viola is eighteen and I am very in love with her. She comes from an orthodox-Jewish family but she feels that this strict education is exaggerated and out-of-date. We meet secretly on the outskirts of the town and from there undertake excursions with

the motorcycle, which I was allowed to keep because of my work in road construction. For the daughter of an orthodox family, it is already bold to walk out with a young man; riding on a motorcycle is considered impossible.
In 1940 Viola moves with her parents to Prague. When I visit her there, her parents suggest to me that I emigrate with them to Palestine. I think of my parents and brothers and sister and decide in favor of my family. I am the oldest son and must remain.
At the end of 1940 I get to know Eva Bock. She has just completed, in preparation for Palestine, a Hachsharah, a practical course on an agricultural farm. In the beginning we are always with other young people and discuss politics, literature, philosophy. We also occupy ourselves with psychoanalysis. Freud and his dream interpretation especially fascinate us. It is at least a way to overcome a part of our inhibitions. We all act as if we understand everything and try, with the wisdom just acquired from books, to impress the girls. At this time we have few other possibilities, so we test ourselves in this intellectual way. And the competition is very strong in these days. To talk about work in road construction would exert little attraction. With Freud it is different.
I succeed in impressing Eva. We like each other and we see each other every day. In bad weather I visit the Bocks at home and "teach" Eva shorthand. How good that I know shorthand!
The year 1941 brings little new for the Jews in Uhersky Brod. Most of the men under forty-five are required to work. They work on building, road construction or as assistants in private firms. From time to time there are raids by the Gestapo. Single persons are arrested and brought to the Gestapo prison in Uherske Hradiste. Later they are sent to concentration camps.
Since Jews have long been forbidden to own radios, the latest news from foreign stations is passed on to them by Czechs. In the Café Smetana, the only official meeting point of the Jews in Uhersky Brod, it is discussed. Among others, I remember a report according to which the Jews, who were deported via Theresienstadt to the east, were forced to work in sulphur pits without gas masks. As a result they were gradually poisoned, the report stated.
Theresienstadt, the old fortress and military town, is the big assembly point for the Jews from the Protectorate of Bohemia and Moravia and from Germany.[4] Many remain there, especially older people. However, for the major-

---

[4] The Theresienstadt Ghetto had a special place in the system of the persecution of the Jews. It served chiefly as a collecting point and transit station for the Jews from the Protectorate, who were deported from Theresienstadt to the east. As of spring, 1942, Theresienstadt was above all a "Ghetto for the aged" among prominent and privileged Jews from the German Reich. The chances of survival, however, were hardly more favorable than in other camps, as the following balance shows: From the altogether over 141,000 interned there, 88,000 were deported and for the most part exterminated. About 33,500 people died in Theresienstadt, scarcely 17,000 were liberated by the Red Army on May 7, 1945.

ity Theresienstadt is a transit camp before the deportation to one of the extermination camps in Poland.

At the beginning of 1942 most of the Jews from Uherske Hradiste are removed to Uhersky Brod. The Jewish lodgings are overcrowded, provisions are increasingly scarce and the reports that reach us about the fate of those already deported are very bad.

Nonetheless, Eva and I try to minimize the seriousness of the situation. That's easy when one is young and confident. We're in love and trust in our luck. Despite the threatening outlook, we make plans for our future life. After my work, until the eight-o'clock curfew, we have only an hour to talk, to dream. We don't want to violate the curfew. Our friends Ilse Jellinek, Ernst Schoen and Adolf Rosenfeld have already been arrested for this reason.

In 1942 the transports that roll via the Theresienstadt Ghetto are in full swing. Today they are assembled in one town, tomorrow in another. Escape is out of the question. Also for us. A man in Uhersky Brod has contact with people who smuggle Jews into Slovakia for a fee. From there one can perhaps reach Palestine via Hungary and Turkey. My brother Erich passes on the address of this man to a young man named Lazarowicz. Three days later my brother is arrested. He is tried, brought to the Gestapo prison in Uherske Hradiste. Then to Brno. To the notorious Kaunitz-College - a Gestapo prison with methods of torture which could not have been worse in the Spielberg Fortress above the town in the Middle Ages. Will we ever see Erich again?

My mother cries very often. We comfort her as best we can. The beginning of September, Eva and I decide to marry. We want to stay together after the transport, too. We go to the rabbi and settle the formalities. The marriage ceremony is in the trend of the times. Above all, the absence of my arrested brother burdens us, especially as we don't know if he is still alive.

We move into a rented room, more exactly, into half a room. The other half belongs to the landlord and is separated by a folding screen. In our imaginations we plan a wonderful honeymoon trip that we want to make to a distant country after the war. And we dream and dream. We don't see the approaching danger. We don't want to see it. We love each other and forget for the moment the war, the Gestapo prisons, the rolling transports.

On January 24, 1943 the hour has struck. The summons of the Security Service (SD) that we hold in our hands ends the month-long tension. On January 27 we must present ourselves in a school near the station. We are to bring all documents, a list of objects left behind us must be drawn up. At home we make final preparations. At least we young people feel our lot at the moment as not particularly hard. It affects us all, we're together, we can work, we've always worked. And in Theresienstadt - and none of us wants to think further - are many acquaintances, relatives and friends of ours. There we will surely not have less to eat than there is for us now.

In the school we are distributed among the various classrooms, are registered, and this personal record, with all possible data, will remain with us from now on. In late afternoon we board a passenger train that is to bring us to Theresienstadt. I am numbered for the first time. The number that I carry around my neck is CP 510.

Theresienstadt, end of January, 1943.

A great multitude. Jammed into barracks. Transit room. Straw on the floor in place of beds. Names are called out. For evacuation to the east. Transfer to another barracks. For a night. A damp, moldy vault crammed to the brim with human beings. No, with "subhumans."

East – labor assignment, one calls it. We're all together, all except Erich: My parents, my wife, two brothers, my sister, sister-in-law. In eight days I'll be twenty-three. For four years accustomed to road construction and quarry. The last weeks in the sawmill. The thought comforts me. Physically I can take a lot. It won't be so bad. Father thinks so too. He paid his taxes punctually. In the First World War three years at the front for King and Emperor. Never deliberately defied regulations.

Transport numbers are distributed. Hung around the neck. CU 210, 211, 212, 213, 214, 215, 216, 217. A thousand women, men, children. Drag themselves along. To Bauschowitz. Passenger train waits. One by one we're called up. Get on board. Ten to a compartment. Somewhat crowded. Surely can't be so bad: After all, a passenger train.

East – labor assignment. Assignment? Why not simply labor? Departure. It is nine o'clock in the morning. See ruins. Hear Saxon. Discover jottings on the wall of the railroad car. Departure Theresienstadt 9 o'clock, then Dresden, Bautzen, Goerlitz, Breslau, Brieg, Oppeln, Hindenburg. Then nothing. Day and night. Along the way we detect Jews. In civilian clothes. With Jewish star on their jackets. With shovels. We throw bread out the window. They pounce on it. Shove each other. Labor assignment? Will we look like this, too? Act like this? One more day. And half a night. The train screeches to a stop. A thousand men, women, children. The escort-troop surrounds the train. We must stay inside. Not for long. A column of trucks approaches. Suddenly strong floodlights illuminate the ramp. SS-Officers and guards are waiting. We are at the death-ramp of Auschwitz-Birkenau.[5]

Auschwitz-Birkenau, death-ramp, midnight of February 1, 1943.

Everyone out! Leave everything! Panic. Everyone tries to stuff as much as possible into pockets. The SS-men roar: Get moving! Faster! One more shirt is put on. One more sweater. Cigarettes. Perhaps an exchange article. Men on this side, women on the other side, women with children on the trucks. Men

---

[5] The Auschwitz Concentration Camp consisted of three complexes with 38 subsidiary camps. Auschwitz I, erected on May 20, 1940, was the main camp and headquarters. Auschwitz II (Birkenau) existed as of November 26, 1941 and after January, 1942, was an extermination camp, in which the "selection" on the arrival-ramp took place. There the large gas chambers were located. Auschwitz III (Monowitz) served as of May 31, 1942 as labor camp for the Buna-Plant of the IG-Farben Trust.

and women who are poor on their feet can ride with the trucks. Many apply.
The rest are lined up in rows of five. A woman tries to come over to us. Probably she wants to speak to her husband or son. An SS-man tears her to the ground with his cane. By the neck. She remains motionless. Is hauled away. Labor assignment?
An SS-officer stands before us. Obersturmfuehrer (equal to the rank of captain in the Wehrmacht). Is so addressed by a guard. Presumably a doctor. Without white coat. Without stethoscope. In green uniform. With death's head (the SS-emblem). We come forward separately. His voice is calm. Almost too calm. Asks age, trade, whether healthy. Makes us show our hands. I hear some replies.
Locksmith – left.
Administrator – right.
Doctor – left.
Worker – left.
Warehouse-keeper of the firm Bata – right. An acquaintance of ours. Buechler from Bojkowitz.
Carpenter – left.
Now it's my father's turn. Worker. He goes the way of the administrator and warehouse-keeper. He is fifty-five. Probably the reason.
Then I come. Twenty-three, healthy, worker on road construction. Callouses on the hands. The callouses are so good. Left.
My brother Ernst: twenty, plumber – left.
My brother Edgar: seventeen, shoemaker – left.
Try to detect my mother, wife, sister, sister-in-law. It is impossible. Many trucks have driven off.
Formation in rows of three. An SS-guard asks for Czech cigarettes. I give him some. He answers my questions. Children go to the kindergarten. Men can visit their wives Sundays. Only Sundays? That's enough! It has to be.
We march. Along a narrow street. See a brightly lit square. In the middle of war. No blackout. Watch towers with machine guns. Double barbed wire. Floodlights. Long, flat huts. SS-guards open a gate. We march through. We are in Birkenau.
We remain standing in front of a hut for ten minutes. Then we're let in. From the transport of one thousand men, women, children only 155 men were chosen for work. Several prisoners sit at tables. Money and valuables are to be handed over. For anything concealed there are severe punishments. From my shirt-collar I unrip a ten-dollar note. From my father-in-law. As a reserve in emergencies. The names are registered. I ask whether I should keep the identity card. The answer is no. We will get new ones. We come into the open. Then another hut. In a room we take off our clothes. We keep only shoes and belt. All our hair is cut off. And shaved off. Because of lice. We are sprayed with Cuprex, for disinfection. Come into a very warm room. Laid

out in steps. Like a sauna. We're naked and are glad of the warmth. We look outlandish. Comical. Bald heads, a belt around the bare middle and we have shoes on. A prisoner in striped clothing enters. Introduces himself to us. We inquire about the women, children. "Go up the chimney"! We don't understand him. We take him for a sadist. We don't ask any more.
The room gets increasingly hot. Suddenly an iron door is thrown open. Leads to another room. Prisoners with special functions roar: Get moving! Faster! . . . just like the SS on the ramp. Seems to be the camp idiom. With blows from cudgels we are driven into an ice-cold room under showers. Ice-cold room. Ice-cold water. After the warm sauna. Attempts to dodge the cold jet are answered by cudgel blows. After ten minutes the water is turned off. There are no towels. Instead clothing. Unfamiliar clothing. Civilian clothing with a broad red stripe on the back of the jacket, a stripe on each pant leg. Looks like oil paint. There is a jacket, pants, underpants, shirt, socks. No coat. No cap.
February 2, 1943.
My brother Edgar is tall. Six feet. The sleeves of his jacket are too short. Much too short. He requests a substitute. Is punched in the face. Falls on the concrete floor. I help him to his feet. The jacket remains the same. So that's the labor assignment. How long can one stand it?
We line up outdoors. Wait for half an hour. The door of a disinfecting station is open. We see two prisoners. They finger the pieces of clothing for sewed-in money and valuables. Throw the money on a heap. Mainly dollar bills. Seem to be worthless here. We wait and freeze. At last it goes on. We march. Come into a hut. Three-tiered plank beds. Six prisoners to a bed. The prisoners on special duty roar: March, march to the beds, shoes stay on the floor. We climb onto the beds. Without straw, without covers. We can't sleep. Let's pray, someone suggests. We pray. Shema Israel . . .
Get up, get going, faster, the supervisors bellow. Several search frantically for their shoes. Many don't find them. Old shoes are there that don't fit. They ask the supervisors. Blows are the answer.
Our only concern is the question: Where are our parents, wives, brothers and sisters? Where are the children? Where are they?
Line up in front of the hut! We're freezing. It is still dark. The ground is muddy. To our left is the barbed wire. Electrically charged. Skull and cross bones. Underneath: "Danger." I am desperate. We'll get shovels. Dig our own graves. Those are my thoughts. I speak them out. My little brother comforts me. I should be his prop. Electrically charged barbed wire. Only a touch – finished. Doesn't hurt. My little brother asks: Do you want to leave me alone?
Line up! Pack of swine! The Block Elder screams. The supervisors scream. Try to push the rows into the right order. An SS-man comes. The Block Elder reports the number. We are counted. Remain standing another half hour. March off into another hut. It's completely empty. We stand around. Another

group comes a few minutes after us. Jews from Poland. From Pruszana. A table is brought in. Several prisoners in striped clothing come. With registration cards. With tattoo-needles. Names are called out. For the last time. Later only the numbers will count. The left underarm is the name plate. Edgar 99727, I 99728, Ernst 99729. Our brand. As with cattle. So they won't get lost. The prisoners with the tattoo-needles are very adept. That comes from the experience. By the ninety-nine thousand seven hundred and twenty-eighth time one has experience.

We wait another hour. Line up outside. We march once more. To a new camp. Two endless rows of stables. Mud is everywhere. Slightly frozen. The camp is deserted. So we're the pioneers. The entire picture is somewhat ghostly. Two long rows of huts. Mud, barbed wire. From the distance one hears the sound of diesel tractors. Tuck, tuck, tuck, tuck ... Inside we're ordered onto the plank beds. We know them already. Three-tiered. For six people. No covers. Bare wood. Here the Block Elder has command. A German from the Reich with a green triangle: a criminal.[6] He speaks to us. Birkenau is no sanatorium. Discipline, cleanliness, diligence. The only way to survive.

The hut has gates on the front sides. On one side is the sleeping place of the Block Elder. The rations are brought here: bread, margarine, jam, soup, a black liquid that one calls coffee or tea. On the other side is a toilet. A prisoner is appointed as "shit-master." He is responsible for order and cleanliness. Since yesterday evening we have had nothing to eat. It is now noon. For two hours we stand around between two huts and do nothing. We move our arms, jump, so as not to freeze. The beginning of February without coat. Without hat. Without food. Without parents. Without brothers and sisters, wives. Without home. Without help. Without hope.

The evening roll call comes. Already for an hour we've practiced lining up. Attention! At ease! An SS-man appears. As usual, the Block Elder reports the count. We are counted. After the roll call we go into the hut. Receive a ration of bread. One sixth of an army loaf. When we work there'll be more, we're told. A tablespoon of beet-jam and black liquid. Good table manners are forgotten. After 24 hours. Most of us eat greedily. I too. We discuss. We talk of comradeship, solidarity. Our brothers in the faith from Pruszana hold together. We too. An instinct, developed in two thousand years. To unite in times of need. We unite. And yet we are two groups. From east and west. Our accents are different. Perhaps our lifelong habits, too. Lifelong habits?

It is already very dark outside. An alarm-whistle pierces the quiet. Shouts reach us. Outpost line close in! From now on we can't leave the hut without

---

[6] The prisoners in concentration camps were characterized by different colored cloth triangles, according to catagories, that were sewn on the clothing: among others red for political prisoners, green for so-called professional criminals, black for "Antisocial elements", pink for homosexuals, violet for "Bible Scholars" (Jehovah's Witnesses).

being shot. The first night fall in quarantine camp. Upon the order of the supervisors we climb onto the beds. We huddle together. To get warm. Bobby Alt lies to my right, to the left my two brothers. I cry and pray. Both I do secretly. In four days I will be twenty-three. My parents . . . Shema Israel Adonai Elohenu . . .
February 3, 1943.
Out of bed! Get moving! Those on duty run between the rows of beds. They hold cudgels in their hands. For the present these are struck against the plank beds. A kind of gong. Wash! We go past two huts. An outdoor water-faucet is there. No water comes out. Perhaps frozen. We return to the hut. Get black liquid. Otherwise nothing. Then we're summoned to roll call. Just like yesterday evening. There is a big difference in temperature between hut and field. Especially in the morning we feel it acutely. When we're cold - and we are often cold - we embrace each other and rub each others' backs with our hands. We rub ourselves warm and tired. We line up in rows of five. Stand and wait. For an hour. The Block Elder comes out. The supervisors, who made us line up in exact rows, make up the first row of five. Kind of celebrities. For a piece of bread they perform this duty. A piece of bread means a lot in Birkenau. Bread is the most frequent word in our conversations. At once, when someone mentions bread, everyone listens intently. Since getting up we have been waiting for bread. Perhaps we will work soon, then there'll be more.
The SS-Blockfuehrer (Block leader, lower SS rank) comes. Attention! Hut 18 lined up with so many prisoners, the Block Elder announces. His report is short and brusque. One must note this tone. All "old-timers" here talk like this. Uniform, yes, the uniform is the reason. Be it only the uniform of a prisoner. Of a prisoner with a green triangle. All are still alive. The count tallies. Get moving!
We stand outside until noon. Then there is beet-soup. We have tin pots that hold one and a half pints. In the afternoon we get strips of linen, needles and thread. We write our prisoners' numbers on them. In front we draw a star of David. Now the numbering is complete. On the skin and on the jacket. The afternoon is quiet. The water-faucet functions. There is water for washing. Only for washing. We drink nonetheless. Wash only face and hands. There is no towel.
February 4, 1943.
The third day brings something new. After the roll call we remain standing between huts 18 and 19. We come to hut 19. The 20th is also occupied. A transport of Jews from Berlin. Tattooed numbers over 100,000. Where are the 99,000? Where are they? How many didn't get registered?
Now three huts altogether are occupied. Three times four-hundred makes twelve-hundred. Judging by the number a respectable village - in three stables. During the day the frozen mud between the huts thaws. Command to lice roll-call: Take off shirts! Search for lice! Danger of typhoid fever. Thus

the quarantine. We search – don't find any. A prisoners' doctor comes. Also searches for lice. He too finds none. The Block Elder comes. Line up in rows of three. Hut 19, forward march! In mud it's very hard to go forward. He orders double time. Takes back the command because of the mud. My neighbor, Dr Rabinowitsch, loses his galoshes – he has no shoes, they've been stolen. It is impossible to pull them out of the mud. He marches now with his feet wrapped in foot-rags. He loses those too. No, we're not cold now. The movement and the fear about what will or can happen next make us warm.

Does Erwin Rosenblum, whom everyone calls Ruzicka, which means little rose, still think of the Grand Hotel Pupp in Karlsbad and the fine menus that he enjoyed there before the war? This morning he delivered a speech to us on his sojourn in Karlsbad. Some took it for sadism. The others let him have the pleasure of looking back. On a time without barbed wire. Without mud. Without hunger.

Now we are there. A barbed-wire fence. In the midst of a big barbed-wire fence. At one point an open space. Twenty inches from the ground. If one stoops, one can crawl through. We inch through. For the Block Elder we're too slow. He assists with kicks. We're at a gravel-pit, prisoners in striped clothing are shoveling gravel. Emaciated. Covered with wounds from blows. A Capo (supervisor) shouts and beats the prisoners with the handle of a shovel. Actually they're walking skeletons. Will we one day look like this, too?

Get going, the Block Elder yells. Take off jackets! Turn them around! We button each others' jackets. The buttons are on the back. Crazy, I think. We must fill the back side of the jacket with gravel. With our hands. Some don't take enough. According to the Block Elder. He kicks the prisoners in the stomach. New gravel. Now he's satisfied. The Capo from the gravel-pit comes to the barbed wire. We must crawl through. With the gravel. It's not easy. If we support ourselves the gravel falls out. Everyone who crawls through receives one or two blows. With the handle of the shovel. Whoever spills gravel has to go back again. New gravel. New blows. How long can one stand it?

Back to the hut. The gravel is dumped between huts 18 and 19. To make the mud dry. Four hundred prisoners – four hundred shovels of gravel. A drop in the ocean. The senseless game is repeated twice more.

February 5, 1943.

Today we must fetch gravel only two more times. Now we know what to expect. On our return the camp Capo awaits us. He is classified as antisocial and has a black triangle. He has invented an odd game. Running the gauntlet. With the gravel. Two rows of prisoners, approximately ten on each side, stand facing each other. Hold shovel-handles in their hands. The others have to run between them from one end to the other. And must be beaten. I am assigned to the beaters. I lift my arms to strike without really striking. Don't notice the Capo watching me. I collapse under his shovel-handle. My back

hurts. With ten Berliners I accomplish much more than with you, you pack of swine!
So that's quarantine. A kind of fitness-test. An elite. An elite of skeletons. It can't last much longer. We're well on the way. The low calorie liquid diet and the undrinkable water cause diarrhea. The run on the two-seated latrine is great. The "shit-master" does very well. Anyone who slips him a slice of bread is given precedence. Those who have none must wait. Until it's too late. From then on they will always hoard bread. As toll. The sick kneel before the doors of the oven and thrust in their hands. Burned wood is to replace animal charcoal. So there's a crowd and a struggle before the oven.
We line up for the evening roll call. Then we get bread and margarine. And blankets. Real blankets. Colored blankets. Different colors. They stem from a transport from Holland. As indicated by the label. Everyone gets a blanket. All are happy. Maybe we're really needed. East – labor assignment. We have blankets. One on top of the other warms better. Bobby Alt and I sleep under two blankets. Warm wool blankets. From Holland. Whose owners are perhaps no longer alive. Now we can even take off our clothes. We lay them under our heads.
February 6, 1943.
Today I'm twenty-three. My brothers congratulate me. Next birthday in freedom! The friends join in. I have difficulty holding back tears. Hardship doesn't make one hard. At least not me.
Roll call. Lice roll call. Fetch gravel. Blows. Towards noon we hear loud shrieks from the next hut. A prisoner has cut out a piece from a blanket. For footrags. All three huts, line up. All on account of one of you, roars the Block Elder. Sabotage! The saboteur is beaten, lies before the hut. He won't live much longer. We line up between the rows of huts on the wide, muddy camp road. The Camp Elder, a prisoner on duty and Block Elders run excited and shouting to and fro. They shove and beat. Until they're satisfied. It can't be a special roll call. All stand together. Pell-mell. The tension mounts. What will happen next? The Camp Elder with the black triangle takes over the command. Attention!
He threatens with a hundred cudgel blows, with standing arrest, withdrawal of rations should the incident be repeated. Now he orders us to squat. Up! Down! Up! Down! Up! Down! For the time being he stops. We try to use the tin bowls that dangle on our belts, as seats. Whoever gets caught is beaten. An hour later the first tip over. The prisoners on duty assist with cudgel blows when anyone tries to get up. The cold, the hunger, the squatting. After seven hours we return to the huts. Those who remain lying are dragged to the side. Laid outside the hut. They won't have to line up for roll call any more. They're counted lying. Treated as if they were dead. The Blockschreiber (Block Clerk, prisoner responsible for index cards of prisoners) notes their numbers. Today the Block Elder will have several rations left over. Also margarine. Or sausage. It was my twenty-third birthday. I won't forget it.

February 7, 1943.
Many have fever. "Who must go to the doctor?", the prisoner on room duty calls. Several answer. Stand leaning against the outer wall of the next hut. Some sit down. They wait an hour. Or longer. We have lost all sense of time. Only see if it's light or dark. No day yet with sun. Only clouds. Gray clouds. Clouds behind which we can imagine no sun. Finally the sick are led away. With effort they drag themselves through the mud. We don't see them again.
To the Block Elder the shifting of gravel seems pointless. The area between the huts is still muddy. Today we march in another direction. We no longer have to turn around our jackets. We march to a building site of a special kind. Old prisoners with whom we can exchange a few whispered words disclose its meaning: Crematory. Terminus. A little ash. Strewn over the fields in a strange land.
Each of us must take four bricks. This has to be done secretly. It's called organization. It's not easy to carry four bricks at a time. Not in this condition. In freedom bricks aren't so heavy. A path of bricks must be laid around the hut. Better for us than fetching gravel. There are fewer blows.
Today Dr Beck from Uhersky Brod hides in the hut. He lies on the lowest plank bed with high fever. We carry him out to roll call. We support him. On the next day he is dying. Two prisoners try to take off the shoes of the dying man. He has good shoes. Shoes mean a lot. In this mud. In this cold. The prisoners shove each other. The strongest wins. A few minutes later Dr Beck is no longer alive. We say Kaddish, the prayer for the dead. He is laid before the hut. Counted at roll call. He's not the only one. Several follow him from other huts. A squad to pick up the dead comes by. So it goes day after day. Always more and more. Blows. Diarrhea. Fever. Now I know what quarantine means. A sieve with big holes. Many fall through.
Every day the same. Dead. Dead. Dead. Hunger and the water decimate our ranks. To replenish our hut Jews from Holland come to us. They die like flies. The Jews from Poland are the most resistant. Frequently craftsmen or workers. Physically they're better off. Not as delicate as the Dutch or Czechoslovakians.
The day is filled with standing around between the huts, with lice roll call, waiting for food. The less emaciated prisoners are appointed to fetch food. Often they try to reach unnoticed into the pot. It's easiest to organize potatoes. You stuff one in your mouth. Naturally there are blows here too. One puts up with them.
The night guard in the hut sounds the alarm. A prisoner from Pruszana has intruded into the room of the Block Elder. Two packs of margarine are the booty. The shrieks called forth by the blows of the Block Elder wake the entire hut. Theft from comrades!, roars the Block Elder. We'll discuss this tomorrow! The thief climbs trembling onto his bed. He only wanted to steal what had been stolen. Stolen from the rations of the prisoners – by the Block Elder.

After the morning roll call we are offered a spectacle. The hut has lined up. The arena is the area between huts 18 and 19. The Tiger, a lanky Block Elder from a neighboring hut. His paw is notorious. When he lifts his arm to strike he wears leather gloves. For the effect. The sound effect. Up to now I have observed only one who didn't go down after the first blow. And that really wasn't worth it. This failure enraged the man with the hard fist. He made up for it. His prestige had sunk. He never worked without spectators.
The Block Elder speaks first. That's the lot of everyone ... Theft from comrades ... The delinquent stands with bloodshot eye before the lined-up hut. Twelve yards to the side is a pit. About ten feet deep. With ground water. On this day the soil is muddy. The paw of The Tiger lifts for the first blow. He strikes. The victim falls to the ground. This is repeated several times. Now it's only seven feet to the pit. We recognize the intention. At best two blows. No, one suffices. Our fellow prisoner falls shrieking into the pit. No one can help him. An hour later we see him, covered with mud, climb out of the pit.
Every second or third day a prisoners' doctor comes. The hut must line up. Shirts are searched for lice. We have to stick out our tongues. Whoever has a coated tongue is recorded and allegedly taken to the infirmary in the main camp of Birkenau. Many go away. None return. Our ranks thin out.
March 5, 1943.
My brother Ernst has diarrhea. He has high fever. The prisoners' doctor is there again. We line up. Stick out our tongues. I am standing in the first row. After the check-up we have to step forward. Edgar is in the second row. Ernst in the third. His tongue is heavily coated. The doctor and the Block Elder are just at the other end of the hut. Quick as lightning I pull Ernst forward. Change places with him. For today the danger is past.
Night of March 5, 1943.
Ernst still has high fever. His lips are dry and cracked. He begs for water. We give him something to drink. Night falls. We have two mugs for the night. We place them at the head of the bed. Ask our neighbor not to take the water. It's for our sick brother. He promises. Nonetheless a half-hour later the water is no longer there. In the hut there is no water. If one leaves during the night, one is shot. The barbed wire is only six feet from the hut. Water, water, water ... We have none. Our fellow prisoner has drunk it. Despite his promise.
March 6, 1943.
Get up! Line up for roll call! Pepa Brammer takes off his lined jacket. It is great luck to own such a jacket. He gives it to Ernst. Takes his thin one instead. Edgar and I embrace Pepa. We know him from home. We can't hold back our tears. It's nothing, Pepa wards off. No, it's not nothing. Only a few would do this. Pepa is among the few. Edi would do it too. I - I don't know. We support Ernst and line up for roll call. Stay in the fifth, last row. For reasons of safety. The Block Leader comes. We encourage Ernst. Only ten seconds! Only ten seconds! Everything depends on them. Then we're

through. We let go of Ernst. The Block Leader is gone. With him the momentary danger. Until the evening roll call. Then, too, all goes well.

March 7, 1943.

Twenty prisoners are chosen to fetch blankets from the main camp. Edgar and I are among them. We have hidden Ernst on one of the lowest beds. Covered him with blankets. We'll be back soon. Ten minutes to go – ten minutes there – ten minutes returning. In half an hour we could be back. We march to the main camp. Remain standing before the storage room. We wait two hours. We're impatient. Ernst is alone. Helpless. Then we get the blankets. Ten for each of us. We go back. A group of prisoners is standing by a hut wall. The wall of hut 18. From this point the sick are led away. It is a waiting room for the doomed. We go closer. Recognize the Block Clerk. The Camp Capo. Ernst. He is trembling. Now we know. In the meantime an SS-doctor was here. A selection. Edgar and I beg the Block Clerk, named Wertheimer, to dispose of card No. 99729. Do you think I'm going to be gassed for you?, is his answer. We can't say goodbye. We wave. The approximately twenty doomed men are led off. We cry. Others try to comfort us, he'll be taken to the infirmary.

March 10, 1943.

An SS-doctor comes. He is accompanied by several SS-men. We must strip naked. He stands with feet wide apart in the entrance to the hut. One by one we have to come forward. We run a few yards. Then we stop. Stick out our tongues. Most of us pass. Several are led off. Now we know the procedure. Half an hour later we're brought to the bath. We rejoice. It's a shower. Warm water. Afterwards we go into the open. The icy wind gives no sign of the approaching spring. We line up. Another lice roll call. Bare to the waist, we stand there for two hours.

March 12, 1943.

Again many fall through the holes in the sieve. The days are all alike. We see a black mass approaching us over the wide camp road. It is a transport of Gypsies. Men, women, children. They stay together. Keep their own clothes. Without disinfection. They're lodged in several Blocks. One hears German, Czech or the Gypsy language.

The next day I enter a hut. Children scream, women cry, men curse. I recognize a Gypsy with whom I worked before the deportation in a sawmill in Uhersky Brod. You'll go to a concentration camp, you Jews, he said to me three months ago. Somewhat maliciously. Today we're both here. Do you have any bread for me?, I ask. He nods. Permits me to reach into his coat pocket. There I find bread crumbs. I stuff them in my mouth. With the dirt from the pocket. What luck. I thank him. I thank him again. He doesn't know that in a few days he himself will search for crumbs.

The hunger gets worse and worse. I eat the potatoes with the skins. Those who still have the strength to peel potatoes I keep especially in view. I beg for their potato skins. I eat them. No, I don't eat them. I devour them greedily.

Like an animal. As if I was afraid. Perhaps of the envy of the other skin-eaters. There are several. Before I couldn't drink water from a cup. Only from a glass. I'm ashamed. And keenly observe the potato-peelers.
March 15, 1943.
The six-week quarantine is over. We remain in the hut and wait. The SS-doctor and three SS-men are there. It's the same procedure as a few days earlier. Run. Stick out the tongue. Several stay behind. We line up. March. After an hour we arrive at the main camp in Auschwitz. Over the gate the inscription: "Arbeit macht frei" – "Work makes free."
"Eyes left!" In honor of our guards in SS-uniforms, who stand near the gate. We're counted marching. Come to hut 1. (In Auschwitz the huts were brick buildings.) Disinfection and shower. Our underwear and clothes we throw on a heap. We receive cudgel-blows from the "old" prisoners who reign here, a shower, fresh underwear, striped prisoner's uniform, prisoner's coat, cap. We line up in front of the hut. A prisoner from Labor Assignment comes. Labor Assignment. It was called that in Theresienstadt. So this was right. Actually east, too. No one mentioned the barbed wire and the gas chambers. Probably it would interfere with the discipline.
We're asked to name our trade. Road construction worker. I stick to this. Come to hut 17. My commando squad is called Huta-Concrete Construction. A roaring Block Elder. Everyone is roared at separately. Order, discipline, cleanliness! Clear? Yes!, I answer. "Yes, indeed," it should be. I'm punched in the face. "Yes, indeed," I repeat.
The room is very clean. Three-storied single beds. Straw sacks. Blankets. Warm. A blessing after Birkenau. We are all very optimistic. Maybe the motto "Work makes free" makes us optimistic.
At five-thirty we're awakened. The wash-room is clean, the toilets too. We get a kind of peppermint tea and line up for morning roll call. At "Attention" the entire camp is silent. Several Block Leaders are engaged in counting. The work-commandos line up.
My commando has its assembly point on the camp road near the kitchen. Then the marching out of the individual commandos begins. I look for my brother Edgar. He has registered as a shoemaker. Doubtless I'll find him. In the evening I'll scour the huts that have newcomers. He'll surely do the same. A band plays marches. Could play in any spa. It's that good. They're all prisoners. Now it's our turn. We march as smartly as we can. Left, left, left, left ... Before the gate the order "Caps off! Eyes right!" For this moment we were drilled in Birkenau. So now it comes off well. The man next to me, a prisoner about thirty years old from Pruszana, has spasms in the stomach. He can't keep up. The Capo, a German from the Reich with a green triangle, notices this. Inquires. My neighbor speaks of gastric ulcers, from home, speaks of diet. Capo Helmuth, as he is called by the "Obercapo," promises speedy relief. He has a good remedy. The sick man rejoices over so much readiness to help. I too. By noon surely all will be well.

We arrive at our working place. Canalization. A big area. Sheds for tools. Shovels and pickaxes are distributed. We set to work. Civilian engineers and foremen show us the way. The sick man stays behind with Capo Helmuth. Shortly afterwards I hear screams. The handle of a shovel was the good remedy. The cart for the dead comes at eleven.

The work consists of digging, fetching cement, transporting concrete. The mixing machine is approximately two hundred yards from the place where the concrete is brought. It's transported in small wagons. On tracks. Three men to a wagon. Two former Czech policemen are with me. Red triangle. Political. Eager to help. The civil engineer is from Silesia. We dump concrete into a pit. The transport must take place on the double. Luckily we go down hill with the full wagon. With the empty one it's easier to run. If we think we are unnoticed we reduce the tempo.

When fetching cement, the main street that leads into the center of Auschwitz, has to be crossed. I recognize the street. At sixteen I spent a holiday in Auschwitz; in an Auschwitz without barbed wire and gas chambers. I think of the walks with friends to the Sola river, of evenings in a youth club, of the first girl I had a crush on, who lived in this town. They are happy and painful memories at the same time. Then I drove in a horse and buggy for a zloty from the station into town. It was an important experience for me. The first journey I was allowed to make alone. To Auschwitz. Is this one to be my last? I try not to think about it. Now I don't want to think. Only to survive. At any price. At any price?

The Block Clerk brings good news. We can write a postcard to relatives. To the few who have not yet been deported. I write to my sister-in-law. She is the step-sister of my wife, half-Jewish. All is well with me. I'm healthy. The text is prescribed, sender too. Family name, first name, Waldsee, House No. 17. As if from a health resort with woods and lake. Why not Villa No. 17? I hardly expect a reply. Probably the purpose was to lull those still at home in to a sense of security.

While fetching cement there's a commotion. A man from Berlin named Martin can't carry a hundred-and-ten pound sack of cement. Twice in a row he drops the sack. It lies torn on the ground. Martin receives blows. He's exhausted. He's lost. We know what will soon happen. We drive with the wagon loaded with cement to the mixing machine. Poor fellow, says one of the policemen. We nod mutely.

My cousin, Fritz Gelb from Uhersky Brod, has been in a bad way for several days. With great effort he shovels gravel. He has diarrhea and is very weak. He doesn't dare go to the infirmary. According to the experiences in Birkenau he's right. The next day he no longer comes to the commando. He couldn't hold out.

After a few days my legs and feet are very swollen. Each day more so. Hunger edema. In the evening I press my thumb against the swelling. In several places. Dents remain that fill up slowly. I'm not the only one. In the evening

the feet are swollen, in the morning the face. Feet, face. I have pain in the area of the inguinal gland. Nonetheless I march out with the commando. I can't keep up. I think of the gastric ulcers. Help by noon. Capo Helmuth. Cart for the dead. I pull myself together. Left, left, left, left . . .
My two good angels direct me to simply crouch on the frame of the wagon. My guardian angels. We have outwitted Capo Helmuth. In the evening I report to the infirmary. Despite my fears. The doorman in the out-patients section of the HKB, short for Haeftlingskrankenbau (prisoners' infirmary), repeats my name. Mannheimer. Mannheimer? Where are you from?, he asks. I tell him. At my question, whether he encountered my brother Erich, he is silent. Now I'm sure that he knew him. He doesn't want to speak. His name is Weiss and he comes from Holic in Slovakia. His prisoner's number is 29,000. A coincidence that he is still alive. Jewish prisoners seldom live so long. Maybe it's due to his job.
I have to undress, go under the shower. Then my prisoner's number is written, oversized, with an indelible pencil on my chest. Everything is very well-organized. Different from Birkenau.
Auschwitz, HKB, beginning of 1943.
In half an hour I am to be operated on. Inflammation of the inguinal gland. The pain makes me rather apathetic. My left leg is very swollen. I have difficulty in taking off my underpants. Surgical table. A surgeon. An anaesthetist. Both Polish prisoners. Ether. I count to forty-three. I awake from the anaesthetic. Am bandaged. A paper dressing. Set on my legs I stagger to my plank bed. It's the top of three bunks. As if on a ladder I climb, with the aid of the next bedstead, onto my bed. I feel myself in safety.
The night is very long. Next to me a prisoner groans. I can't sleep. The groaning, the odor of the sick-room with more than 200 beds. It gets light. I'm happy that the night is over. My relief doesn't last long. One of the male nurses calls: Everyone out of bed! Remove bandages! An SS-doctor stands at the entrance. The Haeftlingsschreiber (prisoners' clerk) calls out the prisoners' numbers. The corridor – about seven feet broad and fifteen yards long – between the rows of beds becomes a testing ground. I'm frightened. I'm very frightened. The fifteen yards must be overcome at the double. Those who accomplish it can return to the beds. The others remain standing near the door. My number is called out. Double time! I run, I run, I run for my life. I feel no pain. The few seconds seem to me like an eternity. My arms are bent up, chest thrown out. More exactly the skeleton of a chest. I can go back to bed.
In the groaning neighbor, whose turn it is now, I recognize my friend Riesenfeld. His entire body is covered with boils. The legs swollen. After eight weeks in the camp. He can't run. He drags himself. At the door he is held back. Then several more. The race for life is over. About forty stand at the door.
The numbers are read once more. One is missing. He managed to escape. Escape? He's hauled out of bed. He screams, screams, screams . . .

The skeletons, whom we call Mussulmen in the camp idiom, receive blankets. It's April. With shirts and blankets they go downstairs. Ten minutes later we hear a truck drive off. Those who remain behind know the destination. No one speaks of it. This week there will be no more selections. What will next week bring? How long must I stay here? No one can tell me.

Second half of April, 1943.

I leave the infirmary. My brother Edgar works as shoemaker. He repairs wooden shoes for prisoners. He says, this time I should pass myself off as a shoemaker with the Labor Assignment. Then I would get into his commando. I report. My hut is 14a – my commando: Clothing Workshops. I am together with my brother.

Next day. I march out with the commando. A big commando. Approximately three-hundred-and-fifty prisoners. Twenty minutes on foot. An old factory. Must have been a tannery. A roof over my head. My brother introduces me to the Haeftlingsmeister (master in charge, prisoner). As in civilian life. He supervises the repair of shoes. Is named Lipczak. From Posen. Every day my brother receives five blows on the behind. With a shoe-last. Although he likes my brother. I am to drive a wooden peg into a leather shoe. I have to stoop. Never knew that such a last could hurt so much. I am to cut wooden pegs. With a shoemaker's knife. In the evening there are more blows. Too uneven and too few, the master says. After a few days it gets better. Now the blows are only for appearances' sake. A hobby of the master's. Under the right collar-bone a reddish-blue swelling that is very painful. It is a phlegmona. In the evening I report to the infirmary.

Once more I have to be operated on. Once more the bath, the prisoner's number with the indelible pencil on the chest. A Polish surgeon. I am sent to hut 9. Next door is the Women's Experimental Hut. The fear of a selection overtakes me. I try not to think of it. I am very emaciated. The rations in the infirmary are very scanty. Just before the morning roll call my brother Edgar comes to the infirmary. He whistles. It is a signal from our childhood. The sickroom is on the second floor. I stagger to the window. How are you?, he calls. Fine, I answer. He can't see my body. Catch, he calls. A day's ration of bread flies through the window. His ration. He goes hungry. For me. So I'll get well quicker, he says. Tomorrow he'll come again. After two weeks I'm discharged. My brother is waiting before the hut. He embraces a skeleton. He suppresses tears. I try to do the same.

The Labor Assignment classifies the discharged. As usual. You simply say upholsterer, I'll manage it, Edi said yesterday. Hut 14a – Clothing Workshops. I know the procedure. Upholsterers come forward! The Upholsterer-Capo, a green triangle, likes the "tall shoemaker", as my brother is called in the commando. He is strikingly big, strikingly young. Seventeen and a half now. I have a good job. For how long? I pick wool. Grecian wool. The Jews from Greece brought a lot of wool with them. Olives and wool. A Pole, a political prisoner, supervises the picking. He is amiable and addresses me by

my first name. His name is Oleg. Not all Poles are so friendly to the Jewish prisoners. I scrub the workshop. When I'm finished with washing up, the less friendly "comrade" upsets the pail and gives me a kick on the behind. I fall down. Those present laugh. I don't. At the request of the upholsterer, I'm shifted to the "Hofkommando," where I'm assigned various tasks in the factory courtyard.
September 1943.
Rudi Mueller is a former glove manufacturer from Prague. We're in the same hut, the same room, the same commando. We've become friends. He sorts empty suitcases according to quality. Those still fit for use are separated from the others. Suitcases aren't in demand. There are plenty of them. Every day new transports with Jews arrive. New suitcases. I have something for you, Rudi says. The Senior Capo notices that we are conversing so Rudi Mueller comes to the Hofkommando too. What have you got?, I ask him later in the hut. He gives me a photograph. He found it in a suitcase. In our suitcase. I cut it into two strips. Insert them in my belt that is doubly sewn. My parents, my brothers and sister are with me. They will accompany me.
The work in the Hofkommando consists of sawing wood, sweeping the courtyard and other similar tasks. Today Rudi Mueller and I have to saw wood. It is a warm day. We rest a bit. Dirty bums!, the Senior Capo calls from a window. He had observed us. Come with me! We go to the tannery. A big basin. Red-brownish water. For skins. Water-level twenty inches from the upper brim. We foresee what is in store for us. We are pushed in in our prisoners' clothes. Try to climb out. The Senior Capo tramples on our fingers. Pushes us back. Tramples on our heads. This is repeated several times. Then he says: You're real guys! With effort we climb out. We tremble from cold, from fear. Bronchitis is the result with me. Fever. I manage to get a respite from work. An abscess develops on my chest. I'm afraid to go to the infirmary. There's a rumor that whoever was there three times goes to the gas chamber. The experiences of the last weeks, that only indirectly involved me, have lessened my confidence in survival. Above all, three incidents led to this.
One day, when our commando comes into the camp, the order "Caps off! Eyes left!" is given as usual. We are counted. The music plays, also as usual. Our eyes, which are turned to the left, see the following picture: On slanting boards, that are leaned against the hut to the left of the gate, six prisoners are lying with their stomachs ripped open. Their entrails spill out. Their faces are smeared with blood and unrecognizable. Later we learn that they belonged to an agricultural commando. Allegedly they wanted to flee.
It is Sunday. Music plays for the entertainment of the prisoners. Entertainment? Before the kitchen, gallows are erected. A special kind of gallows. Left and right two thick poles, diagonally across them a steel bar. Several prisoners are brought from hut 11, the bunker. They climb onto the waiting chairs. Nooses are put around their necks. The chairs pulled away with a jerk. The

hanged men remain hanging for two hours. As a warning. The music continues to play. We say nothing. There is nothing to say.
One evening a little old woman stands near the entrance gate. Her husband is standing there too. Before them is a poster board. On it one can read the words: This is the lot of all whose children tried to flee from Auschwitz. So they're hostages. We greet the old people mutely.
One has to get away from Auschwitz. The constant selections. The fear. Over and over again fear. Is it your turn now? The order, all Jews remain standing after the roll call, is the signal for the selections.
It's Poldi Gelbkopf whom I always rely on in this situation. He's very thin, to be sure, but a robust fellow. Farmer, used to hard labor. If I stand behind him I don't look so skinny. My body appears somewhat broader. Because of the frame. The things that occur to one when one wants to survive. And I want to survive. There is a power that sustains me. Perhaps my brother. Certainly my brother. I wonder what sustains the others? I have long since lost faith in God. All this can't happen before the eyes of God. Why this trial, in case it should be one? Why these martyrs? Why?
In Birkenau a transport from Theresienstadt is said to have arrived. In the family camp. As with the Gypsies, the families stay together. My friend Hermann from Troppau is in the Roofing-Commando and is working now in Birkenau. Through him I try to learn whether my parents-in-law, who were able to stay in Theresienstadt at the end of January, are present. For the most part doctors remained in Theresienstadt. Like my father-in-law. The seventy-year-old could possibly be among them. He is. My brother and I send him bread. I send a message too. The joy is great. About my wife and sister-in-law I give no information. Hope is non-existent, I don't want to hurt the old people. Also the hope that my parents-in-law will survive is non-existent. For that I know Birkenau too well.
Weiss, the doorman of the HKB, finally gives in. He knew our brother Erich well. Erich's feet were frost-bitten and he went the way of many. We don't ask more. On the same day we encounter Lazarowicz, the man who betrayed my brother. To the Gestapo. In Uherske Hradiste. We know the methods the Gestapo uses to get prisoners to talk. We speak of unimportant things, of work commandos. What else should we speak of? We're not judges.
The women from the Experimental Hut 10 return from a walk. They're all good-looking, neatly dressed. Their ages could be between twenty and thirty. For the most part Jewish women from Slovakia and Poland. One can't see what happens to them in Hut 10. A professor named Clauberg[7] comes every

---

[7] Carl Clauberg (1898–1957), gynecologist, joined the NSDAP in 1933 as chief physician of the Women's Hospital of the University of Kiel. From 1933 to 1940 Clauberg was a professor at the University of Koenigsberg, then director of the Women's Hospital Koenigshuette in Upper Silesia, not far from Auschwitz. He sought contact with Heinrich Himmler, whom he interested in experiments in sterilization of women without operation. From 1942 to 1944 Clauberg tested in grand style his method of mass

week to the camp to supervise the experiments. Therefore many assume it concerns medical experiments, perhaps sterilisation, artificial insemination or the like.
A transport from Posen has arrived. I think of Albert Goettinger and of the bread we fetched for him in the past from Nivnice. Of his sojourn in Posen. Of the letters full of gratitude that he wrote Eva. So much gratitude for a bit of bread. At the time we couldn't understand it. In the meantime we have learned to. The new arrivals are in a quarantine hut. But one can get in. I inquire about Albert Goettinger. A prisoner points to a very emaciated man in the corner of the room. I address him. Tears come before my words. Albert doesn't know who I am. He has never heard of me. I am Eva's husband. Eva Bock. Now he understands. We sit in silence on the wooden plank bed. I give him a piece of my bread. And a pullover. He is to go on a transport again. To the coal pits. To Jewischowitz. The next day I no longer find him. The transport has left.
October 5, 1943.
We are counted. Afterwards all non-Polish Jews must remain standing. The SS-Obersturmfuehrer from the death-ramp in Birkenau comes. The Block Clerk stands next to him with the card index. Transport, we all whisper. We strip to the waist. About one-hundred-twenty prisoners are left. The Block Clerk calls out the prisoners' numbers. The first selection I'm not afraid of. The main thing is to get away from Auschwitz.
The same doctor as on the ramp. I inspect him closely. I picture him without uniform. He looks exactly like many other doctors. His gaze, he wears glasses, is utterly placid. His face is narrow, profile somewhat sharp. His hands slender, almost sensitive. He is very tall. About six feet four inches. His bearing straight as a dart. We have to show our hands. Stick out our tongues. One after the other. Then we get dressed. The doctor gives the Block Clerk directions that we can't hear. It's my brother's turn: 99727. Then mine: 99728. We're approximately in the middle of the group. The Block Clerk gives me a sign. He is our friend. A Berliner. The sign means: Wait. Only your brother is going, he says. I was afraid of this. The wound on my chest that has not yet healed. The abscess. Something has to happen. I can't stay in Auschwitz alone. My only brother. Away from Auschwitz. Away from the showers without water.

---

sterilization through injection without anesthesia, in Hut 10 in Auschwitz I, on Jewesses and Gypsies. The experiments were accompanied by the greatest pain and often led to the death of the victims. In 1945 Clauberg was deported to the Soviet Union and sentenced to prison for 25 years, for taking part in "mass extermination of Soviet women," but was pardoned in 1955 and released to the Federal Republic of Germany. He was arrested in Kiel in November, 1955 and died in August, 1957, shortly before the beginning of a trial for "continuous severe bodily injury" of female prisoners in Auschwitz. Clauberg had boasted of these "scientific" accomplishments to the end.

Cap in hand, hands on the trouser seam, I step before the lord over left or right, yes or no, life or death. "Herr Obersturmfuehrer, prisoner 99728 requests an audience!" This sentence came quick as a flash. Everything or nothing. Away from Auschwitz. From the gas chambers. Crematoria. Only away. I try to replace my slight Austrian accent by the curt camp tone. "Was wollen Sie?" – "What do you want?" The "Sie," the polite form, surprises me. A small ray of hope. "Herr Obersturmfuehrer, prisoner 99728 requests to be allowed to go on transport. Am completely fit for work." "But you have a wound on the chest!" Amazing this memory. In the meantime I had dressed. One prisoner looks like another. "Open your shirt, I'll have a look. Clerk! Transport!" "Thank you, Herr Obersturmfuehrer!"

One day later. The rations must hold out for two days. Bread. Sausage. Margarine. New clothes. Fresh underwear. Instead of leather shoes there are wooden clogs. Not Dutch. A wooden shoe made in one piece, on the front a piece of canvas. For the tip of the foot. It's not easy to march in these clogs. In order not to lose them the toes must be curled under. We march to the waiting cars. They're railway freight cars. On each side thirty-five prisoners. The center area remains vacant. For the SS-guards. We don't know the destination. The guards don't want to tell us. You'll work, is their only reply. We're comforted. Why should we have otherwise received new clothes, underwear, rations? A ray of hope suffices and already we're perfect optimists. Is it the will to live or naiveté? Through a crack in the car wall someone imagines he can make out that it leads north. For the time being we don't know more. We ride for two days and two nights. Auschwitz is far away. What were we told at the time? The children go to the kindergarten. Husbands can visit their wives on Sundays. The truth was different. There were no kindergartens. There were no visits. There was only hunger, misery and death.

On the Jewish Day of Atonement we arrive in Warsaw. In the Warsaw Ghetto.[8] More exactly: in the ruins of the Warsaw Ghetto. Wagons loaded with old bricks stand on a side-track. They are historic bricks. Witnesses to a battle between the courageous fighters of the Warsaw Ghetto and the superior force of Himmler's SS-troops. We know no particulars. The information that leaked to Auschwitz was scant. Presumably it was brought by Polish prisoners. We stand here now on historic ground. In wooden clogs. Brought here to demolish the remnants of the battle. Day breaks. Everything looks so eerie. Burned out houses. A great stillness. No human being far and wide. We

---

[8] After 300,000 inhabitants of the Jewish residential quarter in Warsaw had already been deported to the Treblinka extermination camp, the remaining 60,000 Jews resisted, from April 19, 1943, the further evacuation of the Ghetto. The SS-units under Juergen Stroop required until May 16 to crush the armed opposition. Thereby the Ghetto was completely destroyed. For the clearing of rubble and to salvage useful material, a separate concentration camp was erected in Warsaw on August 15, 1943. Its prisoners were evacuated to Dachau on July 24, 1944.

line up for roll call. March. The clack of two thousand wooden clogs sounds ghostly. Their echo in the dawn is especially weird. On a street sign we read: "Dr. L. Zamenhof." The inventor of Esperanto. For better understanding between nations. Twenty minutes later we arrive. It is Gesia Street. In the main building is a prison. Behind it a concentration camp is erected. Wooden huts with windows. Looks quite good.

We line up on the roll-call square. A Camp Elder with black triangle is delivering a speech. Discipline, cleanliness, diligence! We know it already. Allocation to the individual huts. One thousand prisoners. Five hundred Greek Jews came before us. Have been here for three months. Criminals from the Reich too. As Block Elders and Capos. The SS is fond of filling these posts with professional criminals. My brother and I come to hut 1. The numbers that we receive in Warsaw are 2881 and 2882. The tattooed numbers are no longer valid. New camp, new numbers. There are still no beds. We sleep on the floor. Shoes under our heads. Without blankets. The many people warm the room. It's only October. So it's bearable. Edi and I are assigned to a Demolition Commando. It's called "Merkel." Presumably the name of the demolition firm. First march out. A Polish overseer. Now we have civilian clothes with red stripes on pant legs and jackets. We receive pickaxes in our hands, climb in wooden clogs onto the burned out or already partially demolished walls and have the task of breaking off bricks from dangerous heights. We clean and stack them. Day after day the same.

The work commandos are often frisked when marching into the camp. The cellars of the burned-out houses frequently contain treasures. Plates, cutlery, various china objects. They are favorite articles of exchange in dealing with Polish civilians. I find a bag of barley. Smuggle it into the camp. Together with friends I cook some. We agree we don't like the taste – but perhaps it's nourishing. In any case: Barley. Better than beet. One day we find skeletons. From the rebellion. Three adults. Two children. Buried alive in rubble. Or poisoned by smoke. Or shot. We don't know. We say Kaddish.

Several prisoners organize a cabaret-group. On a Sunday they have their début in hut 6. A corner becomes an improvised stage. Leading initiators: Herbert Scherzer, actor, and Ernest Landau, journalist, both from Vienna. In the first and second rows sit the camp notables. All professional criminals – Camp Elder, Block Elder, Capos.

The program consists of sketches, couplets. We forget for the moment that we are in a concentration camp. Only a few gained admission. Due to lack of space.

After the performance I see the "artists" come out of the kitchen with a small kettle of soup. Artists' soup. I follow them. Scherzer disappears into a hut. I address Landau. I don't know him. "Comrade, can I have some soup?" "Get yourself a bowl!" I run into the hut, fetch a bowl and can hardly believe my eyes. Ernest Landau is really waiting. He gives me soup. I thank him. This deed will determine my attitude towards Ernest Landau for all time.

November 1943.
They are looking for washers for the laundry. Now I summon up my courage. I have already been a shoemaker and upholsterer. Why not washer? I report. Where did you work as washer? Theresienstadt. He who lies quickly lies well. The laundry for the entire camp. Four prisoners. Two cauldrons. A lot of laundry. Worn for months. By sick people. Disgusting. There are lice. Lice mean typhoid fever. After two weeks the laundry is closed. New commando. Laundry nightshift. In the city. Outside the Ghetto walls. Exciting. It is the firm Winter, Leszno No. 20, Warsaw. The laundry comes from the Wehrmacht and the SS. Two SS-men accompany us. Germans from Croatia. A Polish woman and her daughter supervise the nightshift. Steamheated washing machines. Warmth. Rotating washing machine. Hot-mangle. Everyone is happy. The others in the camp envy us. Secretly we wash our laundry too. At eight in the morning we return to the camp. Evenings we put on dirty laundry. From our friends. Despite the danger of typhoid fever. Anyway there are enough lice now in the camp. For several months no clean underwear.
A friend from the Demolition Commando brings a notebook he found under the rubble. In Polish. I look at it. A diary, written in the last days of the rebellion in the Ghetto. The writing of a young girl. For soup I buy the notebook. Have it translated into German. Lately a civilian works in the laundry. Blond. Peroxide-blond. Young. Pretty. Intelligent. Apart from Polish speaks German, French, English. Her name is Cesia. She is especially friendly to us. That indicates that she is a Jew in hiding. Who lives with "Aryan papers." As one calls them. We don't want to ask directly. On the next evening I inquire about her parents. She cries. Now I know. And understand the bleached hair. I don't tell the others. A change in conduct would be dangerous. She shouldn't go the way of her parents. The diary occurs to me. Cesia will preserve it for posterity. In case we don't survive. Perhaps in a museum. Museums are fairly safe. I speak with her. She consents. Each day she takes several pages with her. The last days of an approximately fourteen to 16-year-old girl. Hunger, no light, no water, filth. Hideout. Constantly exposed to danger.
In the camp a typhoid fever epidemic breaks out. Two huts are turned into an infirmary. Edgar falls ill. Robert Sawosnik, a Norwegian student of medicine, looks after him. Ernest Landau is there as male nurse. He reported voluntarily. Is courageous. Every morning I come to the hut. After the nightshift in the laundry. Slowly Edgar recovers. The dead from the last night lie before the hut. Skeletons covered with skin. Skin with big blue-black spots. Typhoid fever spots.
The SS-command is uneasy. From a Block Elder we learn that already there has been an inquiry in the Reichssicherheitshauptamt (the central security authority of the Reich) in Berlin. Don't liquidate, was the answer. The epidemic is gradually checked. The balance: About 500 dead.

The Greek Saul from Saloniki is employed in the clothing chamber. It is a privilege to be employed there. Once a week he comes into town to the laundry. Accompanied by SS-men. With horse and wagon. He tries to flee. Fails. He is shot at and wounded. Can't run.
On the following Sunday everyone remains standing after the morning roll-call. Next to hut 6 gallows are erected. Saul is hanged before our eyes. His brother Isaak must look on. Breaks down. The prisoners go into the huts. Life goes on. Life?
In the laundry there is a great commotion. Pieces of clothing are missing. No one admits the theft. The dayshift, Polish civilian workers, put the blame on us. On the next evening our commando doesn't march out. We stay in the camp.
Warsaw, December 1943.
Roll call. We are counted. Line up. The dead from the night lie in front of the hut. As every day. The Block Leader counts off. The living and the dead together yield the total. It tallies. Luckily. Get moving! Attention! Announcement: Prisoners who are familiar with office work are to report. Shall I, shall I not? I think of the soap and the towel in Auschwitz. Of the showers, disinfection. The showers without water. (Only later I learned that the "showers" were disguised openings for Zyklon B - prussic acid.) Nonsense! Warsaw isn't Auschwitz. I report. We must line up before the garrison. Seventeen prisoners line up. Before the Obersturmfuehrer. Next to him the Commando Clerk - a prisoner. 16 "Aryans" - "Aryans" from the Reich - one Jew. No chance, I think to myself. Who can stenograph?, the SS-officer asks. Apart from me one prisoner reports. Come forward! My rival understood "photograph." I am assigned to the prisoners' office. Shortly before the beginning of winter in Warsaw. Hope of survival. With deep gratitude I think of my father. He said to me: My boy, stenography is very important. By the way, I didn't once have to write shorthand.
Today many young people learn stenography. For many it is difficult. They complain. Then I say: Stenography is very important. I don't say more. They really wouldn't understand.
The work in the office is easy. We have to remove the dead from the card-index, make lists of the work-commandos and the like. The peculiarity of the card-index is that several prisoners' numbers were used up to three times. When someone died his number was alloted to a new arrival.
Willy V. feeds swine for the SS-kitchen. He comes into the office. A green triangle. Professional criminal. He permits me to write in his name to my sister-in-law, who is still at home. Germans from the Reich can write and receive packages. "Dear Maria, all is well with me in Warsaw. Send me a pair of closed wooden shoes. If possible Eva's yellow wedding dress and some jam. I'm healthy. Hope you are well too." Four weeks later Willy brings a package to the hut. I want to give him something from it. He declines gruffly. Almost insulted. Presumably he is too proud. The package contains various

eatables, a pair of closed wooden shoes, socks, grape sugar, vitamins and a glass of jam. In the jam the "yellow wedding dress" - Eva's gold bracelet and necklace. Maria understood. I knew she would understand. I hope to exchange the bracelet and the necklace for bread. Lots of bread. I give them to a Polish civilian master - Pawel Sikora from Posen. He brings me a single four pound loaf. Allegedly the jewelry was taken away from him at the Ghetto gate by the SS and he gave me the bread from pity. There's nothing I can do.

The relatives of the "Aryan" prisoners have a privilege. They can request the ashes of their relatives. When the time comes. For a fee. For Capos and foremen the time comes sometimes, too. No, they don't die from hunger. Not in Warsaw. From time to time the finding of objects of value is their ruin. Not the actual finding but trading with them. The SS-guards are often partners in selling. They're the salesmen. In Warsaw, outside the Ghetto walls. Usually bring the suppliers vodka in exchange. Vodka loosens the tongue. The Capos brag about their wonderful connections. Not for long. The contractors in green uniform with skull and cross bones like silent partners. "Shot while escaping," is the given cause of death. For the card-index. For the relatives. The crate with the ashes stands next to my desk. I didn't succeed in finding out whether the ashes come from the site of the burning near the building of the former Jewish Council. Or from somewhere else. This time there are four urns to fill. Oberscharfuehrer Mielenz supervises my work. The urns are packed in wooden boxes. On them the prisoner's name and day of death. The calibre of the pistol is missing.

Leon Halpern lived in a "mixed marriage" before his arrest. His wife and child remained in Prague. He wrote for a package. Through a prisoner from the Reich. In the package a letter is enclosed. "Dear Leon," it begins. The official addressee isn't named Leon. Mielenz orders me to search for all Leons in the card-index. He wants to have them in fifteen minutes. I know Leon well. I do just one thing. I inform him. More I can't do. He can prepare himself better. For questions. For blows. Leon must lean over a wooden construction like a table. Receives fifty cudgel blows. He is thin but tough. The German from the Reich is assigned to another commando. Leon asserts he did it without the knowledge of the German. He's a real guy.

In Warsaw a transport arrives. Hungarian Jews from Auschwitz. They occupy the new camp, that was prepared months ago. The office moves too. It's only a few hundred yards away. New SS-guards come. From Lublin. The Ghetto and camp there are said to have been already liquidated.[9] Most of the prisoners are still engaged in demolition work. The political reports that from time

---

[9] The Concentration Camp Lublin, also known under the name Lublin-Majdanek, existed from October, 1941 until the liberation in July, 1944 and had ten camps. From summer, 1942 to July, 1944 it was an extermination camp; altogether approximately 200,000 people were murdered there.

to time leak through to us let us hope that the end of the war is near. Now the only thing that matters to us is to survive. Allegedly there is danger from partisans. The SS, who are allowed to go into town in their spare time, always stick together.

The commander of the camp in Plaszow near Cracow[10] comes to us. From the card-index we must choose skilled workers who are to be transferred to Plaszow. The commander, Goeth,[11] is feared. I tremble when he dictates the transport list into the typewriter. This transport doesn't materialize. Several days later we receive rations for a march. This time no freight-cars are waiting. We will go on foot. In wooden clogs. Westward.

A long column of emaciated prisoners drags itself along the main street. SS-guards, partly with dogs, drive us on. Whoever stays behind is shot. We are in a great hurry. We sense that the Russians are near. The nervousness of the SS is perceptible. Many of us stay behind. They can't keep pace. Although we actually don't march so fast.

Towards evening we rest in a meadow. The first night's quarters. We're confined to a particular area and surrounded by guards. So we won't flee. We're plagued by thirst. Aren't allowed to look for water. The soil here is very moist. That gives us hope. We dig with tablespoons. After three feet reach water. We pounce on it. This way several sources come to light that temporarily quench our thirst. Drink, drink, drink ... Good water. Many pray. Thank God for the miracle.

The next day we go on. Again many stay behind. Hunger and thirst plague us. We reach Sochaczew. A river. Despite the danger of typhoid fever we drink. With and without tadpoles. We can't help ourselves. Aren't even nauseated. Thirst is worse than hunger. Before I didn't know this. It doesn't have to be a desert. A march suffices. We're afraid. Of hunger, of thirst, of staying behind.

Before Kutno we pass the night in a forest. It is raining. It pours. We lie on the ground. With spoons we dig grooves around us. So the water can run off. Our clothes are wet through. Now there's enough water. The rain stops. The day begins. We march to the station in Kutno. Ninety prisoners must find room in a freight car. Forty-five on one side – forty-five on the other. The middle must remain vacant for the two SS-guards. We squat on the floor. Pressed tightly together. The stench of urine and feces is unbearable. The thirst caused by the

---

[10] The Concentration Camp Cracow-Plaszow existed from January, 1944 to January, 1945, had the official name "SS-Work-Camp" and was formerly a forced labor camp for Jews.

[11] Amon Leopold Goeth, born in 1908 in Vienna, was lastly commander of the camp Plaszow, in the rank of SS-Hauptsturmfuehrer (that corresponded with a captain in the Wehrmacht). In August/September 1946 he was indicted in Cracow before the Polish Supreme National Court of Law. Among other crimes he was charged with the assassination of 8,000 Jews in the Tarnow Ghetto. The death sentence was carried out on September 13, 1946.

over-salted rations gets steadily stronger. It's forbidden to fetch water. The SS fetch it. Fill their flasks. We beg for water. A prisoner breaks out a gold tooth from his dentures. He gets water for it. Gold for water.
We have three dead in our car. Pressed to death. Suffocated. Who knows? There is shoving and beating. The guards threaten to shoot. To no avail. The area doesn't get bigger. So it goes on for three days and two nights. With stopovers at unknown stations. Emptying pails. Searching for water. We arrive in Dachau. We draw a deep breath.

Dachau, August 1944.
We drag ourselves into the camp. Exhausted but relieved. Bath. Disinfection. Registration. Edgar 87097, I 87098. Numbered three times and still alive. We remain standing on the big roll-call square. Are distributed among the huts. Quarantine in hut 17. This time it's to last three weeks. My teeth are very loose from undernourishment. I go to the dental-station. The French prisoners' doctor recommends carrots, but doesn't say where they can be obtained. Opposite the dental-station is the dissecting room. Right next to it the mortuary. A Czech prisoners' doctor, Dr Bláha, asks me, do you want bread? I do. Bread from the dissecting room. What does it matter? I don't dare to ask for carrots. I can come again.

Italian officers arrive at our hut. As prisoners. Approximately twenty. Old Social Democrats and Labor Union functionaries come too. Old also in years. One of them must go to the infirmary. I want to show him the way. He declines, almost offended: "I was here already in 1934," is his answer. As an "oldtimer" I couldn't impress him. A seventy-year-old man in Dachau.

Towards evening I am ordered to the office. I must type index cards of new arrivals in the nightshift. At midnight there is gruel. Even cold it tastes good. Allegedly comes from the diet-kitchen. Experiments, gallows, gas chamber[12] – and diet-kitchen? I don't understand.

In Dachau the control of the prisoners is in the hands of the Politicals. Not of the green or black triangles, as in Auschwitz or Warsaw. In the priests' hut there are priests of all nationalities. Germans, Poles, Czechs, Yugoslavs – Catholic, Protestant, Greek-Orthodox. I encounter a priest who knew my father well. He doesn't ask about him. He doesn't want to hurt me.

There's a brothel in Dachau, too. A brothel for prisoners. For "Aryans." Except for Russians. One is admitted by ticket. On advance notice. The allegedly voluntary victims are prisoners from Ravensbrueck.[13]

In Dachau there are many Jugoslavs. One calls them partisans. They were. I speak with several. I admire their courage. These people go into the moun-

---

[12] In the Dachau Concentration camp a gas chamber did indeed exist. However, it was not used for the systematic killing of prisoners as in the extermination camps.

[13] Ravensbrueck (near Fuerstenberg in the district of Potsdam), established on May 15, 1939, evacuated on April 30, 1945, was the largest concentration camp specifically for women (42 subsidiary camps). Over 90,000 women died in Ravensbrueck.

tains. Fight against a regular army. With much idealism and few weapons. Under the hardest conditions. I compare. Them and us. We let ourselves be transported like animals to the slaughter. With numbers around our necks. Promptly we held out our heads. Cattle to be slaughtered resist entering the slaughterhouse. Not us. We obey without protest. Except for the Jews in the Warsaw Ghetto. And the Maccabeans two thousand years ago. Maybe it's because the Jews during this long time in the Diaspora were often treated as second class people, or worse, and therefore, throughout the ages, on the whole submitted passively to all persecution.

After three weeks of quarantine in Dachau we go to Karlsfeld. A few miles from Dachau. The camp is called O.T. Subsidiary Camp Karlsfeld.[14] There are brick huts and three-tiered bedsteads. As everywhere the Camp Elder makes a speech here, too, that we already know. We are assigned to the single work commandos. My commando is named Sager and Woerner. We must build assembly halls on the BMW-grounds. The work consists of carrying cement and steel. It amuses the Commando Leader, SS-Hauptscharfuehrer Jentsch, to set his sheep dog on the prisoners. He gives the order "cease" only when the victim is bleeding. After a few days I fall ill. I can stay in the camp. For "light" work. That's what it's called. Light? With a very old prisoner, Albert Kerner from Munich, I transport corpses with a mule from Karlsfeld to Dachau. To the main camp. For burning. Kerner walks next to the mule, the SS-guard next to me. I must see that the dead remain covered. A sudden gust of wind lifts off the covers. The passersby, mainly women, have frightened expressions. Corpses from the concentration camp aren't a pretty sight.

In one hut there is praying. For the most part Jews from Hungary. They pray every day. On Yom Kippur – the Jewish Day of Atonement – they even fast. Political reports are circulated. The Americans and British are said to be very near. How near no one can say.

In January, 1945 a commando is transferred to the Subsidiary Camp Muehldorf.[15] My brother is part of the commando. This time we're really to be separated. Alone it's harder to come through. Friends are good, to be sure – a brother is better. I remain behind. I think of the good soldier Schwejk, who wants to meet his friend in a Prague Inn ("U kalicha"), at six p.m., after the war. We'll surely find each other, is our mutual consolation.

---

[14] The Subsidiary Camp Karlsfeld of the Dachau Concentration Camp was established on July 11, 1944; the management was in the hands of the Chief Supervision of Construction Dachau of the Organization Todt (OT). The OT, named after its chief, Dr Fritz Todt, was erected in 1938 as a state organization for the erection of military plants and structures of military importance. Above all foreign forced laborers ("Fremdarbeiter"), prisoners of war and prisoners from concentration camps were employed on the OT-building-sites.

[15] The Subsidiary Camp Muehldorf of the Dachau Concentration Camp had five Under-Commands, among them, between August, 1944 and May, 1945 the Under-Command "Ampfing-Waldlager V and VI," whose prisoners built the underground aircraft factory under the management of the OT-Chief Supervision of Construction Muehldorf.

Fourteen days later another transport is put together. Mainly very emaciated prisoners. Cautiously I inquire. Apparently it will go to Muehldorf. For work. I report. The longing for my brother is stronger than my fear. We receive rations. Board a freight train. The trip lasts only a few hours. A small camp. Wooden huts. We are allocated among them. Already on the same evening I find my brother. I foresaw that we would find each other. The commando to which I am assigned is building an underground aircraft factory. The work is hard. The food bad. There are lice in the camp. Where there are lice there is typhoid fever. I become sick. For fourteen days I can't eat anything. In the meantime the infirmary was "cleared out" once. The sick were brought to Camp Kaufering near Landsberg. A death camp.[16]

On April 28, 1945 comes the order to evacuate the camp in Muehldorf. Freight cars stand ready for us on the track. I am very frail and must be led directly from the infirmary into the car. Five weeks of typhoid fever have weakened me greatly. Leaning on my brother, I reach the car. I feel rescued – secure. Several hours later the transport departs. The escort consists not only of SS-men but also of members of the Wehrmacht. That comforts us a little. We stop at every small station. Notice that we are riding westward. In Poing, not far from Munich, we stop for some time. On the next track is a train with anti-aircraft machine guns. Suddenly an alarm sounds. Our guards, who have surrounded the train, have disappeared. An American low-flying attack aims its shots at the two trains. In great haste we leave the cars and run into the fields. Can it be true? Is the war over? In any case we don't intend to return to the cars. Several fellow prisoners are killed in the air-raid. Now, at the last minute. Also a friend of ours. Engineer Najman, from Prague. He held out for five years. In vain.

Our freedom doesn't last long. Suddenly we are encircled. The guards shoot over our heads and drive us back into the cars. The transport goes on. It is April 30, 1945. We stop on an open stretch. In the distance we see a long, motorized column. Once more our guards have vanished. For the last time. We open the cars. The gate to freedom. Several hundred yards from us drives an American military column. We still can't grasp that we are liberated. I am too weak to leave the car.

Next to the train the Americans erect a temporary field hospital. Two first-aid men look after the sick. Lay them on cots. Wash them. Give them restoratives. Ambulances come. The most serious cases are to be brought to a hospital. We are human beings again. We can go to a hospital without being afraid. We are free.

---

[16] The Subsidiary Camp Kaufering consisted, since summer 1944, of altogether nine camps in different places in the vicinity of Landsberg, airfield Lechfeld, Kaufering. Two of these camps served officially as "Sick-Camps." The mortality in Kaufering was especially high.

Eli A. Bohnen

The Shoe on the other Foot
An US Military Rabbi remembers the Liberation of Dachau Concentration Camp

I remember writing my wife after the first day in Dachau. I remember telling her I now had enough material for nightmares for the rest of my life. I was not exaggerating.
The 3rd Infantry Division, together with my own, the 42nd Infantry, had taken Dachau. It is difficult to describe the emotions with which my assistant, Corporal Heimberg, and I approached the concentration camp in our jeep. The area had been sealed off as soon as the shooting was over, probably to avoid contamination and infection from any diseased inmates of the camp. A guard directed us to a harried Colonel who could give us a pass.
"State your purpose in wanting to enter the camp, Chaplain. This isn't exactly an exhibition, you know."
As I thought about it later, I was somewhat embarrassed by my answer. I blurted out the first words which came to mind, the words of Joseph in the Bible: "I seek my brothers." I hadn't meant to be melodramatic. But all that I had heard of Dachau made me lose myself in emotion.
Our first encounter with the camp almost made me wish the Colonel had not let us through. There, on a railroad siding, were the freight cars laden with their grisly cargo. What seemed to be thousands of bodies of Jews were heaped in grotesque disarray. Each of the bodies was clad in what was soon to become familiar to us as the standard uniform of the concentration camp, the thin-striped pyjama suit. Nearby lay a few bodies of SS guards who had been killed in the battle for the camp. In my mind's eye I can still see the figure of an emaciated prisoner urinating on the face of one of these guards as he lay still in death.
We had been with a fighting division. We had seen death at close range almost every day for months. But this was different. For some reason which I find difficult to convey, I did not think for the moment of the victims of this ceaseless massacre which had become a matter of routine for the Nazis. I thought of the executioners. I recall turning to my assistant and telling him that I felt like apologizing to our dog, who was with us, for the fact that we belonged to the human race. As we went further into the camp and beheld the skin-covered skeletons that were its prisoners, and saw the paraphernalia which made it an extermination center, I felt increasingly inferior to the dog; as a human being I was kin to those who were responsible for Dachau.

My faith in man was partially restored a few days later. I was conducting services for our troops in an open field, a few miles east of Dachau. As the services proceeded, I noticed three young civilians standing behind the last row of soldiers, apparently joining in the Hebrew portions of the service. Jewish civilians in Germany during the war were something of an anomaly, so it was natural for me to be curious about them.

I introduced myself and saw that they were in their late teens or early twenties. They told me that they had been prisoners in Dachau, and with the liberation of the camp had joined a group of prisoners who roamed through the countryside stealing food from the farms and clothing themselves in whatever they were able to find in the farmhouses. They met with no opposition. The terrified Germans did not dare oppose these former inmates of the camp about which there had been such terrible rumors.

About an hour before coming upon our services the boys had been raiding a nearby farm, together with their companions. This band of marauders, they told me, was made up of Poles, Russians, Hungarians, Czechs and themselves. As they searched for loot, one of the men cried out from the barn, bringing the whole gang to his side. In the dim light they saw a man dressed in the typical peasant garb of the district, cowering in obvious terror in one of the stalls.

"It's Mueller, it's Mueller," the men cried, as if with one voice. Immediately those closest to him began to pummel him and tear at his hair.

In Dachau, where cruelty was normal, Mueller had been one of the more sadistic of the SS guards. He had obviously been happy with the fate which had made him keeper of these doomed and helpless prisoners. While his cruelties were numerous there was one in particular for which he was notorious in the camp. He would seize a prisoner who had displeased him – it was not difficult to incur his displeasure – and would tie one end of a rope around the hapless prisoner and the other end to a huge anvil which stood out in the open. Taking a whip, he would order his victim to drag the anvil across the prison yard. Obviously, it was impossible for the starved and emaciated unfortunate to budge the anvil. The lash whistled through the air over and over again as screams resounded among the barracks. No one knew how many of Mueller's victims had died under his whip.

One did not need much imagination to visualize the scene as one of the boys described it, his vivid Yiddish somehow adding horror to an already horrible picture. His companions nodded their heads in agreement as he told me of the tortures Mueller had inflicted upon his miserable charges.

"When we saw Mueller there in that barn, all of us had the same thought: the shoe was now on the other foot. We were now the captors and Mueller was in our power."

I half expected to see a look of gloating satisfaction on the faces of the boys as they talked of their opportunity to repay the guard for what he had done. I was soon to learn why this look was not in evidence.

"It seemed we all had the identical idea," the boy continued. His Yiddish was interspersed with modern Germanisms, undoubtedly picked up from the camp guards. I remember thinking how strange it was that the hated guards had had this influence over the speech of these Jews. "We found a rope hanging from a peg in the barn and tied one end around Mueller's waist. There was nothing comparable with the anvil in the barn so we dragged Mueller outside. He was crazy with fear, begging for mercy, his lips flecked with foam."

The boy stopped for a moment and from the faraway look in his eyes I could see that he was visualizing the terrible scene he was describing. One of the other boys took up the story.

"The only thing we could find that was heavy enough was a boulder lying outside the barn. We managed to secure the free end of the rope to this huge rock and then each of us grabbed whatever we could find to serve as a club. There were ax-handles, lengths of chain and whatever else would serve the purpose."

"The three of us were the only Jews in the group and we were always together. Like the others we also took hold of something to use as a club. Like the others we relished the anticipation of doing to Mueller what he had done to so many of our friends."

This was said in a matter-of-fact tone and again I marvelled that there was no indication of satisfaction on the faces of the boys, nor of exultation in their voices as they spoke of their looking forward to repaying the Nazi in his own coin.

"Those nearest Mueller began to strike him as the others closed in on him," the boy continued. "We could see him straining at the rope while horrible screams came from his throat. The three of us, standing there waiting our turn to strike Mueller, suddenly looked at one another. Then, without a word, we threw down our clubs and ran. We continued running until we could no longer hear the cries of anguish of the tortured man. It was then that we came upon this service and heard the familiar Hebrew words which made us stop."

– from volume *Rabbis in uniform*, New York, 1962, pp. 82–86

David Max Eichhorn

Sabbath Service in Dachau Concentration Camp
Report on the First Week in May 1945 by an US Military Rabbi

The XV Corps took Nueremberg on April 20 and Munich, about 125 miles southeast, on April 30. Thus to our Corps went the honor of capturing the two main centers of Nazidom. En route from Nueremberg to Munich, in the town of Treuchtlingen, I was given a large Sefer Torah which had been hidden in the town-hall by a local official on the November night in 1938 when the Treuchtlingen synagogue was burned and all the Jews in Treuchtlingen were killed or driven off into the woods.

The concentration camp at Dachau, twelve miles northwest of Munich, was taken on April 29. I arrived there on the afternoon of April 30. The horrors of this camp have been described by so many in such detail that I shall not dwell at length upon this aspect except to record the following reactions of myself and others who were with me. We saw the 39 boxcars loaded with Jewish dead in the Dachau railway yard, 39 carloads of little, shriveled mummies that had literally been starved to death; we saw the gas chambers and the crematoria, still filled with charred bones and ashes. And we cried not merely tears of sorrow. We cried tears of hate. Combat hardened soldiers, Gentile and Jew, black and white, cried tears of hate. Then we stood aside and watched while the inmates of the camp hunted down their former guards, many of whom were trying to hide out in various places in the camp. We stood aside and watched while these guards were beaten to death, beaten so badly that their bodies were ripped open and the innards protruded. We watched with less feeling than if a dog were being beaten. In truth, it might be said that we were completely without feeling. Deep anger and hate had temporarily numbed our emotions. These evil people, it seemed to us, were being treated exactly as they deserved to be treated. To such depths does human nature sink in the presence of human depravity.

Soon after arriving in Dachau, I met Meyer Levin, the novelist and newspaper correspondent. The next morning, he and I went to Allach, a subsidiary camp of Dachau, about five miles away. The camp Allach was divided into separate sections of Gentiles and Jews, about 3300 Jews and 6000 Gentiles. The comparative conditions in the Jewish and Gentile sections may be understood through one simple statistic: The first day I was there, 40 Jews and 5 Gentiles died. In other words, the death ratio was about 15 Jews to one Gentile. Causes of death were listed as malnutrition and general debility.

Both at Allach and Dachau, death was commonplace. Naked bodies lying outside of barracks waiting to be carted away were a familiar sight. And the bodies did not smell. There was no meat left on them to rot, just skin and bones. While I was sitting on the corner of a bed in the Allach "lazarett" talking to a Professor Schwartz, who had for six years been the only unconverted Jewish professor at the University of Warsaw, the man on whose bed I was sitting died. A doctor came along, saw that the man was dead, covered his head with a sheet and Professor Schwartz and I continued our conversation as calmly as before. Just like that. I did not even get up from the bed. "Poor fellow," said Professor Schwartz. "At any rate, his worries are ended." It was a fitting eulogy.

I presented the Torah from Treuchtlingen to the Jews of Allach. I shall never forget the presentation ceremony and the service which accompanied it. There were quite a number of rabbis and cantors in Allach, including a Czecho-Slovakian rabbi, Dr. Klein, who spoke about a dozen languages. During the service, Dr. Klein thanked me eloquently for the Torah in English, German and Hungarian. Another dramatic moment was the chanting of the "El Male Rachamim" by a cantor from Warsaw with a very beautiful voice. After the service, literally hundreds of people crowded around me, kissing my hand and begging for an "autogram." It was a very embarrassing experience. I felt that it was I who should be humbling myself before them and honoring them for that which they had suffered and surmounted. I kept reminding myself that it was not I to whom they were paying homage but to the wonderful American Army which had delivered them from certain death and from physical and mental torture worse than death. To die from a bullet is so easy and so quick, many said. But to die slowly, in mind and in body, from torture, humiliation and hunger is much worse.

The Administration of the Allach camp was in the hands of a non-Jewish American officer, Lieutenant Schreiber, and a small group of American Soldiers who moved heaven and earth in a mighty effort to get food and medicine quickly to the starving and the sick. They were aided greatly by a fine group of inmates who were organized within the camp into a well disciplined and smoothly functioning committee. Lieutenant Schreiber, in his early twenties, a toughened combat soldier, reacted to the situation with the mind of a brilliant executive and the heart of a saint. The tragedy of these unfortunates became his personal tragedy. To work with such a person was an exalting experience, even in the midst of misery and death.

A few paragraphs back, I wrote of deep anger and of hate. In harboring such thoughts, one must be sure that he is directing his thoughts toward those who are really guilty and not toward those whom he presumes to be guilty. Every time I hear some thoughtless person say that the only good German is a dead German, I think of the hundreds of Germans and Austrians I met *inside* the concentration camps, priests and ministers, lawyers and doctors, Socialists and pacifists, workers and farmers, living skeletons with eyes that burned with an imperishable prophetic fire and a boundless love for their fellowmen. I think of many Germans whom I knew who had saved Jewish lifes at the risk of their own. I think especially of SS Mann Gerhardt Schmidt. Schmidt looked like the kind of man the Nazis bragged about, the perfect typical Aryan, tall, blond and handsome. He was a pilot in the Luftwaffe. He was shot down and wounded and then forced into the SS. He was a patriotic German who loved his country but who hated Hitler and the Nazis and everything for which they stood with a hatred that was deep and true. In the spring of 1944, he was sent to the Jewish section of Allach as "block fuehrer," section leader. He protected his Jewish flock in every way within his power. Every evening he listened in secret to the broadcasts of the BBC and kept the hopes of the Allach Jews buoyed up by informing them of the progress of the Allied advance. When he learned that certain Jews were destined for extermination, he hid them until the danger had passed. When a Jewish inmate would contact typhus, which was a one-way ticket to the gas chamber, he would smuggle the sick person out of the camp in one of the camp's straw-wagons, take him to his home in Dachau where the patient would be nursed back to health by Schmidt's wife and then be smuggled back into the camp. Three days before the American liberators arrived, he hid two machine guns and bandoliers of ammunition in his straw-wagon, brought them into the camp and buried them in the Jewish section. He informed his Jewish brethren (and, God bless him, I write that word deliberately) that he would fight with them to the death against the other SS if they attempted to massacre the Jews before they retreated. Fortunately, the other SS left so fast that there was no attempt at massacre.

SS Mann Schmidt did not run away. He took off his uniform, put on civilian clothes and went home. Three days later, he decided to return to the Jews of the Allach camp. He and his wife walked up to the gate where they were stopped by an American guard and questioned. When Schmidt readily admitted that he had been a German soldier, he was quite naturally taken into custody and destined for a quick trip to a POW compound. His wife came into the camp office and pleaded with Lieutenant Schreiber to release her husband. Some of the Jewish leaders were summoned and they attested to the truth of the facts I have just written down. They said further that the Jews of Allach would be grateful and happy for the privilege of taking their German comrade into "protective custody" so that he could go on working with them as before. Lieutenant Schreiber secured permission from Corps HQ to have Schmidt retained as a worker in the camp. He was released by the military and placed in the care of the Jewish committee. I accompanied Herr and Frau Schmidt from the office to the Jewish compound. It was the home-coming of a hero. The Jews crowded around their beloved "fuehrer," hugging him, kissing his face, his hands, his feet. The big man broke down and cried. So did his wife. So did I. When I left Allach, Mr. and Mrs. Schmidt were living in the headquarters of the Jewish committee and Herr

Schmidt was a key-figure in the manifold relief activities that were being conducted there. A few weeks later I learned that one night the Schmidts had quietly left the camp for an unannounced and unknown destination. It seems that they had heard that some of the bad Germans in the nearby community of Dachau had vowed to kill the "traitors" at the first opportunity. There were and there still are many bad Germans as well as many good ones. The same may be said of every other group of people on the face of the earth.

After two days at Allach, I returned to Dachau on May 3. I was placed on temporary duty there as a member of the camp staff and remained for four days. I roomed in an Army hospital that had been set up just aside the "lager" gates; but practically all my time was spent inside the camp compound. Because of the prevalence of typhus, I received an injection of antityphus serum. Every time I had to go out of the camp, which was about three or four times a day, I was dosed with anti-louse powder. By nightfall I was so full of powder that the inside of my clothes and my body were lily-white. And I certainly needed the stuff. Whether it was the son of the Gerer Rebbe or the melamed from Palestine or the merchant from Prague or the plain ordinary Jew from Lodz, all the inmates were emaciated, filthy and liceridden. Only the Jewish doctors were clean. In some semi-miraculous way, the physicians had maintained the standards of cleanliness demanded by their profession. Another exception to this condition of disease and dirt was the barracks of Hungarian, Greek and Italian Jewish girls, 160 of them, who had been brought to Dachau just a week before. Some of them had been workers in factories and farms, some had been used in German military brothels. They had been treated with so little consideration by the Germans that most of them had lost the female's normal sense of modesty. When, from time to time, my duties brought me into their barracks, they continued to dress or undress in my presence as if they thought I were not there. I used a room in this barracks as a sort of headquarters, not because of the situation just described but because it was the only semi-cheerful spot in all of Dachau. The girls had not been in Dachau long enough to be afflicted with typhus or with lice and, occasionally, some of them smiled. Unfortunately, when these girls were given thorough medical examination in the ensuing weeks, it was discovered that many of them, who looked healthy outwardly, were afflicted with tuberculosis.

I did what I could, in the short time at my disposal, to bring what comfort and cheer was possible to the approximately 2600 Jewish men and 225 Jewish women wo remained among the 34,000 inmates of Dachau. I visited every barrack in which there were Jews, talked to the bed-ridden, miserable unfortunates and tried to raise their spirits. I also tried to act as a liaison between the Jews, the camp's International Prisoners' Committee and the American military authorities. At both Allach and Dachau, I supervised the gathering of a list of the names and addresses of all the Jews in the camps. The overwhelming majority of the Jews at both places were Hungarian and Polish. I met only one German Jew and a few French and Belgians.

I had a very unpleasant experience soon after being assigned to the Dachau staff. The inmates, after liberation, left the camp, invaded the town of Dachau, took whatever food they could find from the greatly frightened Germans of the town and proceeded to eat and eat and eat. Their emaciated bodies could not stand the strain. A number of them literally gorged themselves to death. The American medical authorities decided that, for the protection of the inmates, they must be forcibly detained within the compound in order to get the proper medical attention and to be fed the proper kinds and amounts of food. The effect of this on the inmates is not difficult to imagine. Many of them were not in a proper state of mind to understand the necessity for this action and they thought that their liberators had suddenly become persecutors. Since it was impossible to change many of the disagreeable features of confinement at a rate fast enough to satisfy the inmates, considerable discontent generated rapidly in the compound.

The doctors ordered me to see to it that no inmates got out of the sections in which most of the Jews were quartered. Armed guards were placed around the fences to make sure that this order was obeyed. Some of the inmates were still bringing food they had "liberated" in Dachau back to the compound by means of bicycle, wheelbarrow, donkey cart or any other type of vehicle they could commandeer. Finding the gates locked, they would scurry up to the fence, throw the food parcels over the fence to those on the other side and then quickly scurry away. I was told by the medics that this would have to be stopped. I instructed the guards to frighten away the food-bearers by shooting over their heads. This worked quite well for a while, but, when the food-bearers discovered that the soldiers were not aiming directly at them, they continued their well-meant but harmful tactic. Reluctantly I was compelled to tell the guards that they would have to actually hit one of the offenders in a non-fatal spot on his anatomy in order to protect the health of those in the compound. This was done. The next fellow who tried to throw food over the fence got a well-aimed bullet through his leg, was taken off to the hospital and eventually recovered from the wound. This drastic measure halted all further efforts to get any more food over the fence.

(I had another unpleasant experience of a somewhat similar nature little more than a month later at the concentration camp at Ebensee, Austria. The JDC bought 12 tons of food in Switzerland which was delivered to XV Corps HQ in Salzburg by the International Red Cross. Here it was loaded on Army trucks for delivery under my supervision to the camp at Ebensee. The shipment consisted of such items as raw beef, flour, cocoa, and other normally unedible items. When the camp inmates saw the trucks come through the gate of the camp, their hunger was so intense that they made a mad dash for the food shipment. I was on the lead-truck of the twelve-truck convoy sitting beside the driver. On every other truck was a driver and a guard. Feeling sure that the approaching mob would trample us to death in its determined rush for the food, I ordered the drivers and guards to get off the trucks and to stand in line with fixed bayonets, with the hope that this would put a stop to the frenzied dash of those coming in our direction. Fortunately for all concerned, this did the trick. The mob came within perhaps seventy-five or a hundred yards of us, stopped uncertainly and then slowly retreated. We were able to deliver the supplies to the Ebensee kitchen without further interruption ... About seven or eight years later, I was visited at my office at the national Jewish Welfare Board in New York by a fine-looking young American soldier. "Remember me?" asked he. "No," I replied. "You should remember me," said he, "I tried to kill you once." "That is something I ought to remember," said I, "but I don't." He laughed. "Of course, you don't" said he. "I was one of that mob of hunger-crazed people who tried to run you down at Ebensee." His eyes lit up. "And while those trucks were being unloaded," said he, "I stole a hunk of that raw meat and carried it off to my room and ate it up all by myself. Best tasting meat I ever ate in my life.")

On Friday afternoon, May 4, I held a service in the women's barracks. It was, of course, a very touching experience, as were all such services which I was to hold during the months to come in many DP camps in Germany and Austria. At the end of the service, a lieutenant colonel who had been standing at the rear of the room approached me with tears streaming from his eyes. He introduced himself. "My name is George Stevens. I am in charge of the Signal Corps unit which is taking the official Army pictures of Dachau. When will you hold another such service? I want to get a film of it for the historical record." I told him that a camp-wide Sabbath service was planned for the next morning, Saturday morning, and that he certainly could make a film of it if he wished.

The service was to be held at 10 a.m. in the main square of the Dachau compound. The International Committee had promised to have the platform in the square decorated with the flag of every nation represented in the camp (I think there were twenty-eight in all) and, in addition, every nationality would send a delegation to the service as an indication of its brotherly sympathy for the Jewish people. I arrived at the square at 9 a.m. to make sure that everything was in readiness for the service. To my amazement, no preparation of any kind had been made. I sent for Charles Baum, a young Belgian, the Jewish representative on the International Committee, and asked for an explanation. Greatly embarrassed, Mr. Baum informed me that the service would not be held in the main square. The Polish non-Jewish inmates had threatened that, if a Jewish service were held in the square, they would break it up by force. (This was only one of a number of ways in which the Poles of Dachau showed hostility for their fellow Jewish sufferers. I was informed that, when the Polish Red Cross distributed food packages to the Poles in Dachau, the packages were given out on the basis of one to every Polish Christian and one to every two Polish Jews.) Rather than cause a disturbance, the Jews had decided to cancel the service in the square and to hold the service, instead, in the camp laundry, which was only big enough to accommodate about 80 people and could, therefore, hold only a very small percentage of the Jews who would want to be present. While I was not pleased with the decision, I raised no strong objection as I felt that the Jewish inmates were more knowledgeable in this particular situation than was I and should be allowed to do what they considered proper. So I set up an altar in the laundry and prepared for the limited service.

While the service was in progress, in a jam-packed room with hundreds of others outside crowded around the open doors and windows, Colonel Stevens came in, elbowed his way to my side and demanded to know why the service was not being held in the square. His cameras and crews were ready for action and he wanted the event to go on as scheduled. I stopped the "davaning" long enough to tell him that I would explain, after the service, what had happened. He waited outside until the end of the service to hear the explanation. After hearing the "inside story," he exploded in anger. "I did not give up a good job in the movie business in Hollywood," he bellowed, "to risk my life in combat for months and months in order to free the world from the threat of Fascism and then stand idly by while the very victims of Fascism seek to perpetuate its evils. I am going to do something about this." And do something about it he did. He took me to the Camp Commandant, a fine gentleman of Irish extraction who had formerly been Police Commissioner of Boston and, with loudness of voice and much banging of the table, George Stevens repeated his anti-Fascistic sentiments. The Commandant readily agreed with Colonel Stevens. It was decided that the service would be held next morning, Sunday, May 6, at 10 a.m. under the protection of an American military "guard of honor." As an added "movie" touch, Colonel Stevens requested that I teach some of the girls in the women's barracks to sing "God Bless America" at the service. I did as he asked. That Saturday night I spent about two hours teaching a choir of fifteen Hungarian Jewish girls to sing the Irving Berlin composition; and they learned to sing it quite well, even though they knew not one word of English.

And so, thanks to the decent instincts of an American movie director, the camp-wide service was held in the main square. It was attended by every Jewish male and female whose health permitted. As promised, every nationality was represented by flag and by delegation. There were an estimated two thousand Jews and non-Jews at the service. And ringing the outer rim of the service with faces turned away from the platform and with loaded rifles and fixed bayonets was the American military "guard of honor." They were prepared to deal with a situation which did not develop. No untoward incident of any kind marred the service. (Meyer Levin, who was present at the service, described it in an article in the American press. It is quite likely that the incident with which Irwin Shaw concluded his novel, "The Young Lions," is based on Levin's account of the Dachau happening.)

The program of the day was as follows: The opening remarks were made by Mr. Kuci, formerly Albanian Minister of Propaganda, chairman of the

inmates' International Committee, who said that all the inmates of Dachau were very much aware of the exceptional intensity of Jewish suffering there and elsewhere under the Nazi yoke and that all freemen rejoiced that the Jews of Dachau were, at long last, able to resume their religious life without hindrance. Then the Ark was opened and I recited Shehecheyanu and benshed Gomel and went through a brief Torah service. After being formally introduced by Mr. Charles Baum, I gave a short talk. When I' finished, one of the loveliest of the Dachau girls presented me with a bouquet of flowers on behalf of Dachau Jewry. Then a Palestinian "Chalutsa" came up to the platform bearing a Zionist flag and made an impromptu speech in beautiful Sephardic Hebrew to me and the assembly. Little American and Zionist flags made by the girls from their precious store of remnant materials were presented to me as priceless "souvenirs" of this never-to-be-forgotten occasion. My talk, given in English, was then translated into German by one of the inmates. He must have made what I said sound good because the crowds response was very generous. Then my girls' choir sang "God Bless America" sweetly and enthusiastically. Then Mr. Baum spoke in French and German, thanking all the non-Jewish delegations for coming to the service and also expressing the hopes and aspirations of the Jews of Dachau. The latter part of his speech was so moving that it gave everyone a chance to have a good cry. The assembly joined in the singing of "Ha-tikva," after which I ended the program with a benediction. The entire service, about forty-five minutes in length, was filmed with sound by Colonel Stevens and his crew. While the service was in progress, a wagon-load of naked dead came past the assembly on the way to the crematorium. Colonel Stevens ordered the cameras turned on the wagon and a filmed record made of this weird though temporary addition to the audience. (Several years later I was invited to the Army Pictorial Center at Astoria, L.I., to witness a showing of the film of the Dachau service. The "staged" singing of "God Bless America" was retained in the film. The dead-wagon scene was eliminated. "We had to take it out," the movie people explained to me. "It seemed to improbable that a viewing audience would suspect that the scene had been 'staged'.")
For an hour after the service, I was mobbed, kissed, photographed and signed so many "autographs" that I vowed then and there to give up completely and absolutely whatever chance I had of becoming a movie star. It was a tiring and, as mentioned before, highly embarrassing experience.
The next morning I attended two Polish Catholic masses also held in the main square at Dachau as memorial services for the Polish dead of Dachau. I did so for two reasons: to express my gratitude by this act to the small number of Christian Poles who had attended the Jewish service and to show their less brotherly brethren that we have greater respect for their religion than they have for ours.
On Monday afternoon, May 7, I returned to HQ XV Corps, which, in my absence, had moved with the battle-line about seventy-five miles eastward

from Munich, Germany, to Salzburg, Austria. Here, on May 8, the war in Europe officially ended; but die-hard Nazi units of the German forces did not cease fighting with our units until May 11. On that date, XV Corps was placed in charge of the Austrian Occupation Zone, a mission which it fulfilled until September 1. During this period, I travelled constantly between Innsbruck on the west and Linz on the east, holding services for our widely scattered troops and trying to be of some help to the DPs in the many camps throughout Austria.

The text of the speech which I delivered at Dachau on May 6, 1945 follows:
My Jewish brethren of Dachau,
In the portion which we read yesterday in our holy Torah, we found these words: "Ukrawsem d'ror baw-awretz l'chawl yoshvehaw; yovel hee ti'ye lawchem; v'shavtem ish el achuzawso v'ish el mishpachto tawshuvu" which mean "Proclaim freedom throughout the world to all the inhabitants thereof; a day of celebration shall this be for you, a day when every man shall return to his family and to his rightful place in society."
In the United States of America, in the city of Philadelphia, upon the exact spot where 169 years ago a group of brave Americans met and decided to fight for American independence, there stands a marker upon which is written these very same words: "Proclaim freedom throughout the world to all the inhabitants thereof." From the beginning of their existence as a liberty-loving and independent people, the citizens of America understood that not until all the peoples of the world were free the hearts of all men and all nations would there be lasting peace and happiness for themselves. Thus it has been that, throughout our entire history, whenever and wherever dictators have endeavored to destroy democracy and justice and truth, Americans have not rested content until these despots have been overthrown.
Today I come to you in a dual capacity – as a soldier in the American Army and as a representative of the Jewish community of America. As an American soldier, I say to you that we are proud, very proud, to be here, to know that we have had a share in the destruction of the most cruel tyranny of all time. As an American soldier, I say to you that we are proud, very proud, to be with you as comrades-in-arms, to greet you and salute you as the bravest of the brave. We know your tragedy. We know your sorrows. We know that upon you was centered the venomous hatred of power-crazed madmen, that your annihilation was decreed and planned systematically and ruthlessly. We know, too, that you refused to be destroyed, that you fought back with every weapon at your command, that you fought with your bodies, your minds and your spirit. Your faith and our faith in God and in humanity have been sustained. Our enemies lie prostrate before us. The way of life which together we have defended still lives and it will live so that all men everywhere may have freedom and happiness and peace.
I speak to you also as a Jew, as a rabbi in Israel, as a teacher of that religious

philosophy which is dearer to all of us than life itself. What message of comfort and strength can I bring to you from your fellow-Jews? What can I say that will compare in depth or in intensity to that which you have suffered and overcome? Full well do I know and humbly do I confess the emptiness of mere words in this hour of mingled sadness and joy. Words will not bring the dead back to life nor right the wrongs of the past ten years. This is no time for words, you will say, and rightfully so. This is a time for deeds, deeds of justice, deeds of love ... Justice will be done. We have seen with our own eyes and we have heard with our own ears and we shall not forget. As long as there are Jews in the world, "Dachau" will be term of horror and shame. Those who labored here for their evil master must be hunted down and destroyed as systematically and as ruthlessly as they sought your destruction ... And there will be deeds of love. It is the recognized duty of all truly religious people to bestir themselves immediately to assist you to regain health, comfort and some measure of happiness as speedily as is humanly possible. This must be done. This can be done. This will be done. You are not and you will not be forgotten men, my brothers. In every country where the lamps of religion and decency and kindness still burn, Jews and non-Jews alike will expend as much time and energy and money as is needful to make good the pledge which is written in our holy Torah and inscribed on that marker in Philadelphia, the city of Brotherly Love.

We know that abstractions embodied in proclamations and celebrations must be followed by more concrete, more helpful fulfillments. We do not intend to brush aside the second part of the Divine promise: "V'shavtem ish el achuzawso v'ish el mishpachto tawshuvu." Every man who has been oppressed must and will be restored to his family and to his rightful place in society. This is a promise and a pledge which I bring to you from your American comrades-in-arms and your Jewish brethren across the seas.

"You shall go out with joy, and be led forth in peace;
The mountains and the hills shall break forth before you into singing;
And all the trees of the field shall clap their hands.
Instead of the thorn shall come up the cypress,
And instead of brambles myrtles shall spring forth;
And God's name will be glorified;
This will be remembered forever,
This will never be forgotten."

Amen.

Hermann Langbein

Work in the Concentration Camp System

From the beginning, one of the principles in the National Socialist concentration camps was that every prisoner had to work. For this purpose, all the prisoners were grouped in labour units supervised by one prisoner as a "Capo", or foreman (in the case of larger units, there were several Capos or foremen who were under the control of one Capo). The "leader of the unit" was a member of the SS who supervised the work and whose commands the Capo had to carry out. How he did this was up to him; if he beat those under him, this was viewed favourably as a rule. If one died as a result of the beating, the Capo had only to make sure that the death was properly reported, since the roll-call had to be right. The Capo was not asked why the prisoner had died.

The work unit to which he was allocated was decisive for the chances any prisoner had of survival – whether he had to do heavy physical work in the open, exposed to all weathers, or whether he was able to work indoors; whether the work made it possible to acquire something to eat, for instance in agricultural work, in an abattoir or in the kitchen, or whether he was working in a quarry or a gravel pit, where there was no possibility of organizing anything edible. Also decisive was whether corporal punishment was practised. In the case of work in the open for which no qualifications were needed, where each man was under constant surveillance, corporal punishment was supposed to increase the speed of work, the SS made sure of that. If a man was employed as a skilled tradesman at a machine, then corporal punishment was not considered a suitable method for improving the speed of work.

When the men were admitted into the concentration camp, the occupation of the prisoner was entered into his record card. As a general rule, a trade was useful, as metal workers, bricklayers, carpenters and the like were constantly requisitioned by the leaders of the units. A lawyer, or anyone who had some other intellectual profession, on the other hand, was not in demand. In addition, the SS preferred intellectuals as the objects of their cruelties. Even wearing glasses could suffice for the wearer to be maltreated by the SS. Those who had any experience when taken into a camp, such as those who were moved from one concentration camp to another, stated their occupation as one that could be expected to have better chances of being allocated to a particular work unit. Anyone who had good connections to fellow prisoners in the labour system (that is, to the office which assembled the work units) could try to have his occupation changed on his record card. Of course, there was a big risk involved in this, and not only because such a deception could be discovered, since, if it transpired in the work place that the person in question did not have the professional qualifications claimed and the others and the Capo did not cover him until he had learned his way, he had to reckon with the worst.

Some few had the opportunity of getting themselves a better unit in this way; another way was to bribe a Capo, and this became more and more possible after the end of October 1942, when Himmler permitted "Aryan" prisoners (except Russians) to receive parcels – this was the result of the changing situation in the War and the necessity this brought about of making more camp labour available for the armaments industry. But the fact remained that there was always only a small number of "good" units and that the vast majority was allocated to units in which heavy physical work and corporal punishment prevailed and where there was hardly any opportunity of organizing anything to eat.

Thus the prisoners were forced into a struggle for survival. Anyone who had enough energy tried to get a place in a good unit; and anyone who was allocated to one, tried to smuggle a friend, a like-minded person or a compatriot into this unit. Only too often this was possible only by barring the way to others, to people one did not know. The camp command deliberately exacerbated this battle; it did everything to make any agreements among the prisoners impossible and it established a hierarchy for this purpose. At the top of this there were always Germans, and they could usually expect to get a good position when the percentage of Germans in the camps was small. In many camps, it fell to below 10% in the last few years, in Auschwitz it even fell below 2%. The Jews were always on the lowest rung of this hierarchy. They were to be allocated to the heaviest work, indeed it was often forbidden as a matter of principle to assign someone who was forced to wear the Star of David on his zebra-striped uniform to a good unit. That this principle was not always adhered to everywhere can be attributed to the fact that there were Jews whose skills were essential for an armaments factory (and to the fact that it was observed as long as they were still capable of working in a way that made their qualifications usable). Finally, there were exclusively Jews in some of the subsidiary camps, so that in the last phase, there were even Jewish Capos and Camp Elders.

This situation forces all those in the concentration camp who still had the strength to contemplate resistance to try to reduce the conflicts among the various categories of prisoners and nationalities if at all possible. This was no simple task, but one that those who were seeking ways of improving the conditions of life in the camp and who felt obliged to do it could not shirk. If this was to be achieved, efforts had to be made to gain influence over the centres of so-called prisoner's self-administration.

The expression "prisoners' self-administration" which has become usual in the specialist literature is not correct. All the prisoners who held a position always had to obey the orders of the SS. If they were slow about this, then they lost their position. It was only within the framework of these orders and directives that they had any chances. These increased as the camps became larger and thus more difficult to keep under surveillance.

In every camp, those prisoners who were involved in the deployment of labour were in key positions. For it was here that the assignment to particular units took place. As a rule, the SS used German prisoners here; not only because of the language, but also because – in accordance with the "racial" thinking of the National Socialists – even as prisoners, they counted more than foreigners, to say nothing of those who, for "racial' reasons, were not merely regarded as inferior but as having no right to life. In every camp, it was crucial to the general atmosphere whether the key prisoners in the labour deployment section were responsible people or had been corrupted by the camp command. It is true that they were all equally subject to the commands of the SS. But they probably all took advantage of the fact that the camp commands placed great importance on lists, card indexes, statistics and other bureaucratic methods. They extended this red-tape as much as they were able, made it as obscure as possible and thus themselves all but indispensable. Naturally, the SS could remove some people from the labour deployment section if they fell from favour; but to change all those working there at once would ultimately have been completely impossible for the SS; left to its own devices the SS would rapidly have lost track of things entirely.

Another important key-function was that occupied in every camp by the unit deployed in the prisoners' hospital (also called prisoners' sick-bay in some camps). This unit was in great demand, as it had many advantages. Those who were assigned to the staff of the prisoners' hospital generally did not have to appear at roll-call. They got more to eat (among other things because notification of deaths were often made with delays, so that the rations for the dead continued to be delivered to the hospital for a short time). And not the least aspect was the fact that they had an activity that appealed to their feeling of responsibility. The better they did the job, the better it was for the sick. The difference between the feeling that one's work was assisting one's enemy on the one hand, and being free from such pressure in one's work on the other, can hardly be overestimated.

For a long time, the SS would not allow a prisoner who was a doctor to work in the hospital. Later, when doctors were able to be on the staff, the position of Camp Elder of the Hospital (in some camps he was called the Capo of the prisoners' sick-bay) was occupied by prisoners who were not doctors; here the hatred of intellectuals may have played a role as well. Only Auschwitz was an exception in this regard, where two doctors occupied this position in succession from August 1943 onwards – they were both Polish.

While one might be able to help in the labour deployment section by assigning someone to a better unit (this, however, only ever succeeded in a few cases), in the hospital it was possible to help – within the narrow framework decreed by the SS – not only by providing better treatment, but also because once a prisoner had been admitted to hospital, it was easier to organize a change in the unit to which he was attached. When he was released from hospital, it was easier to arrange for him not to be assigned to his old unit without the leader's noticing it.

In the first phase of National Socialist rule, only Germans were interned in the concentration camps. The camps were also smaller and thus easier to patrol. At this time, work often had a different function. There were no other opportunities for work apart from the activities carried out for the maintenance of the camp and in the workshops (where moonlighting for members of the SS was engaged in at all times; this provided opportunities for corrupting the SS). But the principle that every prisoner had to work needed to be adhered to, and so totally pointless work was often ordered. Prisoners had to pile up stones very exactly, to build a wall. Then they had to carry the stones to another place and erect the wall again there. All this had to be done at the double. In fact, prisoners at that time were often commanded to run at all times. It is obvious that such a clearly senseless activity was an additional burden in combination with the exhaustion caused by the haste. This was precisely the reason for commands of this nature.

When foreigners were admitted to the camps in growing numbers, the situation changed. The camp command deliberately built up the prisoners' hierarchy described above. The first foreigners to arrive in the concentration camps were numerous Austrians on 2 April 1938. But since they were considered Germans according to National Socialist doctrine, it was the transports of Czechs brought to the camps in relatively large numbers even before the war who were the first to provide the camp command the opportunity of starting to play one group of prisoners off against another, that is, to give the Czechs worse jobs than the Germans. This was a system in which they soon gained a wealth of experience and virtuosity.

After the armies of the National Socialist German Reich had subjugated one country after another, the stream of foreigners began, which made the concentration camps become what they are generally known and described as. The different nationalities were played off against each other, the Slavs being treated worst, and among these, the Russians worse again than the others. The Czechs stood a little higher in the hierarchy, mainly because many of them understood German, and a knowledge of the language was important for allocation to a better unit. The conflicts between the groups of prisoners were "maintained and stirred up as assiduously as possible", writes Rudolf Hoess, the commandant of Auschwitz. "Divide and rule" was the way to run a concentration camp.

The latest group to be admitted to the camp was always given the hardest work. It was on them that the camp command concentrated its harassment and cruelties. After Hitler had attacked the Soviet Union as well, a campaign began which the National Socialists called by the code word "final solution of the Jewish question". This was the organized mass killing of Jews in extermination camps. Soon gypsies,[1] too had to share the same fate. In the extermination camps at Treblinka, Sobibor, Belzec and Kulmhof there were only a few hundred who were not herded straight into the gas chambers. Their fate was one that begs comparison – they were forced to serve the machinery of murder, to cut the hair off the corpses, to break out the gold teeth and burn the dead. In Auschwitz, prisoners grouped into a special unit immediately next to the crematoria with their built-in gas chambers and completely isolated from all the others, were forced to do the same work. Periodically, they themselves were killed too and replaced by a fresh intake from a newly arrived transport of Jews. As they were bearers of secrets, they were not to remain alive.

It has not yet been sufficiently acknowledged – indeed, it is not widely known – that the prisoners who, in the two extermination camps at Treblinka and Sobibor, had to exist in conditions that were beyond the imagination of even other concentration camp prisoners, found the strength to organize uprisings and carry them out successfully. This occurred in August (Treblinka) and October (Sobibor) of 1943, when the Russian front was still a long way off. The prisoners forced to work in one of the four Auschwitz crematoria also staged an uprising on 7 October, 1944. It was not successful, but the prisoners were able to blow up one crematorium and thus reduce the capacity of the murder machine.

When the "final solution" began, the German armies had already suffered tangible set-backs. The hopes for further rapidly-won victories and a speedy final victory were thus buried. More soldiers, more weapons were needed and so also more workers in the armaments industry. For this reason, the SS decided not to send all the Jews deported to the extermination camps from the regions that lay under Hitler's power straight to their deaths in the gas chambers. Those who appeared to be capable of working were taken as prisoners into the concentration camps in order to serve as slaves in armaments. The concentration camp at Auschwitz, which had hitherto differed from the other camps only in that mainly Poles were interned there, was designated as the centre of this campaign – selection of those fit for work and extermination of the rest.

This meant that Auschwitz became the largest place of extermination as well as the largest concentration camp. Since the number of Jewish prisoners taken into the camp was constantly increasing despite the particularly high death rate, Himmler decided that all Jewish prisoners were to be assembled in this, the camp with the worst living conditions. Indeed it was for this reason that they were to be brought there. In the autumn of 1942 all Jews with

---

[1] In these pages 'gypsy' is a translation of the German *Zigeuner* and has to stand for Sinti, Roma and other groups of travellers who were jointly so designated by the National Socialists and persecuted on racial grounds (trans. note).

very few exceptions who were in other camps were moved to Auschwitz. As early as 1941, the IG-Farben works began constructing a large chemical factory not far from this camp in order to exploit the labour of the prisoners. The Buna works in Monowitz erected an subsidiary camp immediately adjacent to the factory so that the exploitation of the prisoners' labour would not be diminished by the long march from Auschwitz, and so that diseases prevalent in the camp at that time would not be spread into the factory.

This example was later followed by others, not only in Auschwitz but in all the concentration camps. Around each one grew an ever increasing circle of subsidiary camps, the majority for armaments factories. The principal focus was on factories working on V-weapons (the new "long-range weapons", with which the National Socialists hoped until the last gasp to win the turning point in the War) and for the aviation industry. Secrecy was the supreme commandment here, and this could best be guaranteed not by having "foreign workers" and prisoners of war forced to work there, but totally isolated concentration camp prisoners. German workers had already been hard to come by for a long time. Those who were still available were obliged to work as tradesmen and foremen so that the foreigners – and this is what the concentration camps contained more and more – could be forced to devote their entire labour to the cause.

When the factories in Peenemünde, in which the production of V-weapons was concentrated, had been successfully bombed in August 1943, their production was moved to other factories, supposedly protected from further Allied air attack in mountain-tunnels. Other important armaments factories were also moved into similar subterranean production sites.

Prisoners were forced to dig these tunnels, to fit them out and to work underground there. The most notorious camp of this type was Dora, constructed as a subsidiary camp of the Buchenwald concentration camp immediately after the destruction of the facilities in Peenemünde; this soon attained such proportions that it became an autonomous concentration camp. In the first phase, the prisoners deployed there were not permitted to leave the tunnels after they had finished work.

While the prisoners at work had had to endure harassment, cruelties and corporal punishment in the previous phases, these methods were reduced to a certain extent, but not abolished entirely. The place of pointless cruelty – or all too often in addition to it – was taken more and more by urging to greater production: the use of prisoners "must be exhaustive in the true sense of the word, in order to achieve maximum production", was the wording of an order issued to all concentration camp commanders on 30 April 1942.

In these factories, a system of rewards, in addition to the terror, was to ensure successful work. The SS were forced to acknowledge the experience of old that slave labour is unproductive. On 15 May 1943 therefore, a further order from the centre decreed that the prisoners were to be given bonus certificates if they worked to the satisfaction of their superiors. The fact that these measures were put into effect in such a way as could hardly be expected to achieve the purpose intended, was part of the system that had developed in the camp commands. Very often, the SS-men in charge of the units responsible for the distribution of the bonus certificates did not give them to those who had done the best work; instead they gave them to prisoners who had "organized" something for them, that is, acquired something illegally. And, as a general rule, there was hardly anything that could be got in the camp for the bonus certificates that was of real use – only such food items as were no longer useful to the SS and apart from that, toothpaste, and such things as toilet paper.

There was another circular to all camp commandants that had been sent out earlier, on 5 December 1941, and this had much more positive consequences in reality – for the "Great Buildings of the Führer" – which were to be erected after the final victory, bricklayers and stone masons would be required in far larger numbers than were currently available. Schools for bricklaying were therefore to be set up in all camps. Selected prisoners were to be motivated to join these schools "by additional food and clothing, if necessary". At this time, bricklayers' schools were in fact established in many camps. Young prisoners in particular were allocated to these, in Auschwitz even Jews. This "only asylum for young people", as Thomas Geve calls the bricklayers' school in Auschwitz, counted boys "between 13 and 18" among its pupils. These schools enabled the survival of quite a few men.

The necessity of having increasing numbers of prisoners working in armament factories finally forced the SS to give up one of its principles. Originally, all the concentration camps in the "Altreich", the old German regions, were to be "judenrein", free of Jews. This is why the Jews imprisoned there were deported to Auschwitz in the autumn of 1942. But from April 1944 on, Jewish prisoners were transported back into the "Altreich" so they could be put to work in the subsidiary camps erected near the armaments factories. The ever-increasing influx of Jews deported to Auschwitz also added to the numbers of those selected as fit for work during the arrival selections. This formed the greatest reservoir from which the SS could draw new labour. In the last year of the existence of the camps this reservoir grew immensely.

Himmler had to report regularly to Hitler on how many concentration camp prisoners were being used in the armaments industry, and it was his ambition to state increasing numbers in spite of the high death rate. For this purpose, all the camp commandants were obliged to report how many prisoners were allocated to units not engaged in work for armaments. The number of these had to be constantly lowered, and so they were reduced all the time. As they were generally "good" units, the prisoners sought ways of increasing them. There was thus a constant tug-of-war: cunning and corruption of the SS personnel on the one hand, rigorous measures by the camp command acting under pressure from the central authorities on the other. During the Nuremberg War Criminals' Trials, a competent witness, who had been working in the SS central office, stated that approximately 500,000 concentration camp prisoners had been deployed in the armaments industry in the final phase of the War.

When it became known after the War that many armaments factories had profited from the labour of the concentration camp prisoners, some companies tried to imply that this had been forced on them. Against this must be held the statement of the senior resident doctor at Auschwitz, Dr. Eduard Wirths, who once said: "We are now completely swamped with factories which absolutely insist on having prisoners."

Other leading officials of armaments factories tried to gloss over the real state of affairs and asserted that they had tried to make the life of the prisoners easier. The facts contradict this as well. Dr. Walter Duerrfeld, a director of the IG-Farben factory in Monowitz insisted that the camp SS doctor on duty undertake selections in the hospital of this, the largest subsidiary camp of Auschwitz, and had those prisoners who did not seem as though they would be fully fit for work again rapidly, sent back in the full knowledge that this meant death in the gas chamber in Auschwitz-Birkenau – the fate of those who had become unfit for work in Auschwitz. "When the sickness rate exceeded 5% of the size of the camp, I had to undertake a selection of this sort", camp doctor Dr. Friedrich Entress said in a statement; for the IG-Farben factory had to pay the camp command for every prisoner in the subsidiary camp at Monowitz, regardless of whether he worked in the IG-Farben factory or not, and Duerrfeld saw his task in helping the company save money.

Coal was mined for the IG-Farben factory at Monowitz in the nearby mine in Jawischowitz, where another subsidiary camp for prisoners had been built. The manager of this mine, Otto Heine, demanded from the SS not only an extension of the hours of work, but also that no midday meal be distributed in the mine, since the restricted space underground meant that too much time was wasted. Hence the prisoners received food only in the mornings and after work in the evenings. Heine also advocated that prisoners no longer able to carry out satisfactory work be removed and replaced by a new intake. But everybody who worked in the Auschwitz-complex knew that being sent back as no longer fit for work meant death.

If the Siemens-Schuckert factory prides itself on the fact that prisoners working for it in Bobrek, a subsidiary camp of Auschwitz, had distinctly better living conditions than those working in other units, then this was due to their being specially picked skilled workers who could not be readily replaced and were thus to be „most carefully restocked", as senior engineer Kurt Bundzus put it. This expression alone says enough.

Since more and more prisoners had to work in armaments factories, sabotage played an increasing role here, for it is only too understandable that the prisoners could have no interest in boosting the strength of their enemies. The SS were aware of this as well. It therefore persecuted any attempted sabotage with all means at its disposal: with the aid of an army of spies, with inhuman tortures and executions as deterrents. Just a few examples to illustrate this: in the Auschwitz subsidiary camp Blechhammer, a Jewish prisoner was hanged in front of all those who attended the roll-call. He had kept a piece of wire because he wanted to fix his shoe with it. A German foreman saw this and reported him. He had to die as a saboteur. The SS reacted to sabotage attempts most vehemently in the Dora camp, where the prisoners were engaged in the production of V-weapons. Between 10 and 21 March 1945 alone, 118 prisoners were publicly hanged there – mostly Russians and Poles.

But it was not only terror of such proportions that stopped sabotage activity. Otto Horn describes on the basis of experiences in the concentration camp Buchenwald, how a qualified tradesman sometimes felt it as great good fortune to stand at a lathe again after years of excruciating imprisonment and pointless work. So quite a few did not find it easy to contain their pride in their profession and not produce more and better than was absolutely demanded of them. Despite this, however, sabotage took place everywhere where prisoners were made to work on the weapons of their enemies; often this was spontaneous and on an individual basis, but frequently also well-thought out and organized.

This began in the deployment section with the allocation of work. The prisoners who allocated the work assigned prisoners who were professionally qualified to work in a particular factory, to a unit where their qualifications could not be put to use. A different profession was entered into their record cards so that the SS could not exploit their expertise. Private jobs were eagerly carried out for SS members not only in order to corrupt an SS man in charge (which had already occurred frequently before), but also to remove valuable materials from the production line. The SS personnel were only too glad to have things made that were hardly to be obtained anywhere outside the camp during the War. Once, when the Gustloff factory near the concentration camp Buchenwald received a particularly urgent order for armaments, prisoners' doctors falsely diagnosed typhus in some sick prisoners, whereupon the commandant imposed a two-week quarantine period, because he feared the spread of the disease to civilian workers and members of the SS. The order thus had to wait for a fortnight.

Finally, there were individual groups who even dared an open refusal to work: women of the Jehova's Witnesses group in the concentration camp Ravensbrueck refused to work in angora sheep breeding and in the vegetable garden because the wool was intended for army purposes and the vegetables were sent to an SS hospital. They accepted corporal punishment, reduced rations and the deprivation of blankets. When they remained firm in their refusal, they were sent to Auschwitz. Russian women, who had been taken to this women's concentration camp as prisoners of war, refused to work in an armaments factory. It was only after the SS threatened to shoot them that they saw themselves forced to yield. A group of Italian prisoners of war sent to concentration camp Dora after the fall of Mussolini refused to work in the production of rockets, appealing under the Hague Convention. For this, seven officers, who were evidently regarded as the ring-leaders, were shot.

There was a further group of prisoners also refused to carry out the work they were ordered to do, which this time did not serve the armaments of the Hitler armies: 400 Jews deported from Corfu to Auschwitz were ordered to work in the crematorium, that is, to collaborate in the destruction of other Jews. They refused. As a result, they were themselves murdered with poisonous gas on 22 July 1944.

In the concentration camp system, in the SS-state, as Eugen Kogon called it, in the "univers concentrationnaire" as David Rousset described it, work played a greatly changing role in the twelve years of its existence. But always, in conjunction with other methods employed by the SS, its purpose was to destroy the human dignity of the prisoner, to make him the tool of his enemies. Anyone who had the strength and the courage to defend himself against this, who did not want to become devoid of any will of his own, an object of the SS, but wanted to remain a subject, had to find a way, while doing the work forced upon him, of not sinking down to become a faceless slave. That only very few succeeded in this is a result of the murderous system of the National Socialist concentration camp, which was aimed at breaking people before they could find an opportunity of adjusting to such a totally abnormal situation; the fact that a few individuals did succeed shows that even in the most inhuman circumstances, humanity – that is, resistance against this system forced upon the people – could not be completely destroyed.

This may be a source of hope for those who in later times find out about this period and its problems.

Ladislaus Ervin-Deutsch

About Those who Survived and Those who Died
From Auschwitz to Labour Camp III in Kaufering

To those who remained human in times of inhumanity.
To those who remained European in a Europe of blazing funeral pyres.
To the people and the Royal Family of Denmark.
As a sign of homage and of love.

Prefatory Note

From 1944 onwards the building of underground armaments factories in Germany was speeded up with force. The "Organization Todt", under Minister Speer, was responsible for construction and implementation. This government organization also directed private enterprises, such as the Moll Company. The supply of the labor force – concentration camp prisoners, prisoners of war, "foreign workers", (in all 1.36 million workers were working for the OT) – for these "bunker projects" was the responsibility of the SS. Hitler had ordered the deportation of 100,000 Hungarian Jews in the spring of 1944, especially for the construction of underground facilities, since the reservoir of Jewish slave labour in the annexed Polish regions had long been exhausted.
The author of these memoirs, which describe the conditions for living and working in the subsidiary camp at Kaufering, was deported to Auschwitz in June 1944 from Klausenburg (Cluj) in Siebenbürgen (Transylvania), which at that time belonged to Hungary. He was 18 years old and had just passed his university entrance examination in the spring of 1944. Ladislaus Ervin-Deutsch, who is descended from an educated Hungarian family, had also made the situation of prisoners liberated at the end of the War the subject of a play, set in a sanatorium of the UNRRA (United Nations Relief and Rehabilitation Administration) in Gauting near Munich. The author was himself treated there for a year after his liberation ... The play was performed in Bucharest in 1966/67. In other one-act plays, Ervin-Deutsch has also attempted to convey by literary means the world that was experienced by prisoners in the concentration camp.
The memoirs, which Ervin-Deutsch gave the title "On the Living and the Dead", were written in Bucharest in Hungarian in 1959. Some passages were published the following year in the Hungarian literary journal "Utunk". In two places depicting the meeting with Viktor Capesius on his arrival in Auschwitz, the author has made subsequent additions of details to the text for its publication in the *Dachauer Hefte*. The text was translated into German by Stephan E. Osztroviczky in 1969. The translation authorized by the author was to serve merely as a working manuscript for the Historische Abteilung des Internationalen Suchdienstes (the Historical Section of the International Missing Persons' Tracing Service) in Arolsen, to which the translator is attached, and for the Archive of the Dachau Concentration Camp Memorial Site. Ruth Jakusch, the

director of the Site at that time had received the document from Ladislaus Ervin-Deutsch and organized the translation.
Ladislaus Ervin-Deutsch returned to Klausenburg (Cluj) in 1946 and studied chemistry. From 1950 to 1974, he worked as a chemist and Hungarian writer in Bucharest. In 1974, he left Romania and has lived in Hamburg since then. W. B.

In the course of the years, memories fade. Even the events most difficult to bear, even those that wear down the nerves, lose their color and their liveliness, their contours and their acuity, they become grey and blunted, faced with three-dimensional reality they slide into two-dimensional images, into a world of fairy-tale and dreams. In retrospect, one has to think very carefully from time to time to the long-past experiences – as though one had not lived through them oneself but merely read or seen them.
But the distance in time does not only make things pale and veiled, it also distorts. The contours become blurred and they change as well. Time – memory protects, pushes things into the background, drops things, adds others, elaborates and shades. And with distance, the distortion of the memories increases as well ...
For fifteen years, my memories have been maturing, paling and darkening.
I must make haste to put the blurring outlines onto paper as long as I can still see them, or imagine that I can still see the essentials. I must hurry, I must grasp the memories slipping away into the world of fairy-tale and dreams and drag back into the realm of tangible reality those things that matter and are worthy of being dragged back – as an example, as a warning, as a lesson. The images to be conjured up – fairy tales, dreams – were once reality. What in them is terrible and frightening is no figment of the imagination. Reality was like that.

ARRIVAL – five days

I awoke – the door of the carriage was torn open with a great noise. Hurrying, coarse people jumped into the open carriage: "Get out! Faster, faster!" In the semi-darkness of the carriage, where the flickering, silent lights of a town-like object behind the rails shone through the closely barred windows, a confused muddle ensued. Squeezed up, startled people reached for their clothes; they made haste to gather everything and to find their scattered belongings. In the darker corners some people kicked away the clothes and blankets of others and got in each other's way. No-one found what he was looking for. The strangers who were jumping up and down only heightened this confusion. "Faster, faster!" In the semi-darkness, dull blows could be heard – shocked screams of women, indignant protests ... These people had still regarded themselves as human beings despite being transported in a cattle waggon, and they were not yet accustomed to having other humans treat them as inhuman.

In a few minutes, the carriage was empty. To the right and left they fell in double file, the men separate from the women. Dressed in boots and a windcheater, with a rucksack or a small suitcase, in slippers, in shirt-sleeves or pyjamas or whatever was possible in this confusion. Suitcases and rucksacks had to be left behind. The guards said that the luggage would follow. In that moment, it dawned on me that we would not need any luggage where we were going. We began to move. The rows of men and women began to separate from one another without really noticing. I got a fright. Where is my mother? Disappeared! I never saw her again.

Our column marched past a high-ranking SS-officer sitting astride a motorcycle. – "How old? – Healthy? – Sick? – This way. – That way." The direction was indicated by a short movement of the hand – the column was divided. One column meant life in the first instance: the labor camp. The other was the death sentence. At the end of the path was the gas chamber with the inscription "Shower" – asphyxiation lasting six to ten minutes (sometimes even fifteen) awaited those who had been condemned to death by this movement of the hand – the old, the sick, the children.

I arrived in front of the SS-officer at the same time as my brother. "Pharmacist, have you landed here too?" the officer said in faultless Hungarian. "Are you a Jew?" "Yes, a Jew", my brother answered him, also in Hungarian. "Pity . . . I am sorry. Are you healthy? Why are you walking with a stick?" "My toes froze off. Last winter. In Russia". "You had better not tell anyone else that. If you are asked whether you are healthy, your answer should be a clear yes. The sick have to die. And now move on with those fit for work. With your brother . . . don't I know him too?"

Then the officer gestured to a guard to come over and said: "The prisoner with the stick is allowed to keep his stick."

This order was effective for some minutes. We walked on, another SS-man came past our column, and, cursing, he tore the stick out of my brother's hand. His limp became more noticeable, but the selection was over. We were fit.

The SS-officer was Dr Viktor Capesius, formerly the representative of the Bayer company in Cluj. At that time, in the period before the War, he often came to my brother's pharmacy to collect orders and to chat a little. My brother and he had slowly become friends and later Dr Capesius came even when he had no business. Just for a coffee, a glass of schnapps or to play chess. On an evening like that, while they were playing chess, I had got to know him.

Strange, unexpected meeting on the arrival platform in Auschwitz.

Remarkable ambiguity of human nature. One can hardly talk or think about it in any other way than ambiguously: The same Dr Viktor Capesius, who, with a wave of his hand and apathetically, or perhaps with the pleasant feeling of success given by the eager fulfilment of his duty, had sent many thousands of people to their deaths by gassing, tried to save the life of my brother.

Ought my brother to have been grateful to the murderer of my mother? A problem of conflicts. The first, though by no means the last in our career as prisoners. But murder thousand-fold cannot be pardoned by a single exception.
Then we had reached the gates and entered the town shimmering in the lamplight and peculiarly quiet. Blinding light, barbed wire, watch towers, huge blocks of huts arranged like a chess-board, between them, barbed wire barriers. And no movement anywhere, not a soul anywhere. Only at the gate was there a large group of SS-soldiers. Over the gate, the encouraging inscription "Work makes you free!"
The silent gleam, the clean-swept, well-paved, bare path, the locked doors and windows of the buildings called up in my mind fantastic stories of cities under a spell. It was all strange, frightening, nightmarish. I did not know where I was – Auschwitz – Birkenau – I heard these names for the first time then. Why had they brought me here, what is to become of us? Had they brought us here for work? For execution? What could there be in those locked buildings? My disturbed imagination knew contradictory answers to all these questions. In my luggage there were two volumes of Arpad Toth; their conclusion were the last two lines which had been going around in my head during the journey: "No path leads to the meadow any more where primulas flower and the nightingale sings."
Had we come a long way or had we only come a few hundred metres – I no longer knew. We had reached low, long, stretched out blocks of buildings. We were admitted in groups. We had to wait for a long time in front of the entrance. Day broke. We reached a large over-crowded hall. "Undress, pack your clothes together; keep shoes and belts."
In the mass of people, armed SS-soldiers moved around; so did other figures, comically dressed in striped outfits or in civilian suits, armed with rubber truncheons, who rushed up and down, urging us to hurry, pushing and hitting out around them, moving through the helpless people. "Disinfection? Execution?" After a few minutes, the rubber truncheons began to move also. "Faster, faster!" Coming out of the hall, we reached a long, wide corridor. This was where the hairdressers worked. They were Polish Jews speaking Polish and Yiddish and were dressed in striped prisoners' outfits. There were also some who spoke German. "Fancy arriving here in '44 without any resistance. Didn't you know what has happened in Poland, Austria and Czechoslovakia? Didn't you know what was waiting for you here? Haven't you heard of the gas chambers, of the crematoria? Didn't you try to flee or to hide?" I was ashamed of my passivity and ignorance. This was where the path of an unpolitical person living in seclusion led. Helpless and lost, one is dragged along by the raging torrent. Now it was too late for all that. At the end of the corridor, a door with the inscription "Shower" over it. Well – a shower, we thought reassured. Later, we discovered that somewhere in another camp building similar inscriptions were intended to be just as reas-

suring. But awaiting those who passed their doors was not a shower, but the gas chamber.

In that other building where the gas chamber was, my mother died. Perhaps at the same time as we entered the shower. At that stage I did not know the circumstances. I did not know where and how, but I did know that she had died. Dr Capesius had informed my brother.

He came after us, he had looked for and found my brother, he wanted to speak to him. I can no longer remember where he found us. Probably in the overcrowded hall, before we got undressed. Later he would hardly have recognized us. Capesius went next to my brother and said quietly to him:

"They will tell you that families will be reunited. That the members of your families will see each other again. That you should calmly await meeting them again ... But it is not true. And you should not wait calmly. Your younger brother is here. Did you travel to Auschwitz with your mother?"

"Yes", my brother answered him.

"How old is she?"

"Fifty-six"

Dr Capesius looked at his wrist-watch, then said in a matter-of-fact way: "Then she is probably already dead or dying."

Neither of us could say anything. Dr Capesius spoke on, deliberately coolly and clearly.

"The old and the sick have to die. You should impress that upon your minds. You will never see your mother again. Don't have any false hopes. It is better that way. Because then you have nothing you can wait for. Take advantage of every opportunity of getting away from Auschwitz. Regardless of where. It can be no worse anywhere else. Occasionally, people are transported to various labor camps. Volunteer when they are looking for people for any work. Even the hardest work is better than staying here. It should be made clear to you that anyone who stays any length of time in Auschwitz dies. That is what I wanted to say to you. I can do no more for you. Now I have to go. I wish you luck to survive."

The friendliness of a murderer deviating from the execution of his duty. But his clear, even if cruel words, later gave us resoluteness and were to lengthen the life of my brother by seven months.

Dr Capesius turned around and disappeared. We never saw him again. Much later, eighteen years later, I almost had the opportunity of seeing him again. In the summer of 1962, I was called as a witness in the Auschwitz Trial by the court in Frankfurt. As a witness in the Capesius case. At that time, I was living in Bucharest and the Romanian authorities did not approve my application to travel abroad. They were afraid that I might use the trip to flee the country illegally. Thus my never-presented statements as a witness remain a problem in the balance. For or against. Probably I would only have described the facts: Dr Capesius did carry out selections, thus he also murdered. Including my mother. In between times, where he knew and liked the victim,

he also helped. Such as in the case of my brother Gabriel, in the night from 11 to 12 June 1944.
And so, warm shower, not death by gassing. Disinfection. Dressing.
We received tattered underwear, blue and white striped prisoners' clothing made of linen and similarly striped round caps. You could not recognize people. It took some minutes before I found my brother Gabriel and my friend Paul Engel, with whom I had gone to high school for eight years. And they were standing right next to me!
Cutting off our hair, removing our clothing, the arbitrarily distributed, crumpled prisoner's outfit that was tight to bursting point or hung loosely like a sack, the rudeness, the rubber truncheons – all this had created an insurmountable abyss between our past and the present in just a few hours. The first part of the night in sealed cattle waggons, the last four days in locked, half-dark rattling carriages, the heat, the crowding, the lack of water, the perpetual uncertainty and the fear of our unknown destination all these things still belonged to our relatively human past, despite everything. The Hungarian police with the rooster feathers on their helmets and the SS-men who took over from them at the Czechoslovakian border no longer regarded us as human beings, but we did still feel more or less as though we belonged to the human race. Only the locks, the walls, the barbed wire, the iron bars and the bayonets of the police separated us from the other part of humanity. These few hours since we got off the train, from the train to the selection, from there to the gates of the camp, to the bath house and the way from there through the buildings to the exit from the bath separated us more from our civilian past than the hundreds of kilometres from Cluj to Auschwitz. Our arrival was like shutting one's eyes, falling asleep and having a nightmare. When I saw my brother and my friends at the exit from the bath and they saw me, this nightmare was no longer so confused, it had lost its dream-like quality, and become reality, the only reality. The past stayed behind us not only through this change of scene, it had become very far remote in time. Memory equals fairy-tale – where were they, where were they not ... That all this might return one day had become quite improbable. The reality of our existence – prisoners dressed in rags, overseers with rubber truncheons, walls, barbed wire barriers, watch-towers, and behind these fences, abandoned and bare loneliness, a smoking chimney about which it was whispered that it belonged to the crematorium consuming the victims of the gas chambers.
We had to wait for a while at the exit from the bath. It had become lighter. The quiet camp awoke. Everywhere, groups of people dressed in striped clothing appeared. They were all like us, only thinner, unshaven and broken. The overseers were uncouth men, well-fed, though also in prisoners' clothes or civilian suits patched with prisoners' cloth. On their sleeves, they wore yellow armbands with the black inscription "CAPO". We did not know what this inscription meant; we found out later.
Left, two-three-four, left, two-three-four, commanded the CAPOs, setting the

pace, and running up and down the rows; their rubber truncheons hailed down on any who had lagged behind – on older people, but also on younger ones weakened by hunger, by the inhuman work or some illness. "It looks as though this is awaiting us too," said my friend Paul depressed.

Later, we had to stand in a row and were made to move in a zig-zag along the fence between the buildings.

Our path finished at a barbed-wire barrier. The gate opened, the SS-guards counted those entering. Our surroundings did not change. The internal wire barriers simply separated the large camp into smaller sections. This facilitated maintaining order, checking those present, sifting out those who were candidates for death and the immediate stemming of any revolt.

As I later discovered, I was in a sub-section of Camp "C". We crossed a ditch on a board and stood at the entrance to a building. The entrance was not very wide, our rows of five abreast could not get through without jostling. SS-soldiers and overseers kept guard at the wide-open gates, and, with their truncheons and riding-whips, drove the thronging people inside, some of whom lost their footing or their balance. The blows did not even appear to be aimed at keeping order. They merely increased the crowding and the breaking up of the rows and they caused confusion, horror and helplessness. "What is happening? What will become of us? Rubber truncheons and riding whips without any reason or purpose? What has happened to law and justice? Is it quite impossible to defend oneself or to complain? Are there no limits to the arbitrary behaviour of the guards and overseers?" Perhaps it was precisely this helplessness with all the question marks that was the purpose of this inhuman treatment. Knocking down the people's self-esteem with a steam-roller, accustoming them to this nightmare atmosphere, cutting off all opportunities from the beginning, breaking their will, nipping any resistance in the bud.

A lash from the whip had struck a small, stooped man of about fifty. He was a doctor from Nagyvársd, probably no longer of quite sound mind. The ghetto, the four days' journey or perhaps the concentrated events of the previous night hat put him off balance. He was unable to get over this arbitrary action and carry on as usual, he could not adapt to the situation and proceed without a word. It was as though he had lost his senses; and yet his was the reaction of a normal person. He started back, horrified, he looked around him. Then he went over to the SS-man who had struck him. "What do you want from me? What have I done to you? Why did you hit me?"

"You swine," gasped the SS-man, raised his whip and struck the malcontent in the face twice. The whip left two long, blood-red stripes on the face of the man. "You are not a human being, you are a wild beast, no-one can even talk to you in a human fashion. Maybe I can make myself better understood with your own method." With these words, he strode up to the SS-man and struck him in the face. The SS-man staggered against a door post, his mouth opened wide, his face became distorted. Perhaps at that moment the thought that

shot through his brain was – have we lost the war or has a revolt broken out in the extermination camp – and the riding whip fell from his hand. A few moments later, the old, stooped doctor collapsed under the blows of the SS-men and the overseers. The whole thing had taken only a few seconds.
Everyone followed the events as though turned to stone, but no-one dared to interfere. The rows continued into the hut. In the hut, we lined up against the walls, so that a square area remained empty in the middle. Standing in this square, the "Herr Ober" – internal commandant of Camp C, – made his speech. It was translated into Hungarian by a man deported from Holland but originally from Hungary – Uncle Weiss, the interpreter. His mother tongue was now Dutch, but he spoke perfect German, and Hungarian surprisingly well. Only his pronunciation was interesting; in other circumstances I would probably have smiled. But what he was translating was not at all funny.
In his address, he said that all those who subjected themselves without resistance to the instructions of the "Herr Ober" and obeyed the regulations precisely would remain alive. But anyone who disturbed the order would be strung up. Apart from shoes and belt, no-one was permitted to own any personal belongings. If anyone had anything, he should hand it over now. This was the last opportunity. If anything was discovered later, the owner would be hanged, even if he was prepared to hand it over voluntarily. Notable examples were quoted: person "X", who had arrived from Hungary a week before us, had a knife blade hidden in the sole of a shoe. It was found. The "Herr Ober" had this person hanged. "Y" had only a pin hidden in his lapel. The "Herr Ober" had him hanged. Those who had arrived a week before us could confirm this. One night, an argument had broken out in one of the huts. The Block Elder had not been able to restore order and reported it to the "Herr Ober". The "Herr Ober" had then had all the doors locked and sealed air-tight, whereupon the noisy inmates of the hut suffocated. Almost nine-hundred people were crammed into this hut and not one survived. "Because there must be order and all noise is forbidden!" – Uncle Weiss pointed to the proverb written on the wall: "Speaking is silver, silence is golden!" The "Herr Ober" spoke on about discipline, order, about punishments and related interminable examples of those who had infringed discipline and were hanged as a result.
During the speech of the "Ober" and the translation by Uncle Weiss, I had looked at the "Herr Ober". At first, this form of address seemed ridiculous to me. "Herr Ober" ... head waiter ... The similarity of sound in the words forced itself more and more into the foreground: "Herr Ober" – Führer (Föúr – "Führer" pronounced very similarly in Hungarian!) dictator in Camp C. He himself was an outcast too. He too had been interned in the concentration camp. His life had been uncertain, his future hopeless, he himself a prisoner, but inside the camp, he was absolute master over the fate of ten, twenty or even thirty thousand people. At his command, anyone could be beaten to

death, hanged or suffocated. He was tall, brown-haired, solid and with military bearing. He wore sports clothes of good quality, patched with striped material, and high boots. In his hand a riding whip, with which he constantly beat against his boot as he spoke. As was told later, he was a German officer and had been at the Eastern Front until 1943, when it was discovered that his grandfather had been a gypsy. He was demoted, interned and sent to Auschwitz. His background as an officer had been taken into consideration and, as a result, he had been given responsibility for the internal running of the camp; he fully justified this responsibility.

At the end of his speech, the "Herr Ober" had the doctor who had protested at the stroke with the whip at the entrance brought to him. He could no longer stand by himself, two men had to support him. Uncle Weiss translated. The "Herr Ober" said that this man had offended against camp discipline. He had presumed to maltreat a member of the SS-guard. As a punishment, he would now be beaten to death. The „Herr Ober" ordered that everyone was to remain at his place. All were to observe the carrying out of the punishment and to learn that this is what would happen to anyone who attacked a superior. The "Herr Ober" beat his whip impatiently against his boot and called to the overseers standing in front of our rows: "Begin!"

The condemned man was thrown onto the ground and five or six overseers struck him – with rubber truncheons, with thick wooden clubs, one held a short iron bar. There was no cry of pain to be heard. In the silence, there was only the sound of the blows raining down. A quiet groan and after that, only more blows, finish, the end ... This was our welcome to Auschwitz. We returned to the square between the huts, were divided into groups and every group was assigned its quarters.

The huts were gigantic hangar-like buildings made of bricks. Large double doors, with hardly any windows, wet concrete floors, semi-dark, unfurnished. At the end of the room, there were small rooms divided off with boards; these contained a bed, table, chairs, lamp and a small cast iron stove. This was where the Block Elder lived with his wife and two children. They were German gypsies. Compared to us, they lived in a lordly fashion. They had remained together, they lived like human beings, they were not starving and they were not tortured. But in August 1944, or it might have been at the beginning of September – I was no longer there – all the gypsies imprisoned in the camp, whether young, old, man, woman or child were collected one night and carted off to the gas chambers; they were killed and burnt. They had lived there for years. When they had to line up they realized what awaited them. The women cried, the children screamed and some of the men tried to resist. Many were shot. Those who were still in Auschwitz and survived the war said that it had been a terrible night; huge flames leapt from the chimneys of the crematoria from the evening till the morning.

The part of the hut reserved for us was damp and dark even though it was only the middle of June. One could only sit down or lie down on the floor, on the concrete floor and despite this we hardly had enough room. The huts were designed for barely five hundred people lying close together but there were more than nine hundred of us. We could only sit down if we formed orderly rows and moved really close together. After we had arranged ourselves for ten to twenty minutes we succeeded in sitting down – tired, sleepy and without a word. My brother was perspiring from walking and standing around for hours. He had previously spent three years in the labor service in the Ukraine and during this time, his toes had frozen so much that they had to be amputated. Scarcely six months after his discharge from the hospital, he was deported and was still limping very badly. Despite his stick he walked very badly but since they had taken this away from him in the bath house, walking was even more difficult for him. He stared in front of him exhausted and silent. His friends and acquaintances, who had sat down around him were waiting for some encouragement because of his constant humour or at least a cynical remark that would make them smile. But this time they waited in vain, he remained silent.

But the despondent silence did not last long. The Block Elder made a path for himself through the crowd with his stick. Roll-call! Everybody to the square between the huts. The "old hands" leapt up immediately. They knew what this meant. For days, weeks, months, they had practised this at least twice a day, on some days, even three, four or five times. We went out to the large, empty square next to the neighbouring hut and lined up in rows of five along a brick wall in the form of a square. Our Block Elder, his assistants and other overseers with CAPO armbands arranged the rows. Their instructions were accompanied by punches and blows with a stick. Here and there cries of pain could be heard. Here and there a man would collapse. They were carted behind the rows, the overseers kicked them a few more times, carried them back into the huts and listed them as sick.

The rows got into order, those beaten up were dragged away, but the actual purpose, the roll-call, had not yet begun. We stood and waited. Light fog settled over the camp. Our clothing gradually got wet. It began to rain gently. The "old hands" nodded, "We are used to this. In Auschwitz it is almost always wet and foggy. And it rains nearly every day too." We stood in the rain for hours. In the distance, we heard movements coming from the squares between the neighbouring huts. The Block Elders and their assistants became active. They ran up and down between the rows, put them in order and counted those present. Again and again the truncheons came whistling down here and there.

Finally, the "Herr Ober" arrived with an NCO of the SS. "Caps off!" The Block Elder reported to the "Herr Ober", which he in turn passed on to the NCO. The NCO wrote down the number present and moved on. "Caps on! Dismiss!" Roll-call was finished. It hat not ceased raining. But we were not allowed to return to the huts. Maybe later, in the afternoon, when the Block Elder is of the opinion that it is raining hard – say the "old hands". It is not advisable to go inside without permission. It was happened that people have been beaten to death for this.

The ground got soft, it became mushy. We were not allowed to sit down nor to lean against the huts. In 1943 SS-men allegedly shot from their watch towers those who leaned against the walls. But the situation had improved since then and it now hardly ever happened that a guard shot into the crowds between the huts. There was more to be feared from the overseers.

Among the "old hands" there were my old Hungarian teacher and Robi and Erwin, two good friends. They had arrived here a week before me. We had stood a little bit to one side, at the rear of the hut and were leaning against the walls. We hoped that the roof which protruded only slightly would protect us from the increasingly heavy rain. The two friends spoke about huts, about Block Elders, about CAPOs, of the chimneys smoking in the distance, of mass executions. They knew that those unfit for work were sent to the gas chambers immediately after arrival. They knew that anyone under sixteen or over fifty had hardly any chance of remaining alive. Without regard to age, the old, weak, sick, pregnant women and mothers who refused to be separated from their children, were killed. "From time to time selection units arrived, who chose the sick and the weak for the gas chambers. Since your brother limps he has to be careful, he must not attract attention," warned Erwin. "My little sister has certainly been killed", mumbled Robert to himself in despair. I thought of my mother and of what Dr Capesius had said; she was fifty-six, old, grey. I hoped that she only discovered at the last moment what awaited her.

They told of endlessly long roll-calls, of rain, of cold, of the jammed-full huts, of the whips and truncheons ceaselessly thudding down, of the food. They were both hungry – they had been for days, constantly. I had not yet got to know hunger. In the evening in the carriage, I was full and after that, the events following upon one another without interruption claimed my total attention. I was not hungry, although it was certainly late in the afternoon by now.

"Look out! Get out of the way! Move apart!" Robert alerted us at the last moment. An SS guard with a CAPO appeared around the corner of the hut. They caught a youth of about my age, who was also seeking protection from the rain by the wall but did not disappear into the throng in time. Injured by the blows of the CAPO, he fell into the mud with his face bleeding. "That was the SS-man from the kitchen" announced Erwin. "They are getting food carriers." "Tell me what the arm band with the letters CAPO means". "Overseers and the group leaders in the labour groups." – Erwin was so well informed. "The majority of them are criminals, sentenced to forced labour for life. But there are also some who have become more or less mentally unbalanced through interrogations, corporal punishment or other cruel treatment. They were the most reliable people for the SS – sadistic idiots . . ."

After that, we did not seek protection by the wall any more. We stood around in the middle of the square, in the mud. Robi's shoes had got wet. He was wearing canvas shoes with a wooden sole: "I had new ski boots. They noticed this and the Block Elder took them away from me. You are lucky that they haven't noticed yours yet. Be careful. Don't clean them; rather wipe mud all over them. Shoes can mean the difference between life and death here." I followed his advice. I smeared mud on my shoes with a little stick. Robi and Erwin helped me. After that we dirtied Erwin's shoes, since the dirt he had put on in the morning had been washed off by the rain in the meantime. "We are conscientious people who dirty their shoes carefully every morning after they wake up", jeered Erwin. In a few minutes they were so filthy that there would be hardly any SS-man, Block Elder or CAPO who would envy us them.

And then came the food carriers. The food hung in open vat-like containers on two poles. It smelt of dishwater. We stood in rows of five. Each row was given one dirty, rusty metal container, old saucepans, casserole dishes or fairly large tin cans. There were no knives, forks or spoons. Some of the "old hands" produced "spoons" made of flat pieces of wood. There was no possibility of washing dishes and hands unless you did it in the rain. Five people at a time went up to the food carriers and the prisoner on duty filled the container. To eat, we had to go to the other end of the square. Standing in the rain, we drank in turn some of the thin, unappetizing, maggoty contents. The container went round the circle like an Indian pipe of peace. If one of the five had a spoon, then it too was passed round the circle – perhaps they felt one degree more human.

I can't remember exactly what the food in Auschwitz was like. All I know is that it was disgusting. I was able to drink from it only once. "If we want to stay alive we'll have to eat everything" warned my brother. But he couldn't do it either. We were probably not hungry enough yet. The other three in our row, Dr Lengyel, a dermatologist, Dr Engel, area doctor from Zsombor, Paul's father and my friend Paul himself continued to take great pains with the food, Paul stopped last. "I can't do it! But I'm still terribly hungry", he complained. The remainder, about two thirds of the ration, we passed on to our friends who had arrived a week before us. Without even a grimace they ate. They were starved already.

After the meal another roll-call. This time it was much faster. It can't have taken more than an hour and a half. There were some who could no longer endure standing around in the rain – two fell over. Some had to be supported. In the meantime, it had become dark. We had to go back into the huts. There followed the distribution of bread. We got two hundred grams of bread and twenty grams of salami per head. The bread was mouldy but still edible. My brother wanted to give me his salami ration. "I won't survive anyway. The labor service, frost, hunger, ... and limping on top of all that ... I want you, at least, to get home ..." I didn't accept. "We have to get home together." But I did get home alone.

We consumed our rations immediately, although they were intended for twenty-four hours. In this way we were full at least once. The far-sighted divided the bread and the salami into tiny pieces. They ate more frequently but always remained hungry.

After the meal, we arranged ourselves in rows once again in order to be able to sit down simultaneously. We got ourselves into an orderly arrangement. For those who had remained standing outside a row in the semi-dark, no room to sit down remained. Somehow or other, we crowded together even more, to create space for them. Our clothes were wet, we were cold and mortally exhausted. Our situation at night in the dark, overcrowded huts seemed even more hopeless than outside in the rain. Nobody could sleep. Low murmuring filled the room. This monotonous noise was interrupted by a shout; it was the Block Elder. "If there isn't peace and quiet soon, I'll have all the doors locked and you will have all suffocated by the morning."

Then, in a gentler tone: "You can whisper. If anyone has a good voice he's allowed to sing too. But only one at a time." - "He loves good voices", whispered the "old hands".

A gentle disturbance ensued. Somewhere, a man stood up. Quietly at first but then somewhat more strongly, a religious song of lament filled the air. The singer - cantor of a large church in Poland - had an excellent, lyrical tenor voice. We all listened reverently. After this hymn, followed some Yiddish songs, then other prayerful, lamenting hymns. Half an hour later or maybe an hour or even an hour and a half, silence fell. The singer ceased.

The Block Elder spoke again, but this time more quietly and more humanely "Who else wants to sing?" The new voice sounded stronger and sharper. "Valentin's prayer" sounded out. An opera singer from Prague, someone next to me whispered. Some opera arias followed a piece from "Faust".

He doesn't know any Yiddish, he's only learnt the song texts by heart, said the unknown commentator. The last song, "Mein Städtele Beltz", was smothered in sobs. The singer wept and so did the Block Elder. They were weeping about their destroyed home and the members of their families who had been killed. - "A happier song", demanded the Block Elder. The singer from Prague remained silent. A bar-singer from Transylvania arose. He began to sing a hit song but stopped immediately. Once again, he sang the song about home, about the township of Beltz and then he too fell silent. There was quiet. ... The Block Elder went back to his room without a word. Nor was there any more murmuring to be heard. People were thinking back, they were also trying to sleep. Here and there, someone sighed.

I could not fall asleep. I tried to conjure up the distant, very distant images. The bank of the Szamos ... our apartment ... a sixteen-year-old girl, Judith Grünewald, with whom I had been in love for three years and who had been deported a fortnight before me - pictures of her had remained in my suit in the bath. My mother. My mother's face in the door of the carriage as she got out when I last saw her. This image pushed all the others aside. The creases

had disappeared from her frightened and yet resolute face – all expression vanished from it. The face itself vanished ... Between a thousand and many thousands of kilograms – a handful of ash ... and hardly twenty-four hours ago she had been standing next to me in the door of the carriage ...
I could not got to sleep. I remained awake all night. In this night, I wept for the last time. After this, I felt I had matured into an adult. I remained alone.
"Grown up is that person
in whose heart there is neither father
nor mother any longer ...
Who knows that life was
lent to him as a bonus for death ..."
I think my brother slept, perhaps he was weeping too. I did not know, we did not talk about it ...
On the second day, I did not need to be woken, I was awake. The washroom provided new surprises, even though I was to a certain extent safe from surprises after spending twenty-four hours here. It was a large dark building with washing facilities similar to cattle troughs running parallel with the walls. Above these, iron pipes had been installed and from these pipes, at a distance of a metre and a half apart, ran ice-cold water. There was no soap, no towels. In this wash-room, the CAPOs, the Block Elder and their assistants constantly ran up and down. I do not know why washing annoyed them so much. With whips and truncheons, they hit anyone who got in their way. If one wanted to wash despite this, the best thing to do was to retreat into an isolated corner and allow the water to run over one until driven away by the next passing overseer. Then one had to disappear as quickly as possible, wet, and with one's shirt thrown over one's shoulder. Even so, one could not always avoid the sticks and whips or, from a greater distance, stones and bricks hurled at one.
Standing around between the huts. Roll-calls lasting hours and more pointless standing around. Fog, rain. The sun appeared, but its veiled rays did not give any warmth. It vanished again soon and it rained again. The people were discussing the political events. "The great Russian attack ... The invasion in Western Europe ... It can't be long any more ..." The "old hands" interpreted this in the best possible light for themselves. "Russian units will be here in a few weeks ... The Germans will be unable to resist much longer ..." It was as though the suffering and the hopeless situation had given way to optimism. But we, who had arrived the day before, were more gloomy about the future. "The war can't last many months more ... Maybe until autumn, at most, until the onset of winter ... How many will survive that long ... until liberation?" But the war continued for a long time, well into the spring. And only very few survived to see the liberation.
Together with Paul, I brooded on how we might get into another camp most quickly. "There can be no worse place". We agreed that we would volunteer

if they were assembling groups of tradesmen for some other camp – according to the "old hands", that sort of thing happened very frequently. "Perhaps they won't test us and later we'll work our way into it somehow. If it does come to light that we don't have the faintest idea, then we'll already be in another camp". Between roll-call and food distribution, we made a sortie into the neighbouring huts and tried to ascertain whether a relatively large labor group was being assembled somewhere that we might join. There was nothing. No transports were leaving.

During the food distribution we were hungry. We gave away only one third of our portion. It was my brother's view that after three days we would eat everything to the last skerrick, and after a week, nothing would disgust us any more. He was right. In the night, we conversed very little, and even then, only in whispers. No-one sang. I was tired and cold. Sleep did not refresh me. I awoke shattered. It was pouring with rain again. Everything was wet and dirty. "And then having to stand outside all day again, getting soaked, avoiding the overseers, waiting for the evening just so we can get back under a roof and rest a little half-sitting, half-lying on a wet concrete floor." It was with thought-processes such as these that I occupied myself on the third day in Auschwitz. I could not suspect that this day would not be like the two preceding ones. Seeing anything ahead or calculating ahead was impossible. The events that meant life or disaster for us were now determined more or less by blind co-incidence.

The 13 June 1944 dawned. For the "old hands", one day passed without significance into the next; they knew only that it was June. But we new arrivals knew that we had arrived on the morning of 11 June and so far, only the days that had gone by counted. After the morning roll-call, we were watching some balloons flying over the bare area behind the electrically wired fences. "Where have they come from, why?" We pursued pointless thoughts, for which we did not get any answers. The balloons appeared to hang in one spot. We wanted to draw conclusions for our own fates from any signs and from every item of news, even from the appearance of the balloons, from all these events . . .

We were hurriedly summoned to a second roll-call. Hardly an hour had passed since we had lined up in the morning. "What has happened?" The "old hands" were not surprised. "After all, we have only had two roll-calls a day for the last two days – that was unnatural. We stand in our rows. There's nothing unusual about that, it's just uncomfortable."

We lined up. Everything happened as usual. Waiting, rain, overseers running up and down, beatings with sticks, individual screams, someone collapsed half-unconscious and was carried bleeding into the hut. This time the "Herr Ober" appeared, not only in the usual company of the NCO of the SS, but with several SS-officers and one officer who wore a yellow-green uniform and so did not belong to the SS; on his arm, he wore a band with the inscription "Organisation Todt".

We are being collected to work. One of those officers is not from the SS, he belongs to the "Organisation Todt", which carries out work necessary for the "German Army" explained someone behind us. The interpreter appeared. "Doctors and pharmacists fall out!" My brother embraced me and went to the front. Paul's father, Dr Engel, and many other acquaintances did likewise. They lined up separately and were led into another hut. "Tradesmen fall out!" Paul leaned over and whispered to me: "Don't forget that we are tradesmen." We stepped forward. Next to us stood Peter Honigsberg and his father, neighbors from Gyulai Pál Street, Dr Gombos, our Hungarian teacher, Jancsi Kádár and many other people I knew from high school, they must have been from the seventh and eighth year, since those younger were probably no longer alive: I knew that not one of them was a trained tradesman, just as little as I was myself.

We had to line up separately and were led to another corner of the square. Those who remained behind, who had not volunteered as doctors, pharmacists or tradesmen, were lined up opposite. "Unskilled laborers", said the officer of the "Organisation Todt", pointing to those left over. We stood in rows of five again. We waited. Paul's father recommended that we should claim to be bricklayers. "If we stay together, I'll teach you and it won't be obvious that it is not your trade ..."

The "Herr Ober", the interpreter and the officer of the "Organisation Todt" came to our group. – "What is your trade? How old? Where have you worked?" Uncle Weiss translated the officer's questions. When it was my turn, I stuttered something about having been employed concreting an airfield in Cluj. I really did know something about mixing concrete. The officer wanted to see my hands, laughed and waved: – "Unskilled!"

So I had to go to the group standing at the opposite end. So an unskilled labourer is what I became. Jancsi Kádár, Paul and the teacher stood next to me a few minutes later. They had not been believed either. Peter and his father had remained with the skilled tradesmen, as bricklayers. We were envious of them and regretted that we had not succeeded in staying with them as tradesmen. "That group will certainly be given a place to work first. They will work, maybe work very hard, but surely under more humane conditions."

We lined up, were counted and ordered to march "left-two-three-four, left-two-three-four" commanded the CAPOs marching at the side of the group, striking individual marchers with their sticks from time to time. The picture was the same as on the day of our arrival, only now I belonged to those taking part.

"Are we going to start work already? I hardly dare to dream it; or maybe there are too many unskilled workers and we are going to the gas chambers ..." My friend Paul next to me considered this possibility. None of these assumptions turned out to be correct. We were only taken through the gate of Camp C into Camp E, that is, only into another part of this gigantic internment camp.

"Starting from here, the individual labor groups are to be transported to the various parts of the Reich. Those that come here are sent off to work sooner or later. It depends when, from where and how much manpower is requisitioned." The "old" inmates of Camp E provided these explanations.

The group of skilled tradesmen with Peter and his father stayed in Camp C. We were completely separated from one another. I do not know what happened to them. They are dead ... Did they die a natural death or were they murdered? ... I shall probably never know. Since we parted, I have never been able to find anyone able to tell me anything about Peter and his father and their comrades, neither in other concentration camps nor later, after the Liberation. Probably, there are no witnesses of their doom.

When I sat down at my desk about four weeks ago to refresh these slowly vanishing camp memories, they were still moving like dark wraiths of fog in my consciousness. It was as it had been in earlier times, before an examination in my student days. I was busy with preparations, I knew the topic. And yet, when I thought about it, theses, formulae, a heap of confused equations stood before me and it seemed impossible to extract anything from them in order to have a clear structure and connected, clear answers. Suddenly I heard the first question of my teacher and the fog dissipated. Memories stood crystal clear in front of me.

I began to write. More and more new images and contours emerged from this foggy semi-dark. The gloomy place, the depressing atmosphere, the rain and the mood. Occasionally, the events conjured up became three-dimensional reality, the dead rose again. I can remember details again that I had forgotten for years, names I had not been able to recall for fifteen years. When I wrote about the appearance of the "Herr Ober", the name of the long-forgotten interpreter "Uncle Weiss" came back to me ...

When my memories of Camp C were exhausted, I prepared for the second half of my stay in Auschwitz. But then I recalled a small but nonetheless significant episode: letter writing. This took place on one of the three days I spent in Camp C. I cannot remember which one, nor do I know whether it happened at the morning or evening roll-call. When we had lined up, the Block Elder and his assistants distributed cards and pencils. Every person obtained a military post-card and a piece of indelible pencil. The "Herr Ober" spoke and Uncle Weiss translated: "Everybody will write. Those who have relatives, to them, those who do not have family members at home, will write to a friend or acquaintance. Each of you has received an empty card and a pencil. In ten minutes, everybody has to hand in a written card and of course the pencil as well. The 'Herr Ober' will dictate the text. Everyone will write what the 'Herr Ober' dictates, in German. If anyone so much as changes a single word, the 'Herr Ober' will have him hanged." The "Herr Ober" dictated the following text: "We have arrived safely, we are well. We are happy." I still remember one line very precisely: "I am in good health, happy and cheerful". After the name of the sender, came the address.

Waldsee (Forest Lake) - that sounds beautiful. In a place with such a fine name, there can only be happy and cheerful people. The reader imagines sunshine. Anyone reading these lines automatically thinks of lakes and sunshine. But Auschwitz is the exact opposite. An almost uninhabitable, unhealthy, swampy area south-east of Cracow: with fog, swamp fever and destructive, contagious diseases.
The message had to be written. But I did not want to contribute to this deception, to this lying Nazi propaganda. I did not write the name of the sender, nor an address. In this way, it could not be much use. When we returned the card and the pencil, the Block Elder only checked that it was written. He did not notice that mine had neither an address nor a sender.
The last two days in Camp E call forth even more blurred memories than the preceding ones. Once the first shock of the arrival was over, and the nightmare had become something everyday, the exhaustion, constantly getting wet, the filth and the cold decreased our sensitivity. My awareness of the transition was anaesthetized by apathy, and this meant I was not so dismayed by the physical conditions of Camp E.
When we arrived and were allocated our living area, the people in the two huts were already crammed together. It was already getting dark. Food distribution, roll-call, sleep, reveille, smearing shoes, roll-call, sleep. Hardly anyone I knew - of all my acquaintances, only Paul and I got into the same hut - and even worse sleeping conditions than before. The floor of the huts was not concreted. In the dirt on the wet floor stood beds made of planks, several storeys high - seven sleeping places on the bottom, in the middle six and on top five places. When we arrived, there were eight people pressed tightly together and lying on their sides at the bottom, seven in the middle and six on top. One person could not turn around individually, the whole row had to turn at the same time. There was no space for us any more, only on the wet floor between the plank beds, and even there was already over-crowded. I slept the first half of the night and finally woke up because I was cold, my clothes were wet and all my limbs hurt. I spent the second night underneath a plank bed. Perhaps I had found a drier place, perhaps I was more tired, more crushed; I slept through almost until dawn. With my teeth chattering, I longed for reveille so I could get out and warm myself by moving around. I was hoping for a little sunshine, but that turned out to be a vain dream.
In the early afternoon, we were assembled for roll-call a second time. "You are going to work", said an unusually communicative CAPO. We lined up in the square next the hut and waited. "Left-two-three-four" we heard from the path in front of us. Rhythmic steps resounded and then we saw the approaching group. - "There's Dr Lengyel ... my father ... your brother ..." Paul moved nervously, darted now to the right, now to the left side of the group. He was trying to see if there were any other acquaintances among the new arrivals.
It was the group of doctors and pharmacists. They were only now coming

from Camp C. They got their quarters three huts further down. A few minutes later, we had to line up for roll-call. "I have to go there. They'll take us away after the roll-call and I want to say goodbye to my brother." "I am going too", said Paul. Someone, I didn't know who it was, promised to get us when the counting started. Along the huts, we managed to reach the square where the new arrivals were lined up without being seen. My brother and Paul's father were standing next to each other. For a moment, I was almost happy. Then we were told that the counting had already begun in our group. We went back. A CAPO noticed me. He cursed and threw a stick at me.

Immediately after the roll-call there was the distribution of food. Then we had to line up again. Triple salami and sausage rations were handed out and a fruit cube as well. "It looks as though we are to make a three-day journey" I thought to myself. Before lining up, I dashed over to my brother again. We said farewell to each other. It was then, in Camp E in Auschwitz-Birkenau, that I saw him for the last time.

I hoped that he would have better working conditions as a pharmacist in a group of doctors and pharmacists. Perhaps in some kind of health service; in that sort of work, his sick right leg would surely not cause him any too great distress. ... They were taken to dig tunnels in Melk near Mauthausen. My brother worked for six months in a mine. At the end of December he died of hunger, cold and total exhaustion. How he stood it until the end of December at all, how he lived, how he died, I do not know. All his friends also died. Paul's father too. One of our distant acquaintances told me years later that he had been together with my brother in Melk. It was from him that I discovered when he died. ...

When I returned to my group, the others were already in rows of five, their bread and salami rations in their hands. Many had already eaten a part of their three-day ration. I managed to return to my place unseen. After another counting, we were marched off. I looked back once again. The huts hid my brother's group. I saw only one part of a row about eight or ten prisoners in striped suits: my brother was not among them.

Through the door of Camp E, we came to a main road. I think we went past the "bath house" again too. Then we reached the main entrance. It was dusk. Around us there were SS-soldiers moving about with large German shepherd dogs on leashes. When we passed through the gate, we were counted again. The camp lay behind us. I saw again the inscription "Work makes you free." Now I felt its true meaning. An escape from hell. For those marching in, the inscription over Dante's hell would have been more appropriate: "Lasciate ogni speranza, o Voi chi entrate." ("Abandon hope, all ye who enter here".)

Travel nerves ... adventure ... an unknown goal ... I was eighteen years old. I was glad about the change that had occurred, and that something was about to happen; but glad too that we were getting away from Auschwitz. But not only we, the older men were also glad. Only for them, the doubts were greater and the hope smaller.

For a while we walked along the wire barriers that surrounded the camp. Suddenly there was congestion. The first rows stopped – and shocked, we all stopped. "What is the matter? Go on, go on! Proceed!" shouted the SS-escorts, the dogs barked angrily and pulled at their leashes. The people remained unresponsive. They were looking to the right and their gaze clung to the fence as though they were turned to stone. "What are you staring at? Have you never seen a dead man. You can have enough of them. In a little while you can stare at each other!" – "A lazy swine has killed himself. So what? Go on, get moving, march!"

The dogs barked even more furiously. They tried to throw themselves at us, but that could not happen. We were being sent off to work and our train was already waiting. The escort was probably regretting that they could not have a few people torn apart by the dogs. That was their greatest pleasure. They tried to make up for it by hitting the marching men with their rifle butts. A young man screamed and fell over. The SS-man, who had tried to hit him on the back, missed and struck him on the skull. Then he went over to him and kicked him in the face. – "Stand up, you ..." He did not move. "Two men fall out and carry him. Two others can take over later."

Two men lifted up the young man lying on the ground. He was bleeding at the back of the head. His eyes were staring into the distance, his mouth was opening. He had died. They reported this. "Died? That's his affair. Your job is to carry him on. There were two thousand of you who came through the camp gates and two thousand of you will get onto the train. What matters is the number of those present ..."

The column moved on slowly. Next to the rows, two men carried the dead man. They were part of this labour unit as well. "Left-two-three-four, left-two-three-four and a little faster!" After about one hundred and fifty paces, I arrived at the spot where the column had stopped. On the inside of the fence, two CAPOs were busy under the supervision of an SS-guard. They wore thick rubber gloves. They were occupied with separating a prisoner from the electrified fence; emaciated to skin and bone and his distorted face looked like that of a scarecrow. The hands of the dead man – the prisoner with the distorted face was dead – held fast to the wires, as though in a cramp. The two CAPOs tore the corpse by its legs, the strands of wire banged together, but the clenched hands would not yield. – "Dammit, you'll tear the electric wires like that. Here, cut off his hands!" The SS-guard accompanying the CAPOs drew his bayonet and gave it to one of the men. He took the knife but then hesitated. The second man took it from his hand and cut off the dead man's fingers. The corpse fell to the ground and vanished from my view. It was hidden by those who came behind me ...

Later, I found out what those who were marching in the first rows had seen. A shockingly emaciated man in prisoners' clothes had staggered beyond the forbidden two-metre wide strip of ground separating the barbed wire fence, disregarding the calls of his comrades hurrying along behind him. Shots were heard from the watch tower. In the out-of-bounds area, stood two equally frighteningly emaciated prisoners, they had tried to hold their comrade back – one of them fell, groaning. The other limped away. In the meantime the suicide candidate – he surely wanted to commit suicide – had reached the wire fence, grabbed the wires and fallen forward. His face jammed between two strands of wire, his eyes stared glassily in front of him into the distance beyond the fence, into liberty. The electric current had killed him instantly, he was free ... The next day, maybe not for a week or a month, he would have died in the gas chamber anyway, suffering thousand-fold worse pain. Such emaciated, exhausted prisoners had no hope of being sent anywhere else. Day after day, they waited to be carted off to the gas chambers ... Every day, there were a few who put an end to their fate by their own hand. Between the wire barriers, there were a few dead nearly every day. Some were killed by the bullets of the guards, some by the electricity ... This was the simplest way of committing suicide.

After a few hundred metres, we wheeled away from the fences and walked towards the rails. Behind us, in the camp, the lights were being turned on. The squares between the huts were empty. Those who had remained behind, the ones still alive, were going to sleep. We, the labor transport, one thousand nine hundred and ninety nine men and one corpse, had reached the railway station. Probably, we were where we had arrived five days earlier, perhaps somewhere else. I did not know. The confusion of rails, carriages, locomotives and whole trains. Blinding light. We were taken to a goods train. Then we stood in rows of five next to this train and waited. The SS-guards counted us again and were then relieved by a new guard shift. "Look, the new escorts, those aren't SS, they are soldiers of the Army."

The teacher noted this significant change. He was standing next to Jancsi Kádár and me and praised the advantages of the soldiers of the German Army. We climbed into the goods train, fifty people per carriage. Twenty five each into the front and back. The centre part of the carriage, where the sliding door was, remained empty. This was reserved for the escort. Five soldiers climbed into the carriage with us. They divided the centre part off from us by means of narrow boards and sat down on benches they had brought with them. Leaning their rifles against their legs they began to converse with each other.

We took our places too just as we had a few days ago in Camp C, half-sitting, half-lying, pressed close together. There was room to do no more than that here either. We conversed in whispers. After a while, the carriage doors were closed and locked with chains, then an additional lock. It got dark. The guards lit lamps. We waited for an hour or two in this state and then the locomotive whistled, there was a sudden shuddering and the train started to move, for an unknown destination. After a few minutes the lights of Auschwitz and Birkenau had vanished once and for all.

Dachau-Transit

We had been on our way for two days. Virtually nothing happened. The cramped situation, the lack of mobility, put us into a dulled, drowsy state. Standing in one spot didn't help either. There was no room to have any movement. The rations distributed before the beginning of the journey were already consumed. We were hungry and there was no water either. The guards told us that until we arrived, there would be nothing to eat nor anything to drink. One person died. He was sick, he spoke in a confused manner, wept, and then became quiet. On the morning of the second day he was cold and already rigid. There were no doctors among us. We didn't know what he died of. He stayed with us. After all, fifty men hat to arrive in this carriage. There was no corner where we might have laid him. So he remained in the row in which he had been seated. The guards gave us an old blanket with which we covered him.

We stopped for an unusually long time at one station. We could see nothing through the barred windows, and the doors were not opened. Hours could have passed. Night fell. We didn't know what happened. We asked our guards "Where are we?" They gave us no answer. When it had got completely dark, the people discussed with increasing anxiety; "Where can we be? What are we waiting for?" One of the guards called something out of the carriage door and got into conversation with a soldier who was just going past. Briefly, he told us what he had found out.

We are in Dachau. Five hundred people are staying here. The rest moves on. "Who is going to be among these five hundred? . . . Ten carriages . . . The first ten or the last ten? . . ." I didn't know in which carriage we were, the others didn't know either. "If we are in the middle, then we are sure to go on. If we are at one end of the train . . . question of luck." We had all heard something of Dachau already and what we had heard was not even approximate to the whole truth. Everybody shuddered at the thought of staying here. We were in luck. Our guards thought so too. There was suddenly great movement on the station. Hard steps, dogs barking, commands, creaking of locks, whistling of trains and shunting locomotives. Midnight must have been well past when it became quiet again. One of our guards looked through a crack in the door, turned around to us and said "You are in luck. You're going on." After a while, the train did indeed move on.

At dawn we arrived. Kaufering. This was the first time I heard the name of this little town. More precisely, I did not hear it at all, but read it. The train stopped. The sliding doors were opened. We stood on a small, clean railway station. On the front of the main building there was a large sign saying: "Kaufering".

Two weeks had passed since our departure from Cluj. For the first time we saw civilian population again. After the SS men with their German shepherd dogs, after the Block Elders, after the CAPOs, this was a relatively soothing aspect. When we got out, the civilian population disappeared from the railway station. We lined up between the tracks: one thousand five hundred, four to five dead among us. Five hundred had remained in Dachau. At this time, they could really already be reckoned among the dead. No one heard any more about them, no-one knows what happened to them. Not one of them lived to see the liberation.

Behind the railway station, a peaceful little town was just waking up. The War had not left any traces here yet. Perhaps the population of Kaufering had not even seen those transported for forced labour. As we passed, they took their bedding, which they had hung out to air, back inside and closed the windows. In the streets, people pressed themselves against the walls of the houses. We were the outcasts of the civilian world. We now had more contact with our guards than we had with the indifferent citizens, who looked at us inquisitively here and there. Yet this view of the streets we were walking along aroused many memories in me. Then this morning meeting with the civilian population was behind us. We got onto a main road.

"Moll Night Shift" and "Labour Camp Number Three"

Camp Number Three was about four kilometres away from Kaufering. After Auschwitz, it created a friendly impression – a complex in the shape of a brick in between green meadows. Small, round, tin walls, tin roofs, so-called bunkers, larger huts covered with canvas, and some timber huts with kitchen, a rations store and the CAPOs' quarters. Round about, double thick, impenetrable barbed wire, with watch-towers thirty to forty metres apart. The wire fences here were not electrified. On the outside of the barbed wire, there were flowers, gardens and friendly timber huts with green blinds waiting for the guard staff.

Labor Camp Number Three was new. It had only just been finished. It had been built by the prisoners of Camp Number One a few kilometres away. It was waiting for us, empty. When we had settled into our bunkers and huts, we thought that we had come out of Hell into a convalescent home without any transition. Paul and I got into a bunker where there was space for twelve people. The other ten were acquaintances who also came from Cluj.

We were given eating utensils and blankets. Sawdust was spread out on the floor of the bunkers. It was soft. We could stretch out comfortably on the floor and even cover ourselves. We were not cold ... we slept long ... banal pleasures ... from the perspective of normal life, we were still in a miserable position, but compared with Auschwitz, we lived splendidly. Comfortable places to lie, blankets, seven hours' peaceful sleep: it seemed to us that an unattainable dream had now become reality. We slept deeply and peacefully until the morning.

This quiet life lasted two days. We arranged our bunker, we cleaned the paths, rested and talked. In the mornings and afternoons, there was a roll-call, but not lasting hours as in Auschwitz. It was all over in an hour and a half. They counted us more frequently and made us practise removing and putting on our caps.

On the second day, we were divided into labor units, based on time and place of work. Together with Paul and three other inmates of our bunker, I was sent to a building site of the Moll Company and night shift at that. The abbreviation for our camp unit was "Moll night-shift".

In these two restful days, we managed more or less to get our hunger under control. We had starved for the second part of our journey. All the more satisfying were the rations in the new camp. At the beginning, three of us got a loaf of bread (approximately fifteen hundred grams), twenty or thirty grams of salami and ten grams of margarine or fat. Instead of salami we occasionally got artificial honey. In the mornings warm "ersatz" coffee and in the afternoons more than half a liter of warm food. The kitchen staff were taken out from ranks. In the first few days they tried to prove that they knew something of their art. In general, the entire camp command was - at least temporarily - provided from our transport. We were the first inmates of this camp after all. The Camp Commandant called a few men to him at random and from among these, chose those who spoke German well in order to use them as secretaries, Block Elders, CAPOs, head of the kitchen, and camp administrator. In the course of time, there were often new positions and those who already held office appointed the new functionaries. About five to six weeks after our arrival, "expert" CAPOs from Dachau arrived in our camp. For the most part, these were German criminals who had been sentenced to many years imprisonment, just like their notorious colleagues in Auschwitz. The most important positions were taken over by them; for example the Camp Elder, the kitchen CAPO (the head of the kitchen was degraded to cook), the CAPO of the Moll night-shift and the others became leaders of the labour units.

Work started on the third day. Roll-call took place in darkness and after that, individual units went out through the camp gates. "Left-two-three-four ... left ..." This refrain sounded less strict than in Auschwitz "Shift change at night! Back to the huts. Sleep! It's your turn in the evening". The NCO who had recorded the list of those present gave this command. He was a kindly, grey-haired, old man, tired of the War.

At lunch time, we had to clean the paths inside the camp. Afterwards we were relocated in the four large huts covered with canvas. Here there were also plank beds in several storeys. The huts were cooler, windy and less friendly than the little bunkers; but no-one was interested in our opinions. We put our blankets down and then went to the food distribution with our eating utensils. We already ate quickly, but could not be finished by the time we were summoned to roll-call again. The counting was short; there may have been some three hundred people there, allocated for the night shift. We started off, it was hardly six o'clock.

I cannot remember the details of our way, although we passed along it twice a day, mornings and evenings for nearly two months. In the beginning, having slept properly, we were rested and almost in a good mood. Later, increasingly exhausted and crushed. Our steps, initially precise and fast, dragged more and more with time. Despite the constant warnings and beatings of the CAPOs, we were only capable of improving our tempo for a short time. Our walk amounted to approximately five or six kilometres each way and led us through pastures, an isolated part of Kaufering, and then into the middle of the forest. The part of the town we went through each day always stirred up the past; just as the area round the railway station at our arrival did ... the houses, the people in their well-furnished apartments, inhabitants who spoke, lay down, got dressed, ate, rested, conversed with one another or read books – these inhabitants reminded us of home, of our families. Now I see in front of me again a large, tall half-timbered house with a pointed roof. In a window of the first floor, a young man, semi-naked, with tousled hair, a towel thrown over his shoulder, is rubbing his eyes. Later, an older woman takes his place, it might have been his mother. She shakes out a dusting cloth ... this milieu disappeared and melted in with the present landscape.

At seven in the evening, we arrived at our place of labor, an enormous building site in the middle of the forest. We were unable to recognize its purpose or its size. Nor did we discover it later even though we worked there for two months. This complex of buildings was not finished. Roads for cars, tracks for narrow gauge railways, small locomotives, countless carriages, piled up rails, sleepers, huge storage buildings, thousands and thousands of bags of cement, boards, beams and steel supports. The whole effort initially focussed on building a railway to make the concreting works of the great buildings possible. When we arrived, we were divided at once into small groups of twenty to forty men. These groups were guarded by one or two men, each under the command of an NCO or of a soldier of the "Organisation Todt". They gave us instructions and also determined what the individual groups were to do. After a few days, a foreman was appointed within each group, he then became the CAPO.

The first night, I was assigned to concreting. Together with Paul and Uncle Hugo, an elderly relative of Paul's, a few others from Cluj and a group from Transdanubia. Under the instructions of people belonging to the "Organisation Todt", we mixed concrete and poured it into moulds. Around us, there was great noise and confusion. The small railway rattled, a little group worked on laying rails, great concrete-mixing machines crashed and two or three bulldozers angrily tore out the roots of felled trees and piled them on a heap. In the midst of all this noise, there was, in addition, a confusion of languages, like in the building of the Tower of Babel. German machine operators, Ukrainian "volunteers" who had been brought to Germany, a little further on a group dressed in prisoners' clothing speaking Lithuanian and one speaking Yiddish, and then we Hungarians. Uncle Darvas, a sedate farmer of about fifty from Western Hungary, with a moustache and military stance, was always trying to avoid working. He preferred to devote himself to "organizational tasks" and loudly provided us with advice. He ran around pompously and occasionally got into conversation with the "Organisation Todt" supervisor and with the guards. He was trying to get himself a little position in this way. We let him. He was the oldest. We were able to endure the work more easily. Soon he was CAPO and later the Block Elder. He behaved in a relatively humane manner.

Paul and I regarded concrete mixing as physical training, as sport. We breathed regularly, we shovelled with a sweeping movement in a steady rhythm so as to distribute the strain on all our muscles equally. We only had to keep an eye that the work did not proceed too fast. It was to be a sporting activity and not profit the Moll Company too much. One shovel of concrete into the mould and one that missed if the overseer was not looking. The guard was not concerned with the work. He went for walks, he smoked, he lay lazily on his blanket, but had his rifle handy at all times. We worked almost without a break from seven in the evening until midnight. The older men laughed at us and warned "You are working too much, you should have a rest in between." "We are doing a three-month summer training course. The war will be over by then.", said Paul.

During a half-hour break at midnight, we got warm barley soup. Then we worked on until half-past six in the morning. We packed up our tools and returned to the camp. We were tired. On the way we met the group that was on its way to the day shift. When we arrived in the camp, it was already past eight. Roll-call took a fairly long time. The superior of the kindly old NCO had come to the camp to check the roll-call of those returning from the night shift. He was a coarse and, as it later transpired, merciless sergeant, who constantly fiddled with his riding whip. He did not like our "Caps off!" and he had us practise it twenty times. Then the entire roll-call had to be repeated. Although there were only three hundred of us, the procedure took two hours. Then came the distribution of "coffee". But we no longer had any great desire to drink it.

While we washed ourselves, we recovered somewhat. As in Auschwitz, there were iron pipes with holes in them, which were to substitute for taps. The pipes and trough-like washing facilities were in the open and the water did not drip out but poured out in a strong stream. We were able to wash ourselves calmly and without being hit. We just had to sacrifice our sleep time for it. It was probably about half-past ten when we arrived dead-tired in our huts. I stretched out on my plank bed and fell asleep at once; I could not even cover myself with a blanket.

We might have slept for some three or four hours when we were woken up. We were still sleepy and exhausted. The camp had to be cleaned. The chief commandant was coming in the afternoon. The day-shift was at work, so that we were the only ones left to carry out this unforeseen labour. We cleaned.

After the cleaning, we still had about half an hour. We did not even return to the huts. We lay down in the grass. Then came the food distribution, gobbling the food down, roll-call and departure.

Our good mood of the day before had vanished. We marched tiredly and apathetically. In the forest behind Kaufering, we met the day-shift returning from the building site. In the first rows, four prisoners carried a person, bleeding and disfigured to the point of being unrecognizable on a makeshift stretcher. The first casualty of the labor camp. I did not know him. They said that he was deployed laying rails. The supervisor of "Organisation Todt" had struck him over a trifle. Thereupon they exchanged words, in the course of which the supervisor struck the prisoner in the face with a spade. He fell down the slope and got into the scoop of the bulldozer which crushed him.

We continued without a word. We arrived at our work-place in a depressed mood.

"Under rest conditions like these you can't work in a sporty manner", said Paul. "The old doctor was right. We were only ruining ourselves" "You have to dawdle, better play tennis at home, in the autumn." In the second night we too spared ourselves just like the older men.

Uncle Darvas didn't work at all any more. He moved around to help the man from the "Organisation Todt" deploying the men. He then ran pompously between the little groups, screaming, waving a little staff but despite this, encouraging the people lovingly: "Zum Donnerwetter! (Damn it!)" – I learnt this curse from him – "Holy Mother of God! You are to work! Faster, faster! Don't worry if I scream as though I were on the spit. But if I scream then the damned supervisor doesn't stick his nose in anywhere. It's better if I shout; that doesn't hurt anyone. All you have to do is pretend to work when I shout. You have to keep moving. If he is a long way away you don't have to put anything in your shovels. He doesn't see it anyway and the more slowly the building proceeds the faster the war ends ... Well, and now you can have a rest, he is looking in the other direction. When I shout, it means that he is keeping an eye on us again and for you that means that you have to work ..."

Uncle Darvas walked pompously behind the man from "Organisation Todt". We smiled "He will be the right CAPO for us". In fact he really was right: but unfortunately I didn't stay in this group for long. We rested for about half an hour and then Uncle Darvas voice resounded again. He spoke faultless German except for a western Hungarian accent. "Mr Supervisor you can go and lie down for an hour or two. I assure you that the people will work without interruption"

He roared again. That was a warning that we had to work. His voice came from the railway embankment. The supervisor must have been satisfied with what he had seen. Everybody worked as though his life and liberty depended on it. I tell you that they are working here, said Uncle Darvas to the supervisor and then he screamed at us "Go on, go on! Keep it up! You only have to move a little bit longer. Now you have to put a bit of cement on the shovel – he is coming to you now. The son of a whore. For God's sake! Faster, faster! He's so tired that he'll die soon. He's just waiting to be asked. But he'll go straight to the devil –. When he does, you can take turns at sleeping yourselves. Go on, go on! Keep it up! I've got quite hoarse from all this yelling and this swine still won't go away! Ah, at last he can bring himself to do it. He's turning around, yawning, you see his eyes are shutting already. Off he goes, faster, faster, I don't mean you this time, I mean him. In five minutes the first of you can go and sleep, but if possible between the trees, in the darkness. The others have to stay at their places and move around a little. You don't have to be afraid of the guard. He's a decent chap. He comes from Vienna. He's only interested in the number present. As far as he's concerned the whole gang could sleep until morning. He's not interested in the work. He's had enough of the war. We only have to watch out for the supervisor, that arse hole. And I will watch out for him! If anything happens you'll hear my voice, don't worry!"

We didn't doubt it. We had heard old Darvas' voice from miles away. He shouted louder then the rattling of the train, the noise of the machines and the voices of twenty rough supervisors shouting orders. I stood around until food distribution at midnight, leaning on my shovel. Whenever anyone came past I worked. Paul was asleep under the trees and with him every second one of us. After the food distribution, the others were to keep watch and we, the second half, ought to have been able to sleep. But it didn't happen that way. The "Organisation Todt"-man got up to eat and didn't lie down again. After the food distribution everybody had to work until the morning.

During the day, we were able to sleep for only four hours. A short dog fight took place above our huts. English fighters shot down a German plane and the burning wreck fell onto the fence of our camp. The crew was incinerated. We of the night shift had to remove the pieces of wreckage. The wire fence had to be repaired as well. After that, food distribution, roll-call and then, we marched off. This procedure was repeated day after day. Half the time rationed to us for rest, sometimes two thirds, was denied us. There were always some jobs to do.

If we were able to sleep for two or three hours while on the building site of the Moll Company, it was all tolerable. But sometimes even Uncle Darvas' cunning didn't help. Sometimes the supervisor was on our backs the whole night. Sometimes a control came to check the work. Then we had to work the whole night through: Eleven hours, the way to and from about three hours, three perhaps three and a half hours work at the camp, one hour roll-call, five and a half or at best six hours remained for rest, for sleep, for eating and for washing etc. At the end of the first week, we were exhausted. We could hardly wait for the Saturday night in order to sleep in peace and quiet at last. We had been told that the night before Sunday was free. But after roll-call came the awful surprise. "Moll night-shift, line up" there was no respite from work. We had to march off again. And another new week without hope for a peaceful night.

"Perhaps we can stay in camp next Saturday," we encouraged each other. But the next Saturday was a long way off – seven nights and seven days separated us from it. Finally they too passed, and the next Saturday evening arrived. We did not go to work. After the food distribution we returned to the huts. I was not sleepy but very tired. I lay down. Paul lay down on the neighbouring bed. We talked, mainly about memories of home. I fell asleep. Paul talked on for a while before he noticed that he no longer had a listener. In this night, I dreamed about my mother for the first time. We were at home, in the dining room, at the table. My brother was there. So was my uncle who ate with us every Sunday. The soup was brought in. Golden yellow, steaming, meat broth. My mother served ... Later this dream often recurred. Nothing ever happened. We were just all together, sitting around our dinner table. The dream never went beyond serving the soup.

On the Sunday, we went to the roll-call rested. It didn't even bother us that it took a long time. We had time and leisure to wash ourselves comfortably and to wash our clothes. Around noon, we lay down in the grass next to the huts. The sun shone and it was pleasantly warm. It was pleasant to think of the evening, especially as we still had some five hours before we marched off. We talked with the people of the day shift. About two weeks had passed since we had talked with them. We left every night before they got back and when we returned to the camp in the mornings they were already gone. I made some new acquaintances: Two young men my own age from Transdanubia, Josef Hausner and Laci Vajda. Like Paul and me, they had done their university entrance examinations in the spring of 1944, shortly before their deportation. It turned out that we lived in the same hut, and that they were also working night-shift for the Moll Company. They also liked discussing literature. Laci Vajda wrote poems himself. I think he was very gifted. As Josef told us, the poet Aprily praised Laci's poems, of which he had seen a number. He ranked him with the most talented young poets in Transdanubia. Later, we were frequently together. Laci Vajda had exchanged a few sheet of paper and a pencil for food with somebody on the building site. He often wrote. If he was not too exhausted and hungry, he would also recite his poems, his own poems or some by Karinthy, Babits, Kosztolányi and Aprily, mostly the "Antigon" by Aprily. He thought this fitted our situation best ... I shall never forget the refrain: "Dark is the sand of Acheron – Haimon, best beloved, here I must die."

He did not believe that we would survive the end of the War. He did not believe that he would get home again, and he did not get home again. His father, his old uncle, Dr Vajda and he all died in January 1945. I do not know exactly when. I had typhus and could scarcely walk for three weeks. When I recovered, I began to look for my friends who had also been ill. Laci Vajda and the greyhaired Uncle Vajda were not there ..."

On that Sunday evening, we went to work in a good mood. Days and weeks passed. It happened less and less often that we were able to rest for an hour or two during the night. The building activity was being pushed ahead. The "Organisation Todt"-man checked the work strictly and spent more and more time among us, cursing, threatening and driving us to work. One night he saw a prisoner – somewhat older than me, from Dézs – throw half a shovel-full of cement between the trees. He leapt at him, tore the shovel out of his hand and hit him on the head with the sharp edge. "Damned swine, I'll teach you what it means to sabotage our war!" The shovel struck the young man on the forehead; a dull thud and blood flowed from his split head. The young man fell over, unconscious. Our guard from Vienna watched this scene from where he was lying. It had only lasted a few minutes. He stood up, went over and hit the work supervisor in the face.

Wild animal! The supervisor looked shocked at the guard soldier, turned without a word and walked away. Two or three days later, this guard was replaced. A sickly Prussian from Danzig, evidently no longer fit for service at the front, with a gloomy gaze and shaking hands, was put in his place. He kept on asserting that the English and the Jews had started the war with the aim of destroying Germany. But they had not reckoned with the Fuehrer! – As far as he himself was concerned, he tried to take vengeance on the Jews. The English were too far away for him. The good Viennese guard had vanished. He was said to have been sent to the front line. The battered young man from Dézs was carried back to the camp by other prisoners on a stretcher. He was treated in the hospital for a few day, but he did not regain consciousness, and died. Naturally, no-one reported that "Organisation Todt"-man to start proceedings against him. A single blow to the face was the only punishment for murder. And for this blow he was even vindicated. A humane German soldier may well have paid for it with his life.

Later, months later, at the beginning of winter, this work supervisor who had become a murderer headed a group of timber cutters who were to fell trees in a snowed in fir forest. He marked the trunks that were suitable for building and had to be cut down. Somebody accidentally bumped him, whereupon he fell over and at that moment was killed by a tree crashing down. It was an accident – he died in the fulfilment of his duties for Fuehrer and Fatherland. An inquiry revealed no suspicious circumstances. All we knew was that the tree that fell on him was cut by the group from Dézs. Perhaps they were friends of the murdered young man . . .

On the building site our life was made hell by the new guard. The "Organisation Todt"-man could have slept if he had wanted to, the guard drove us on without a break. He never slept for a moment and only very seldom did he take a rest. At most, he would sit on his greatcoat for a quarter of an hour at a time, cursing or whistling military marches. Otherwise he was constantly among us to check whether our shovels were full enough. He would constantly run his shaking, freckled hands through his pale red hair and complain, his face turned heavenwards, because we were working so slowly. "Work faster! Much faster. This is no home for lazy-bones! Get on with it or else the devil will get you!" In order to give his words more weight he would slash around him with his dog whip at those that he could reach. Sometimes he struck people in the ribs or on the arm with the but of his rifle if he thought that they didn't have enough cement on their shovels.

We didn't even get any peace in camp during the day, although the time was supposed to be for rest. After the wreckage from the plane crash, there was something new every day. There was some work or other for the night shift to do almost every day instead of resting. If there was nothing else, well then, sweeping the paths or spreading gravel on the paths between the huts so that everything might be beautiful and neat when the camp commandant made his daily rounds. Ultimately, it made no difference what they made us do and it was actually all the same to us whether it was heavy or easy work. We had to be on our feet anyway and hadn't had an opportunity to sleep properly for weeks ... the weaker men staggered with tiredness and the Sunday we all longed for often brought disappointment. Almost every second week we were deprived of our day off ...

On the way to and from work, people dragged their feet, stumbled and occasionally fell over. At work our movements became fumbling, many dropped their tools – in our group, things like that were punished by a blow with the rifle butt. There were also some who fell from scaffolding or while carrying sleepers, who tripped over the rails and got under the wheels of the trains. Illness increased as did accidents. A death no longer caused much of a stir, nor did it arouse any pity unless it was a close friend. Illness, accident, death were daily events we had become as accustomed to as we had to the roll-call and the work. Constant exhaustion made people indifferent. On those Sundays when we remained in the camp, when we had a break from Moll nightshift we spoke less and less with one another. We washed ourselves slowly, we washed, dried and repaired our filthy, sweat soaked, patched and torn underwear. We slept a great deal. If the weather was fine, we lay down in the grass next to the huts and gazed silently into the sky or talked, tiredly and haltingly of home or of our dreams: "What it will be like when the war is finished. It will be fine ... but we won't be there any more" – Laci Vajda now only wrote despairing and gloomy poems and read from them. We discussed how we might get away from Moll night-shift. But we found no practicable solution.

We were not skilled enough ... there were some who changed to another labor group or to a different unit after four of five night shifts. But there were not many of these, it was only the sly and those able to cope with life. They knew in time where more workers were required next or a new labor group was assembled, or where someone had died and his job become vacant. They immediately applied to the group leader responsible, sometimes they simply moved into the hut of the other labor group or else they exchanged their job for a part of their rations, sometimes in instalments dragging on for weeks. There was always somebody ready to do that. It did sometimes happen that everything went smoothly, but it also happened that a supervisor complained to the Camp Elder and that they took very strict measures against the man who had offended against work discipline. These punishments were beatings, being locked up and deprivation of rations. Those punished often died during the punishment. Uncle Darvas was among the first to get out of the Moll night-shift. Only a few days after the replacement of our Viennese guard. I don't know how he did it; one evening he remained in the hut and then moved into another one and didn't go to work any more. Later, on a free Sunday, I discovered that he had become deputy Block Elder in one of the huts. In the winter he was promoted to Block Elder.

Almost two months after beginning the Moll night-shift, I at least managed to be transferred to another night-shift group. When we were lining up before marching off, the CAPO of a group working on the railway embankment began to shout that he was one man short. This CAPO was a German criminal sentenced to forced labour and had arrived from Dachau not long before. I chose quickly, ran over and stood in the row. The CAPO did not know his people yet. He thought that I belonged to him and had only run late. He picked up a stone and threw it at me but missed. He cursed for a while but finally got over it. The other prisoners said nothing. A few minutes later my former CAPO began to rant and curse "Wretched bunch! When I counted just now the number of those present was correct and now there is a man missing, has somebody absented himself?"

My former comrades said nothing. Others did not see me when I ran from their rows. The CAPO got furious and threatened to break the bones of the absent man or have him locked up without food or drink for ten days. Perhaps he would be merciful and just have him hanged. He thrashed around himself with a stick and ran up and down among the other groups checking the faces. I hoped he wouldn't recognize me. I had hardly had anything to do with him. I was in luck. The old NCO arrived who wrote down the number of those present. He asked what had happened. "No doubt somebody felt ill just before lining up and hasn't been entered into the sick list yet." That was to be checked.

He was right. A few minutes before line up a young man had fallen unconscious onto the path that led to the night-shift workers' huts and had been carried into the sick bay. He had not yet regained consciousness. Thus the number present was in order. I could stay in my new group, in the group from which the unconscious man came. My old group marched off with one man absent. The CAPO thought he had made a mistake when the number present was correct at first count.

I was now away from Paul. I regretted it. I felt very lonely. But I wanted to get away from this half-mad raging guard. After a few days, Paul also managed to change his labor group even if still within the night-shift. But we didn't get together despite that. One or two months later, in the autumn, we accidentally met in the same work place, in a gallery and in the night shift. My new labor group was working on the track of the narrow gauge railway. We were building the embankments, we carried the sleepers and laid new rails. The building site was spreading out more and more and so the railway lines had to be extended, since this railway – it transported the soil, the gravel, the sleepers and the rails – was also the supply line on the site. Cement, bricks, mortar, timber were transported. The work was tiring and much harder than mixing concrete. I had to get used to it first. Shovelling I could do. Now I had to learn to balance sleepers on my shoulder – if you didn't balance them properly they were twice as heavy –, had to learn to carry them without a break along the narrow embankment between the rails, between the rocks, between the sleepers already laid. I had to learn to tip dump-trucks, unload rails from the carriages and carry them in step with eight, ten, or eleven other workers without stumbling: build embankments with the soil brought by the dump-trucks, the gravel and clay which had to be flattened and stamped firm before the next load arrived. In addition, there was the constant need to watch for trains coming and going and leap clear, since if one were too late one got under the wheels hopelessly ... but it had been worth it. I got far away from the hated guard from Danzig. The guard here was only rude on the way, on the site the "Organisation Todt"-officer did everything. Our guard had transferred all his work to the supervisor and spent the entire night smoking his pipe behind the embankment. I had got out of the thin concrete in which I had stood for six, seven or eight hours at night. Gradually it was eating away my thick shoe soles. The supervisor of the "Organisation Todt" was energetic but despite his determined expression he was kindly and an honest man.

In the beginning I thought that it would be impossible or at least very risky to do any damage or to loaf occasionally at my new job. But I was wrong. Once in a while the supervisor himself gave us an example of how one might cause damage. As I discovered from the other workmates in this group, he had been a railway man before the war. When he declined an invitation to join the Party, he was conscripted into the army, sent to the Eastern Front in 1941, was wounded and after his convalescence sent back to the first line of battle. After being wounded a second time he was unfit for combat and for this reason was allocated to the "Organisation Todt" for railway work. He did not believe in the Fuehrer nor in the victory of the Nazis. He was withdrawn and quiet. He hardly talked to us and if he did, only when it was absolutely necessary. Occasionally, mostly after midnight, when there were no Germans in the vicinity, he himself tipped a dump-truck over with such force that the gravel or clay fell not on the edge of the embankment but behind it, into the depths. With teeth clenched, he cursed as though the whole thing annoyed him, although he had done it on purpose. Now and again, he saw one of us allow the load of a truck or a sleeper to slide down the embankment, or when carrying cement, trip and fall into a puddle. In cases like this, he growled or, cursing loudly, said that we should work more carefully. He was cautious. But he reported nobody, nor did he hit anybody. Nobody was friendly with him, but everybody respected him; perhaps one or other of us liked him a bit too. We liked the work of building the railway embankment, even though it was hard work: You could hardly have a rest because the trains passed at regular intervals. We caused damage where we could. You had the feeling that you had at least done something, something positive in the battle. You were contributing a little bit, even if it was only very tiny and insignificant in reality, to undermine the Hitler regime. We envied the soldiers who were able to fight against fascism with their rifles in the front line.

My new job cheered me up a little. I was in a better mood but even that could not stall the ever-increasing exhaustion. The hours of work were not reduced, the intensity of the work was increased more and more and the breaks during the day were cut again. The night-shift workers were isolated. Their external appearance was also different to that of the other camp inmates. Later, at the end of autumn and in the winter, when the cold began and food rations were reduced, people died like flies. The loaf of bread, which in the beginning was to fill three people, became smaller and was divided among six, then among eight, in December even among twelve. By this time, the salami and the Sunday sweets had vanished without trace. Most of the dead were from our ranks. Of those who had spent the summer in a rotating shift with the Moll Company, only about eight to ten per cent were alive in the spring. Not even half of those would have lived to see another summer, the summer after our liberation in 1945.

The fact that my shoes had collapsed in the meantime contributed to physical degeneration in my case. The cement had had its effect, the triple sole had gone through, and no-one knew where it might be repaired. The top part too began to rip, the leather broke, in some places it became hard and rough. I got blisters on my feet. On the way to and from work, every step hurt. My entire concentration was directed to walking and to the small unevennesses on the path. The forests and meadows, the little town we walked through with its petit bourgeois atmosphere, it open windows, some of them lit up, the people behind the windows in their everyday civilian life – all disappeared behind the stinging pain. And yet this route was the only thing that made me feel bound to the past, that kept the past awake in me and shook me awake from the nightmare of Auschwitz, that reminded me what there was in the world and that there would come a time without nightmare. The last few days of the third week in the embankment group consumed me with pain. It was raining as well and it was dirty. The water and the dirt got into my shoes. I had to consider every movement and tried to work in one spot as long as I could. If possible I shovelled. I moved to one side only to get out of the way of a train. One night, there was nothing more to shovel, so that I had to carry sleepers. I had to walk. I was giddy, I must have had a fever. I stumbled between the tracks, stood in a puddle, up to my knees in thin mud, I fell over and the sleeper slipped from my shoulder onto my arm. I don't know who helped me to stand up, but he also helped me to put the sleeper back on my shoulder. I carried it on. I don't know how long it took, I don't know how many sleepers I carried around in that night. I thought it would be good to fall over and have a train roll over me. That would put an end to everything. Then the train came . . . and I moved two paces away from the rails. The rain stopped, the sky cleared, and the stars shone in the sky. Later, probably past midnight, the sirens howled. The lights went out, no more trains came, work stopped. We could have a rest. We went to the bottom of the embankment. We pulled the bottom boards out from a stack of boards and lay down on them. What bliss . . . From a long way away, we heard the sound of motors, bombs exploding and the roar of cannon. I paid no attention to it. I fell asleep. Munich or Augsburg were being bombed. The bombers had probably flown over Kaufering. The alarm cannot have lasted long. It was still before dawn when the lamps glared again and the locomotives began to whistle. Work went on. My comrades had to wake me. I was still exhausted but the short sleep had refreshed me a little and I recovered. I carried sleepers until the early morning. I regretted that Kaufering had not been bombed. They probably did not know that there was a building site of the Moll Company here. If they had bombed here we would have been able to sleep until the early morning, or for ever . . .

As far as I can remember, I only worked two more nights on the railway embankment after the alarm. I got into a group which dug trenches also on the Moll Company building site and again in the night shift. I cannot remember how I got into this group. Nor can I recall whether it was the beginning or middle of September, I did not ask for it nor did I want it, but I did not have anything against it either. I didn't care. I can't remember my workmates either, none of my friends was in this group. I can only remember that we were in a forest and dug ditches winding between the thick roots of the old trees. We were told that they were for some pipes. We had little light, we were constantly working in the semi-dark. There were many small accidents. The men stood close together and it occurred more than once that the injured each other with their shovels. The wounds often became infected. But I didn't have to walk too much and that made up for everything. My shoes got wet anew every night because the ditch was covered with a layer of mud, even if it was fine weather. The NCO of the "Organisation Todt", our supervisor, was a crude Saxon from Transylvania who had an evil temper. He swore in Hungarian and drove us on for most of the night, except for the one or two hours when he left us in the care of the guard, so that he could have a sleep himself. Nearly every morning he sent a written report to the camp commandant saying that X or Y would need to be punished because he hadn't worked hard enough. Ten to fifteen strokes with a stick were the result and the fact that the punished man was unable to work better or walk

or move. And yet the work had to continue even if more slowly and agonizingly ...
In the ditch, by the trunks of the old trees, in the constant semi-dark, I tried to get as far away from the lights as I could. The large trees caught the light, I learnt to sleep standing up. I supported my hands and my chin on the shovel pushed into the dirt and slept in an almost upright position, sometimes for two, three or even five minutes until the shout of the supervisor "get moving" resounded in my vicinity. Sometimes I also woke up because in the dream, my muscles relaxed and my knees sagged. Then I started, stretched my muscles with short, jerky movements and continued digging. A few times, maybe four times altogether – I had spent almost three weeks digging in the forest – it happened that I simply did not wake up when my muscles relaxed, so my hands slipped from the handle of the shovel and I fell down. I came to, at the bottom of the ditch, wet and dirty. The workmates next to me helped me to stand up, they rubbed my back and went on shovelling. Their laughter was not ill intentioned, it was more full of pity and instinctive. They knew why it happened, they knew how unpleasant it was to have to wait for morning filthy and in wet clothes. It had probably happened to all of them. In these cases, I shook the whole night, tried to work faster and not to fall asleep again. But I didn't succeed in warming myself up until the morning in the camp under my blanket.
Maybe three or four weeks passed in this way. In between there was only one interruption to the night work, from Saturday to Sunday in the second week. On Saturday night after roll-call, the night-shift workers went to their huts immediately almost without exception exhausted and hungry.
With two daily rations of bread in my hand and on them the twenty grams of margarine for the next few days and eight sweets in my pocket – there were some acid sweets on that Saturday – I went straight to my bed. I had decided to eat myself full and to sleep in. If need be I'd eat everything and on Sunday I'd just have to make do with one coffee and the soup at night. Although my foot hurt a great deal I was very satisfied with my decision. I awaited the evening piously as though it were a great feast day. During that time of constant hunger and exhaustion, there was hardly a greater holiday than a quiet night when you could eat your fill and have a rest. I had made my bed and straightened the blanket. I asked Paul for his knife made from a tin can. Paul sat next to me on the bed, ate and swung his legs contentedly. I cut the two-day rations of bread and spread the entire margarine equally thinly over them. Then I undressed. I folded my clothes and put them under my head. I stretched out covered myself with the blanket and began to eat my prepared margarine sandwiches. Paul took his knife back and said, shaking his head "Your'e getting your bed full of crumbs." – "I'll shake my blanket out in the morning. Now I want to feel good, so don't give me a lecture. I'd rather you told me a story". – "The story has died. But somebody, I think Laci Vajda has a tattered book: Anatole France 'Thais'. About sixty pages. Jancsi Kádár

found it on the way to work. If I can find it I'll read to you from it". – "That would be nice."
I continued to eat my bread and margarine, chewing slowly, almost sucking each individual morsel. It tasted better than my favourite cakes had in the past: rum and chestnut cake or almond cake. In the meantime, Paul had got to the last bite of the ration he had allowed himself for this night; Paul divided his food rations very carefully: and he put an acid sweet into his mouth. He went around between the beds looking for the book about Thais. Laci Vajda really did have it and lent it to us. Two minutes later he got into the bed next to me with a victorious look and held the yellowed torn dirty pages under my nose. A book: a strange feeling went through me, these tattered pages stirred up the past in me again. This was the first time I had seen a book since before my arrival in Auschwitz. It did not have a fresh print smell, no soft satin cover, no rustling paper, nor did it have a title or a beginning or an end, but it was a book. Melancholy thoughts from far away filled the book, which had been so closely bound up with my earlier life that it almost became one with it. It was a book, a messenger from old, happy hours, an image and a memorial. When Paul held it under my nose it caused me almost painful sensations. My eyes became blurred for a moment, my throat tightened, I couldn't swallow and then the tension eased. Paul sat down in his bed and I continued to eat my bread and margarine.
The first few words were incomprehensible. The beginning of the sentence got lost somewhere in the big, wide world. "That doesn't matter, read out the first few words too. Don't let a single word get lost from this fraction of a book". Paul began to read: "... coups de fouet, la musique et la prosodie, et elle flagellait avec des lanières de cuir ces jambes divines, quand elles ne se levaient pas en mesure au son de la cithare ..."
I was able to remember these words for a long time. But when I read this novel again years later, this time from beginning to end, and I came upon this part on page 115, it aroused paradoxical feelings in me. These words which, in Kaufering, conjured up memories of my civilian life, now evoked the atmosphere of the concentration camp. I knew about Thais' childhood, her love of Lollius; but the beautiful story which on that Saturday evening transported me into a happy dream world now made memories crash in upon me and opened a path into the past, to images I did not like to see.
The pages we had in our hands then came from the second part of the novel. The title of the chapter decorated every second page: "Le Papyrus". Paul read on about Thais who learnt by being smacked how to make music, to recite, to dance, in order to amuse the rich in Antioch. She danced and played. Lollius, the son of the pro-consul fell in love with her and she with Lollius. They loved each other for six months, until the spell suddenly broke and Thais felt empty and lonely. They became extranged and Thais left him. It is sad to stay with somebody that one has greatly loved, sad as though she had never loved him. Later she became an actress, very beautiful and very

talented. Porters and street sweepers gladly gave up their bread if this meant they could affort a ticket to see Thais acting. At the climax of her success, she returned to Alexandria where she had been born. The whole town lay at her feet. The beautiful young men, the rich old men and the scholars. Among them Nicias, a rich, still young, sceptical philosopher. But his doubting wisdom was a challenge to the beautiful artist and worried her. Thais did not doubt, she believed in everything. She believed in Christ, in Syrian idols, she was superstitious, believed in miracles, in saints, in Kaldeus magus, in black magic, in false prophets and in all manner of deceivers. Nicias' words, which doubted everything, did not help against her fear of death, nor did his wisdom, which scorned everything. Thais wanted proof, she wanted sure knowledge and no doubts. She wanted to know the secrets of life and began to read the philosophers; but she did not understand them ...
My friend did not speak good French, his pronunciation was not perfect. While he read, he hesitated and despite this, the words sounded in my ears. It was a real holiday, unexpected and with a ceremony which I had not even hoped for, and which Paul, without knowing it, performed like a High Priest.
One page followed after another and the missing events, which made a gloomy picture at first, became brighter and brighter.
With the blanket pulled up to my ears, I warmed up and the slowly eaten bread and margarine satisfied my hunger. Calmly relaxed in the warmth I yielded to Paul's words and enjoyed the mixed taste of margarine and bread. When the slices I had spread were finished, I began to nibble the remaining uncut bread of my two-day ration. Although it was hard and black, not fresh but musty, it tasted good even without margarine. Paul's words gradually merged together, the pictures conjured up vanished, they became cloudy and independent of the words ... Thais began to read the philosophers but she didn't understand them ... I heard that, then I fell asleep. Paul continued reading for a while. The next day he told me that he had looked over to me while turning a page and had only then noticed that I was asleep. Apparently I was smiling. Next to my face was a relic of bread. I must have fallen asleep very happy. The Sunday passed like all the others in which we had been able to sleep the night before, with washing, laundry and resting. We arranged a poetry reading with Paul, Joska Hausner, Laci Vajda and Jancsi Kádár in front of the hut on the grass. We read out the fraction of the book of Thais, which unfortunately did not proceed without interruption since a few pages were missing inside this part. During the reading Jancsi Kádár wept. "I can't stand it any more ... I want to die ... I've had enough ... I can't go on ... ." He repeated these words again and again at intervals of about half an hour and he wept. He was greatly weakened and the strength of his nerves diminished; nonetheless he did endure it for months. When he did die in the winter, it was not a natural death, he was murdered. But that happened much later.

The Sunday meal that remained for me consisted of a piece of bread, a bitter black coffee in the morning and a soup in the evening. In addition, there were the eight acid sweets that I sucked lying in the grass. Although I was hungry, I thought contentedly of the night before.

On the Sunday night, when we marched off again to work for the Moll Company, I marched somewhat more rested and also more hopefully. My abused foot hurt me the entire time and yet I still had the desire and the strength to admire the idyll of the open windows of Kaufering. The mood of happiness I had experienced on the Saturday night warmed me for two or three more days, but then it was crushed by the pain, the work, the exhaustion. The festiveness disappeared in the every-day world. Monotony reigned, blunt and with numbing exhaustion.

It might have been eight to ten days or rather nights after that Saturday that it happened. It was darker in the trench than usual, because two of the lamps intended for us were urgently needed on another building site. The man working next to me in the semi-gloom – I can no longer remember his face or his name, only his glasses, his stooped, debilitated figure and his grey hair – accidently struck my arm with his shovel. He had a good, fairly sharp shovel. It cut through the sleeve of my jacket and penetrated my forearm. Not a lot of blood flowed. I tore off a piece of my shirt and bandaged my wound with the help of my shocked, guilty comrade. He apologized and offered to take over my work too when the supervisor was not there. But there would have been no point in that. After all, even with my injured arm I was still better able to shovel than he. I worked on, only more slowly, more clumsily. In the following nights more and more slowly and clumsily. The wound became infected, my arm swelled up first to the elbow and later to the shoulder. The supervisor of the "Organisation Todt" began to get nasty. I developed a fever. Even lying in bed in the morning, I felt wretched. One morning I didn't return to the hut to lie down. I reported to the so-called sick bay to the camp doctor. He had a look at my arm, shook his head, measured my temperature: 38.7°. He released me from work for two nights. I still had to take part in roll-call but after that I could return to the hut and lie down. For two days and two nights I didn't have to work, I was able to sleep, to rest and I could have read about Thais. But I felt too terrible to enjoy this good fortune sufficiently. I was no longer in a position to read. When I wasn't asleep, I heeded the throbbing in my arm tried to relieve the pain with wet bandages, and looked into the sky watching the early autumn clouds. The colour of the sky, the clear light and the smell of winter heralded autumn.

The pain in my arm was slightly diminished on the second day. I went to the camp doctor again. My temperature had sunk to 38° and the doctor said I was fit for work: "with that much fever you can go to work. The labor camp is no sanatorium, you don't need to strain your arm though. Spare it as much as you can."

My holiday was over. The two days I had spent in the camp were too short to be a convalescence. But the rest I had had in that time gave me the strength to slave away for a few more weeks. This accident had another splendid result, one I had hardly even hoped for: It liberated me from night shift for the Moll Company. This is how it happened: On the second night I didn't have to go back to work because the doctor's certificate was still effective and as of the morning of the third day, I was not officially sick any more. Thereupon, at the morning roll-call, I was assigned to a work unit where there was a man missing. I didn't have to do anything. Everything resolved itself and, what's more, turned out to be better.

New people

I can't remember the name of the new work group nor the new path to the job site, although of course I was now going to work in the bright early autumn morning hours, and had the opportunity of looking at the new area. But in the evening when we returned to the camp it was so dark you could hardly see anything.
This work unit was small. There can't have been more than twenty-five to thirty people. Our job site was at the edge of the forest somewhere in the vicinity of Kaufering. If I were to go there again I would certainly not find it. We cut branches off from felled trees, sawed them into pieces and split the larger ones. The large, intertwined roots were cut into pieces with wedges and heavy hammers and later with axes to be used as firewood. For this reason the group got the nickname "wood unit" – the name just comes back to me now.
We had a guard, a CAPO as the unit leader and his deputy. The "Organisation Todt" supervisor only came over from the neighbouring job site occasionally to check our work. Our guard was an apathetic, tired, old man, sick of the war, and paying attention to nothing. All he did was to check the number of those present three or four times, other than that, he sat on his coat, ate, smoked his pipe and occasionally conversed with the CAPO. The CAPO was a German criminal, he stole, he robbed, maybe he even murdered, I don't know. He came to us from Dachau. I don't remember what he was called, Heinrich perhaps. He was small, lean and had thin black hair on his child's head, a lined face, narrow lips and a high piping voice. These characteristics did impress themselves on my memory. Not one other person of this wood unit has remained so vividly in my memory in the last fifteen years, even though there were a few people I liked. He screamed a great deal, actually all the time, but he only struck us very rarely when the guard was nearby and then only the small, weak, frightened people. He was afraid. He tried to force the pace with yelling and threats or by reporting us. The deputy CAPO a strong, angular man deported from the Székler-country (southern Transylvania), a baker's or miller's apprentice. I have forgotten his name. He was

always boasting about his strength and measured it in terms of sacks of flour which he had carried about with ease at home. He did not work, he laughed all the time. (He was related to or friendly with the coarse, inhuman camp cook, Friedmann, who exploited his position. I can only recall his name with scorn and fury; probably, he has remained in the memory of every single camp inmate for this reason. This is why the deputy CAPO was well supplied by the kitchen from the rations of those who were not related to or friendly with the cook.) If he wasn't eating he ran around the CAPO in order to ingratiate himself with him. On the other hand, he didn't make any difficulties. It was just that it was difficult to watch while he ate, and it seemed to us that he was eating non-stop, while we were continually hungry.

I found new friends among the other deportees who were working with me. I got to know Biener, always ready to help, a young man of my age with his father and his uncle, Nandor Grünberg, a sick but tough bootmakers' apprentice able to cope with any situation: and his colleague and friend the strong, optimistic Lemmi Friedmann – I did not know his real name –, who sang happy songs even if he was tired and hungry, who worked for his weak comrades, who once carried a comrade for miles on his back because he could not stand on his injured leg, and who collected mushrooms wherever he went and always shared those he had fried or prepared in some other way, and who once all but died from mushroom poisoning. This shocked the whole group out of its lethargy. Everyone wanted to do something good for him, to save him. We worked together for four or five weeks. We got used to each other and learned to respect each other. Then the wood unit was disbanded. Chance determined who went where, it depended on the mood of the Camp Elder, of a unit leader or the order of the CAPO. In my next work unit I was together only with Lemmi Friedmann and then I lost him from view as well. Later, much later, I discovered that he died in the course of the winter. Hunger, cold and exhaustion killed him, maybe he fell victim to typhus. I do not know. He disappeared without trace, almost unnoticed like so many others. You hardly noticed if and when a friend vanished if you didn't work immediately next to him. For weeks, we had no opportunity to make enquiries, nor did our strength permit us to; and then, when we began to search, we became aware that he no longer existed and that nobody knew what had happened to him. If you were separated from somebody for just a few days, it was mostly forever. I lost sight of the three Bieners. I never met them again, I don't know what happened to them . . .

Constantin Goschler

Controversy About A Pittance
The Compensation of Forced Laborers from Concentration Camps by Germany's Post-War Industry

In January 1986 the company Feldmuehle-Nobel AG, formerly part of the Flick cartel, transferred DM 5 million (approximately US $ 34 million) to The Conference on Jewish Material Claims Against Germany. This is how the company intended to compensate forced laborers of concentration camps whom they had employed during the Second World War. Thus the Feldmuehle-Nobel AG, which had been bought by the Deutsche Bank shortly before, joined the small group of companies which up to that point had been willing to compensate the prisoners for their work as well as for the damage to their health. So far only seven out of several hundred companies which had helped themselves to the labor reservoir of concentration camps had been willing to make a more or less comprehensive settlement of this debt.

Among the forced laborers employed in Germany, concentration camp inmates - quantitatively speaking - were a relatively insignificant group. Workers from abroad - so-called foreign workers - among them both civilians and war prisoners, made up the principal share. However, foreign workers cannot simply be put into the same category as forced laborers. There were differences both in terms of the workers' origin and the respective phase of the War. In mid 1944, when the forced labor system, which had been increasingly refined since the beginning of the Second World War, had reached its climax, prisoners of concentration camps employed in the war industry accounted for a half million[1], civilian foreign workers for 5.74 million, and war prisoners for 1.94 million workers[2]. The figures given for concentration camp prisoners employed as forced laborers, however, have to be multiplied because they indicate only the number of prisoners employed at a certain point in time. The essential characteristic of that group of employees, however, was high 'fluctuation' resulting from the fact that they were earmarked for annihilation, and that exploiting their work and life potential to a maximum was seen solely as a final stage before death. This continued to be

---

[1] Cf. Alan S. Milward, 'Der zweite Weltkrieg. Wirtschaft und Gesellschaft 1939-1945', Munich etc. 1977, pp. 231; Dietrich Eichholtz, 'Geschichte der deutschen Kriegswirtschaft 1939-1945', Vol. 2: 1941-1943, Berlin (GDR), 1985, pp. 224.
[2] Cf. Ulrich Herbert, 'Fremdarbeiter. Politik und Praxis des Auslaendereinsatzes in der Kriegswirtschaft des Dritten Reiches', Berlin etc. 1985, p. 11.

the essential feature of this group of forced laborers, even though the work conditions of foreign workers and those of prisoners from concentration camps became – to some extent – very similar, especially towards the end of the war[3]. The forced labor aspect certainly was a phenomenom of the war industry, which also affected a large portion of the population not persecuted by the National Socialist regime. But the particular circumstances under which the prisoners of concentration camps, and in part civilian foreign workers and war prisoners, were forced to work should not be dismissed with an 'all-in-the-same-boat' interpretation[4].

Claims by former forced laborers of concentration camps for compensation of their wages and damage to their health do not fall within the framework of the restitution and indemnification laws in the Federal Republic, which consists of both redress of private property lost during persecution by the National Socialists and restitution for personal damage suffered as a result thereof. In addition there are a number of bilateral treaties with various countries, the most important of which are those with Israel and The Claims Conference signed in Luxemburg in 1952[5]. Within this complicated sytem of restitution, in particular as a result of the 'Federal Indemnification Law' (BEG), at least some forced laborers received compensation. However, according to the norms (and in the language) of this law, restitution was a term which referred solely to damage to life, body, health, freedom, property, assets and business interests due to National Socialist persecution for reasons of race, political conviction or religion[6].

Thus, a former forced laborer might be entitled to receive compensation for deprivation of his personal freedom due his work, but not for withheld wages or damage to his health resulting from it. This meant that prisoners of war who had been employed as forced laborers were not entitled to compensation in the first place since deprivation of one's personal freedom is in keeping with martial law. Nor were civilian foreign workers, according to the criteria applied, considered to be persecutees, not even if they had not come into the country voluntarily, as was sometimes the case. In this case it was usually assumed that they had been forced to work not on account of their political conviction, race or religion, a precondition for consideration as a persecutee under the National Socialists, but on account of their nationality. Thus they most often fell into the problematic category of 'National Persecu-

---

[3] Ibid, p. 359.
[4] A tendency towards such an interpretation is found in 'Ein Stoffabzeichen mit weisser Schrift auf wattierten Jacken: Flick und die Zwangsarbeit', by Guenther Gilessen; in: 'Frankfurter Allgemeine Zeitung' (hereafter referred to as FAZ), Jan. 09, 1986.
[5] Cf. 'Die Wiedergutmachung Nationalsozialistischen Unrechts durch die Bundesrepublik Deutschland', edited by the Federal Minister of the Treasury in cooperation with Walter Schwarz, 5 Volumes, Munich 1974.
[6] Cf. Otto Kuester, 'Erfahrungen in der deutschen Wiedergutmachung', Tuebingen, FRG, 1967, pp. 12.

tees'[7]. Naturally, the majority of prisoners from concentration camps fit the compensation concept of the Federal Indemnification Law. Thus some of the forced laborers of concentration camps were legally entitled to compensation. For every full month of deprivation or restriction of their personal freedom the BEG granted DM 150 (approximately $ 90.00) compensation[8]. But, as outlined before, this did not solve the question of compensation for wages and health damage resulting from forced labor but only from deprivation of personal freedom due to confinement in a concentration camp. This is why those affected have undertaken efforts since the early 1950s to receive compensation for this kind of damage as well.

It was Norbert Wollheim who initiated the campaign when he filed a lawsuit against the German company I. G. Farben in Liquidation in 1952[9]. In 1943 Mr Wollheim of Auschwitz concentration camp was 'hired out' as a forced laborer to I.G. Farbenindustrie AG at Monowitz. For his work there he claimed DM 10,000 in compensation. I.G. Farben justified its position by stating that the company had been coerced by the German Reich into employing forced laborers, that is to say that it had acted on instructions given by the Reich. In this way the company intended to rid itself of any responsibility and place it on the Federal Republic of Germany as the legal successor to the Reich.

In doing so I.G. Farben presented a pattern of justification which from then onward all companies confronted with such claims were to use, in as much as they were at all willing to reveal the true number of forced laborers they had employed. Subsequently, all companies without exception rejected any legal or even moral obligation to compensate forced laborers they had employed at the time. Oftentimes, they prided themselves on the argument that the employment of concentration camp prisoners in their companies provided the prisoners with greater prospects of survival. Thus compensation was all the more out of question. To this day that argument plays an important role when these companies defend their policy of exploiting the concentration camp prisoners at the time. Mr Otto Kranzbühler, the defense lawyer acting on behalf of various companies involved in the matter, said in a 1984 TV interview: "I will by no means accept the assertion that an unusually high number of people from concentration camps who were employed in the industry died. On the contrary. They were more than happy to work for the industry because they were properly fed there and had a chance to survive, a

---

[7] Cf. Wolfgang Jacobmeyer, 'Vom Zwangsarbeiter zum heimatlosen Auslaender. Die displaced persons in Westdeutschland 1945-1951', Goettingen, FRG; 1985, pp. 236.

[8] Cf. Heinz Klee, 'Die Entschaedigung wegen Schadens an Freiheit', in: 'Wiedergutmachung Nationalsozialistischen Unrechts', Vol 4, p. 459.

[9] See Wolfgang Benz, 'Von der Feststellungsklage zum Vergleich (In Sachen Wollheim gegen I.G. Farben)' in: 'Dachauer Hefte 2' (1986), pp. 142; Benjamin B. Ferencz, 'Lohn des Grauens'. 'Die verweigerte Entschaedigung für juedische Zwangsarbeiter. Ein Kapitel deutscher Nachkriegsgeschichte', Frankfurt etc. 1981, p. 60.

chance which – as we all know – they did not have in the extermination camps[10]."

As far as the prisoners' improved prospects of survival through employment as forced laborers is concerned, one must bear in mind that the prisoners were often forced to work under conditions which, in the long run, did not improve their prospects of survival in any way. Other essays printed here are clear and direct on this matter. Nor can the assertion that German companies had been coerced into employing concentration camp inmates by the Reich be justified. Benjamin B. Ferencz, in his important book dealing with this matter once again presents the most important documents quite clearly. They provide evidence of the fact that certain German companies played quite an active role in recruiting labor from the reservoir of the concentration camps[11].

In German courts in which claims by concentration camp prisoners formerly employed as forced laborers were ruled upon, a basis for decision-making took shape in the course of several trials which briefly designated all claims to compensation for wages and detrimental consequences to health as having been made either too early or too late. However, they did not deny that, in principal, the claims were justified. The first case was that of the large group of those forced laborers, not only those from concentration camps, who were citizens of a country which was an enemy of or occupied by the German Reich[12]. This interpretation rested on the 1952/53 London Debt Settlement Agreement on Germany's foreign debts, according to which part of the Reich's debts had expired while another part was submitted to a halt to claims. Article 5, II of that agreement stipulates that "... an examination of claims resulting from World War II and made by countries which were at war with or whose territory was occupied by Germany or by citizens of such countries against the Reich or any individuals acting on instructions of the Reich ... will be deferred until a final settlement in the matter of reparation payments has been agreed upon"[13]. Wage demands made by former forced laborers were considered part of precisely that part of war debts. In the negotiations leading to the London Debt Settlement Agreement it was assumed that wage claims by foreign workers and forced laborers would have a considerable impact on Germany's solvency. It was therefore agreed – in spite of its non-agreement with general principle of international law as laid down in The Hague 'Landkriegsordnung (land-based war regulations)' – that such

---

[10] Otto Kranzbühler in: 'Vernichtung durch Arbeit', TV documentary by Lea Rosh, broadcast on Nov. 04 1984 by 'SFB'.
[11] Cf. Ferencz, 'Lohn des Grauens', pp. 266.
[12] See decision by the Berlin 'Supreme Court' in Ellfers and 115 other vs. Telefunken and Hagenuk from 23 Feb. 1959; decision by the Federal Supreme Court in Staucher vs. I. G. Farben from Feb. 23 1963.
[13] Agreement on Germany's Foreign Debts, London, 27 Feb 1957, in: 'BGBl', 1953, II, p. 340.

wage claims were to be deferred[14]. For those affected by this temporary solution it means that a ruling on the problem has been postponed to this day. The argument that the claims were made too late, in contrast, affected, above all, the German plaintiffs. Initially they were in a more favorable position to file a lawsuit since their claims could not simply be dismissed by referring to the London Debt Settlement Agreement, which had, naturally enough, made provisions only for Germany's debts to other countries. Claims put forward by the Germans were usually recognized as being basically legitimate. Yet in the end these claimants were rejected, again by referring to the fact that the limitation periods in Germany had elapsed by then[15].

To this day no former concentration camp prisoner has succeeded in sueing a German company for adequate compensation of forced labor in an final hearing. To be accurate, there was one exception which should be mentioned; it, however, only serves to verify these observations in its own way. In 1965 Adolf Diamant sued the Buessing company at Braunschweig District Court. As a Jewish prisoner of the Auschwitz/Birkenau concentration camp he was selected by an engineer of the Buessing company in the summer of 1944 to do forced labor for the company in a concentration camp commando at Neuengamme[16]. The Braunschweig District Court sustained the plaintiff's claim for compensation of the wages withheld and carefully computed the time the plaintiff had worked for the defendant. For the more than six months Adolf Diamant had worked for Buessing 1,778 hours were calculated. It thereby concluded that – according to the wartime wage controls – the appropriate pay scale was one Reichsmark (RM) per hour worked, thus totalling 1,778 Reichmarks (RM) in withheld wages. The Court then converted that amount to the currency value of 1948 and devaluated it by a ratio of 10:1. The plaintiff thus wound up being legally granted the amount of DM 178.80[17]. Ferencz called the verdict a Pyrrhic Victory[18].

Other trials involving forced laborers of concentration camps against various companies also ended successfully. These successes, however, were usually reversed through appeal hearings pursued by the companies, so that claims made by forced laborers were at latest brought to an end before the Federal Supreme Court. The German lawyer Edmund Bartl, for example, who had been 'hired out' by the Sachsenhausen concentration camp to the Heinkel

---

[14] Cf. Arthur Bergmann, 'Fremd- und Zwangsarbeiter – Ansprüche nach dem Londoner Schuldenabkommen und in der Sozialversicherung', in: 'Rechtsprechung zur Wiedergutmachung', 30 (1979), p. 42.
[15] Cf. 'The Federal Supreme Court's Decision in Bartl vs. Heinkel from 22 June 1967; Decision by the Berlin Supreme Court's Civil Division in the Helen R. and Rachel B. cases, represented by Karl-Heinz Schildbach, vs. Rheinmetall AG from 15 Nov. 1959.
[16] In the case of Adolf Diamant vs. Buessing, cf. Ferencz, 'Lohn des Grauens', pp. 214.
[17] Verdict by the Braunschweig District Court in Diamant vs. Buessing from June 20 1965; also see Bulletin of the 'Comité International des Camps' (CIC), Nov. 19 1965, p. 8.
[18] Cf. Ferencz, 'Lohn des Grauens', p. 214.

company, fought successfully before both the Augsburg District Court and the Appellate Court at Stuttgart[19]. This success raised high hopes among many former forced laborers that their claims would also be paid. Conversely the companies involved became increasingly alarmed by a possible shift in position in the legal system, which would present them with enormous costs. The West German Ministry of Finance seemed to share their concern because the former prisoners protested the Ministry's consultation and support of the Heinkel company[20]. Yet the verdict handed down by the Federal Supreme Court at Karlsruhe in a final court hearing ended all speculations about a possible shift in the prevailing jurisdiction practice regarding this complex of disputes. On 22 June 1967 the court dismissed Edmund Bartl's lawsuit once and for all. Since the plaintiff was in this case a German his claims could not simply be dismissed by referral to the London Debt Settlement Agreement. The Federal Supreme Court justified its decision by stating that Dr Bartl had made use of his rights too late and that his claims did not lie within the limitation period, and that in view of his experience as a German lawyer he could be assumed to know about the applicable legal situation[21]. Norbert Wollheim, in his suit against I.G. Farben AG in Liquidation also managed to attain a trial success which was at the time considered to be a sensation. The Frankfurt District Court surprisingly sustained the charge filed by Wollheim and his attorney, Henry Ormond[22]. This was certainly made possible by the fact that I. G. Farben had been branded by public consciousness due to its particularly close association with the National Socialist regime, to which the company's exemplary condemnation by the Nuremberg Military Tribunal had contributed. One of the reasons for condemnation was the abuse of slave work[23]. However, Frankfurt High District Court, which I.G. Farben had appealed to, no longer maintained such a clear position. It now suggested a settlement between I.G. Farben in Liquidation and Wollheim, who had meanwhile received the support of the Conference on Jewish Material Claims[24].

---

[19] Cf. The Augsburg District Court's decision in Bartl vs. Heinkel from July 31, 1962; The Stuttgart Appellate Court's decision in Bartl vs. Heinkel from May 19 1965; weekly magazine 'Der Spiegel', May 13 1965, pp. 59: 'Entschaedigung. Sklaven des Reiches'.
[20] Cf. CIC bulletin, April 04 1967, pp. 1; daily newspaper 'Sueddeutsche Zeitung' (hereafter referred to as: SZ), June 20 1967, p. 3, 'Unterstuetzt Bonn ehemalige Sklavenhalter?', by Dieter Lau.
[21] Cf. Federal Supreme Court's decision in Bartl vs. Heinkel from June 20 1967, p.10; SZ, June 24/25 1967, p. 10. 'Keine Entschaedigung mehr für Zwangsarbeit'.
[22] Cf. Frankfurt District Court's decision in Wollheim vs. I.G. Farben from June 10 1953.
[23] The members of the board of directors, Krauch and Ter Mer, were found guilty in this matter, seven other members of the board were set free; cf. Trials of War Criminals before the Nuremberg Tribunal, Vol. 8 (The I.G. Farben Case), Washington 1952, pp. 1167
[24] Decision of the Frankfurt Appellate Court in Wollheim vs. I. G. Farben from Oct. 21 1955.

A group of Polish forced laborers who had worked for I.G. Farben when they were at Auschwitz concentration camp and whose interests were not represented by the Claims Conference also filed suit in the hopes of obtaining some measure of redress. Their suit, however, was ultimately dismissed by the High District Court which referred to the London Debt Settlement Agreement. In this case the court supported I.G. Farben's assertion that the company had been an instrument of the Reich and concluded that all claims made by Polish forced laborers were to be deferred until the problem of reparation payments was solved[25].

Thus those German companies which had employed prisoners of concentration camps have not had much reason to be afraid of the courts. This was the reason why Hermann Langbein who, among other things, had also supported the latter-mentioned Polish group in their efforts to obtain compensation, filed a suit in 1969: "The companies involved attempt to skip out of their moral obligation to paying compensation with newly invented excuses, hoping that the jurisdiction was in their favor and that subsequently they could not be legally forced to pay[26]."

Those few selected examples illustrating the large number of unsuccessful lawsuits to obtain compensation for concentration camp laborers make it clear that in the final analysis going to court had proven to be the wrong way to gain redress. Moreover, the plaintiffs, who were in most cases very poor, were hardly in a position to go through a lengthy trial against the powerful companies. Thus Edmund Bartl's case ended in complete financially ruin[27]. This was also one of the reasons why organizations of former prisoners took the initiative. The few settlements reached between former forced laborers or their representatives and the companies which once had helped themselves to their labor, however, were all the result of out-of-court settlements. In those settlements the companies steadfastly refused to acknowledge any legal or moral guilt.

In every case it was only by threatening to draw public attention to the companies that a willingness to pay could be forced. That could be effective insofar as German industry, on its way to reintegration into the world economy after World War II, had to beware of the effects of image-hostile campaigns, especially in the United States. At the same time it meant that the various individual groups which had developed from the circle of former forced laborers were not equally able to pursue their claims in this way. The organization which came nearest to success was the Conference on Jewish Material Claims against Germany, a consolidation of 23 Jewish organizations from all over the world, founded in 1951.

---

[25] Descision by the Frankfurt High District Court in Staucher vs. I.G. Farben from Feb 23 1963; also see Ferencz, 'Lohn des Graunes', pp. 84, pp. 168.
[26] CIC bulletin, 03 September 1969, p.13
[27] Cf. CIC bulletin, 15 July 1967, p. 10.

The Claims Conference's first president was Nahum Goldman, who also played a leading role in the 1952 negotiations in Wassenaar near The Hague which took place between representatives of the Federal Republic of Germany on the one hand and of the State of Israel and the Claims Conference on the other[28]. The latter organization primarily represented the interests of Jewish forced laborers against the German companies involved.

Other organizations working for compensation for forced laborers of concentration camps were, in particular, the 'Internationale Auschwitz Komitee' (IAK) and the 'Comité International des Camps' (CIC), founded in 1963. At its Paris conference on 4 and 5 October 1963, the CIC called upon "the companies which at the time had taken advantage of the slave labor of concentration camp prisoners to give compensation to the victims without distinction"[29].

The driving force for compensatory claims in both organizations was Hermann Langbein who, for ideological reasons, gave up his position as Secretary General of the 'Internationale Auschwitz Komitee' in 1962, while continuing his work as secretary of the 'Comité International des Camps'. Owing to the fact that both organizations represented, in particular, claims made by foreigners, among them Eastern Europeans, it was much harder for them to mobilize effective public pressure against the laborers' erstwhile "employers". But mere appeals had been ineffective up to that point.

If one considers the few successful settlements regarding compensation for forced laborers of concentration camps in context, a series of long and weary negotiations and spectacular moves to influence the public becomes evident. The first and so far most important case of that kind was the agreement reached between I.G. Farben AG i.L. and the Claims Conference. After Wollheim and Ormond had been unexpectedly successful with their suit before the Frankfurt District Court, the Claims Conference became active in the matter as well. I.G. Farben developed a certain willingness to negotiate since confirmation of that verdict by an Appellate Court would have had unforeseeable consequences for them and for all other companies which had employed concentration camp laborers. Moreover, it was not the right moment to aggravate the American public with such an issue; this could have jeopardized efforts made to have confiscated German foreign property in the United States released[30].

In 1954 negotiations between the Claims Conference and I.G. Farben were initiated. Walter Schmidt, who was entrusted with the company's liquidation as decreed by the Allies, met with the director of the Claims Conference's

---

[28] Cf. Ernst Katzenstein, 'Jewish Claims Conference und die Wiedergutmachung nationalsozialistischen Unrechts' in: 'Die Freiheit des Anderen'; edited by H.-J. Vogel and others; publication in honor of Martin Hirsch; Baden-Baden 1981, pp. 219.
[29] CIC Bulletin, 7 Feb. 1964; p. 4
[30] Cf. Ferencz, 'Lohn des Grauens', p. 72.

Liaison Office, Herbert Schoenfeld, and soon after with Benjamin B. Ferencz, incumbent director of the organization's German branch. But during these initial contacts, the ideas of the parties involved of the financial dimensions of such an agreement differed by a power of ten. While Schmidt had a maximum of DM 10,000,000 in mind, Ferencz spoke of DM 100,000,000. The first thing I. G. Farben's overwhelmed representative did was to retreat for consultations. He also consulted the Federal Association of German Industries, the Bundesverband der Deutschen Industrie, and the Finance Department in Bonn, which had encouraged him to conduct the negotiations[31]. Finally, after the Frankfurt District Court had in October 1955 called on both parties to make a settlement, negotiations were resumed in early 1956. "Schmidt announced that I. G. Farben was prepared to set a maximum amount in order to treat all claims equally, both Jewish and non-Jewish. The company's estimate of non-Jewish claims was no more than five percent ... Moreover, the agreement had to contain a clause that the company was not legally responsible for the events which had taken place at the time[32]." A further condition put forward by the company was that it intended to withhold a fixed amount of money from the total to be agreed upon in order to satisfy claims made by non-Jewish workers. In the end I. G. Farben made an offer of DM thirty million from which the company planned to withhold three million for payment to non-Jewish claimants, and an additional three million to be held in reserve in case of further litigation. Furthermore, only those forced laborers who had been employed at I. G. Farben's plant at Auschwitz were to enjoy the proceeds of this agreement. On this basis a tentative agreement with the Claims Conference could be signed on 06 February 1957[33].

A few other hurdles had yet to be overcome, before an agreement could to go into effect irrevocably. In particular, I. G. Farben asked for a guarantee that by means of that agreement all claims would be taken care of. For that purpose, a special federal law was passed, stipulating that the registration deadline for all claims by former forced laborers concerning this company was 31 December 1957[34]. Last but not least, the consent of I. G.'s stockholders' meeting had to be won.

One particular problem which resulted from the argreement was that the Claims Conference was neither authorized nor willing to represent the interests of all former forced laborers, but only of former Jewish workers, who in this case, however, accounted for approximately 95% of those concerned.

In addition, I. G. Farben had at least planned to include non-Jewish claimants as well. But the Claims Conference opposed the fact that these claims

---

[31] Ibid; pp. 68.
[32] Ibid; p. 72.
[33] Ibid; pp. 73.
[34] Law on the appeal to claimants of the I. G. Farbenindustrie AG from 25 May 1957, in 'BGBl', 1957, I, p. 569.

would reduce the total amount of money negotiated. On the part of this organization I.G. Farben's concern for non-Jewish claimants was interpreted as a tactical maneuver to play off the various groups of claimants against each other[35]. In any event, to this day this agreement has remained the only one to take non-Jewish claims into account.

Yet part of the former Farben forced laborers felt the agreement put them at a disadvantage. Representing the latter, the Internationale Auschwitz Komitee (IAK) initiated negotiations with I.G. Farben and the Claims Conference at Frankfurt in June 1957. It demanded that all former inmates be treated equally without distinction and that at least the closest dependants of those slave workers who had died as a result of working for I.G. Farben in Auschwitz be considered for reparation[36].

After an interruption the negotiations were resumed on 29 November 1957 and 24 Februar 1958[37]. The IAK's inability to push through its demands led to a crisis which at various stages of the negotiations seemed as though they would jeopardize the entire agreement. But despite the unresolved difficulties the agreement went into effect on 1 April 1958 as planned. The problem of compensation for close dependants of Farben slave workers, was to be taken into consideration in part after 1965 when a Hardship Fund was set up from undistributed money of the Claims Conference's share. Is was from this fund that some of those affected were able to receive compensation after all[38].

Yet the largest dispute developed on the matter of the so-called National Persecutees. The agreement between I.G. Farben and the Claims Conference stipulated that compensatory payments were allowed to be made only to those persecuted for racial or political reasons. In the case of Polish inmates, for example, it was assumed – to their disadvantage – that they had not been persecuted for political but national reasons. As a reaction to this, as had been said earlier, a group of Polish forced laborers, with the support of the IAK attempted to push through their claims in court to ultimately fail even before the German Supreme Court. Thus Polish, Czech, Hungarian and Yugoslavian forced laborers made an effort to prove the fact that "they had worked in I.G. Farben plants in the Auschwitz district and had been incarcerated in the Auschwitz concentration camp on account of their hostile attitude towards National Socialism ..., their race (gypsies and "non-professing" Jews ...), their religious confession ... or political reasons ... [39]." Until the summer of 1961 an investigating committee, appointed by I.G. Farben,

---

[35] Cf. Ferencz, 'Lohn des Grauens'; p. 74.
[36] Cf. Information Bulletin of the 'Internationale Auschwitz Komitee' (IAK), November 1956; pp. 2: 18 June 1957, pp. 1 f.; 14 Sept 1957, pp. 1; Cologne Newspaper 'Kölnische Rundschau', June 05 1957; 'Auschwitz-Komitee fordert Verbesserungen'; Newspaper 'Deutsche Woche', June 12 1957; 'Auschwitz Häftlinge verhandeln mit I.G. Farben'.
[37] Cf. IAK Information Bulletin; December 4 1957; pp. 1.
[38] Cf. CIC Bulletin: 19 November 1965; p. 9: Ferencz, 'Lohn des Grauens'; pp. 90.
[39] IAK Information Bulletin, Warsaw; Sept/Oct 1961; p. 2.

screened 796 claims made by this group, from which 323 were approved while 473 were rejected. Approximately DM 1.5 million was paid[40]. The main task of distributing the money, namely 27 million of the total of DM 30 million granted, was put into the hands of 'Compensation Treuhand' – an organization set up by the Claims Conference especially for this purpose – which was in charge of the screening and approving of Jewish claims.

However, the interpretation put forward by both the Claims Conference and Compensation Treuhand which stated that only those would receive payments out of their funds who still shared the Jewish religious belief, i.e. the so-called "professing Jews", caused protests. Among others, even Henry Ormond, supporter of Wollheim, protested against such an interpretation of the agreement with I.G. Farben[41]. The various requests had to be carefully examined in order to comply with the strict provisions of the agreement. It so happened that only I.G. Farben laborers from concentration camps but not those from work camps were allowed to receive restitution. Anyone who had worked at the Buna plants for up to six months, received DM 2,500, beyond that DM 5,000. All in all DM 27,841,000 was distributed from the Claims Conference's Farben fund, since the original amount, which, however, had been reduced by DM 750,000 in favor of non-Jewish victims, had accumulated interest. The 5,855 Jewish forced laborers and borderline cases, for whom a decision was finally made, came from 36 different countries, whereby Israel and the US accounted for the largest groups. Thus together with the non-Jewish claimants (among them also the "non-professing" Jews), who separately received compensation from I.G. Farben, approximately 6,500 former forced laborers at the Buna plants received compensation from the DM 30 million[42].

In 1954 negotiations for compensation with Alfried Krupp were also initiated. Before the Nuremberg Military Tribunal he had among other things been charged with crimes against humanity and forced laborers[43]. But as early as 1951 the American High Commissioner John McCloy had pardoned Alfried Krupp and had his private assets returned. When former Krupp laborer Mordechai S. filed a lawsuit to obtain compensation with the Essen District Court against the company owner, who had regained his property and honor, the Claims Conference picked up on the matter and approached the company owner with suggestions for an agreement. Jacob Blaustein, vice-president of the Claims Conference, via his old friend John McCloy tried to make Alfried Krupp give into this claim. At the same time, though, his organ-

---

[40] Ibid.
[41] See Henry Ormond's letter to the Claims Conference from July 9 1957.
[42] Cf. Ferencz, 'Lohn des Grauens'; pp. 264.
[43] Cf. Trials of War Criminals before the Nuremberg Military Tribunals; Vol. IX (The Krupp Case); Washington 1950; pp. 1396.

ization compiled evidence in order to be equipped for a fierce confrontation. After some time had passed – and it seemed to the Claims Conference that Krupp was not seriously interested in an agreement – it changed its strategy. Personal intervention was intensified, but at the same time it approached the US government to request it to warn Krupp of its obligation to sell its steel property at Rheinhausen as had been previously agreed. Threat to jeopardize its world-wide economic expansionist activities pointed in the same direction[44].

After five years Krupp finally gave in. On 23 December 1959 an agreement was reached between the Friedrich Krupp company at Essen and the Claims Conference. DM 6 million was to be made available to those Jewish inmates who were able to produce evidence of their former employment with Krupp. If the number of those entitled to compensation was large enough this amount could be increased to a maximum of DM 10 million, as in fact turned out to be the case. Conversely, the Claims Conference accepted the obligation to keep all further claims by Jewish forced laborers and their dependants away from Krupp. At the same time the agreement ruled out the possibility that by paying Krupp recognized any legal obligation or that the position of other German companies was thereby prejudged. Friedrich Krupp understood his payment to the Claims Conference to be a voluntary contribution towards the relief of suffering for which National Socialism had been exclusively responsible[45]. As could be expected, the fact that non-Jewish Krupp laborers were not included – in contrast to the I.G. Farben agreement – immediately caused protest to arise among them. "Such a distinction is not only unjustified but also serves as a feeding ground for anti-Semitic tendencies", the IAK contended[46]. Hermann Langbein presented this demand to the Krupp works, upon which he was told that the company had not maintained any plants at Auschwitz at all[47]. Following this, Langbein presented documents to Krupp works' legal department which provided evidence of the fact that until October 1943 Krupp had employed Auschwitz inmates to do forced labor[48]. Krupp works finally admitted that this was true, but did not undertake any further action[49]. The company blamed the Claims Conference for the exclusion of the interests of non-Jewish forced laborers, which – so the argument goes – had refused to consider them in the negotiation process due to lack of a mandate[50]. After all, the real problem more than likely was that non-Jewish forced laborers and/or their organizations often were not accepted as partners at the negotiating table. This group was simply not rele-

---

[44] Cf. Ferencz, 'Lohn des Grauens'; pp. 107.
[45] Ibid. pp. 117; pp. 264; IAK Information Bulletin; Feburary 2 1960; p. 3.
[46] IAK Information Bulletin; 14 January 1960; p. 3.
[47] Cf. IAK Information Bulletin; 25 March 1960; p. 1.
[48] Cf. IAK Information Bulletin; 17 May 1960; p. 3.
[49] IAK Information Bulletin; 17 June 1960; pp. 4.
[50] Cf. Ferencz, 'Lohn des Grauens'; p. 120.

vant for the agreement which as far as Krupp was concerned was not so much motivated by moral problems as by the avoidance of economic disadvantage.

The task of distributing the payments to the Jewish forced laborers was in turn taken on by Compensation Treuhand. Once again strict regulations had to be complied with. The large number of civilian foreign workers and war prisoners, for instance, who had done forced labor for Krupp, were excluded from the agreement. Only inmates from concentration camps were to be paid. In this way 3,090 individuals from 33 different countries who had filed a claim received a total of DM 10,050,900. Here the maximum amount paid to a single forced laborer was DM 3,300[51].

Germany's major electrical concerns Siemens, AEG, and Telefunken, had also employed forced laborers from concentration camps during the War. In contradistinction to I.G. Farben and Krupp, though, they were not held responsible before the Nuremberg Military Tribunal so that it was difficult to provide evidence of their involvement. Yet these companies were also confronted with their burden of guilt for having employed concentration camp laborers. AEG was to be first. At the request of several former forced laborers who had worked for the company Henry Van Dam, Secretary General of the Central Council of Jews in Germany, wrote to AEG at the end of 1957, calling on it to make compensation payments to this group. After a short period of writing back and forth AEG rejected the idea of an agreement. Van Dam became resigned and passed on the matter to a lawyer[52]. At the same time a test case against Telefunken had begun. But on 23 February 1959 the Berlin Appellate Court decided in a second hearing in the Case Ellfers vs. Telefunken that the claims deriving from forced labor had to be considered restitution claims, which could not be dealt with until a peace treaty with Germany had been signed[53].

While test cases against Telefunken and AEG were being undertaken without much success the Claims Conference approached the companies directly. Due to the fact that AEG had bought Telefunken in 1941 it spoke on behalf of both companies. Beginning in March 1960 Ernst Katzenstein, President of the Claims Conference in Germany for some time now, negotiated with the AEG chairman of the executive board of directors, Hans C. Boden, and his legal adviser Hellenbroich. Influenced by the I.G. Farben agreement the negotiations resulted in a simple exchange of letters that same year. AEG paid DM 4 million without recognizing any legal obligation or setting an example for other companies. The money was to help restitute damage the Jewish inmates of concentration camps who had been employed in the plants of AEG and Telefunken might have suffered. Once again the Claims Confer-

---

[51] Ibid. pp. 264.
[52] Ibid. pp. 140.
[53] Decision by the Berlin Supreme Court in Ellfers vs. Telefunken.

ence had to guarantee that with this payment the companies would be dismissed of any further obligations towards Jewish claimants[54].
Compensation Treuhand encountered great difficulties in paying effective compensation, since it had to draw on extremely low funds. It distributed a total of DM 4,312,500 among 2223 Jewish claimants. Initially payments of $500 per claimant were made to later decrease to a mere $375[55].
In 1961 the Claims Conference initiated negotiations with Siemens. Upon the discovery of a report originating from the Siemens company itself undeniably proving that at least 3,900 inmates had worked in the company's main plants, the Siemens leadership gradually gave up resisting a settlement. On 24 May 1962 an agreement was reached, according to which Siemens was to pay DM 5 million for the Jewish workers from concentration camps, whereby the amount of money was to be raised to a total of DM 7 million if the number of claimants was large enough. Other than that the agreement again contained clauses following the familiar pattern: no recognition of any legal or moral obligation, prevention of any further Jewish claims through the Claims Conference etc. Compensation Treuhand finally paid DM 7,184,100 from the Siemens fund to 2203 claimants from 28 different countries, whereby they managed to have DM 3,300 per claimant approved[56].
Here too, in the case of agreements with the electrical concerns non-Jewish forced laborers protested strongly. "These companies have stated their willingness to grant Jewish inmates compensation. However, they continue to refuse to pay the same amount of compensation to non-Jewish inmates as well. In addition, they have only compensated inmates of the Auschwitz," concentration camp to date, however, not these from other camps[57]. The Comité International des Camps therefore contemplated forcing these companies to make equal compensation payments by conducting test cases. It mailed out questionnaires to all former inmates who had so far turned to the Comité International des Camps in their effort to obtain redress from German companies, for which they had to do forced labor. Apart from the companies Krupp, Siemens, AEG and Telefunken, which thus far had compensated Jewish inmates only, a particularly high number of claims could be collected against companies which had not yet made any compensatory payments up to that point. Among those were the German companies Messerschmidt Works, Heinkel Works, Hanomag, BMW, the Borgward Works etc. In addition claims against a number of Austrian companies, in particular against the Saurer Works, the Steyr Works and the construction company Negrelli could be collected. The largest group to return the questionnaires and grant the CIC power of attorney came from Poland and Czechoslovakia.

---

[54] Cf. Ferencz, 'Lohn des Grauens', pp. 148.
[55] Ibid. pp. 264.
[56] Cf. ibid., pp. 153; pp. 264.
[57] CIC Bulletin, Feb. 02 1966, p. 11.

It was in these countries that survivors of concentration camps had thus far been excluded from compensation[58]. CIC evaluated several hundred claim packages and informed the companies affected. They, however, without exception, declined to pay compensation settlements, as CIC vice-president, Eugen Kogon, outlined at a press conference in Frankfurt on 17 January 1967[59]. Thus CIC placed all its hopes in a test case. Yet the outcome of the trial Bartl vs. Heinkel which was awaited with great suspense and which the aircraft company was finally to win before the German Supreme Court, proved anew how 'dull the weapon of test cases' had been and at the same time served to reassure the companies affected that their attitude of wait-and-see had proven right. Once again no holds were barred in the battle of the Rheinmetall Berlin AG Case. The attempt made by former forced laborers from concentration camps to achieve a favorable settlement through the courts failed according to the familiar pattern. On 15 November 1959 in the case of two Jewish claimants who, as inmates of the concentration camp at Buchenwald, had done forced labor for Rheinmetall under inhuman conditions, the Berlin Appellate Court decided that their lawsuit had been filed too late for consideration since the limitation period had already passed[60]. In the appeal hearing before the German Supreme Court in 1964 the verdict was confirmed, but on different grounds. As of then their claims were considered restitution claims which would be dealt with after a future peace treaty had been signed[61].

Meanwhile Ernst Katzenstein, acting on instructions from the Claims Conference, made efforts to engage the Rheinmetall company in settlement talks, but to no avail. It was not until it became known that Germany's armorer planned to sign a $50 million contract with the US Army to deliver canons that the Claims Conference had an ace to play. B'nai B'rith, one of the Claims Conference's 23 member organizations, placed itself at the disposal of the Claims Conference in order to exert influence and in this way thwart the arms deal, should Rheinmetall be unwilling to give in on the matter of compensation. This organization, with half a million members in the United States, then initiated public campaigns and lobbying activities with this goal in mind[62].

These efforts seemed to bear fruit so that Rheinmetall finally consented to sit down at the negotiating table. Otto Kranzbühler, Rheinmetall's vice-chairman of the board of supervisors and former defense lawyer for I.G. Farben in the Wollheim case – under the influence of the impressive and powerful campaign

---

[58] Cf. CIC Bulletin, 31 March 1966, pp. 9.; 20 July 1966, pp. 10; 25 November 1966, pp. 11; Feb. 02 1967, pp. 8.
[59] Cf. CIC Bulletin, 02 Feb. 1967, pp. 11; see also CIC Bulletin, 11 April 1967, pp. 1; 02 October 1967, pp. 1.
[60] Cf. Footnote 15.
[61] German Supreme Court's Decision in Helen R. and Rachel B., represented by Karl-Heinz Schildbach, vs. Rheinmetall AG, of 17 March 1964.
[62] Cf. Ferencz, 'Lohn des Grauens', pp. 168.

– began presenting initial offers. In the difficult negotiation process – in which the US Department of Defense and the German Ministry of Defense also took a background role, and Phil Klutznich, US Ambassador at the United Nations was the go-between – Hans Wilhelmi, acting on instructions from Rheinmetall, negotiated a settlement with Ernst Katzenstein. Wilhelmi finally gave his word to transfer DM 2.5 million to the Claims Conference as soon as the US Army had definitely agreed to the purchase of the canons. This in turn depended on an end to B'nai B'rith's campain against Rheinmetall. The agreed amount was in fact paid promptly after a decision on 13 May 1966 had been made in favor of the canon purchase[63].

The settlement left it to the Claims Conference's discretion to distribute the money, but the amount of DM 2.5 million was so small that compensation payments had to be made very restrictively. Numerous former forced laborers of concentration camps who had worked for Rheinmetall wound up not receiving anything. All in all the money was distributed to 1,507 recipients, each of whom received DM 1,700[64].

Once again the non-Jewish forced laborers had not been taken into consideration at all, so that Hermann Langbein, acting on instructions from the Comité International des Camps, turned to Rheinmetall Berlin AG in order to claim compensation for that group as well. Rheinmetall refused and, in addition, made it understood why it had made the payment in the case of the Claims Conference. In a letter to CIC it stated "that the payment to the Jewish Claims Conference, with which you are familiar, was made solely in view of an order for canons which had been promised to us[65]. Thus Rheinmetall did not at all consider the payment as compensation of forced laborers, but rather as ransom to hinder the campaign against the canon deal. This is why the letter ended with: "The company's payment was thus based on a service in return"[66].

The thus far last and largest chapter in the history of compensation of concentration camp laborers by German industries can be titled Flick. In a separate trial (the fifth of a total of 12 hearings which followed after the International Tribunal of major war criminals) Friedrich Flick as one of the leading industrialists of the Nazi period had to justify himself. His defense lawyer was the by now familiar Otto Kranzbuehler. In 1947 Flick was found guilty of looting, employment of forced laborers and financial support of the SS and sentenced to seven years imprisonment[67].

---

[63] Cf. ibid., pp. 179f.; see also SZ, 23 May 1966, p. 5, 'Rheinmetall zahlt an fruehere KZ-Haeftlinge. Entschaedigung wird mit amerikanischem Ruestungsauftrag in Verbindung gebracht'.
[64] Cf. Ferencz, 'Lohn des Grauens', pp. 264.
[65] CIC Bulletin, 31 March 1969, p. 9.
[66] Ibid.
[67] Cf. Trials of War Criminals before the Nuremberg Military Tribunals, Vol. 6 (The Flick Case), Washington 1952, pp. 1194.

In 1951, having been pardoned by American High Commissioner John McCloy he was released from the prison at Landsberg. He reestablished a significant economic empire, which included the Dynamit Nobel AG company. For the production of ammunition during the War, this company had employed numerous forced laborers from concentration camps, e.g. from Buchenwald and Gross-Rosen. At the time Flick had been one of the company's directors[68].

It was in 1963 that the Claims Conference first sought to establish contact with Flick in order to confront him, in his function as the principal company director of the Dynamit Nobel AG, with the issue of compensation for the company's former slave laborers. For this purpose Hamburg banker Eric Warburg arranged a meeting between Erich Katzenstein and Fabian von Schlabrendorff as Flick's representative, which took place on 20 June 1963. Surprisingly Schlabrendorff promptly agreed to draft a settlement with the Claims Conference so that a contract could be negotiated immediately. The contract provided that any claimant who could prove that he or she had worked in any of the three designated Dynamit Nobel plants, would be entitled to receive DM 5,000. A total of between DM 5 million to 8 million was discussed. Schlabrendorff stated that he would present the draft to the owners of Dynamit Nobel AG for debate[69].

After this quick initial success, however, a long phase of maneuvering began. In 1964 the draft was slightly altered and a final payment of DM 5 million agreed upon. All that was missing was Flick's signature, but once again, nothing happened. In 1967 Schlabrendorff - who had played the role of an honest broker - resigned in his capacity as Flick's representative, since he had been appointed judge at the German Supreme Court. From then on the Claims Conference had to deal with Flick's authorized representative Eberhard von Brauchitsch, who was considered to be an opponent to such a settlement. In the end not even the personal intervention of former High Commissioner McCloy, who had pardoned Friedrich Flick, could not prevent the latter from pronouncing the contract obsolete once and for all[70]. When Friedrich Flick died in 1972 the entire matter seemed to have been ended.

On 4 December 1985 Friedrich Karl Flick, Friedrich Flick's son and heir, made a surprise announcement that he planned to sell his industrial empire to the 'Deutsche Bank'[71]. Robert Kempner, former deputy plaintiff in the Nuremberg war crimes trials, took advantage of this occasion to bring up the old demand for compensation of Dynamit Nobel forced laborers once again. He had done so as early as 1982 and 1984 under less favorable condi-

---

[68] Cf. Ferencz, 'Lohn des Grauens', p. 199.
[69] Cf. ibid, pp. 200.
[70] Cf. ibid, pp. 203.
[71] Cf. FAZ, 5 Dec. 1985, p. 13. 'Der Flick Konzern wird aufgelöst'.

tions, but this time his effort was to have the matter dealt with once and for all. On 10 December 1985 Kempner sent a letter to the Deutsche Bank spokesman for the board of directors, Friedrich Wilhelm Christians. Among other things he wrote the following: "From a moral, political and legal standpoint it seems to be necessary to free the Flick Works of the stigma of nonpayment to the victims of the company's surviving slave workers who have suffered great damage to their health. Now that most of the Flick cartel will be purchased by the Deutsche Bank, numerous personal and economic commitments must be fulfilled. This also includes the amount of money in question, which accounts for less than 1% of the selling price"[72]. Following this appeal by Kempner, the Claims Conference sent another letter to the same address on 18 December. In it the Conference expressed the hope that following the Deutsche Bank's takeover of the Dynamit Nobel company the commitment made by the Flick company to pay between DM 5 million and DM 8 million for Jewish forced labor during the War many years ago would be fulfilled[73]. Werner Nachmann, chairman of the board of directors of the Central Council for Jews in Germany, now also supported these claims. On 27 December 1985 he wrote to Deutsche Bank and expressed his expectation that Deutsche Bank would now fulfill the commitment made by Flick company and a moral obligation as other German companies had already done earlier[74].

At the end of 1985 Christians, the speaker for the board of directors, continued to brush off the appeals addressed to his company and explained that this was not Deutsche Bank's, but Mr Flick's problem, if one could speak of a problem at all[75]. Yet Deutsche Bank soon found itself faced with a situation in which it could no longer afford to be so carefree about the matter. Since early 1986 public attention had increasingly focused on this problem and even the German Bundestag and the European Parliament announced that debates on the topic 'Slave Labor in the Third Reich' would be held[76]. In this situation it was Hermann Fellner of the Christian Social Union Party (CSU), a delegate in the Bundestag and CSU speaker on internal affairs, who - in an interview, 'poured plenty of oil into the fire', thus accelerating

---

[72] Kempner's letter to Christians from Dec. 10 1985 in: 'Aufbau', Jan. 17 1986, p. 2. 'Eine spaete Geste der Wiedergutmachung'.
[73] Cf. 'Allgemeine Juedische Wochenzeitung', Jan. 03 1986, p. 1, 'Moralische Verpflichtung.'
[74] Ibid.
[75] Cf. FAZ, Jan. 06 1986, p. 4. 'Galinski mahnt Entschaedigung auch bei der Deutschen Bank an'.
[76] See debates of the German Bundestag, Stenograph. reports, Vol. 136, 187th Session on 16 Jan 1986; On 16 Jan 1986 the European Parliament handed down two decisions in reference to industry. With regard to the most recent payment by Feldmuehle-Nobel AG to the Claims Conference total payment was considered to be insufficient, and compensation of all former forced laborers demanded; cf. official publication of the European Communities, No. C 36, 17 Feb 1986, pp. 129.

developments immensely. On 4 January 1986, in the Cologne 'Express' he stated that as far as compensation claims by Jewish forced laborers during the Nazi period were concerned they were based neither on "legal nor moral grounds". In addition, such claims conveyed the impression that "Jews are quick at hand when it comes to money jingling in German cash registers"[77]. This statement caused considerable protest. Finally even Federal Chancellor Helmut Kohl dissociated himself from these statements, though not very emphatically. At the federal press conference on 9 January 1986 he advised Fellner that this had been 'neither the right wording nor the appropriate language ...' [78].

However, the matter had already been resolved the day before. On 8 January 1986, Feldmuehle Nobel AG, with the consent of its new owner Deutsche Bank, announced that it was willing to pay the DM 5 million demanded by the Claims Conference, which it then did immediately[79]. One can only speculate about what lay behind this decision. The strong public reaction certainly played a role. It is also conceivable that the decision was made to create a favorable atmosphere for the pending visit by Israeli President Shimon Peres, who visited Germany in late January. The Feldmuehle Nobel AG's board of directors itself called the decision a "humanitarian solution" and in this context erroneously explained that Friedrich Flick and other colleagues had expressly been acquitted of the charge of having participated in the slave work program in the Nuremberg trial[80]. At this juncture the unfortunate tradition was continued, namely to give to the certainly justified compensation payments for former forced laborers of concentration camps the undertone of giving alms to the poor.

At this point the Claims Conference is occupied with examining claims and organizing the distribution of the DM 5 million. In the past a total of 1,200 to 1,500 former Jewish inmates who had been employed as forced laborers with Dynamit Nobel have turned to the Claims Conference[81].

After the payment by Feldmuehle Nobel AG had become public, the Comité International des Camps decided to make another attempt and addressed a number of companies concerned with the as yet unresolved problem of compensation of their former slave workers. The response to this 'attack' has varied in each case. At this juncture no conclusion has been reached[82].

Maybe the rekindled debate on the problem can aid even those former forced laborers of concentration camps who are still alive and who have so far been excluded from compensation in realizing their right to compensation of wages and damage to their

---

[77] Cited in: 'Aufbau', 31 Jan 1986, 'Fellner entschuldigt sich'.
[78] FAZ, 10 Jan. 1986, p. 2 'Politische Umschau des Kanzlers'.
[79] Cf. FAZ, 9 Jan. 1986, p. 1, 'Feldmuehle Nobel leistet Entschaedigung'.
[80] Ibid.
[81] Cf. 'Aufbau', Jan. 17 1986, p. 2 'Eine späte Geste'.
[82] Note by Hermann Langbein to the author from Aug. 08 1986.

health. They make up the majority by far. The exact number of those forced laborers of concentration camps who have thus far received compensation from the German industry cannot yet be given at this point since payments from the Feldmuehle Nobel fund have not been made in full yet. However, by a rough estimate, the total number of those compensated until now probably is no more than approximately 16,000[83].

---

[83] A survey on the payments by Compensation Treuhand made until 1973 to Jewish forced laborers from concentration camps can be found in 'Lohn des Grauens' by Ferencz, pp. 264, According to the survey, the organization was able to pay compensation to almost 15,000 former slave workers until 1973. The non-Jewish forced laborers, who were paid directly by I. G. Farben, and the Jewish forced laborers, who are to be paid now, along with the most recent payments made by Feldmuehle Nobel AG, must be added to this number.

Barbara Distel

In the Shadow of Heroes
Struggle and Survival of Centa Beimler-Herker and Lina Haag

The twelve-year history of the concentration camp Dachau is almost exclusively the history of men, since only in the final phase were there also female prisoners and guards in some of the subsidiary camps. In the years 1933–1945 more than 200,000 men were registered as prisoners in the main camp of Dachau and its subsidiary camps. After the liberation only a tiny fraction of them wrote about or gave accounts of their experiences. Only in individual cases did the fate of Dachau prisoners become the subject of historical research. Mostly it was then a so-called prominent prisoner whose story of persecution was included within the framework of an examination of his life story. However, the history of the women among these prisoners has practically never been written or researched. They were often with their husbands in the resistance. Practically all of them had to suffer persecution and discrimination during the imprisonment of their husbands, many were themselves interned in prisons or concentration camps, and not a few women died there.

In Munich there are living today two women whose stories are parallel in that they were the wives – in the meantime the widows – of former Dachau prisoners both of whose stories have been documented and made known. There are many other analogies in these personal records. Both grew up in the Germany of Wilhelm II in politically conscious working-class families and thus almost inevitably became a part of the workers' movement. Both lived under forces and conditions which must be difficult to imagine for young women today. In their youth, at the end of the 1920s, both tried to break out of their poor living conditions and "get away", and both were induced to return by their husbands. A return which only a few years later led to prison and the concentration camp. The life of both has remained until today marked and determined by the experience of imprisonment and persecution. And both have had to conduct their struggle for survival alone, since their husbands, who were pronounced Nazi opponents long before 1933, were arrested before they were and disappeared behind walls and barbed wire. Each has consistently gone her own way, and both women still live and act according to convictions to which they have remained loyal. Even in old age – again on their own – they still take on what they view as their duty, mostly with little regard for their own wishes or needs.

But despite all the things the two biographies have in common, they are nonetheless two different stories of the survival of two very different personalities, and it is not easy to find a form of portrayal which does justice to both of them. It is hoped that the chronological representation of events does not appear too schematic, and that each story in itself can be seen as a sketch standing in contrast to the picture of women as passive and suffering, a picture which is still common today.

"Nothing is free. Nothing is given away either. We have had to fight for everything."

Centa Dengler is born in Munich on 12 March 1909[1]. Her father is a construction worker, and her mother, who is already forty years old at Centa's birth, must supplement the family income by washing and cleaning. A year and a half later she is joined by a sister, Maxi. She is a twin, but the brother dies at birth. Maxi is consumptive and, especially during her childhood, always sickly and in need of care. From the beginning Centa always has to be the stronger one; she also has to take the thrashings for both. Thinking back on her childhood, she can recall no nice experience, she actually only remembers the social privation which, as she says, "didn't leave room for love or for what one calls a happy childhood."

The mother is a strict Catholic and under the father's influence breaks away from religion only slowly and with difficulty. The father is active in trade unionism and at first a member of the Social Democratic Party (SPD). Later he changes over to the Independent Socialists (USPD) and then to the Communists (KPD). He takes both daughters from an early age with him to political meetings and events. From the very beginning the social environment of both girls bears the imprint of politics. The family spends its free time in the circle of "free thinkers", and early on both sisters are taken into a Communist children's organization. In contrast to her sickly sister, Centa is a good student, and during her time at elementary school, through the mediation of a Catholic teacher of religion, she is offered the possibility of being adopted by a French family. Thus the way to a higher education would have been open to her. Already at that time Centa would have gladly escaped from the narrowness and poverty, but her mother strictly refuses the offer. "No, she said, even if I have to take my children on my back and go begging, they're not going to be taken away from me." The offer becomes invalid anyway, since the father makes the decision at about the same time to take the children out

---

[1] The account about Centa Beimler-Herker is essentially based on five long conversations which the author held with her between November 1986 and February 1987, as well as on the transcript of an extensive interview which representatives of the Association of Victims of Nazis (VVN) held with her in September 1977. Centa talks about herself and her feelings only with the greatest reservation. The drama of the story of her life is concealed behind extremely objective language which always attempts to keep her own personality in the background.

of religious instruction. He makes no attempt to explain this decision to his daughters. "He said, just get out. You don't need that. Religion is the opium of the people. Children don't need that."

Centa has only a few isolated memories about the time of the revolutionary government in Munich. "Father hid his gun at home and my mother was naturally afraid that the 'Whites' might come and then something might go wrong. But he did it anyway. He thought, nobody knows when you might need it. And then when the White guards really came to Munich from Dachau by way of Schleissheim – we were living in a rear house in Schleissheim Street – they called out 'Heads away from the windows, close the windows, or else we'll shoot.' And in the front house was a man with his family, he looked out of the window anyway and was killed by a shot from the street. There was naturally a terrific uproar."

Centa is fourteen when Hitler tries to seize power in 1923 with his march on the Feldherrnhalle. "That really interested me, and I went into the city without permission. And when the shots fell in Max Joseph Square, I was in front of the post office on the corner. When the mounted police came and the Nazi demonstrators began to shoot, I went into the post office with the crowd, and the people closed the door. When the police or the military opened the door again they were standing there with rubber truncheons. Well, they didn't hit me, but those with the swastika armbands, they got a good beating. Then I went home and told them everything, and my father said, you're good, you rascal, how did you get the idea of going there. You could have been done in."

After the conclusion of her eighth year at school Centa has to start earning money at once. To begin with she works for a pittance in the office of a company which manufactures beer bottle caps. At 16 she then officially leaves the Catholic Church and joins a Communist youth group. She buys a second-hand bicycle, paying for it in instalments, and can for the first time fulfill a material wish. And with that she is able, at least in her free time, to join the other members of the youth group and escape the cramped conditions at home. They spend their weekends at the Ammersee where they sleep in haystacks; on looking back, memories of these excursions are among the pleasantest of her youth.

Centa changes her job and works for two and a half years in a lawyer's office. A young man who she meets there and who emigrates to the US, to start work as a waiter and then to make his fortune there, offers her his help in case she wants to join him there. Centa already has her emigration papers, but until she's 21 she needs the permission of her parents and they again refuse to give it, she has to abandon the plan.

In the meantime she takes an ever greater interest in political events. Max Holy, the director of the Bayerische Rote-Hilfe-Organisation [Bavarian Red Help Organization], employs her to do office work, and finally she gets onto the editorial staff of the Communist daily newspaper Neue Zeitung. The newspaper is produced at night and Centa works at times simultaneously for three editors, until she suffers a physical breakdown. "Politically that was a highly explosive time, there were many elections, and many governments were dismissed. The party naturally always had a lot to do. I wasn't only working on the editorial staff, in the evening I was also at meetings. Or in the party office sending out election material. Until I couldn't go on any longer. Then I got a short holiday to recover. And then things were changed anyway and the newspaper wasn't produced at night any longer."

She encounters Hans Beimler for the first time in 1925 when, after his return from a trip through the Soviet Union with the first workers' and farmers' delegation, he speaks at a spontaneous demonstration at the Munich railway station. "Suddenly a beer barrel was rolled in from somewhere and Hans stood on it and then for the first time I heard him speak to the masses. He told them briefly about his experiences in the Soviet Union and you could see that deep down he himself was absolutely convinced of his ideas. He had a certain appeal."

In 1928 Hans Beimler, who she later cames to know better through party work and whose wife has commited suicide, asks her to move in with him and to take on the care of his two children, nine-and-a-half-year old Rosi and seven-and-a-half-year old Hans. Hans Beimler is 14 years older than Centa. "Because of his political work he was almost never at home. But when the mother is missing and the father isn't there either, then the children are missing something, that isn't good. Then I decided to do it. But for me that was a sacrifice, since I had to give up my job. But naturally at that age one gets along better with the children."

At the end of 1928, Hans Beimler is sent to Augsburg by the party leadership in order to reorganize the local chapter there. At first Centa stays with the children in Munich, and they seldom see Hans, since he is very intensively involved in the party work in Augsburg. In the end he wants Centa and the children to join him in Augsburg and to marry her. In the meantime he is well-known. Centa's parents have met him, and at least her father has no objections to the union. "Only my mother, she thought I was crazy, at my age with the children. She thought I wouldn't be able to cope. And since at that time you had to have your parents' written consent to marry before you were 21, we just waited until I was 21."

Centa was not in such a hurry for marriage and family life either. "I also thought about that. If I marry now and take on this family for good, then my personal wishes and interests have to go totally into the background. And I said I first want to escape, as you say, for a year and work at a real job. If possible in some party operation. And then we came to an agreement, Hans helped me, otherwise I probably wouldn't have been able to do it. The wife of a comrade, who was then imprisoned in the fortress Niederschoenenfeld, and who had a small child, was meanwhile to take charge of the household and the Beimler children."

Thus, on 1 November 1929, Centa can go to Hamburg where she works at the Russian trade agency. As before, the free evenings are reserved for honorary party work, but Centa, who until then has hardly ever been out of Munich, likes it there. She enjoys the new surroundings. Her place of work is in the free port where she can look at the big ships during her breaks, and she feels comfortable with her colleagues and comrades who show her Hamburg in their few free hours. Hans Beimler immediately regrets having let Centa go to Hamburg, and writes to her begging her to come back at once. When she refuses and reminds him of their agreement, she receives a telegram the day before Christmas from a friend of Hans': "Come immediately, Hans seriously ill." She gets on the train with the firm intention of returning to Hamburg directly after the holiday, but Hans Beimler – healthy and uninjured – has already given notice by telegraph to her place of work in Hamburg and ordered her things to be sent back. "You're disappointed at first of course. But the children said, you're here again at last. That was really what decided me. They were really inconsolable when I was away. And they begged, please stay with us now. Then I said, well, ok. And with that my odyssey was over."

Centa and Hans Beimler, who is in the meantime Town Councillor in Augsburg, marry in July 1930. Centa, who at first felt very foreign in Augsburg, settles in well and makes many friends. The center of political work and also of social life is the "workers' home" founded by Hans Beimler. It is a two-storey house which the party rented from a brewery. This house also accomodates rooms used by the Party and a youth association, together with a restaurant, which serves good, inexpensive meals.

Very soon Hans Beimler becomes the Communist Party representative in the Bavarian Landtag (parliament) and then in 1932 the representative in the Reichstag and the leader in charge of the Communist Party in southern Bavaria. They have to return to Munich. Centa only reluctantly gives up her party work and her friends in Augsburg. After being away from Munich for years she has first to make contacts again. Hans is practically always away, and their economic situation is far from rosy. "A Communist Party secretary was just a poor dog, they got very little money. And when he was a representative he had to hand over his daily allowance and was able to keep only a little sum, maybe 50 marks, for books and expenses. One time I said, I don't have a single mark left. At that time he was just leaving Augsburg for Munich, to take the express to Berlin. And then he said, I'll see what I can get. Come to the train, I'll throw it out as we pass by. I then went with Rosi to the railroad in the Fasanerie where we were living at that time. But at that speed the air pressure of the express train tore the rubber band which held the box together and all the coins were scattered around. We crawled along the tracks and gathered our money. I even don't know if we found it all. But any way, for the time being we were out of the mess again."

The political situation is becoming critical, and Centa and Hans discuss with friends and at party meetings what precautions have to be taken in regard to the threatened National Socialists seizure of power. However, after January 30, 1933 the Beimlers share the opinion of many people in the opposition that Hitler and his government would only be around for a short interlude. "One believed it may perhaps last for a few months, but no longer. The trade unions will call a general strike and with the help of the strong workers' parties the brown spook will quickly be done away with. Actually, each of us thought that way."

Efforts are made to bring party addresses, important papers, typewriters and stencil printers into illegal accomodations, and Hans Beimler is also looking for a place where he can go into hiding if need be, although at this time Centa doesn't know that. On March 5, 1933 he is once again elected as a representative to the German Reichstag, but in the morning of March 5 he is warned by a policeman from his city quarter that after the polling centers are closed all leading members of the Communist Party are to be arrested. In a great hurry Hans and Centa pack the most important things on a cart and go to their illegal quarters, a small garden cottage in the section of Munich called Großhadern. The children stay in the care of Centa's parents and sister.

In that cottage they have already hidden a typewriter, a stencil machine and a lot of paper and they begin immediately to produce illegal material, especially leaflets which then are brought, mostly by Centa, to arranged meeting places. Centa also secretly goes back to her apartment which is in a terrible condition after being searched. Since they don't have money any more for the rent, the apartment has to be given up, and the children move to Centa's parents' apartment.

"Financially that was very bad since one didn't have anything in reserve. Nobody had money in a bank account or anything like that. Of course, the party tried to collect membership fees in its illegal existence too, but there were naturally comrades who didn't hand over anything any longer. Then one only got a few mark from time to time for the most important things. One really had to fight one's way through. I still remember that we had carrots and a few potatoes in the garden cottage. I think I got them at my mother's. I fixed a vegetable stew, and we ate it with great hunger. And Hans said, hopefully it won't be our last meal before execution. And on the next day he was arrested."

Hans Beimler is betrayed. On April 11, 1933 he goes to an arranged meeting place to receive party funds. It isn't his contact man who is awaiting him there, but a police car. When he doesn't come home, Centa goes to the apartment of the comrade who was supposed to meet Hans. He assures her that Hans didn't keep his appointment, but Centa doesn't believe him. Her suspicion is confirmed, a few days after Hans Beimler's arrest, when a young, unknown man comes to Centa's parents, without saying a word gives them Hans Beimler's belt, and again disappears immediately. On the inner side of the belt Hans Beimler had noted down how horribly he was mistreated in the police headquarters and that he is convinced that the man he wanted to meet has betrayed him. Centa passes the belt around because the comrades must be warned. In addition, through contact with a Catholic priest, the reports about torture of political opponents are to be made known to a broader public[2].

Centa is arrested ten days after her husband in her parents' apartment. Until then she has not thought much about what an arrest would mean for her, although Hans spoke with her about it during the weeks when they lived in the garden cottage. "He pointed out to me that it is possible that one will be physically mistreated, and that one has to be courageous. In no case must one give names or addresses. But really, as soon as you became a member of the party, you were taught that a Communist doesn't make any statements to the police."

She only really becomes afraid when she has to go after dark along an unlighted cemetery wall to get to the garden cottage. And this fear becomes her doom when she decides, on the evening of 20 April, rather to seek shelter at her parents' than to go along this dark way. As she tries to leave the apartment unnoticed the next morning around five o'clock, she is picked up by two police investigators and taken to Munich police headquarters in Ettstreet. At first she is on the floor under the cell where Hans Beimler is being held prisoner, but already two days later she is moved to the prison Muenchen-Stadelheim. Written news of Hans is delivered to her twice more before he is taken to the concentration camp at Dachau.

Hans Beimler is one of those opponents of the new regime who are persecuted with implacable hatred. Nonetheless, he succeeds in fleeing, first from the camp at Dachau, and then from Nazi Germany. In the summer of 1933 he writes about his experiences. The pamphlet, "The Nazi Murder Camp of Dachau – Four Weeks in the Hands of Hitler's Hell-Hounds", appears in August 1933 in German, English and Russian at the publishing association of foreign workers in the Soviet Union and becomes one of the first internationally known documents about the system of terror in Germany.

But the hatred of the National Socialists doesn't only extend to Hans Beimler himself. After his arrest the children are not given permission – contrary to the usual practice – to visit their father. And like the wives of other political functionaries, Centa is imprisoned as a relative without being charged or having a trial and is treated like a criminal. And after Hans Beimler succeeded in escaping from the concentration camp Dachau in the night of the 8 to 9 May 1933, even Centa's father is time and again taken into custody and cross-examined for days. The son of Hans Beimler is forcibly brought to a youth educational institution in Wasserburg, and the 14-year-old daughter Rosi is allowed to stay in Munich only because she is already doing an apprenticeship.

---

[2] See: Otto Gritschneder: Die Akten des Sondergerichts über Stadtpfarrer Dr. Emil Muhler, in: Beiträge zur altbayerischen Kirchengeschichte. Band 29. München 1975

Finally, in September 1933, Centa's sister Maxi, who has also worked illegally with her friend, later her husband, is delivered to the prison Muenchen-Stadelheim. And then, when even Centa's mother, who is accused of supporting the forbidden Rote-Hilfe-Organisation [Red Help Organization], has to serve a ten-week sentence in the correctional institution Neudeck, all the family members have become victims of the ineffective rage of the persecutors from whom Hans Beimler escaped.

Centa herself remains in prison for two years and nine months in Muenchen-Stadelheim. There she becomes familiar with all aspects of prison life. At first she is put in a solitary cell and only sees the other 'political' women during the daily walk in the courtyard. "But as happens in all prisons, we soon had a good relationship, we exchanged political news, and since newspaper were allowed there, we were naturally informed about further developments." Thus she first learns from a fellow prisoner about the flight of her husband from Dachau concentration camp. However, she can only believe it when she herself is cross-examined about it. "There I said, why are you asking me about it? I'm imprisoned here, what am I supposed to know about it, behind bars here?"

After some time the solitary confinement order is repealed, and Centa is put into a communal cell with six other women. "We had an unusually good, comradely life together, sharing our joys and sorrows." And then when, after a few months, the women were assigned to work, the connections to other political prisoners were intensified, also those toward the outside. Centa works in the laundry and finds many chances there to send on or take in news which is hidden in the laundry. In the same way illegal tracts, which are smuggled in from the outside, also reach the imprisoned comrades.

When Maxi comes to Centa's cell, she takes her under her care again. Maxi works in a cleaning squad and thereby has access to the quarters of the authorities. "She got hold of all sorts of things, even paper and pencils, which was of course forbidden. Then in our cell we made ourselves a card game out of small cards. And suddenly in the evening – one could always tell by the way the doors were unlocked – there would be a check of the cells. Everything was always ripped out, and they looked to see what they could find. All right folks, what do we do now? Since we were working outside, we had to take our dishes for the meals with us into the cell, and they weren't standing in front of the door, but beside it. The food was awful stuff which we mostly didn't eat. So we throw our playing cards into the soup. Of course they were ruined. But otherwise there would have been a punishment report and perhaps a few days arrest. And afterwards we just made ourselves new ones."

The political prisoners in the men's division mostly come, after serving their sentence or without any trial, from Stadelheim into the concentration camp at Dachau. Centa has contact with many of them. She learns what is going on outside, who is arrested, who is released, who appears before the court, and much more.

Through encoded messages she also finds out that Hans Beimler has managed to escape abroad. From there, with the help of comrades in Germany and his daughter Rosi, now 15 years old, he organizes the abduction, on 24 December 1934, of his son Hans from the educational institution 'Maria Stern' in Wasserburg and the transport of the children to Switzerland, from there to Czechoslovakia and finally to the Soviet Union. The children meet their father once again during their journey through Czechoslovakia. It is their last meeting with him.

Centa once again receives the confirmation of the successful escape of the children through the interrogating officials of the Gestapo who question her about it. She is calmed and relieved, above all this means that a financial burden has been taken away from her parents who only have her father's tiny invalid's pension to live on. When he dies in 1935 after a serious illness, the Gestapo doesn't allow even one of the two daughters to be at the burial, even though the Director of the prison Muenchen-Stadelheim had supported them on this point.

At the end of January 1936 Centa and Maxi, together with three other women, are unexpectedly brought from Stadelheim to the Munich police prison. At first they hope that this may perhaps mean their release. But after two days they are shipped on by rail via Hof and Halle to Hannover without knowing where they are being sent. It is the first transport from Stadelheim to the first women's concentration camp Moringen, which at this time is not yet under SS authority. "A man in a loden suit with a little feather on his hat 'received' us and told us that this was a women's prison for 'politicals'. Pretty soon we found out that the whole camp was a workhouse with a few hundred men and around twenty women. In the coming weeks we were joined by old familiar faces from Munich, and also our comrades from Franconia were brought to Moringen. Thus the 'Bavarian Hall' came into being. At this time there was also a 'Jews' Hall' and one where the Jehovah's Witnesses were housed[3]."

During the winter months, Centa first has to sort peas and lentils, later she works in the tailoring shop where the clothing which has been collected for the 'Winterhilfswerk' [Winter Relief Organization] is cleaned, sorted and repaired. The prisoners are freezing and the food rations are poor. "It was limited to beans, peas and lentils, apparently because they grow well there, and the only ray of sunshine was Sunday when there were always meat-balls and potatoes."

But the solidarity of the women with each other in Moringen is perhaps even closer and warmer than it was in Stadelheim.

There were seven of us in a four-man cell, as close as lifelong friends. Of

---

[3] See: KZ Moringen – Männerlager, Frauenlager, Jugendschutzlager. Eine Dokumentation. Herausgegeben von der Gesellschaft für christlich-jüdische Zusammenarbeit Göttingen e. V. und dem evangelisch-lutherischen Pfarramt Moringen o. J.

course that means sharing personal joys and sorrows. For example, we had a comrade who wasn't married and had an illegitimate child. The boy came into an institution, and she suffered a lot because of being from her child and was often depressed. Although she was otherwise a happy person. When letters or other things depressed her, then we just tried to cheer her up again, and we always managed to do that. And this community of solidarity helped us to endure the time in prison more easily. It was the same with the parcels we got from outside. My mother would not have been able to send me any more parcels, but the solidarity on the outside made it possible for her to bake a cake once in while and buy something for us, which she then sent off at once. Although she herself mostly lived on the food in the soup kitchens. But other prisoners got things from home more often, and everything was shared in solidarity to the last crumb. No one had more and no one had less."

In the spring the women voluntarily report for work out of doors. They work at the cultivation of mulberries which are needed for breeding silkworms. After being shut up for years, they are all happy to be outside. But the food continues to be atrocious. "At noon a man came from the workhouse with a soup pail on the cart and a ladle. We had our Bimmel – that's what the dish was called – and then everyone got a scoop of the contents of this pail. But first we had to shove aside the grubs and the worms. We stacked them up nicely around the edges and showed them to our guard who was unwilling to believe that there were maggots in the cabbage soup."

Centa and her comrades also find ways and means in Moringen both to receive illegal messages and to smuggle them out of the camp. The permitted correspondence is censored, but with the help of released prisoners in particular, relatives and also the women in Moringen receive real information. In this manner Centa learns that Hans Beimler has volunteered for the International Brigade in the Spanish Civil War. "It filled me with a certain satisfaction to know that Hans was fighting with a weapon in his hands for the Spanish Republic and didn't have to suffer the fate of the many thousands of anti-fascists murdered in concentration camps."

When the imprisoned women hear about the actions of solidarity which are being carried out in the world for the members of the International Brigade, they organize a collection of money among themselves and the sum is taken illegally to Spain.

"It must have been the end of January 1937. One day I noticed that women standing around in groups of three or four stopped talking whenever I joined them. I was shocked. After this had happened two or three times, I asked, what's the matter, what have you got against me? It looks as though you don't trust me, if you stop talking every time I come along. Then one comrade said, we can't keep it secret from Centa, we've got to tell her. We got illegal news, your Hans fell on 1 December 1936 in a battle in the university quarter of Madrid. – Well, I just had to come to terms with it. The solidarity and sympathy of the other comrades and also of the rest of the women was a big help. In the evening, when there was usually quite a lot going on in the room where we slept, one of the comrades announced that she had something to say. She officially told the women and said a few sentences about Hans' life. Then, at the end, she called on them to sing a Communist song. We did that then – quietly, of course. And after that not a word was spoken, somehow everyone was preoccupied with the news. But of course I couldn't show anything to the outside world, because the news wasn't official. A few weeks later I was called to the Director of our camp. In his room he offered me a seat and said, Frau Beimler, I have some sad news for you. I have learned that your husband has been killed in action in Spain. Unfortunately, he was on the wrong side, because if he had fought on the right side, today you would be a celebrated woman. What was I supposed to say? Probably he expected me to say something or show some emotion. I said, thank you for the news. I didn't say anything else. Then he said there was something he wanted to tell me in private, that from time to time he had to listen to enemy radio stations for official reasons. And he had heard that at the funeral ceremonies in Barcelona half a million people were present. I should find comfort on the fact that so many people had admired him. And then he also said – he was somehow embarrassed because I hadn't shown any emotion – actually the reason for your arrest is now over. The next time I am at the Reichssicherheitshauptamt [Main Security Services Office] in Berlin I will use my influence to secure your release. I said, thank you for that."

About three weeks later Centa is, in fact, released. But in Bavaria she hasn't fallen into oblivion. On the order of the Gestapo-Leitstelle [Main Gestapo Office] in Munich, against the petition of the camp doctor in Moringen, she has to return to Munich with a group transport which is underway for eight days with stops at various prisons. Like every other released political prisoner, she has to sign a statement that she will speak to no one about her experiences in prison or the concentration camp. And beyond that she has to report to the Gestapo every day for a year.

During the years of her daughters' imprisonment, Centa's mother had become a fearless opponent of the regime who made no secret of her opinions. "Naturally, I wrote telling her that I was being released and that I was travelling with a transport and that it would therefore probably take a few days. Then she went to the Gestapo every day and asked if I was there already. When I arrived there, they said, now your mother, she's a tiresome woman. She came here every day asking, well, isn't my daughter here yet? And why isn't she here yet? My mother was by then rather old and she was naturally terribly happy when I finally got back. She said, now we have to get busy and see that Maxi also gets out soon."

Centa's sister Maxi is released from Moringen in June with a group of Bavarian women. She is able to work again as a saleslady in a consumers' co-operative and in July 1939, shortly before the outbreak of war, she marries the boyfriend of her youth, who at the time of her release from Moringen is still imprisoned in the concentration camp at Dachau.

After a lot of effort, Centa herself manages to obtain work with the Upper Bavarian coal-mining corporation. Every day she has to make her way to the police to register there, even on weekends she is not allowed to leave the city. She is unable to accept a favorable job offer outside Munich. "They always said it was because of the danger of escape. I said to them I didn't intend to escape since my mother and my sister were in Munich. I knew, of course, they would have taken it out on them. And, besides, where should I have gone? Ridiculous."

She cautiously tries to establish contact with old friends and learns that, in the meanwhile, many of them have been arrested. After the unsuccessful attempt on Hitler's life in the Munich Buergerbraeukeller on 8 November 1939, she is also arrested again. "I didn't have a radio, because it was almost dangerous to have a radio. And then, of course, I didn't know anything about it. Early in the morning, around 5:00 or 5:30, the doorbell rings, and they say, State Police, get dressed and came with us. But, why? We don't know ourselves, come on. O.K., O.K. You get your toothbrush and of you go. Little by little, about sixty people, all well-known Munich Communists, arrive at the Wittelsbach Palace. And they say, there has been an attempt on Hitler's life. Then we said, we're going to be in a pretty mess if it's proved or suspected that it was done by our side."

After four weeks Centa is again released after her employer, in a company important for the war economy, has used his influence to secure her release. "My sister also worked very hard to get me out. She kept going to the Gestapo making inquiries. No, they said, no information. She'll came home again, if it turns out that the Communists haven't had anything to do with it. She also brought me little parcels, but wasn't allowed to visit me. Well, four weeks. They passed by. Again I presented myself at the company. It had become known there that I had been in prison for four years for political reasons. The head of personnel said, I suggest that you first take a little vacation. You will naturally be employed with us again. You were arrested without being guilty. And at the same time he paid me my salary for these four weeks. Of course, I was very happy."

Occasionally Centa receives news about her step-daughter, who is working in a factory in the Soviet Union and at the same time going to schools to improve her education. She doesn't know, however, that the young Hans Beimler has left the Soviet Union in 1936 and made his way through to France. He also tries to join the International Brigade, but he is too young to be taken and he stays in Versailles until the outbreak of the war. From there Centa then one day receives a letter from him. Only years after the end of the war does she learn that Hans Beimler junior has been able to go to Mexico from Marseille with one of the last civilian ships to leave Europe, because one of the passengers recognized him as the son of Hans Beimler.

At this time, she herself has only very little contact with her old friends and comrades. Those who have been released from concentration camps under severe injunction are very cautious, and it even happens to her that old acquaintances cross to the other side of the street when they see her. At the beginning of the war several Munich Communists are again arrested and taken to concentration camps. "At the beginning, at the time of the so-called lightning victories, we were of course disheartened. We wondered how it was possible for the whole world to put up with it. Of course, even before that the annexation of Austria and the occupation of Czechoslovakia had been followed with alarm. We kept thinking that the other western countries would do something. But they weren't prepared for war at all and had been attacked without warning. And we said, in the end there's the expansion toward the East. That's something Hitler had already written about in *Mein Kampf*. And then there were discussions among our people. After the Hitler-Stalin pact too. For example, we met at the Ammersee or in somebody's flat. Later on the Gestapo they blamed me for that. We know quite well where you all meet and that you listen to enemy broadcasts. I replied then, if you explicitly forbid me to meet friends I met in prison, or who I know from the past, then I'll follow the order. If you don't explicitly forbid it, I don't see any reason why I shouldn't get together with them.
In 1941, when Hitler had begun the war against the Soviet Union, it was clear to me all at once – and to all our friends – that it was now over. He won't conquer the Soviet Union. One still couldn't guess how long it would last, but we knew that was coming to an end."
In 1941 Centa is approached by an old friend who tells her about the underground links between Vienna and Berlin and asks her if she can find a contact address in Augsburg, where the organization has so far not established any contact. "I said, that's not so easy. I don't know anyone outside our Party. I'll first have to try to speak to our people. Maybe they know someone. Then I went to Augsburg three times. To Frau Proell, whose husband was in Buchenwald, to Frau Wagner, whose husband was in Dachau, and to Frau Wuerzinger, whose husband was also in Dachau. Then I cautiously presented my request. I said, we can't do it. But maybe you can think of someone. But independently of each other. You don't know where I'm going next time. Later the Gestapo told me exactly which days I was in Augsburg and who I was visiting. I said, all right, those are old friends of mine. Is it forbidden, perhaps, to keep in touch with old friends? That is the only reason I can give."
On 14 March 1942, Centa is again arrested. "Yes, it was the same procedure. At 5:00 in the morning the Gestapo officials came and picked me up. The interrogation official received me especially nicely. He said: Well, well, the Beimler women just can't give it up. But this time we laid out the noose, you put your head in it, and now we only have to draw it together."
Already in February 1942, the Gestapo had in Berlin, Munich and other cit-

ies, arrested members of various resistance groups, who had maintained a loose contact with one another. In Munich the 'Hartwimmer-Olschewski-Group' named after their leading members, was still in the beginning of building up conspiratorial cadres. All groups were betrayed by spies.

Five members of the Munich group are sentenced to death. Three die before sentencing after being severely maltreated whilst under arrest[4].

Centa spends seven months in detention. She works in the Munich Gestapo prison, first in the prisoners' kitchen and then in the officials' kitchen, as a dishwasher. Thus time and again contacts are made with other prisoners. She also once sees two Dachau prisoners who she knows from earlier. "They run across the courtyard, and I think, it's not possible, I know these two. I go out to the back and say, well what are you doing here? Defusing mines. That was a work squad. Called the suicide squad. And they also told me that the SS guard where they work doesn't stick his neck out. And people slip them something when they say they are Dachau prisoners. And when they arrive at the Gestapo prison they also get something to eat. But then they are always brought back to Dachau."

In the Gestapo prison Centa meets the man who later becomes her second husband, Hans Herker, who is also a codefendant in her trial. Since the beginning of the National Socialist period he had also been a member of the Communist resistance. He was sentenced to two and a half years in prison in 1935, and then after serving his sentence he was imprisoned in the concentration camp at Dachau until the middle of 1939. When Centa meets him he is one of a group of manual laborers who are kept in detention at the Gestapo prison to carry out routine repair work.

Centa spends six or seven months of her detention in the Gestapo prison. She is only once brought for four weeks to the prison Muenchen-Stadelheim, when an official has seen her going alone from the prison into the Gestapo building. After the conclusion of the interrogations she is released, again through the efforts of the management of her firm. Her colleagues were allowed to visit her during her imprisonment thereby reassuring her that they had pressed the managing director, the so-called war economy leader, to do something about her release. She can return to the company. However, this time she doesn't receive any money for the time of her imprisonment, and the Gestapo gives the order that, if she attracts the attention of the Gestapo once more, she is to be fired without notice. In addition, she takes care of the old and sick mother of Hans Herker, who is only released from detention after a year and a half. In January 1944 he is called up to Battalion 999, the so-called rehabilitation unit of the armed forces, although he had been classified as unsuitable for military service.

After suffering bomb damage in September 1943 Centa's company ('Ober-

---

[4] See: Hartmut Mahringer: Die KPD in Bayern 1919–1945 in: Bayern in der NS-Zeit, Band V, hrsg. v. Martin Broszat und Hartmut Mehringer. München 1983, p. 278.

kohle') is evacuated from Munich to Penzberg where one of the company's own mines lies. Centa moves to Penzberg, "a little bit out of the firing line", where she first shares a room with a colleague. Very quickly she again falls under pressure to do things which could cost her life. "It was like this. Our office was on the first floor. The widow of the mine director lived in the lower rooms. And there was a lovely big garden. Two men from the Soviet prisoners' camp had to do the garden work. We saw them from upstairs. They were in an awful condition, very thin, and also poorly clothed. No proper boots, just the famous wooden clogs. We talked it over with colleagues, and everyone thought we should do something to help them a little. And then they said to me, we're willing to give you money and meat ration cards, if you'll see to it that those two get something. So I took charge of that and left something for them in the cellar in a pit. Although that was not without danger. Then we made gestures to them, very crudely, that there was something to eat, down there. Sometimes, a few cigarettes as well and a bit of chocolate. And that went on for a long time, almost until the end."

In July 1944 – before the events of 20 July – the trial against 18 defendants, among them Centa Beimler, takes place before a court in Munich, more than two years after the arrest and investigation. The defendant Hans Herker does not take part in the trial. His senior officer in the army had told the court that he had been transferred to the front. Centa is sentenced to one and a half year's imprisonment for aiding and abetting the preparations for high treason. They cannot prove anything against her. The three women from Augsburg testified in agreement with one another that Centa's visits had been of a purely private nature. "I still have to laugh, even today. In my case it was said that I was being sentenced because as a trained Communist, I didn't tell the Gestapo about these illegal organizations."

The rest of this sentence is, again through the intervention of the management of Centa's firm, reduced to probation until the end of the war, and Centa is allowed to return to Penzberg. Her relationship to Hans Herker becomes constantly closer after his release from detention. Thus, she also learns that he hadn't been sent to the front, but that his senior officer just wanted to protect him from taking part in the trial. Hans Herker's sentence is also reduced to probation until the 'final victory'.

In Penzberg, a small miners' town about forty kilometers south of Munich, the National Socialists had never really been able to gain a foothold. In 1934, in the prison Muenchen-Stadelheim, Centa had already met miners from Penzberg who had been sentenced in one of the largest trials in the early times of National Socialism in Bavaria, for possession of concealed weapons, meaning preparation for high treason[5]. Most of them later came to the con-

---

[5] See: Klaus Tenfelde: Proletarische Provinz. Radikalisierung und Widerstand in Penzberg/Oberbayern 1900–1945, in: Bayern in der NS-Zeit, Band IV, hrsg. von Martin Broszat, Elke Fröhlich und Anton Großmann. München 1981, p. 247.

centration camp of Dachau, where in turn Hans Herker came into contact with them. Thus Centa, when she comes in September 1943 to Penzberg, has a number of reasons to make contact with the local people. In addition, the name Hans Beimler also means something to the Penzberg Communists.

Centa brings her mother, who has been bombed out of her quarters in Munich, to stay with her and, for a time, her sister too. She learns that Hans Herker, who finally was nonetheless sent in the direction of the eastern front, is lying wounded in a military hospital camp near Rosenheim. He had been hit by shell splinters, without having himself been involved in battle action. She also brings him to Penzberg in the hope that he can find a place in the miners' hospital there.

In the meantime people in Penzberg, as in other places, are waiting for the end of the war. Just as in Dachau, in Penzberg too on 28 April 1945 they finally hear the call of the 'Freiheitsaktion Bayern' ['Bavarian Freedom Action'], on the radio from Munich, summoning the people to lay down their weapons and put an end to the senseless destruction. As in Dachau, a group of opponents to the regime then goes to the Town Hall in Penzberg to remove the officials holding office there. As in Dachau, this action takes place a few hours too early. In Dachau, the insurgents are shot by a returning SS-unit. In Penzberg a group of the 'Volkssturm' [civilians, mostly young boys of 16 and old men, drafted at the very end of the war] sets up an execution squad, which puts to death seven people in the afternoon of 28 April. Hans Herker was also supposed to go to the Town Hall, but Centa was of the opinion that his health still wouldn't allow that. She didn't let him go thereby saving his life.

Otherwise than in Dachau, in Penzberg the execution of the insurgents brings no end to the final senseless killing. In the night of 29 April, a group of the so-called Werewolves hunts down 'traitors' according to prepared lists. Many are able to hide but nine more people from Penzberg fall victims during this night of murder. On the following day the American troops march into Penzberg and take it without a fight[6]. "The people were waiting with every fiber of their being for the Americans to move in. After this night of murder, the grief in all Penzberg was terribly great. Because it affected almost every family. And the events were such a burden that it paralyzed people."

Of course, Centa is needed immediately. First, as a victim of the Nazi regime and the widow of Hans Beimler, she has to dissuade the American occupiers from seizing her living quarters and those of her colleagues. Then she is called to the Town Hall by Sepp Raab, a Communist miner, who was able to escape abroad, and who, after his return, was chosen by the Americans to be mayor of liberated Penzberg. She is supposed to take over the management of the savings bank. "The savings bank was closed, since the people who worked there were practically all members of the Nazi party, except for the

---

[6] Tenfelde, op. cit. p. 369.

apprentice – he had a clean record. Now the savings bank was supposed to be re-opened for business. Then I was asked to go to the Town Hall. Mayor Raab wants to speak with me. He had the idea that I should manage the savings bank until things got going again. I said, for God's sake, how do you think I'm going to manage that? I don't know anything about it. Well, he said, do you imagine I was born to be a mayor? The Americans said, you do that now, and I just have to do it. Then, together with the apprentice, I re-opened the bank and the customer service began again. That lasted a few weeks until someone came from Munich. It's strange, when you're just simply shoved into a responsible position. But the boy was quite good. He was the son of a Penzberg Social Democrat, with whom I'd had contact earlier, because he had also provided food for the Soviet prisoners of war."

On 24 August 1945, Centa and Hans Herker marry. He goes back to Munich to look for an apartment. Centa stays with her company until the end of the year, and then she gives up her job there in order to start a new life with her second husband.

There is no break for a rest. Hans Herker, who is politically uncompromised, is named as the director of the food office in Muenchen-Schwabing. "That was terrible. He suffered a lot because of that. The need was so great. And the families who didn't have anything, who were really the worst off, they came to this distribution office. He said, you're supposed to distribute something you haven't even got. You always had to say 'no'. There isn't anything to give out."

Together with other women in her part of the city, Centa sets up a sewing shop where old pieces of clothing, primarily from military supplies offered by the American occupation authorities, are taken apart and worked over for civilian use. "A lot of women worked there. Four master tailors were in charge, and we did the necessary preparation work. My mother also helped. And even women who had been in the National Socialist women's organization offered their services. There was one woman among us who was very skilful in making house shoes out of raffia material. We made a lot there. It was all for children and adults who didn't have anything. A comrade who was a master baker and delivered a lot to the Americans set aside some things for the children's afternoons, which we also organized. They were naturally very popular. Then there was also a puppet show or there were Christmas events, all mainly for the children. I was totally absorbed by this work. That went on until July 1948, when my daughter was born. Then there was peace and quiet for some time."

Against Centa's wishes, Hans Herker gives up his position with the City of Munich in 1947 in order to work as the secretary for the Communist party in the city council in Munich Town Hall. "He just let himself be talked into it. That was even more work than before. You didn't only have the people in the Town Hall with their petitions, they would also be waiting for him at home. And then after the currency reform, it was all over. The city councillors said, yes, Hans, but we don't have any more than you do - 40 marks. Now you'll have to look for something else. Then he slowly began to work as a painter again. In the beginning of 1950, he set up in business on his own."

Their daughter, Christa, grows up with the political work of her parents and every sort of problem is discussed within the family circle. She is barely sixteen years old when her father suddenly dies of a heart attack. "He worked too hard. You just used to think we need a refrigerator or a new item of clothing, and above all, we have a child, and she needs all sort of things. And then from one hour to the next, he was dead of a heart attack. He was only 58 years old, and it hit me very hard. I had an excellent relationship with my husband, and then it ended so abruptly. And I think - maybe that's not fair - a child can't replace a husband. We had so many plans. Hans always said, when we retire we'll do this and that. But he just worked too hard, and on top of it all he also had the political work. He was very thorough, he never did anything superficially."

After the war, Centa was able to re-establish contact with the Beimler children. The contact with Hans Beimler junior, who had established himself in Mexico as a film producer, first came about through an appeal in a magazine published by Oskar Maria Graf. Hans had married a North American in Mexico, and they had two sons. When he learned that Centa had a daughter, he sent her, via a charitable organization in Switzerland, parcels with things which he supposed that she couldn't get in Germany. "He thought what I might need as a mother was baby oil and diapers. And once a big parcel of safety-pins arrived. Then we really had a good laugh."

In the Soviet Union Rosi had married an Austrian, with whom she returned to Vienna in 1946. He had a son from his first marriage. In the early fifties, Rosi and he are able to visit Centa for the first time in Munich. Then in 1957 Centa goes to Vienna for the first time. After that she develops a warm relationship with Rosi and her family which has lasted until today.

After the Federal Compensation Law comes into effect, Centa and her husband apply for imprisonment compensation. Beyond that, Centa tries to make a claim for health problems as the result of imprisonment. "That was in 1954. Then it was discovered that I have a malignant tumor, and I was treated for five weeks in the clinic. My claim regarding damage to my health was rejected. For cancer or tuberculosis, there is no compensation. Every mortal person can have that. I did get a pension for being unable to work, but after some time it was taken away again. I wasn't prepared to accept that without any protest so I appealed. I went before the social court, and in my arrogance I said, I don't need a lawyer. I can defend myself and also dispute with the expert. That, of course, was all wrong. He talked so much that I didn't know who I was anymore. I became so upset that I wasn't able to say anything. Then I lost. Maybe I should have fought on. But my husband had the point of view, why should you let yourself be dragged around there. You only get upset. We're managing all right by ourselves, we don't need that. So then you just gave up. He felt so well himself that he didn't even make any claims for health damages."

But Centa is able to achieve one success, however. She fights with the help of an official defender for compensation for Hans Beimler's children. After two and a half years of negotiations, each of the children is awarded an indemnity of more than five thousand marks for educational disadvantages. Hans doesn't want to have the money. He invites Rosi and Centa's daughter, Christa, to Mexico, and the money covers the costs of their flight.

After doing very well in her final school examinations, Christa breaks off her business administration studies after a short time, to rush into a marriage which quickly breaks down. In disillusion she goes to Canada, where she marries a second time and has two children. Together with her husband, she is active in trade union work. The relation to her mother is very close and warm, but it's a long way from Munich. "I should fly over. But the older you get, the more problematic it is. She has often suggested to me that I should move over. If I were twenty years younger, I probably wouldn't have any doubts about it at all. But as an older person, you're a burden on the young. I see it that way. I've also tried to learn English, but I didn't get far. And, oddly enough, my Christa didn't teach her children any German." Since the death of her second husband, Centa has worked for the Association of Victims of Nazism (VVN) in Munich. "At that time, my comrades said, we've got to get her some work, then she'll get over it more easily. And that was true. I started in January 1965, and I've worked there ever since then. It was very good. It helped me."

She is now 78 years old and not in the best of health, but she can't contemplate 'retirement'. Even when her daughter Christa in Canada and her stepdaughter Rosi in Vienna urge her to treat herself to more rest and free time and to reduce her obligations. But the organization of the Nazi victims is as dependent on her work as is the Ludwig-Feuerbach Home for the Aged in Munich, where former Nazi victims also live and which she also helps to care for.

Over the course of the years she has also been increasing taken up with her role as a witness, who can report from personal experience about resistance and persecution. However, the Communist Hans Beimler has never been granted the same esteem in the Federal Republic as in the DDR, where there are books and films about his life and where Centa, as his widow, has been repeatedly honored.

Then one day Hans Beimler the third, who lives in California, stands at her door. His father has never spoken with his children about the past. He has therefore set out to ask his grandmother about it himself. He knows practically nothing about the history of his grandfather, whose name he bears. A name which even in far removed America, often makes people stop and think to become attentive and ask him if he's any relation.

Centa has a difficult time with this grandson who has grown up in a completely different environment. And in addition she cannot speak English, nor he German. Hans would like to make a film about the life of his grandfather. For the time being, however, a short, very concise documentary film develops out of this meeting. It is produced by a German filmmaker and friend of Centa, together with her, her sister Maxi, her daughter Rosi and young Hans. "Hold on, girls," Centa's mother had called to her when she was in the prison Muenchen-Stadelheim. And with this as a title, the film depicts the efforts of the three women to show the young American the places of German history and to bring it to life.

At the end of the film Centa is seen sitting alone again in her kitchen. She is exhausted from the filming and the confrontation with the past, which, as she says, is again causing sleepless nights. But in her tiredness, there is no sign of resignation. You know that on the next day she'll again be where she's needed[7].

"It is good luck that one kept one's head, and that the head still works[8]."

A few months ago Lina Haag celebrated her 80th birthday[9]. Her appearance does not betray her eighty years or the years of suffering and persecution she lived through. She is attractive and elegantly dressed and you have the feeling that she enjoys this and has a talent for it. She is still a good-looking woman, and she enchants the people who come to her readings with her open and warm manner. Her public appearances are still always difficult for her. At first she is nervous and shy when she stands face to face with strangers. But time and time again she feels she finds reward enough in the manifold response her personal story of her fight against injustice and brutality evokes. She has for many years received letters from all over the world and numbers of unknown people have come to her home to thank her personally.

Her story, which she wrote in 1944 in the form of a letter to her husband at a time when she herself was still living underground and had no idea of his whereabouts, has lost nothing of its direct forcefulness, even after forty years. The book appeared in 1947 under the title "A Handful of Dust". Next to Eugen Kogon's "The SS-State", it was, after the war, one of the first publicized documents about the German resistance. The writer Oskar Maria Graf, who happened to come upon the book in New York, turned then to her and offered to write a preface for the second edition. Until his death, he then

---

[7] "Halt durch Dirndl!" – Stories of the Bavarian resistance. A film by Carin Braun, Munich, televised on Channel 2 (ZDF) in May, 1983.
[8] "Ich liebe und ich lebe" [I love and I live] interview with Lina Haag, aired in Radio Bremen on 5 September 1984.
[9] The narrative about Lina Haag is primarily based on quotations from her book – Lina Haag, Eine Handvoll Staub [A Handful of Dust] Frankfurt 1977. With her clear and concise language and her direct testimony, the book is captivating. Lina Haag has no shyness about showing her feelings, and even short excerpts of account are moving. Her story has been supplemented by three long discussions, which the author had with her in April and May, 1987, as well as by newspaper reports about her and by her own correspondence.

visited the Haags whenever he was staying in Munich. In the meantime, Lina Haag's story has also appeared in England, in the DDR, in the Soviet Union and in Hungary. Taking all editions together, a total of 348,000 copies of it have been printed. Until today she has declined to use the royalties for herself, but is pleased and proud when, above all, young people write to her and tell her how the book moved them.

Lina Haag is born on 18 January 1907, in Hagkling/Wuerttemberg. It is only on her first day at school that she discovers in the most embarassing fashion that her mother had brought her into her marriage as an illegitimate child.

"At that time no one bothered much. That was a joke. I came to school as a little six-year-old, quite innocent. My brothers were all named Haselmeier. I didn't know that my name was Jaeger, I was just the Haselmeiers' Lina. So, we are all standing there in a row. The teacher calls out our names, and as she does so, we have to sit down on the benches. She calls out, Pauline Jaeger. Who is Pauline Jaeger? I'm not Pauline Jaeger. I'm standing there on my own, the last one. And the teacher says, she's so dumb that she doesn't even know her own name. Everybody laughed. Children are really cruel. Filled with shame, I shoved myself onto the bench."

Today Lina has little interest in talking about her childhood in Schwaebisch-Gmuend. "There's nothing specially interesting about it, the usual things for a worker's child. I had four brothers, one died, three are still living today. My father was a Social Democrat, and after the war he joined the Independent Socialists (USP) and then the Communist Party. He worked as a grinder in a metal goods factory, rather hard work. We were a real proletarian household. My mother was out a lot, doing cleaning and washing. She had to earn money, too, there was never enough. We had to struggle on the lowest level. Already at thirteen I was sent to the factory, and I didn't like it at all. I worked in various factories as an unskilled worker; that was child labor. I was just sent along from one factory to the next. I went quickly wherever where the pay was highest, and worked. Then I turned over everything at home. Later I met Fred, and it was the same with him."

She gets to know Alfred Haag at a Communist youth group she has get into through her father. They marry when she is 19 years old because her daughter Kaete is on the way. It is the time of great unemployment. Alfred Haag has to live from his unemployment compensation, with which he also has to support his mother. He is politically very active and works as the publisher of a weekly magazine of the Communist youth group. "Working all the time, but with no income. It was utter wretchedness. I wanted to get out of this misery. I had an uncle in South America, in Buenos Aires, and I thought we could get out of all this if we went over there. He didn't send tickets for both of us, only for me. And the child was also there already. And then Fred promised me that he would come over with the child as soon as I had paid off my ticket and earned enough for his. Nothing came of that. I worked under the most difficult conditions over there, first as a nursery governess and then as a general servant. I did everything. I even took in other people's laundry for to iron at night in order to earn a few more pesetos. And then Fred wrote that he was not coming. The political work in Germany was too important. Something terrible was brewing up. He said I should come back. So I did." Lina doesn't talk to Fred about her disappointment. She has come back and doesn't question this decision any more. Only in her notes does she come back to this unsuccessful attempt to get her family away from the misery of Germany. She describes how, in her German prison cell, her stay in South America appears to her as a mirage of sun and freedom. "Did that really happen, so much sun, too much sun sometimes, so that one had to escape into the shade? ... When I stood at the railing gazing at the horizon for a while, I had the feeling I was standing in a glass ball, then the colors of the sea and the sky were one tone, one light. I couldn't see where the sea ended and the sky began. It was overwhelming. I have always avoided thinking about it, thinking about my South American trip, because it was one of our many missed opportunities. If you had come over too, things would be totally different today. But it seems as if it has to be like that – we were never able to experience something nice together. We aren't even allowed to endure the difficult and bitter things together, as you see ... I wanted to have you with me. And abroad. As though I had a premonition of what was awaiting us. We have gone our necessary ways. You to Dachau. I via Buenos Aires here to this solitary cell. You out of defiance. I out of love. You as a political person. I as a woman. Now I am alone again. As before."

On the day after Lina returns to Schwaebisch-Gmuend to her husband and daughter, Fred tells her that he is going to the Soviet Union for a nine-month course of instruction, and she is again without him. After his return he first works as the editor of the Sueddeutsche Arbeiterzeitung (Southern German Workers' Newspaper). A short time later he is elected as the youngest representative to the Stuttgart Landtag (Regional Parliament). This does not improve the family's economic situation, however, because he gives his daily allowance as a member of parliament to the party, except for a sum which he would earn as a carpenter. However, the work load increases substantially again, also for Lina, who takes care of her husband's paperwork in the evenings.

On 10 February 1933, Alfred Haag is picked up at home by SA men. First he is brought to a prison and then, afterwards to the first Wuerttemberg concentration camp on Oberen Kuhberg close to Ulm. Lina herself is arrested four weeks later. "They take me because the Reichstag is burning, because they need a reason to destroy the Communist Party. I belong to the Communist Party. Therefore they take me. I haven't committed any crime, but they take me into custody like a criminal. They see that lunch is cooking, that I have a child, that I can't just drop everything. Nevertheless, they rush me. They give the child to a neighbor. They take my coat off the hook and throw it at me. 'Get a move on', they say."

In her notes she comes back time and again to the behavior of her acquaintances in view of the oppressive measures which were apparent to everyone, and she closely records the turning away and the indifference of the neighbors. "As we go down the stairs, I hear doors closing everywhere, very quietly and carefully, but I hear them. On the street, a chill runs down my spide. I feel the stares at my back. People are watching me from all the windows. I don't see this, I know it. Everybody is doing errands, as always in such cases. Everybody is getting milk or coming from the market. Obviously, it has to be that way."

She remains under arrest for ten months, then she is released and allowed to go home. She doesn't allow herself any rest with her little daughter and her parents, but immediately begins her fearless and untiring fight for the release of Alfred Haag. This fight will be interrupted for years by her renewed imprisonment. But at first she puts all her hopes again in the family's emigration to Argentina. She sells the contents of her home in order to be able to finance the trip. She succeeds in being admitted to the Wuerttemberg Minister of Justice, and with the help of exit papers and ship's tickets she is able to get him to use his influence for the release of the prisoner Haag. But on the order of the Wuerttemberg Reichsstatthalter ['Reich's Governor'] the Gestapo does not release the prisoner. Lena's attempt to call on him personally fails as does a trip to Berlin where she hopes to gain something at higher levels. On 11 July 1935, Alfred Haag is brought from the Oberen Kuhberg to the concentration camp at Dachau.

Lina is also picked up again. "I am brought to the Gestapo. It is warm outside. The first spring sun is shining. Through a narrow opening in the window at the driver's seat I catch a glimpse of a shining world, I feel the promise of the coming spring. In the small opening where I can look out, the pictures fly past in colorful succession. The streets are filled with people. The first bright spring clothes shine out of the crowd. Baby carriages are standing in the parks. Trees and bushes are touched with a hint of green. Everyone is happy and in high spirits. I never knew that the world can be so beautiful. I could touch it with my hands, there is just the bodywork of the car between it and me. And yet it is unattainably distant." She is told that there is a search going on for an official of the Communist Party who has gone into hiding. She is supposed to inform the police immediately if the man should come to her seeking shelter. Lina knows that she now finds herself in a situation where there is practically no way out, a situation which can only end in her being arrested again. "That is now clear to me. This knowledge is so terrifying that I just stop and stand in the middle of the street. (Probably, I did stand there.) Then suddenly someone grabs me by the arm, and a car passes me with screeching brakes. In a moment people surround me, a man cries out excitedly that I had nearly been run over. As though that would have been so terrible. The man is obviously disappointed and insulted because I am staring at him in astonishment. What else could I do? Am I supposed to scream, too? Am I supposed to tell him that sooner or later I'll be arrested, separated from my child and imprisoned? Unjustly and illegally? Only because a subordinate ambitious Gestapo spy wants to make himself important? And that none of these curious women, who are standing around me now with so much sympathy, will be shocked or outraged? Such is life. My life is so. Is that life?"

It happens as was foreseen. Some time later, the unknown man is standing at Lina's door. She warns him and not long afterwards is arrested. She spends twenty months in detention in the Stuttgart Gestapo prison. In her account there are penetrating reflections about this time and about life in prison, how the prisoners swing between hope and despair and about her own, very private efforts not to give in.

"During the interrogation, one is utterly calm, indifferent, hard. The reaction afterwards is worse, when you're on your own in the cell. You're shaking all over, you can't control your quivering nerves. You have to hold on to the table, or lie on the floor until your nerves slowly become calmer again, and you fall into a deep sleep, like being dead. That's what it is like with me ... Dreams are good, and they are bad. Good, because at least for a short time one can escape from reality. Bad, because reality takes bitter revenge for this escape. One has to go back to reality. It sobers one not carefully, but brutally with all of its misery ... I am sentenced to light deprivation. I had never been in a dark cell before. At first, I don't see anything out of the ordinary about it. It is just night. You doze a bit, think angrily about the privileges which are probably going to be taken away from you. The slate board, which you've grown used to having, the newspaper, which I could have subscribed to later, the quarter pound of butter, which I could have bought extra for myself, the books from the library. Gradually, this eternal darkness becomes loathsome. You shut your eyes and try to sleep. It doesn't work. You stare again into the terrible darkness. Time stands still. The quietness is dangerous. You can hardly bear the feeling of being totally alone. Then comes the fear. Then come the attacks. The feverish thoughts. The anxiety. The crazy ideas. The hallucinations ... Your heart pounds. Around your stomach you have a terrible feeling of emptiness. Then, all at once, you think you aren't alone anymore. Someone else must be in the cell. You want to call for help. You start to talk to yourself. 'What do you want,' you say, 'you silly woman!' You swear and rage. That works. 'If it hadn't been for that filthy creature, that guard,' you say, 'then this wouldn't have happened.' 'That pig!' For some time things are better again. Then your heart starts pounding again ... You don't know how long you are tormenting yourself. Later you doze off again. When you wake up, it is night. Night? Oh, that's right, you're sitting in a dark cell. Then it starts all over from the beginning. But then it does become light again. I come back to the good old cell. In a cell full of light. My eyes become moist. Not only because they are blinded by the light."

During the time of her detention, Lina is continually affected by the fate of

her fellow prisoners. Lilo Herrmann, who is imprisoned in the cell across from her, is the first woman to be condemned to death by a National Socialist court. Lina is very upset and writes in moving words about her shock and her helplessness in the face of this verdict. "In the evening Lilo Herrmann whispers through a crack in the door across the hall to me that she has been condemned to death.
I am lying prostrate on the floor with my ear pressed against the door. I can only utter a groaning sound, no word of comfort, nothing. The horror shakes me. I cower on my plank-bed like a dog who is freezing. Condemned to death. A mother. A young woman. A twenty-six-year-old mother. Just because she doesn't want the war which Hitler wants. Going to death on the scaffold. In the name of the people. In the name of all the mothers of this people, of all the women, of all the loving people. To death. I'm driven half crazy by the hoarse, drunken voice of a stable guard continually bawling out the song 'When you leave, quietly say good-by' in the barracks across the way. I put my hands over my ears. It doesn't help. The melody won't go out my head any more. It is awful. Since then, I'm afraid of this hit song. During the night the whole building hears the news. Cell after cell. A prisoner next-door has a screaming fit. Her piercing screams alarm the house. Unrest fills the halls. As the guard unlocks Lilo's cell, there is loud crying in many cells. I'm crying, too.
The next day is Sunday. By mistake an assistant guard does not lock my cell. I notice it immediately and suspect a trap. However, when the guard on duty locks the corridor door, I am sure that it happened by mistake. Now the whole hall is 'clean'. I knock on Lilo's door. What should I say to her, what can I say to her? Tears are sitting in my throat. I have eight tablets against pain tightly pressed in my hand. That is all I have. In the long months of my imprisonment I begged for them under all sorts of pretexts and saved them for difficult nights. Now I shoved them, one at a time, under Lilo's cell door. 'They're sleeping tablets,' I say shaken. 'Nice of you,' Lilo says in a calm voice, 'thanks very much!' I ask if I can do anything else for her. No, she says, there's nothing more I can do for her. She'll be going away tomorrow, anyway, probably to Berlin . . . to the end, yes. And she wishes everyone the best."
Lina herself does not spend the whole time in solitary confinement. There are fellow prisoners who cheer her up and who help her to regain strength and overcome her depression.
"Life comes into my damned penitence cell, a life which I don't know anymore or which I haven't met yet. Lively, laughing with coquettish movements and a voluptuous figure, red cheeks and full lips. 'I'm Fritzi', the pretty blonde girl says. She places herself cheerfully in front of me, 'and you?' I need quite a bit of time to get over my astonishment. I'm completely taken by surprise with this uncommonly cheerful breath of life. 'Why are you staring so,' laughs Fritzi and reaches for her hair-do, 'is something wrong?' Now I

have to laugh as well. 'Well, good,' says Fritzi, satisfied, 'I thought you couldn't even laugh.' She looks at me critically, grabs me suddenly by the shoulder, turns me a little toward the light and says, 'But I think you need a little bit of amusement. Don't worry, I'm just the right person.' ... Sometimes our ward supervisor spies around and eavesdrops. She is a determined snooper. Fritzi hates her with real fervor. She also shows her that openly. Whenever that repulsive woman is listening in, she tells the most cunning stories with great glee. We pretend that we don't know anyone is listening. I let the sewing machine whiz, with well-played eagerness Fritzi sorts the laundry and, while doing so, she cries out so that the snooper outside can certainly hear it, 'You know,' she cries through the clatter, 'such a piece of filth like our supervisor is actually a pitiful wretch, don't you think? She'll never get a man into her bed in her life. Will have to die an old maid. Isn't that awful?' The shadow disappears from the door. Fritzi laughs. She makes an enjoyable scene out of the most miserable situations."

But Lina also hears life stories in her cell which are so horrible that she can't do anything exept record them with sorrow and anger.

"Maria. I don't know her, but I'm glad when I see her. She is ten years older than I, seriously ill with her gall bladder, tested by sorrows, a fine, brave person. They want to try her for high treason. I'm allowed to stay with her for eight days. During these days, I hear of a fate which touches me very deeply ... Willi was clever and showed a lot of ability in the organization of the 'Rote Hilfe' [Red Help]. He also had luck. Within one short year in Berlin he put numerous local chapters on their feet. Now he was supposed to build up the same organization in Hamburg, because he knew the city and the comrades there from earlier times. He wanted to be back again, at the latest, in two weeks. But he never came back again. At the memory of this, Maria presses her hands to her mouth. I feel it more than see it. It is evening. Twilight fills the cell. The beds have already been let down. We squat on them with our knees drawn up. I think about you.

When Willi hadn't returned after some weeks, Maria went to Hamburg. There she was told by some comrades that Willi had already gone home. She returns immediately to Berlin in the certain expectation of meeting him there again. But Willi had not come. And he did not come. Instead of him, the Gestapo came and arrested her. 'No doubt you were expecting Willi?' said the gentlemen from the Gestapo in an easy-going manner. 'You would really rather have Willi than us,' they joked, 'but he's been unavoidably delayed.' 'Imprisoned?' she asked. 'Oh, no,' laughed the jolly men, 'by no means.' – 'But?' she fearfully asked. 'That's a question,' the men laughed. 'Dead, of course,' they added casually. She didn't believe it. 'When we say that,' they assured her, 'you can believe it.' But she thought it was a trap. 'A funny person,' the men laughed, 'she doesn't believe that Willi is dead.' They found it a good joke. And because they had a sense of humor, they went to the cemetery with her and had Willi's body dug up. Then she saw him. Maria's voice is quiet and moaning. Perhaps I am the first person she has told this terrible story. Perhaps it is a relief for her to tell me about it, I don't know. In the growing darkness I only see the white gleam of her face.

Thus, she saw now that he was dead. Beaten to death. She was still able to recognize him. She recognized the blows made by the police, the blood-streaked welts from his ears to his throat. 'Well, said the men with pleasure, 'do you believe it now?' - 'Why was he beaten to death?' she asked tonelessly. 'Because he was obstinate at the interrogation,' the gentlemen said. And they added jokingly: 'Hopefully, you will be more intelligent!' He had not betrayed his Hamburg comrades, that was what they called obstinate. He was arrested at the barrier of the train station in Hamburg, as he wanted to go to the Berlin train. He had been denounced by a spy.

Now it is dark in the cell. We can hear the horses stamping over at the barracks. Otherwise, it is silent. 'Since then,' Maria continues, 'I've been in prison.' Nothing can be proved against her, she didn't have anything to do with Willi's work, but they're bound to find something."

In March 1938, Lina Haag is sentenced by a Stuttgart court to two years imprisonment; the twenty months of detention are to be included in this sentence. After the verdict is announced, she is brought to the prison Gotteszell in her home town, Schwaebisch-Gmuend, where she is supposed to serve the rest of her sentence. Filled with joy and impatience, she awaits her release to freedom.

"In a few days I'll be with Kaetle again. I'm looking forward to that. I can't even say how much I look forward to that. My whole being is transformed. I want to leave all the bitterness, all the spiritual torment, and all doubts about the future behind me here when I go. Sometimes I completely forget that I'm still here, I think so intensively about all that. The days are becoming too short for my many plans and dreams. On the day before my release I am called into the office. For two years long I have looked forward to this moment, for two years I have thought about how I will behave. I'll be officially informed about my release, and I'll be given a few golden rules of life to take along. Actually, I wanted to be hard and let the officials and the supervisors feel my boundless contempt. But now my heart beats with joy. I walk into the room smiling."

She had rejoiced too soon. Lina Haag also has to go the way of most political prisoners, who after serving their sentence without any further court proceedings, without being given any reasons, and without their relatives being informed, are delivered into a concentration camp. Nothing comes of the reunion with her daughter she has dreamed of. Her daughter is growing up with grandparents, and her first attempts at writing are letters to her mother in prison. Lina is taken to the women's concentration camp Lichtenburg near Torgau in a prisoners' transport which takes four weeks and during which she has to wait for the continuation of the journey at various penitentiaries and prisons.

"Lichtenburg is Torgau's old fortress, a mighty medieval castle with many towers, wide courtyards, dark dungeons, and endless halls, a frightening, gigantic construction with mighty walls, not a bright castle, but the ideal concentration camp. From Gotteszell to Lichtenburg is like a tale about the Holy Grail.
We are drawn up in one of the inner courtyards. About thirty women, political prisoners, Jews, criminals, prostitutes and Jehovah's Witnesses. The women guards of the SS circle us like gray wolves. I see this new ideal of the German woman for the first time. Some have vacant, some have brutal faces, the mean set of the mouth is the same in all of them. They go back and forth with great strides and flapping gray capes. Their commanding voices resound over the courtyard and the large wolf-hounds, which they take with them, tug threateningly at their leashes. They are fantastic, and pitiless, calling morbid ancient legends to mind, and probably much more dangerous than the brutal male SS torturers, for they are women. Are they women? I doubt it. They can only be creatures, creatures with gray dogs and with all the instincts, malice and wildness of their dogs. Monsters.
It is at any rate clear to me from the first moment that here another wind is blowing, a sharper, more dangerous wind. Everything is different, new, more complicated than in prison. But I'm lucky. In my ward I meet Trudl Gessmann again. I was with her for a long time in adjoining cells in the Stuttgart detention prison in Weimar Street. We hardly ever exchanged a word with each other, but we communicated in Morse code, and we saw each other during walks in the courtyard. Now we greet each other like good old comrades who have known each other all their lives. All at once my insecurity has vanished, I have a person who knows her way around here and whom I can depend on."
Lina spends almost a year in the concentration camp Lichtenburg, a terrible year, not to be compared with her time in prison. She survives this year and writes down what she has experienced and seen, also to keep alive the memory of the women who she sees dying there. "We find the fact that Hitler's creatures are recruited not from the antisocial, but from the petty bourgeois element of society, horrifying and upsetting. Then they are not born sadists, not professional criminals, not impassioned murderers, but rather philistine petty bourgeois. Like everyone else. The same organizational talent, which on the outside tries to raise public health with lining-up and vitamin drops, drives the death rate to new heights here in the camp. Hardly a day goes by without a dead woman being discovered in the early morning in a dark cell. They are 'discovered', although the prisoners who are working in the quarters often have already on the day before to remove the clothes from the cell of those who are marked to die in the night. The dead women lie naked on the floor with battered bones and blood-stained bodies. Some have tried to push themselves under the plank-beds, or to flee under the tables, in order to escape the death blows. Crumpled, beaten, stiffened beings, who once had

names, husbands, children, homes, lie there with unfathomable fixed stares. That is the hell of the dark cell with its insane horrors. It is the end of the world. Honor to all these nameless people. A thousand times honor to them."

Time and again her thoughts lead her to the people who lead a normal life outside of the barbed wire, untouched by the suffering and death of the prisoners. With her comrades, who are able to give her the only support and a little comfort during this time, she always comes back to the question, how is it possible that they have become outcasts who can't expect help from anywhere?

"Sometimes we ask ourselves if there isn't anyone outside who thinks of us and why no voice is raised against all this? It must gradually seep through what is going on here. Not only here, but in all camps. Do really all those who are released keep quiet when they are outside? Or do the philistines not want to listen to them? Or do people not hear them in the victory frenzy of the nation?"

On 4 April 1939, she is finally released from Lichtenburg concentration camp because she succeeds in startling the camp commander and challenging his 'SS honor'. She meets him one day when she is used for a short time to take care of paperwork, and after he hears her name, he remembers her husband from the camp at Dachau. He boasts that he had had him flogged. Then he inquires about Lina's 'conduct' in Lichtenburg and says that maybe she can be released. "I am thunderstruck. Everything spins around me, disintegrates, becomes blurred. Maybe can be released! It's enormous. The fear, that those could be only empty words, tears me out of my stupor. I can only see that he is going to leave. I can't let him go. I feel instinctively that the promise would have been forgotten in the next moment. Maybe can be released! A thousand thoughts race through my head. I don't know what all I am thinking. A desperate fear brings me to the right idea. 'Unfortunately that won't be possible,' I burst out. It practically turned him around. 'What?' he barked, 'what won't be possible?' 'That you release me.'

He stares at me amazed. His face is blue, no longer red. 'Because my local Gestapo in Stuttgart,' I say hastily, 'is against it. And they are the higher authority.' 'What?' he yells, beside himself with rage, because I dare to put him down as a lower authority in front of his own officials. 'The Stuttgarter! Higher! What are they then in Stuttgart, huh?' And with a 'We'll see,' he storms off. This time, for good. The door crashes shut behind him."

After that, Lina doesn't even have time to say goodbye to her fellow prisoners. She has escaped from the hell of the concentration camp and returns to life. "I am free. – For the first time in years I'm again sitting in a train unobserved and ride into the spring evening toward Leipzig. The carriage is filled with people who appear strange and festive to me. Have they, who are from this region, never heard anything about Lichtenburg, don't they know anything about concentration camps and the inhuman actions of the SS? And if they don't know about it, why doesn't anyone tell them? Why don't I tell them about it? Why don't I shout it out and burst into their silly conversations, shout it into their foolish heads, into their empty hearts. I'm a coward, I'm a wretch.

Oh, for heaven's sake, why not? Because I want to live. Because I want to have Kaetle again, see my parents again and live with you again. When I'm home, I will go immediately to Berlin and fight for the Gestapo to release you before you die in the quarries at Mauthausen. I was shocked to learn that you've recently been sent to Mauthausen."

In fact Lina does not treat herself to any rest or recovery period. After she has spoken with friends and comrades who were imprisoned with her husband in the concentration camp at Dachau, and who now urge her to do something about his release, she again leaves her daughter with her parents and goes to Berlin, firmly determined to do everything to approach Heinrich Himmler direct. She finds lodgings with friends in an attic room and takes on work in a metal factory in order to support herself. Then she starts with her efforts, persistent and ever renewed, to get the center of power.

"It is worst after the futile pilgrimages in Prinz-Albrecht-Street. To be precise: They are not pilgrimages. You mustn't think that I wail about anything to people there, or that maybe I even break out in tears. That wouldn't affect the men in the Sicherheitshauptamt [main security office] in the least. They live on tears. On tears and blood. There you have to be more inventive if you want to achieve anything. I have put together an exact plan for myself, and I only go there when I have a good day, a clear head, a quiet heart. It's always the same. The guards know me by now. At the counter I fill out the slip, it's always the same embarrassing questions, I know them by heart and I write down the answers briskly and certainly. Also, that I want to speak to the head of the SS, is now a familiar matter for me, although it costs me an effort every time, to write it down, because I know that it is to no purpose. People don't even laugh about it. I only always draw back from the question 'on what business?' It shows me, more clearly than the cold, contemptuous looks of the guards, the evident insanity of my undertaking."

The account of her fight in Berlin reflects the ups and downs of her frame of mind. Although she herself now lives again in freedom, she feels alone and shut out and longs for warmth and human closeness. She needs all her strength in order not to give up, and finally she succeeds in doing that which even today still seems almost unbelievable: Heinrich Himmler receives her. As with her meeting with the camp commander in Lichtenburg, Lina instinctively finds the right words. She doesn't try to be on familiar terms and she doesn't deny her conviction. "You are honest," Himmler says to her, "one has to grant you that." And so she wins the fight for the release of her husband which she had begun seven years earlier and in whose successful conclusion she herself had often no longer believed.

On the order of Heinrich Himmler, Alfred Haag is released from the concentration camp at Mauthausen. Lina is informed that she can pick him up at the Gestapo building in Prinz Albrecht Street.

They take their daughter away from Schwaebisch-Gmuend and live for about a year undisturbed in Berlin. Lina trains to become a physical therapist, and Fred works in a small handicraft firm. Then the war overtakes them, and he is drafted into the army, although he had been declared as 'unworthy for service'. At first he works in squadron of manual laborers, then he is sent to the eastern front.

"Alone again. How easily that is said. Your coffee cup still stands on the table. Your old jacket is hanging there on the hook. If you ever will come back? There is a hopeless emptiness within me. Despite the fact that I have Kaetle. Because I have Kaetle. This year and a half with you and Kaetle was so lovely. This time was so abundant. And now everything is as it was before. I am waiting again. As before. This time it hurts very much. I don't have the nerves for it anymore. I'm tired from all the waiting. I've waited a whole lifetime. I've waited through the best years of my life. Now you are gone again. Not in the concentration camp. In the war. In a war which is being waged with no mercy and to the bitter end. That has been clear to us for a long time."

Lina observantly registers the mood swing in the population which becomes noticeable with the signs of the defeat of the German army.

"When I then get a few days of vacation I go with Kaetle to my parents. In the small country town one notices the mood swing, which is gradually taking place, more clearly than in Berlin. The pace of the big city covers over the signs of uncertainty. Here, I am suddenly greeted by former adversaries. With advisable caution, to be sure, but they do greet me. Our neighbor is standing on the steps when we come home, just as before, when the Gestapo took us one by one. At that time she looked down on us with spitefulness and malicious pleasure. Now she practically falls all over me with extravagant joy in seeing me again."

Lina works at this time as a nurse in a Berlin military hospital camp. She sees the wounded soldiers dying, experiences the deaths of the civilian population in the nights of bombing and confirms: "Even the bombs don't arouse these people. No storm of fire kindles any hatred in these apathetic, exhausted masses against the instigator of this destruction. It doesn't even suffice for outrage. It only suffices for the organization of bomb shelters."

When her daughter Kaete is almost buried under debris, she takes her back to her parents in the small town. After a short time, when the Berlin hospital is bombed, she has herself transferred to southern Germany. Lina Haag spends the last months of World War II in the Hotel Riessersee in Garmisch which had been converted into a military hospital camp.

"Our cities are destroyed, our armaments factories and railroads are destroyed. Traffic comes to a standstill, the economy comes to a standstill and breathing comes to a standstill, only the war doesn't come to a standstill.

. . .

Although many gradually have their eyes opened, many others still believe in the final victory. Many mothers are still proud of their soldier sons or of the uniforms, the little stars, the little crosses and the little ribbons of their soldier sons. In their incredible pride they are sometimes even more dangerous than the professional comptrollers of the war morale who prowl around in all sorts of disguises. Those who still don't see that we are being pushed to the abyss, don't want to see it and can't be persuaded anymore. Before you even see what is happening, you have a rope around your neck for 'undermining military strength'. But I don't want a rope around my neck, I want to experience this end. That this won't be so easy is something I know. I've never doubted the absolute determination of Hitler and his accomplices for total destruction. The millions of dead are still not enough. In order to lengthen their reprieve by weeks and days, thousands upon thousands are sacrificed, also thousands of women and children. These depraved people want to drag the whole nation with them into the abyss. They don't want to leave anything behind except 'scorched earth', only a field strewed with corpses. When they make their exit, they want to slam the door behind them so that the world is terrified. I know that. Therefore I'm afraid. Therefore I fear the end, which I nonetheless wish for with all my strength."

In this situation she decides to write down her experiences, despite the danger involved in that. Writing is a remedy for her against the isolation, against the despair and the fear of being arrested again, after she has learned from her mother that the Gestapo inquired about her. "I can't allow myself to become weak. Therefore I write. I have to unburden myself about the whole misery of the past years. Maybe it then becomes easier to bear. Maybe in that way I can come closer to you. Perhaps, then the waiting is no longer so difficult. I've already been waiting too long. I've been waiting for eleven years. I've been waiting since the 10th of February, 1933. Since the time when they took you."

On 1 May 1945, American army units reach Garmisch, and with that the 'Third Reich' also comes to an end there. Hotel Riessersee becomes a hotel again and serves as quarters for the American occupation officers. In the course of routine questioning Lina meets a German-speaking officer who is responsible for cultural activities. She gives him her notes to read, and, when she later hears nothing from him for weeks, she fears that her account has been lost. When she sees him again, he encourages her to try to have it published and promises her his support.

"I thought then in Garmisch, as much as I love my parents, I'm not going back to Schwaebisch-Gmuend for the time being. I still don't have the necessary distance for that. I was so angry about the Gmuendener, these swine. Directly after Fred was arrested in 1933, there was a rally in the market-place of Schwaebisch-Gmuend. One man standing on the speaker's platform shouted, last night they arrested the drunkard Haag. And everyone shouted, 'drunkard Haag, drunkard Haag'. And yet everyone knew that he doesn't drink, not a drop. They lied in opposition to their own common sense."

Lina moves with her daughter to Munich, where friends of her husband help her to find an apartment. She works as a physical therapist, and her daughter starts an apprenticeship as a cosmetician. In 1947, the first edition of her book appears, and in the spring of 1948, she is invited to Frankfurt am Main for the first German Writers' Congress; she speaks on the topic 'Women and Pacifism.'

Just at this point in time she receives mail for the first time from her husband who is in a Soviet prisoner-of-war camp. Finally, in autumn of 1948, he is able to return to Munich.

In the meantime, Lina, together with a few friends, has opened a Socialist bookstore. "My book had then already come out from Nest publishers. Through that I had chances to get into the business. Then they gave me a certificate that I was allowed to run a bookshop. But it didn't last long, then we had to close it again. My God, I had to earn money, and we couldn't hand out any wages. We tried to add a circulating library, but that also wasn't the right thing."

After Fred's return home, they try to rebuild a family life which had suffered so much from war and persecution. Their daughter marries very young, and the four of them acquire a small house. "We all worked terribly hard at saving. At that time the claims for compensation were in process, and we could give complete proof about our time in prison. We were paid 150 mark for each month. Without even buying a bar of chocolate, we put this money immediately into the purchase of a small piece of property. We had the house built in an unfinished condition. As a carpenter, Fred finished the interior himself, steps, floors, window frames and so on. Then the four of us paid off the house."

Alfred Haag first works as a carpenter, then he gets a position as an employee of a health insurance company. From the beginning he is active with the Association of the Victims of Nazism [VVN], and when he is retired he finally devotes all his strength and energy to the work for the victims. He trains to become a specialist in questions of compensation legislation, and for several years he offers legal advice for compensation claims. He is also closely involved, from the beginning until his death, with he formation of the memorial site at Dachau and the development of the work there. Old age does not moderate his combative attitude, he doesn't try to avoid any argument when he senses political danger from the Right. Only little by little does he tell Lina about his experiences during his years in the concentration camps at Oberer Kuhberg, Dachau and Mauthausen. "I also learned from him about all the daily routines. When we first went to Mauthausen, to this fortress, there he said to me, look, I had to help build that. When he gave tours of Dachau, he always came out with a pounding heart. He suffered more under nervous stress than I did. Also at night while dreaming he sometimes sat up and groaned. I calmed him then. That didn't harass me as much as it did Fred."

Lina is only marginally involved in her husband's work. She is the hostess for many visitors, especially foreign delegations, and she is always available when help is needed at memorial ceremonies, at events and meetings of victims' organizations. Everyone who visits the Haags is pleasantly affected by the warm atmosphere of the house where they live together with their daughter, their son-in-law and the granddaughter Susi, who is especially loved by her grandfather more than anything else. The strong family bonds are to be felt by everyone. Their daughter Kaete leads a retired life, and Lina is convinced that she still suffers from the consequences of the fear which she, as a child, had to endure in connection with her parents. Kaete strictly refuses today to talk about this time. "She says, thank God, Mommy, it is over."

In 1977 the second edition of Lina's book appears in the Federal Republic, and in the Soviet Union the account is also published in large numbers. Later she is asked more and more to give readings from her book and to speak about her experiences. It is primarily women who feel themselves addressed by Lina's book and who reach out to her. A series of radio and television interviews are produced.

On 8 August 1982, Alfred Haag dies at the age of seventy-seven after having two strokes. Lina does not recover from this loss. But she begins to think again of her own strength, which has helped her for so many years to endure difficulties. And she is able to share some of this strength with other, younger people, who haven't experienced those years, and to give them courage to master their own life struggles.

Anise Postel-Vinay

A Young Frenchwoman's Wartime Experiences

I. The Resistance

On 10 Mai 1940, the German army invaded Holland and Belgium. The fall of Paris followed on 13 June.
Although Paris was our home, my mother, my three brothers, my sister and I had taken refuge in the town of Rennes, in Brittany. My father, on the other hand, opted to stay in Paris and continue his work as a doctor.
On 17 June, Marshal Petain announced in a trembling voice that France would not defend herself to the last. We felt shattered, horrified, deeply humiliated. My father drove down to Rennes to join us. We scarcely recognized him: he had aged ten years in the space of a week. His cheeks were sunken and he was seething with anger, with the kind of dumb outrage that one only sees in people of his normally quiet disposition. My father was the son of a peasant family in the Jura mountains, and in addition to the mountain-dwellers' natural calmness and patience, he had inherited their capacity for violent rage.
My mother's family was from Alsace. After the annexation of Alsace by the Germans following the war of 1870, her father and her uncle left the province. She was a tall, blonde, attractive woman with a fiery temperament and an exceptionally keen intelligence; her attitude to the Germans was hostile, and she hated the Nazis. With a mounting sense of unease she had observed the rise of Nazism, as documented not only in the newspapers, but also in the publications of anti-Nazi Catholic thinkers such as von Hildebrandt and F. W. Foerster. In Paris she had taken in and helped a number of Catholic and Jewish refugees from Hitler's Germany.
My mother was familiar with the books of Rauschning, Strasser and Ernst Erich Noth, and with the French literary scholar Robert d'Harcourt's *The Gospel of Violence,* and had given them to us children to read as well. Both my parents were firm Christian believers and staunch Republicans. To them, respect for one's fellow human beings was a sacred principle for which one should be prepared to risk one's life if necessary. The fact that France had fallen to the Nazis deeply depressed me and my family. We knew that this was the beginning of an era of hitherto unparalleled terror and violence.
We did not ourselves hear General de Gaulle's BBC radio broadcast summoning the French people to continue the struggle against the Germans. However, with or without de Gaulle, we would have continued to defend

France to our dying breath. Who was this general with the heroic-sounding name who had set out to salvage France's honour? At the time, we knew nothing about him, apart from the fact that he was saying things which urgently needed to be said.

Deeply dispirited, we returned to Paris. My father bought a new radio, the very latest model available, and immediately the BBC broadcasts from London became the focal point of our lives, despite the Germans' constant attempts to jam the transmissions.

I had begun to study German at the University of Rennes and continued my studies at the Sorbonne. As the autumn semester began, the anniversary of Armistice Day on 11 November was approaching, the traditional day of remembrance for the dead of the First World War. Although any public assembly of more than three people was strictly prohibited, the students decided to hold a march up the Champs Elysees to the Arc de Triomphe and attempt to lay a wreath at the tomb of the Unknown Soldier. That year, Remembrance Day fell on a Monday. The previous day, I had been on a long hike with a troop of Boy Scouts in the countryside near Paris. Keeping pace with the long-legged boys had been far from easy, and on that Monday morning the muscles in my legs ached so much that I could hardly walk. Nevertheless I set off to the Metro and took the train to the Etoile station. After struggling up the stairway, I emerged at the exit on the corner of the Avenue de Wagram and found, to my astonishment, that the Place de l'Etoile was completely deserted. I walked on a few yards and suddenly caught sight of several groups of German soldiers hastily assembling machine guns on the pavement at the end of the Champs Elysees. I tried to run back to the Metro, but my legs were hurting too much, and all I could do was to hide, unheroically, behind the trunk of a plane tree. Salvoes of machine gun bullets came sweeping up the street, skimming the surface of the road. The students fled down the Champs Elysees, raising their hands in surrender to the Germans. To my horror, I recognized one of them; he was a Jew, and I had an uneasy feeling that we would never see him again.

The demonstration had been entirely futile. I felt that gestures such as daubing the Cross of Lorraine on walls were silly and infantile; the practice of collecting and passing on jokes about the Germans seemed equally ridiculous. Apart from reading a few leaflets and banned periodicals which fell into my hands, I had no contact with any of the Resistance groups which were being formed at the time. How, I asked myself, could I make a useful contribution to the Resistance movement? I decided that the best thing to do was to try to get to England and join the Free French army. My mother was prepared to support this plan on condition that one of my friends went with me. However, I was desperately disappointed to find that not one of my friends, either at the university or in the Scout movement, was prepared to go along with my suggestion. Eventually I fell in with a girl from Alsace who had fled to Paris and was highly enthusiastic about the idea of going to

England. Unfortunately, though, the plan failed: despite long and involved enquiries, we were unable to find any means of putting it into practice. One day my mother revealed that one of her friends was involved in Resistance activities and suggested that I should go and see her. Her name was Simone Lahaye; she was a professor of philosophy, and one of her colleagues, a teacher of English, had put her in contact with a former Navy officer who was passing military secrets on to London. I was given a sheet of instructions with the abbreviated designations of all the various weapons used by the German army, and my first task was to find out the type of gun mounted on the German tanks based at Fort de Vincennes. It was a task for which I was wholly unfitted: I could hardly tell a corporal from a general, let alone distinguish between different types of cannon.

Summoning all my courage, however, I rode out on my bicycle to the Vincennes woods and set about measuring the width of the tank tracks in the mud with a tape measure. My descriptions of the guns with which the tanks were equipped were anything but exact. Something told me that this was not the way to tackle the business of resisting the Germans.

My second task was to find out all I could about one of the barrage balloon units near Paris and enter the information in a map. Again, I went on my bicycle, this time with a fellow-student from the Sorbonne. Together, we recorded all the details of where the balloons were moored, the type of balloons used, and their Luftwaffe serial numbers.

The map in which we entered the information, and which I had compiled with the help of one of my younger brothers, was to be photographed on microfilm. Together with a number of further documents supplied by other members of the group, it was to be smuggled in a matchbox into the unoccupied zone by a priest who was sympathetic to the aims of the Resistance. From there, via Lisbon, it would eventually end up in London.

At the end of July 1942, I was sent to Le Havre to observe movements in the harbour and at the railway goods depot. The main aim of this exercise was to find out exactly where the bombs had landed in the recent English air raids.

On 15 August 1942 I succeeded in crossing the border of the restricted zone along the coast, travelling in an overcrowded train and carrying in my rucksack a map of Le Havre containing the information which I had been asked to obtain. The sun was shining when I got out of the train in Paris. My orders were to ring up the leader of our group, a Navy officer, before handing over the information. I had never actually met this man, who was surrounded by an aura of mystery and massive importance, and I was extremely shy about the idea of encountering him, so I decided instead to go straight to my friend, the English teacher. This failure to obey orders was to prove my undoing.

II. Arrest

When I reached the apartment block where my friend lived, I noticed a beautiful red open-top sports car parked by the side of the road. I thought to myself: 'Since driving on a Sunday is prohibited, the owner of the car must be a German.' But then I dismissed the idea as over-cautious. There was an official pass on the windscreen, which indicated that the car might belong to a doctor on his rounds. In high spirits, proud of myself at having come back with a new collection of military secrets, I climbed the staircase up the five floors of the building and rang the doorbell.

A tall young man in shirt-sleeves opened the door. Inside, another man was rooting around in my friend's possessions, which were spread out all over the floor of her apartment. I immediately realized what was going on, but it was too late: I felt my face go white with fright.

'You've gone quite pale,' said the Gestapo man. Playing for time, I answered: 'Well, it isn't exactly a pleasant surprise to come visiting a friend and discover that her apartment is being ransacked.' My cheekiness fooled nobody. I tried to escape by racing back down the stairs, but the Gestapo men were fitter and faster than me. A driver materialized on the scene, and the three of us got into the back of the red sports car. My rucksack was on my knees, with the rolled-up map of Le Havre sticking out of the top. The sun was still shining as we drove onto the Pont de la Concorde. I decided to snatch out the map and throw it into the Seine. But as soon as I began to move, my captors pushed me roughly back into my seat.

When we arrived at the Gestapo's headquarters, located in the offices of the Ministry of the Interior in the Rue des Sussaies, I began to despair. My map disappeared into one of the offices. I waited all afternoon. The police didn't seem at all curious about me and the document I was carrying: they knew the whole story already. In the evening, the Gestapo men reappeared and held a murmured conference, occasionally pointing in my direction as they talked. I gathered from the conversation that they were going to deport me to Silesia. Once more, we got into the elegant car, and I looked at the wonderful evening sky over Paris with the melancholy feeling that I might perhaps never see it again.

An unseen hand opened the heavy iron-bound door of the La Santé prison and closed it again behind us.

III. The French prisons

La Santé

In the prison reception area my watch was taken away from me and a list was given me to sign. To my horror, I saw that the name before mine on the list was that of my father. How had they managed to arrest him so quickly? And it was all my fault.

Men with pale faces, some of them clearly betraying fear, leant against the walls of the grey, dirty cell. It took all the energy I could muster to fight back the sense of despair which threatened to overwhelm me. As the hours passed, I began to hear the voices of men and women talking: at least there was some sign of life in this huge tomb of a prison.

Eventually the door opened with the loud rattle of a key turning several times in the lock, and a German soldier informed me that I was to be shot the following morning at half-past four. I was by no means surprised: I had been engaged in military espionage, and the normal penalty for that was death. I also now understood why the Germans had not interrogated me. But the prospect of dying at twenty – or at any age for that matter – is difficult to accept. I had no desire whatever to become a martyr. Why, I asked myself, had I not simply got on with my studies, keeping well clear of any trouble? But on the other hand, as I told myself a moment later, it would have been entirely wrong to surrender to the enemy – especially this particular enemy – without putting up a fight. Although I was as yet unaware of the full extent of the Nazis' crimes, I rejected Nazism utterly. There was just one more night to get through. I tried not to think of my mother and how desperately worried she must be; instead, I endeavoured to see myself as simply one more small cog in the machine of the war which was shaking the world to its very foundations.

The great clock of the La Santé prison struck every quarter of an hour. That night, time seemed to stand still. At about three o'clock I knelt down by the iron bedstead and began to pray. I said one Hail Mary after another, the only prayer which seemed suitable for the occasion, since it ended with the words 'in the hour of our death.' All other thoughts were extinguished as I concentrated on fighting back the fear which gnawed at my bowels.

Half past three, a quarter to four, four o'clock, quarter past four, half-past four ... I was waiting for my executioners, having combed my hair and smoothed down my skirt. Nobody came. Quarter to five, five o'clock ... and still nobody arrived. At about seven o'clock, the prison began to stir. At last the door of my cell opened. My heart was thumping in my chest. But all that happened was that somebody brought me a cup of coffee. I began to realize that this time, at least, I had been spared. Either my death warrant had been countermanded, or I had been the victim of a standard procedure for demoralizing new prisoners.

In old prisons like this one, the lavatories in the cells – the 'Jaruzel', as it is called in today's prisons in Poland – consisted of only a hole in the floor with no flushing device. In order to speak to your neighbours, you had to lift the wooden lid and stick your head inside the hole, watching out for the lumps of excrement in the water. Using this means of communication, I often spoke to Dédé, a young and militant Communist of seventeen or eighteen. He was an exceptionally brave boy with a wonderful sense of humour, as lively as a pack of monkeys and twice as cheeky. It was the third time he had been arrested; he was in a cell on the second floor, in handcuffs. But Dédé was a skilled metal-worker who had been working in factories since he was twelve, and using a piece of wire from the broom used for sweeping out his cell, he had managed to make a key which would open his handcuffs. As soon as the guard had done his rounds, he would have the handcuffs off in a trice. He had made another key for the prisoner in the next cell, smuggling it in by hiding it in a pile of dust and rubbish. On one occasion he had briefly caught sight of his neighbour while his cell door was ajar. 'Tall, fair-haired, distinguished-looking, a proper intellectual,' was his description of the man. 'We'll call him René,' he suggested. René was a high-school student who whistled one Brandenburg Concerto after another, all day long.

Dédé had broken off one of the flaps in the ventilation outlet of his cell and suggested that we do the same. He would jump up like a cat, grab hold of the bars on his window, just below the ceiling, and entertain the two of us by telling us a constant series of jokes and stories. He succeeded in making contact with 'Auguste', an older Communist of whom we were very much in awe. All we knew about him was that he was a former plumber from Paris who had fought in the International Brigade. One after another, Auguste and his comrades had been dragged before an examining tribunal and come back to their cells, condemned to death. They were waiting to be executed, with no indication of when the sentence would be carried out. Every evening Auguste climbed up and spoke to his comrades through the ventilation system, particularly addressing the younger members of the group. Time and time again, he told them what a normal thing it was to die for the freedom of one's brothers and sisters, that noble causes often demanded the sacrifice of one's own life, that their deaths as martyrs would encourage others to take up arms against the Germans, and that their country, France, was worth dying for. These stirring words deeply moved me, and I added a silent, heartfelt prayer for each of these young people. It was the first time I had encountered real live Communists. And these people were supposed to be materialists? I was quite astonished.

Very early one morning, several cell doors were opened at once, with a loud rattle of keys. From each of the cells, interrupted by the shouting of the guards, came the sound of voices singing the 'Marseillaise'. Then the whole prison fell silent. We never heard Auguste's comforting voice again.

Dédé resolved that the prisoners in our 'corner', as he called it, should not go meekly to their deaths; instead, he proposed that we should make one last desperate attempt to escape. His idea was to use the cover of a stormy night, when the noise of the rain would prevent the sentries from hearing us. René, whose cell was at the end of the corridor, was to lure one of the guards into his cell, knock him down, take his key and open the cell doors of eleven prisoners. The rest would be child's play. Dédé provided a club, patiently removing one of the legs of his iron bedstead, which was to be conveyed to René's cell by means of the 'sock'. This was Dédé's personal goods lift, which he had made using one of his socks and a rope manufactured out of odd bits of cloth. One unforgettable evening he had used the 'sock' to lower down to me two pieces of buttered spiced bread from a food parcel sent by his mother. This time it would contain the leg of the bed, which had to be manoeuvred into the ventilation outlet of René's cell. The problem was that it had to be lowered past the cell of another prisoner who could not be let in on the secret. This man, who had been arrested for selling flour on the black market, and whom Dédé had christened 'The Miller', had shut himself off in his cell in the hope of getting remission for good behaviour.

This escape plan was foiled by the fact that several of the people involved were transferred to other prisons: the women were taken to Fresnes.

Dédé and René remained in their cells on the second floor. Meanwhile things were looking bleak for René, and Dédé decided to try and escape with him via the roof. Every evening he would lower the 'sock' with the bedpost down to René's cell so that René could saw a bar out of it, kicking up a rumpus in his own cell in order to disguise the noise of the blunt hacksaw. The guards intervened several times until they finally realized what was going on.

The two boys were beaten until they were half-dead and then handcuffed hand and foot. After several days of trying to get at the food which had been deposited in tin containers on the floor, they were both struck down with fever: sweat poured off them, mingling with the urine and excrement which seeped through their clothes. A week later they were rescued by being transferred to Rennes.

René was shot four months later. His real name was Lucien Legros, and he was a lycée student from Paris. Dédé survived Schirmeck, Dachau and the typhus which he caught in the last days before the liberation of the camp. His real name is Désiré Bertieau and he is now a professor at a technical university. 'Auguste's' real name was Raymond Losserand. A street was later named after him in the 14th *arrondissement* of Paris where he lived.

The cries and groans of the prisoners in the cells adjacent to mine filled me with horror. They would come back from interrogation sessions with swollen and sometimes dislocated limbs. I was terrified by the prospect of being interrogated myself. I had dreamed that they might question me in my own cell, which they sometimes did, bringing in a table and a typewriter. In my dream, I had tamed and fed one of the rats which scuttled around in the sanitation system and hidden it under the washbasin, throwing in the faces of the Gestapo men when they entered my cell.

However, my interrogation took place in the Rue des Saussaies. Somebody from my group had talked. The Gestapo knew almost everything. Instead of going to London, my intelligence reports were sitting there on the table. In addition to the map of Le Havre, a notebook with a sketch of a street in Chantilly had been found in my possession. In this street, the ambassadors Abetz and de Brinon lived in two large mansions directly facing each other.

There had been a plan to have the two of them assassinated by the Resistance. I had simply entered the initials A and B on the map of the street, in the assumption that if anyone asked me about the notebook, I would easily be able to find some innocent explanation of what I had been up to. But in the interrogation room, my mind went completely blank. All I could think of was the names of the two ambassadors, and I realized how easy it was to betray information unintentionally. The tone of the interrogation sessions became increasingly unpleasant, but to give the man questioning me his due, no violence was used. His name was Weinberger. One thing I did resent, though, was the fact that he had stolen my father's brand-new radio, which was sitting in front of me on his desk. Who was the person who had betrayed us? This question was finally answered after the end of the war as a result of the detective work done by a female comrade, the anthropologist Germaine Tillion. All the men in our group, apart from my father, who was deported first to Buchenwald and then to Dora, met their deaths in Mauthausen. Germaine Tillion's mother, who had been arrested at the same time as us in August 1942, was interned in the so-called 'Youth Camp' at Ravensbrueck and sent to the gas chamber at the beginning of March 1945. Germaine was absolutely determined to find the traitor in our midst, just as she had been determined, before our arrest, to discover the identity of the person who had betrayed the 'Musée de l'Homme' group. It eventually transpired that the traitor was a young clergyman from Luxemburg, the vicar of the parish where the Tillions lived. He had offered his services to the German counterintelligence service: he had a number of expensive mistresses and needed money. I never found out exactly when the matchboxes with the microfilms landed in the Rue des Saussaies. Father Allesch was condemned to death after the war and executed in 1949.

Another thing which I only found out after returning to France was that the small anti-Nazi group to which I had belonged and which had been smuggling military secrets to London was part of an intelligence network which called itself 'SMH Gloria', SMH being the initials of His Majesty's Service spelt backwards. In 1941–42, the expressions 'reseau' (network) and 'Resistance'[1] were unknown to us. We simply regarded ourselves as part of a group of people who were engaged in 'certain activities'.

---

[1] Although De Gaulle used the word 'Resistance' in his broadcast of 18 June 1940, the word did not pass into common parlance until after the liberation of France. The underground broadsheet published by the opposition group at the Musée de l'Homme in Paris was entitled *Resistance* from 1940 onwards, at the suggestion of the museum's librarian, a Protestant woman from the *département* of Drome who remembered that the word had been scratched on one of the stones of the Tour de Constance in Aigues-Mortes by the Protestant women incarcerated there by Louis XIV.

Fresnes

On 13 October all the women from La Santé are due to be transferred to the prison at Fresnes, a suburb south of Paris. The dream of escaping together recedes into the distance. I am furious and decide immediately to escape on my own, under cover of the confusion caused by us all arriving at Fresnes together. I shall use the plan hatched by Dédé: the next morning, when the wardress opens my door for me to sweep out the cell, I shall lure her into the cell on the pretext that there are bugs in the bed. And then I shall creep up behind her and give her a mighty whack on the head with the handle of my brush (which happened to be made of a very hard wood). The idea is merely to put her out of action, though – I don't want to kill her. I shall stuff a piece of cloth in her mouth to stop her from screaming, take her key and her white uniform blouse with the German eagle on the breast pocket, carefully lock the door behind me and walk calmly to the gate.

The following morning, the clock strikes eight, half-past eight, nine o'clock, nine-thirty, and nobody comes to open my cell door. The waiting is unbearable. As I stand there behind the door, with my brush in one hand and the gag in the other, my courage begins to ebb away. Do I really want to go through with this? Fear gnaws at my nerves. At last the key turns in the lock and a wardress of indeterminate age appears. She readily allows herself to be lured into the cell to look for bedbugs. I quietly close the door behind her in order to shut out the inquisitive gaze of potential onlookers. She bends over the bed, an ... bang! ... I hit her over the head. But the blow fails to knock her out, and she starts to squeal. I struggle to stuff the gag into her mouth, but there is something in the way: her false teeth, as I later discover. I attempt to force the screeching woman down onto the bed so that I can lift it and push it up against the wall. She fights back. We are both wrestling with each other on the bed when suddenly the cell door opens and in come the prison commandant, his adjutant and another soldier, all three of them looking quite astonished. They lock the door behind them. I can't possibly take on three big strong men. Getting up off the bed, I realize in a flash that they don't know that I was trying to escape. (I was taking a calculated risk: the penalty for trying to escape – three weeks under close arrest with no mattress – was relatively mild.) The wardress gets up as well and starts wailing on about being attacked, but the officer tells her to shut up and turns instead to me. 'What's going on here?' he asks. I am struck dumb with astonishment; after all, I never expected that I would be called on to explain what I was doing. Gradually getting my breath back, I answer in the German that I had learned at the Sorbonne, pronouncing each syllable slowly and carefully: 'I hit her because she deserved it ...'

'Why?' the officer asks. 'She beat me at La Santé when she had no right to do so,' I reply.

On hearing this outrageous lie, the wardress starts to protest. Again, the officer tells her to be quiet. They leave the cell without further ado, without heaping insults on me or beating me.

My punishment consisted in being handcuffed, having my mattress taken away and receiving nothing to eat for three days. The adjutant even came by several times to adjust my handcuffs or take them off in order to allow me to wash and eat. Yes, to eat! For several of the wardresses secretly brought me soup. They were very cautious, not daring to cross the threshold of my cell. I heard from them that their colleague had been punished by being transferred to another prison.

Paradoxically this incident earned me the respect of the prison commandant. He occasionally came to my cell and talked to me. At that time the Allies were just beginning to score their first military successes: they had retaken the small Mediterranean island of Pantelleria, and although the Germans were still advancing into Russia, I prophesied to the commandant that his side would eventually lose the war. This seemed to amuse him: he didn't believe me. It was probably him that I had to thank for the fact that I was allowed to receive food parcels. Prior to this, my poor mother had always been told that the Gestapo knew nothing of my whereabouts and sent away. For a time, she had assumed that I had managed to escape to England, in some sort of connection with the Dieppe raids. A woman from an adjacent cell in La Santé, the wife of the film actor Harry Baur, eventually told my mother that I was in prison, after she herself had been released.

Via the parcels I managed to remain in contact with my family. With the help of an outside accomplice, I hatched a new escape plan which was foiled at the last minute. I had asked for a file to be smuggled over the wall, but the guard was reinforced at the particular point where this was due to happen. In comparison with what awaited me in Germany, the prison at Fresnes was thoroughly civilized. There was little to complain about, apart from the fact that I was completely isolated from my comrades and had no idea of how our resistance effort was progressing. And I feared that at any minute the door might open and I would be told that I could see my father for the last time before his execution.

Romainville

At the Fort de Romainville, which was a cross between a prison and a concentration camp, I was allowed to see my father. He was very pale and covered with ulcers caused by starvation, but his blue eyes still testified to his unbroken spirit. Instead of being executed, he was deported to Germany. He managed to escape from Buchenwald at the beginning of 1944 with the aid of comrades from the *transport noir,* but was interned again at Dora, the concentration camp in the Harz mountains where the inmates were put to work in a subterranean munitions factory. With working underground, the ulcers got worse and worse. My father was 63, and his hair had gone completely white. His French comrades called him Papa Girard; the Russians in his working party took pity on him and used to hide him in a corner of one of the tunnels while they were working. One day, there was a call for a surgeon to operate on an SS man who was extremely ill with an inflammation of the mastoid glands. This operation, which involved opening up the patient's temporal bone with a hammer and chisel to drain off the pus, was my father's speciality. The SS man's life was saved and my father was transferred to the camp hospital, where he performed a further fifty-two such operations. When he eventually got back to France, he found that his skills had been rendered obsolete by the invention of penicillin.

I spent the three summer months of 1943 in one of the barracks at the Fort de Romainville, near Paris. The fort held several hundred prisoners, both men and women; it was run by the Wehrmacht, which meant that the regime was reasonably liberal. On 2 October, however, we were horrified to see two buses taking a number of men to be executed who had been held prisoner in the bunkers surrounding the fort, to be used as hostages in case of necessity. The day had now come when they were to die. Some of them were married to women in our group. Dawn had scarcely broken. The windows of the buses were barred, but we could nevertheless see the men, each of them seated between two soldiers and looking as pale as death itself. After the war was over, we learned that the men had numbered fifty in all, and that they were being executed in revenge for the death of Dr Julius Ritter, the head of the French office of the German authority which supervised the deployment of forced labour, who had been assassinated by the Resistance on 28 September 1943.

I was eventually deported to Germany on 21 October 1943, a month after my father. I had thought of trying to escape at the Gare du Nord, but abandoned the idea for fear that the Germans might arrest my younger brother in my stead. I was haunted by the sight of the hostages on their way to be executed. On my return to France, however, I found out that the kind little SS man who had been put in charge of us and whom I had entrusted with a note to my mother had indeed visited my home. He would have let me go, and they could have hidden my brother. So my scruples had been in vain.

There were twenty of us, all women. We travelled in comfort, in an ordinary railway carriage, guarded by SS men. Sitting in one of the compartments was Germaine Tillion, who had come direct from Fresnes. This phenomenal woman, with her tremendous sense of humour, literally took me under her wing; every day for the next eighteen months she gave me a piece of her own bread ration, on the grounds that I was younger than her and would, as she said, one day be going home to get married and have lots of children.

In the course of the year which she spent at Fresnes, Germaine Tillion managed to have some of her files brought into the prison and spent her time editing her manuscripts, like Rosa Luxemburg. These documents now lay at her feet on the floor of the compartment, in a green sack made of coarse linen. We both wondered where the Germans were taking us to. 'Well, let's find out from our SS man,' said Germaine. 'I'll show you how to tame a savage.' From her capacious sack she extracted a photograph of a cute little desert fox which she had tamed and which had been her constant companion during her last field trip. She approached the guard and gently tugged at his sleeve, once, twice, three times. At first he roughly shook off her hand, but eventually he turned round and looked at the photograph which Germaine was trying to show him. In the most atrocious German she began to tell him all about the habits of this fox and the customs of the Berber tribes.

Within twenty minutes we knew where we were going: to Aix-la-Chapelle and thence to Fuerstenberg. None of us even knew where Fuerstenberg was. After about ten days sleeping on straw – at least it was fresh straw – in the prison at Aix-la-Chapelle, where we were joined by a further twenty Frenchwomen, we were put on a train bound for this mysterious Fuerstenberg place; again, we travelled in an ordinary carriage, just as if we had been tourists.

It turned out that Fuerstenberg was not in Silesia but in Mecklenburg, north of Berlin. We arrived there on 31 October 1943. It was still light, and we were feeling reasonably cheerful. But as we approached the camp, our hearts gradually began to sink.

However, we were determined not to show any sign of weakness, and so, with heads held high, we entered the camp, carrying our various possessions, including Germaine's green document bag.

IV. Ravensbrueck

The sight which met our eyes suddenly took us back several centuries in time. There were seemingly endless lines of women in grey striped prison uniform with white headscarves, dragging through the mud in wooden shoes, marching round a large square, away to the rear of the camp and back again. With their pale faces and dull eyes they seemed sunk in apathy, although some of them succeeded in conveying through gestures that pity was the last thing they wanted. All one heard was the endless tramp of marching feet, interrupted now and again by the screeching of the women overseers. How could such noises come from the throat of a human being? We would have to get used to the dreadful sound of their voices. That evening we had to strip off and surrender all our personal belongings, even wedding rings, photographs and treasured mementoes such as a letter written to one of the women by her son before his execution. The only thing we were allowed to keep was a handkerchief. One of us, a small plump woman, had her head shaved. She wept as she stood under the shower, and her tears mingled with the water coursing over her naked body.

We had nothing, not even a single towel, with which to dry ourselves. From a heap of clothing on the floor we each had to sort out a set of underwear, a blue-grey striped dress and a jacket. I found a pair of thigh-length underpants of the kind our grandmothers used to wear. They were clean, but made from a type of material which seemed far too good to be worn by prisoners. I inspected the underpants closely. They had curious black ribbed stripes running down them and fringes at the side. Suddenly I realized that they were made from a Jewish prayer shawl, although I had never seen such a shawl before. It was sacrilege, a typical example of Nazi behaviour.

In quarantine

The prayer shawl was a case of straightforward theft. Only a few days later I was to hear of far worse things from a new inmate who arrived from the camp at Lublin in Poland, where she had been working in the sick-bay. At Lublin, as in Ravensbrueck, the sick-bay was situated directly opposite the kitchens. One evening the SS ordered that all the women with small children should be given a ration of milk. The women turned up at the kitchens in groups of five, carrying their children or leading them by the hand. Suddenly a group of SS men with machine guns appeared in front of them, and another group of guards waded into the rows of screaming women and tore their children away from them. They threw the children onto trucks, where two SS men held them in check with their heavy boots. Within minutes the trucks were full and drove off. The young Polish woman, whose hair had turned white overnight after this incident, assumed that the children had been shot and buried outside the camp. Later, however, it transpired that there had been several gas chambers in operation at Lublin. It was entirely possible that the children had been gassed.

The pseudo-medical experiments

While I was still in quarantine, a young, very blonde Polish girl appeared one day and climbed through the window of our hut and told me the following story. "You must know, the French people must know, what the Germans are doing to us here. It all started in August last year, when they told ten or so of the young girls in our hut to report to the guardroom. For several days we had no idea what had happened to them. Then a Czech woman discovered them in a small side room. They were ill, screaming with pain and fever, and their legs were covered with open wounds. Some of the wounds more or less healed up, and several of the girls came back to the hut; the others died. Then another group was summoned to the guardroom, and yet another – and so it went on until last month. We don't know who the next victims will be.

When the third group was called up in the summer, the young girls – everybody here refers to them as the 'guinea pigs' – refused to go. For a whole day the three hundred women in our hut had to stand to attention outside. By the evening the SS men were furious. They drove us back into the hut and set about boarding up the windows. Prior to this they had advised the Germans in our hut to leave. However, although the Germans were not political prisoners but so-called antisocial elements, they refused to leave us in the lurch. For three days we had neither light nor food in the hut. Then the Germans came and hauled off the girls who had been chosen for the experiments. They were dragged off to the bunker and operated on there and then, in the dungeon."

The young Polish girl spoke excellent French. She had been sent to me by the group of surviving 'guinea pigs', so that I would pass word of the experiments on to France. At this point, unbeknown to me, the 'guinea pigs' had already sent three similar messages to London, to the International Red Cross in Geneva, and to the Catholic Mission in Fribourg in Switzerland. Two further messages were buried in the woods outside the camp by one of the working parties. The blonde Polish girl's name was Joanna Muszkovska; today she works as a kidney and bladder specialist in Gdansk, where she is Lech Walesa's family doctor.

Altogether some seventy-five women, including seventy Polish girls in a detail from Lublin which arrived at Ravensbrueck in September 1941, were subjected to these operations, which involved amputating sections of muscle and bone. Some of them were subsequently treated with sulfa drugs, others were simply left to their fate.

The Russian, Polish and Czech doctors among the prisoners, who had been at the camp longer than us, wondered what the purpose of these barbaric experiments was supposed to be. The answer was eventually supplied in the course of the 1947 Nuremberg trials by the SS professor Karl Gebhardt, who spoke without interruption for a whole week and took a visible pleasure in his erstwhile activities. A former classmate of Himmler, Gebhardt was Professor of Orthopaedic Medicine at the University of Berlin; he also ran a large private clinic near Ravensbrueck which was patronised by members of the Nazi top brass. In 1942, Reinhard Heydrich, Himmler's deputy and the governor of Bohemia and Moravia, was assassinated in Prague. Hitler ordered Gebhardt to Heydrich's bedside, but Heydrich died of gangrene a few days later. Hitler was beside himself with rage: 'Losing Heydrich is the equivalent of losing twenty battalions,' he allegedly roared. He summoned Gebhardt and then refused to receive him. His personal physician, Dr Morell, murmured: 'Of course, if only *my* sulfa drugs had been prescribed. . . .' Morell owned a number of factories producing a sulfonamide known as Ultraseptil. In order to get back into favour with Hitler, Gebhardt had provide conclusive 'scientific' evidence that sulfa drugs did not work with certain infections. Himmler provided a ready supply of 'patients', and Gebhardt obtained gangrene, staphylococcus and streptococcus cultures from the SS Institute of Hygiene in Berlin. These bacteria were injected, under anaesthetic, into open wounds in the legs of the 'guinea pigs' following which the medication was administered or withheld, depending on the state of the 'patient' after the injection of the bacteria. The whole point of the exercise was that the treatment should fail. It was medical research turned back-to-front.

Dehumanization

At this stage we were to some extent protected by being in quarantine: we did not have to work, and the conditions under which we lived were relatively civilized. However, from the windows of our hut we often saw utterly wretched figures, women referred to by the Nazis as the *Schmuckstücke* ('jewels'), who were constantly leered at and tormented by the guards. One evening, as I was looking out of the window, I saw several hundred women returning exhausted from work. As they trooped past with their bent backs, filthy clothes and wooden shoes, I thought I recognized one of my compatriots at the end of the line, a middle-aged Frenchwoman whom I had previously seen in La Santé. Her cell-door had been ajar, and to my horror, I thought for a moment that she was my mother, but I was mistaken, thank God. Via the 'telephone' I discovered that she was the widow of a retired doctor from Normandy.

In the dusk at Ravensbrueck, the woman was scarcely recognizable. She had aged twenty years, her hair was grey, she was covered with dirt and dressed in rags. As she approached my window, she raised her skirt to show me a wound on her thigh the size of a persons's hand. At the same time she begged me with outstretched hands to give her a piece of bread. The scene called to mind the very worst episodes from medieval times in my school history book.

From my window I was able to observe the guards' classic game of kicking over the soup canister and then gleefully watching the inmates come running to lap up the soup from the mud, like dogs. Would we too allow ourselves to be degraded and dehumanized in this way? We had no way of influencing whether it would happen or not. Beyond a certain level of malnutrition, sickness, exhaustion and physical abuse, the struggle for survival becomes so desperate that one's self-control evaporates.

Disease

At the end of 1943, the camp was still a relatively clean place: Ravensbrueck was in the top category of concentration camps. We each had a straw mattress with a chequered pattern on the cover, plus a duvet cover, which was also checquered and into which blankets were inserted. And what was more, each of us had a bed to herself – a luxury of which we were soon to be deprived. To warm us both up, Germaine Tillion used to slip into my bed after lights-out. After we had been in quarantine for three weeks, Germaine fainted one day during the morning roll-call. It turned out that she had diphtheria. The following week it was my turn to faint: I had scarlet fever. We were given rudimentary medical care by Russian and Polish doctors in the sick-bay. Germaine's leg and mouth became paralysed. Her Czech neighbour in the next bed, who had already begun to recover, saved her life by forcing her to drink. This Czech woman, a tough and generous personality, was one of the leaders of the Czech Communist group in the camp. Her name was Hilda Synkova. People accused her of indifference to the fate of the Jewish prisoners, who often had nothing to eat, and of belonging to the bunch of Communist hard-liners who had sworn to tie Margarete Buber-Neumann[2] to the stake if and when the Russians liberated the camp. However, Hilda Synkova was always very friendly to the French prisoners, whatever their political persuasion. She committed suicide in 1948 after the Communist putsch in Prague.

When I emerged from the delirium caused by the scarlet fever I promptly contracted a painful ear infection. In the rare moments when I could still think straight, I was furious at the idea that I, the daughter of an ear, nose and throat specialist, should die of mastoiditis. Fortunately I succeeded in arousing the interest of a Polish doctor, who cured me with Prontosil.

In the sick-bay I witnessed the suffering and death of an old Czech peasant woman whose life contained two great loves: for her goat and her son, a technician. This anonymous death – would any of her nearest and dearest ever learn how she disappeared in the Nazi's ash-heap? – taught me to believe in the notion of eternal life. It seemed impossible that this modest life so full of love could be snuffed out forever.

Another of the patients in the sick-bay was a nine year-old boy called Peter, whose mother and little brother used to come and try to catch a glimpse of him through the window. The sadness of this child, who had to be coaxed into speaking and from whom I never managed to raise even the ghost of a smile, left a deep impression on me. His parents were Jews from Riga. The mother and the two small boys stayed in Ravensbrueck until they were sent to Bergen-Belsen shortly before the liberation of the camp. It is conceivable that they survived.

---

[2] Margarete Buber-Neumann was the companion of Heinz Neumann, the German Communist leader who was imprisoned and disappeared to Moscow in 1937. Margarete Buber-Neumann was herself arrested a year later and deported to Karaganda. Following the Hitler-Stalin pact she was handed over to the Gestapo at the beginning of 1940 and interned at Ravensbrueck. She has published two volumes of memoirs and now lives in Frankfurt am Main.

Work

After my stay in the sick-bay I was transferred to one of the worst huts at the edge of the camp. These huts were dirty, overcrowded and noisy, and theft and fights were regular occurrences. Eventually I met up with Germaine Tillion again, and together with her and a few of the other women, I endeavoured to keep up at least a minimum standard of civilized behaviour. Meanwhile the other comrades who had come with us from France had disappeared. They had been packed off to Barth, on the Baltic coast.

One day in February 1944 we saw them return, a small, dejected group with dead eyes; their faces and hair were sprinkled with iron filings. In Barth they had been installing pilots' cabins in Heinkel aeroplanes; one of them had slapped a wardress's face, and they had been collectively punished by being deprived of both food and sleep.

When I had recovered from my bout of scarlet fever, some of the Polish women had suggested to me that I should join the work detail which looked after the prisoners' clothing. The work was easy and clean, and it would have given me an opportunity to wash and change my linen. I hesitated, disliking the idea of working under better conditions than my other French comrades, and in the end I turned the suggestion down. However, if I had to choose again today, I would accept the offer. One simply had to seize opportunities of this kind which gave one a chance to help one's fellow prisoners. The *good Capos,* the 'trusties' with red armbands, performed an invaluable service, and the view that they were all no more than SS underlings is quite mistaken.

Hence I too was put to work transporting earth and stones. The containers used for this purpose were positively antediluvian in design, consisting of a simple wooden box with long carrying handles at either end, as in the days when the Pyramids were built. Each day we feared that we would be unable to hold out until the evening. But somehow we managed to carry on and get through the evening roll-call. After this I was transferred to a working party whose job it was to transport a load of heavy machinery to the tailoring workshop in the camp. I greatly admired the beautiful, strong girls in this working party, but I soon realized that the composition of the party was continually changing. Within a few weeks the girls were half-dead from exhaustion and fever. Many of them contracted a severe form of tuberculosis which carried them off within a couple of months. I was rescued by a Czech Capo called Milena Seborova[3], a wonderful woman who drafted me into the tailoring workshop, where the prisoners made uniforms for the SS. Cases regularly

---

[3] Milena Seborova was arrested in Prague in 1941 and charged with resistance activities in collaboration with the British. Having survived internment at Ravensbrueck, she was arrested again after the Communist putsch in Prague in 1948, brutally tortured and sentenced to five years' imprisonment. Although she was forbidden to leave the country, she managed to escape to the West in 1954. She has recently finished writing her memoirs and is currently looking for a publisher. She lives in the USA.

arrived containing fur jackets which had been confiscated from Russian and Polish peasants and which often bore traces of dried blood, together with the coats of Jewish men, women and children. Our task was to remove the linings and flatten down the fur, which was used to line the SS officers' long raincoats. Sometimes we found theatre tickets in the pockets or jewelry sewn into the hem of one of the coats. It was highly unpleasant work, but at least it was less arduous than loading bricks, transporting earth or pushing wheelbarrows under the eye of a whip-carrying guard.

Unfortunately, even doing this relatively easy job, I contracted tuberculosis. Thanks to the solidarity of my fellow prisoners I was then transferred to the gardening detail, so that I could at least be out in the open air, which would be better for my lungs. Yes, the *gardening* detail – all around the gloomy huts and the prison building with the cells which saw so many crimes there were flower-beds containing sage and asters. The SS who supervised the gardening detail was a courageous individual who had retained his Catholic faith: officially there were twenty women in the working party, but he was satisfied if ten of us were working at any given time. We took it in turns to rest or sunbathe behind the huts, and by the time the camp was liberated my lungs had completely healed up.

Nacht und Nebel

Given that I was a so-called 'N. N.' prisoner, it was astonishing that I was still alive in April 1945. Prisoners in this category ('N. N.' was the abbreviation for *Nacht und Nebel,* meaning 'under cover of Night') were marked down for liquidation and were allowed no contact with their families. They were prohibited from sending or receiving letters and parcels, and if their families or the International Red Cross in Geneva made enquiries about their welfare, the stock answer was that the individual in question was unknown to the authorities.

The *Nacht und Nebel* measures, initiated by Hitler and carried out by the Wehrmacht in December 1941, were directed against political opponents of the Reich in the occupied countries who were suspected of belonging to resistance movements. Many of the 'N. N.' prisoners were beheaded; others were sent to men's camps such as Hinzert, Natzweiler-Struthof or Gross-Rosen, where they were barbarically maltreated.

Paradoxically, the ' N. N.' prisoners in Ravensbrueck tended to be given preferential treatment. The commandant had appointed one of his most loyal stooges as the head of our hut: a German woman, not a political prisoner but a common criminal and a notorious informer, whose main ambition in life was to be the head of the best-run hut in the camp. Since she used her influence with the camp authorities to secure adequate supplies of soup, shoes and blankets, conditions in the hut were relatively decent. As well as political prisoners from France, Belgium, Holland and Norway, the inhabitants of the hut included gypsies and Russian and Polish women, with no 'antisocial elements'. We were joined by the Polish girls who had survived the medical experiments and by two hundred young women from the nursing corps of the Russian army, who by rights ought to have been treated as prisoners-of-war. We all helped each other out, paying special attention to the oldest and the youngest among us; we recited poems to each other, and on national or religious holidays we held little parties. We had banished from our minds all thought of our forthcoming execution. One evening, though, we were summoned outside to a roll-call at which our names were called out – the normal practice was simply to count us. This seemed like a bad omen, and that evening I was just as terrified as I had been that night at La Santé prison after the guard had told me that I was to be shot the following morning. I was gripped by the fear of death, a special kind of fear which takes possession of one's whole body. Germaine Tillion, who was standing next to me, sensed what was going through my mind. She took my hand and told me: 'My dear, always remember that whatever happens in life, even when all seems lost, there is always a five to ten per cent chance that things will change, a five to ten per cent uncertainty factor. That is a fundamental law of human life.' Oh, how I clutched at the straw of those percentages. And, to my relief, after an interval of several hours we were sent back to our huts. At the time we were unaware that in the men's camps, the Russian prisoners-of-war were often the first victims of the gas chambers.

In Ravensbrueck, it was the 'guinea pigs' who were the first to be selected for liquidation. On the evening of 2 February 1945 we heard that the guard was to be reinforced the next morning, that an alcohol ration had been issued in the SS canteen, and that two large trucks were standing parked outside the commandant's office. Our brave Polish comrades were facing their last night alive. Dismayed as we were, we tried to find them cigarettes and extra food. Their compatriots and the Russians persuaded them to make a last desperate attempt to hide. Although we were strictly forbidden to leave the hut, we spent the whole night organizing hiding-places and swapping round numbers. The next morning, before the roll-call, we let the girls out of the window. By a true miracle of solidarity they were able to hide away from the guards until the camp was liberated.

A month later, on 2 March 1945, it was the turn of the 'N. N.' prisoners from Western Europe to be liquidated. Instead of disposing with them on the spot, the SS sent them to Mauthausen with a group of gypsies. But against all expectation, they did not go to the gas chamber. Nobody ever found out why – perhaps the reason was that there were too many half-dead men waiting to be gassed, and the daily capacity of the gas chambers was exhausted. Those women who escaped the guards' bullets on the way from the railway station to the camp and the Allied bombardment of the station at Amstetten, and who were not sent to Bergen-Belsen, where so many prisoners died of typhus, were freed on 23 April by the International Red Cross and taken to Switzerland.

The selection procedure

Let us return, however, to 2 March 1945. Together with the gypsies we were locked into the punishment hut, where we sat waiting to be taken off to Mauthausen. Germaine Tillion mistakenly thought that this new situation might afford an opportunity to get her beloved mother to safety. Mme Tillion was a wonderful old lady of seventy-two, with a kindly, cheerful twinkle in her big blue eyes. For a whole year Germaine had succeeded in preserving her mother's health, but she had recently caught dysentery. Mme Tillion was not an 'N. N.' prisoner and lived in another hut, but Germaine managed to smuggle her into our group when we left for Mauthausen.

So there we were, up in the 'loft' of the punishment hut: the three-tier beds were desperately overcrowded with an additional 700 women on top of the 200 who normally lived there. Germaine had a painful abscess in her jaw and was running a high temperature. Unable to stand the pain any longer, she got permission from the SS guard to go to the sick-bay for treatment. Night fell, and I was alone with Mme Tillion, surrounded by women weeping with exhaustion and hunger, unable to turn round for lack of space. Unlike Germaine I was far from optimistic about being transferred to Mauthausen. The presence of so many gypsies was a bad sign. I had great difficulty in preventing my courage from evaporating. Did I start to pray? I am not quite sure, but I know for certain that I swore a solemn oath that night: if I ever got out off this terrible place alive I would continue to tell the world, to my dying breath, what I had seen and experienced in the camp. At the same time I knew that people would never believe my story of the ordeals we had undergone at the hands of the Nazis.

At last the dawn came. It was impossible to wash in the midst of such confusion. We had to line up in rows on the broad road leading through the sleeping camp. A friendly little French girl, the daughter of a Communist deputy who had been shot in Normandy, took Mme Tillion's other arm to support her. Well, I say 'support': it was the gesture which counted. The girl, Simone Sampaix, had been in Auschwitz; she was seventeen but she was so thin that she locked more like a twelve year-old, and it was unclear who was supporting whom.

Suddenly I feel someone barge straight into me. Under the eyes of the vainly protesting 'trusties' I am dragged away from Mme Tillion and hauled off at the double to a space between two of the huts, where a Czech woman[4], the

---

[4] Anicka Kvapilova worked at the City Library in Prague, where she hid members of the Resistance. She was arrested in 1941. After the 1948 Communist putsch she had to flee from Czechoslovakia. She found sanctuary in Norway, where she is still involved in the running of an organization which helps Czech refugees.

leader of the work detail which repaired the sewing-machines, hastily ties a red armband round my arm and whispers: 'Run off and hide in your hut, they're going to gas you in Mauthausen!' She disappears and I start to run. But what about Mme Tillion? Germaine has entrusted her to my care, and I can't just go off and leave her in the lurch. I walk along by the side of the huts, wait in hiding for a few minutes and then charge into the crowd between two guards and drag Mme Tillion off; Simone follows. The three of us run to the edge of the camp. I hide Mme Tillion in one of the huts where a few Frenchwomen still remain. As soon as it is safe to move around in the camp I go to the sick-bay to tell Germaine what has happened, but I can't see her there. The other patients promise to pass the message on. In the late afternoon, to my horror, I hear that the selection procedure for Mauthausen is to be extended to cover the entire camp. I leave my hut and walk over to the hut where Mme Tillion is hiding. I suggest that she should hide in the 'fourth floor' of the hut, i.e. between the ceiling and the roof, but she refuses. Trusting in providence, she is resigned to her fate. Ignorant of Simone's whereabouts, I feel desperately alone. In the crowd waiting for the selection procedure to begin, I recognise a Frenchwomen called Sylvie. Her face has a deathly pallor; her lungs are wrecked, her legs have been broken by her torturers and she has difficulty in standing up. We smile at each other, and a vestige of hope returns. We slap each other's and Mme Tillion's cheeks to give them a rosy glow. Sylvie almost succeeds in walking normally. We try to get Mme Tillion to walk as fast and as lithely as possible, and hide her white hair under her violet scarf. We take each other's arms. I am the first of five women on the right-hand side of the crowd, near the awful Winkelmann, the doctor in charge of the selection procedure.

The line of women begins to move. Under the electrified barbed wire, rows of agitated Capos and SS men with machine guns stand on either side of the line. We walk quickly towards Winkelmann, who is surrounded by a group of other doctors, plus the camp commandant and the matron of the sick-bay. I stand as tall and broad-shouldered as possible, trying to avert the doctors' gaze from Mme Tillion. But no: Winkelmann moves away from the group; lowering his head, he pushes through the line and points with his fat, stubby finger at the old lady. I pretend not to have noticed and walk on, pulling Mme Tillion with me. The guards come and drag her away. My heart stands still. The women around me are screaming and pushing, and I have to move on. My head is swimming.

The line dissolves and I find myself able to think again. What I have to do is find the 'chimney squad': they can't have reached the youth camp[5] yet. I

---

[5] The 'youth camp' (*Jugendschutzlager*) was a small camp for German juvenile delinquents, a mile or so away from the main camp. It was the place where the candidates for the gas chambers were assembled before going to their deaths.

must get hold of an influential Capo who can secure Mme Tillion's release. My eye falls on Big Carla, a Polish aristocrat who, like Mme Tillion, is an art historian: surely she will help me. But no: she is out to curry favour with the SS, so she doesn't want to know, and she shoves me roughly away. I can't expect any help from her. I can see Mme Tillion in the line of those marked down to die, with SS men and members of the camp police force watching over them. The only thing I could do would be to join her and go to my death with her. But I am afraid. And what would Germaine say? How, above all, would Mme Tillion herself react if she suddenly found me at her side? Surely she would be horrified, furious. I feel like a coward, all the more so because my cowardice is based on reason and logic. Torn between several conflicting impulses, I decide to try, at all events, to get word to Germaine. She had just been operated on and was herself about to undergo the selection procedure – the weakest patients in the sick-bay were also to be sent to Mauthausen. One of her fellow-patients was Margarete Buber-Neumann, who was recovering from an illness and hid Germaine in her bed by lying on top of her. The doctor carrying out the selection failed to notice what was going on.

How ever did I manage to communicate the terrible news to Germaine by shouting through the window of the sick-bay? How could I go back to my hut and throw myself on the straw mattress for which I only had luck to thank?

That night was the worst of my entire life. I suffered terrible agonies of guilt and remorse, and I could hardly bear to think of Germaine. Here was the final proof that I was no hero. After all, Germaine Tambour[6] had voluntarily joined the death squad to keep her sister company. But I had let Mme Tillion go to her death alone. . . .

Some years later at the theatre I had occasion to relive my sense of shame when I saw the scene in Georges Bernanos' play *Dialogues de Carmelites* in which the young Blanche de le Force selflessly opts to accompany her comrades to the scaffold with no thought of thanks or recognition.

Mme Tillion and the death squad were taken to the youth camp. There the selection procedure was repeated, and the chosen victims were carted away in trucks. There was a great deal of to-ing and fro-ing from the youth camp to the main camp. Germaine[7] tried everything to rescue her mother. But

---

[6] Germaine Tambour was a wonderful, hugely talented actress, a former pupil of Charles Dullin. She used to transport us miles away from Ravensbrueck by declaiming French poetry to us.

[7] The anthropologist Germaine Tillion was arrested in Paris in 1942 and charged with working for the Resistance. She spent several years researching the history of the Ravensbrueck camp and has published a book on the subject: *Ravensbrueck* Paris 1973. Following this she returned to her specialist area: the anthropology of the Mediterranean region. She is an Honorary Professor at the Ecole des Hautes Etudes en Sciences Sociales and a Grand Officer of the Legion d'honneur.

Mme Tillion was never seen again. I assume that she was gassed either that same evening or the following morning.

Seven weeks later we were freed and taken to Sweden by the Swedish Red Cross, and on 8 May 1945 we heard that Germany had finally surrendered to the Allies. But we were unable to rejoice: Mme Tillion and so many others had been taken away from us.

Meanwhile I was anxiously awaiting news of my father and my brother. I knew that one of them was in Dora and the other in Buchenwald. Eventually I heard that they were both still alive, but the same letter contained the news that my sister had been shot by the Germans near Paris on 27 August 1944. She was just twenty-three years old.

The Odyssey of the Women from Rhodes

On 20 July 1944, at seven o'clock in the morning, the Germans who had occupied Rhodes ordered all male Jews to register at German headquarters. Although they were told that they were being called together for work, they were all arrested. Shortly afterwards the women received the same order: if even one of them had failed to register by 10 o'clock on 21 July, all Jews would be executed. First Lieutenant Costa - a Jew himself - let it be known that the Germans had issued an order that the Jews were to take all their valuables with them: they might enable them to buy whatever was necessary for survival later on.

On the island of Rhodes itself the inmates were all locked in the office rooms of the air force command, and they were given nothing to eat or drink. Afterwards they were taken to the port to be shipped out. During the journey they had to walk around with their heads lowered, and were on no account allowed to look up. Anybody who dared to do so would be executed on the spot. Then all of them (men, women and children) were locked in the coal storage room of the ship: they were so crammed together that they were not even able to sit down. Finally the women were allowed to sleep on deck. In spite of the rain they preferred this to near suffocation in the filthy storage room.

Shortly before their departure the inmates were helped by a group of Italian

---

The Greek island of Rhodes, since 1921 de facto and since 1923 de juri part of the Italian Confederation of States, was the home of approximately 2.000 Jews. They were unmolested as long as Rhodes was under Italian rule. After the overthrow of Mussolini, however, the island was occupied by Germany in September 1943, and in July 1944 two SS officers arrived - together with the German commander of the East Aegean Islands, Lieutenant General Kleemann - in order to make arrangements for the deportation of the Jews of Rhodes. Unrest among members of the German 'Wehrmacht' was suppressed on the General's order, which stated that the 'Jewish question' could not by any stretch of the imagination be judged by the limited horizon of a soldier. 'In the interest of the measures initiated' any further discussion was to be refrained from (Nuremberg document NOKW 1801).

The death toll of Greek Jews and especially of those deported from the islands was extremely high. Not only did they suffer particularly from the climate, they also encountered greater difficulties with the language at Auschwitz than most other groups.

The fact that the Greek Jews were in bad condition upon their arrival (the percentage of those who were able to work upon arrival at Auschwitz averaged only 15%) was later also confirmed by Rudolf Hoess (see 'Kommandant in Auschwitz, Autobiographische Aufzeichnungen von Rudolf Höß', with an introduction and comment by Martin Broszat, Stuttgart 1958, p. 159).

sisters, who tried to make them believe that soon things would turn for the better. The boat trip from Rhodes to Piraeus took ten days. During the first three days no food was handed out, but in Leros (Lero) the Wehrmacht commander had food from the stocks distributed, some of which had been confiscated in Piraeus.

On the way from Piraeus to Chaidari the women were forced to strip in front of the SS men: if they hesitated to follow the order, because they felt embarrassed, they were brutally beaten. A body search was conducted to see whether they had concealed gold or jewelry. (In the meantime they had been robbed of everything they had brought along from Rhodes: cigarettes, crockery and even their underwear.) Finally all of them - women and men separately - were locked into barracks. (The men were left standing outside in the hot July sun all day long to wait for the patrols.)

Some of the rooms in which the men were kept did not have running water, and the Germans did not even consider having water brought over to these rooms. The men were so thirsty that five of them died. In a gesture of solidarity those men who were kept in rooms with running water broke a hole through the wall and put a pipe through. Since they did not have a container, they proceded to fill their mouths with water and spit it into the pipe. Those on the other side sucked it up. The Germans took malicious joy in pouring gasoline into Laura Hasson's elderly father's face; the gasoline got into his eyes and caused an infection, which lasted for several days.

As if they did not have to suffer enough as it were, their shoes were taken away from them if they were in good condition. They were beaten incessantly when they boarded the ship, then on the march and finally when they climbed up onto the truck. Even women and children - out of pure sadism - were whipped in the face.

They had departed from Rhodes as a group of 1,800 people. Because the severely sick were also taken along, approximately ten people died on the trip, and another fifty, among them mothers with children, died in Piraeus or Chaidari on account of the constant beatings. No member of the entire Jewish community on Rhodes was left behind. When they were locked into the small rooms, Laura Hasson asked one of the SS whether she could get her father something to eat. The SS soldier answered that she could do what she wanted to if the girl 'was nice to him'. Laura was not the only one to receive such offers. The other girls received them as well and more than once.

In Chaidari, when everyone in the courtyard screamed and begged for water the SS told them that they could all go to a nearby well and get themselves some. All of them ran there, but when three or four persons were standing at the well, the SS began beating the others who came running towards the well on the head with clubs and leather belts - regardless of whether they were women or children - in order to hold them back. The SS considered it to be some kind of game and repeated it several times that day to entertain themselves.

The deportees had to spend a further three days in Athens. There they were fed by the Red Cross. Then they left by train for Auschwitz in Poland. They traveled in cattle cars which held 70 persons each, both men and women. The Red Cross had had food and water delivered to the individual cars. During the trip, which took more than fifteen days, the prisoners were allowed to leave the cattle cars only three or four times. They all had to defecate and urinate into tin cans – right in front of everybody else – which were then emptied out of the window.

When they arrived at Auschwitz they had to undergo a selection process by the SS doctors: the young men and women who were able to work were waved to one side; the elderly, children and mothers with small children in their arms to the other. This group of the so-called 'unworthy' were taken to another place and exterminated. All those young people who did not want to leave their parents alone, men who did not want to leave their young wives and babies behind, and mothers who did not want to be separated from their children also died in this manner.

Laura Hasson carried her young nephew in her arms. At Auschwitz railroad station a Greek from Saloniki whispered into her ear, "Give the child to another woman, but make sure that it is an old one!" Laura did not understand what the Greek was trying to tell her, and instead gave the child back to its mother, her twenty-year-old sister-in-law . . .

The girls ended up being led into filthy barracks, which, in addition, were besmeared with excrement. Again they had to undress in front of the SS and the other inmates, and were allowed to take only a cake of soap and a toothbrush with them. Completely naked they were led into a different room, where female barbers shaved their entire body. In a room next door they were then disinfected with a rag soaked in kerosene, which heavily irritated the freshly shaved skin. They then had to take a shower, but received nothing to dry themselves with. They were each given a ragged dress without any regard paid to length or size. When they asked if they could exchange their dresses for ones which were better fitting, gypsy prisoners beat them. They did not receive any underwear. Thus the dresses they were wearing had to serve both as undershirt and panties, both as handkerchief and towel. At four o'clock in the morning they were allowed to leave the disinfection rooms. Their feet were clad with wooden shoes, in which they had to walk to the already overcrowded barracks. There were no beds in the barracks, only wooden boards. Twelve people had to make do with less than two square meters. The boards were set up in three stories and so poorly attached that they often fell on the boards beneath.

A Jewish inmate told them: 'You are suffering, but the elderly will not suffer'. An Italian Jew from Rome warned them: 'Never tell them that you are sick. Even if you have a fever of 104, never tell them'. They soon understood the meaning of these words.

They remained at Auschwitz for two and a half months. Every morning they had to kneel in the middle of the block road for hours. Of the block personnel one Polish Jewess by the name of Magda, called 'The Wild One' was to be remembered for her cruelties. She would beat them on the head, in the face, and beat their fingers with a riding whip. (The personnel was made up of Polish and Hungarian women.) The young women's work consisted of car-carrying roofing tiles. A 15-kilogramm load had to be carried over a distance of two to three kilometers. Had it not been for the cold, the bad nutrition and the wet tiles, it would have been tolerable. At times they even had to move barrels or do other harassing jobs.

Any contact with other inmates was prohibited. Even if they were neighbors, they were not allowed to help or console each other. One young Hungarian woman was executed on the spot when she was caught talking with her mother in a neighboring camp.

Food was as follows: in the morning there were two cans of so-called 'coffee' for 800 people, which meant that not everyone got some; at noon a roll call of sorts for the distribution of the soup took place; however, this could happen at any time of day, either at nine o'clock in the morning or at five in the afternoon, you never knew when the soup was to be distributed. One liter of soup had to suffice for five people. Nobody had a spoon, so all of them had to drink out of the same bowl, sip by sip. So there were quarrels and some serious clashes. The soup was so disgusting that none of the women who have told this story felt able to eat it for the first three days. All the women who worked in the kitchen attested to the fact that an SS woman from the dispensary – presumably a nurse – added some chemical substance to the soup which was to be given to the deportees. It gave the soup a bitter taste and caused a burning feeling in the mouth, the stomach and in the intestines. Moreover, it caused itching in their stomachs and manifested itself in swellings and red patches, which looked like long and straight scratches.

Every other day a female SS doctor came to see the women in the barracks, had them undress (they did not wear any underwear) and checked the swellings and patches. All the inmates had the same symptoms, though not all at the same time. In the case of all women, however, the chemical immediately stopped menstruation.

Furthermore, almost all of the women had actual holes in their mouths and deep cracks on their tongues. In some cases the effects were so bad that they no longer wanted to eat and died of starvation. This was the case with all those women who already had holes had in their throats thus preventing them from swallowing.

Those women in whom swellings and patches had developed, were transferred to the dispensary, where they had to undergo tests. All of them enjoyed going there, because then they did not have to work for a few days. Only then, after they had not eaten the soup with the powder added for ten weeks, did menstruation return, as was the case of two of the women who tell their story here; however, this was not the case with the two others, in spite of the fact that they were twenty and thirty years old respectively. These two women believe that the SS orderlies' attempt to sterilize them without having to operate was unsuccessful simply because they were at Auschwitz-Birkenau for only two and a half months, and moreover, because they intentionally ate as little of the soup as possible. They tried to stick to the raw potatoes they stole from the supply cars. Giovanna Hasson explained that she ate potato peels when she was released from the dispensary – that was how hungry she was. The others did the same: they gulped down unwashed potato peels. It was precisely because many ate raw potatoes and unwashed peels that the most widespread disease in the camp was dysentery. Its effects were so bad that it could sometimes not be cured and resulted in death.

During the whole time the women were under arrest their hair was cut off once only. Only when they were full of lice were their bodies entirely shaved and disinfected once again. They received underwear only once, on their departure from Poland for Germany. They received no more underwear. The SS-doctor Blanka, who had been sent by the camp dispensary, accompanied the women on their 'pilgrimage'. He conducted the selection process outdoors. The women had to stand barefoot and without coats in snow and ice, the temperature several degress below zero. In this way he could discover whether or not the women were still strong enough. If they turned pale and passed out they were put on the transfer list. This also happened to the four women reporting here. They had already reached a state of complete exhaustion.

They were taken to 'camp 2' in Kaufering, Germany. There they stayed for six weeks. Their job consisted of shoveling snow into a shed, pushing carts loaded with dying people, doing the dishes in the kitchen, at times assisting the SS or cleaning the toilets. If they were assigned work outside the camp they had to walk eight kilometers each way. At four o'clock in the morning they were woken up, and at six o'clock at night they returned to the barracks.

'Camp 2' was a real inferno. There was no 'break' (i.e. an interruption from work to eat the additional piece of bread which was sometimes distributed to those who worked). The barracks were disgusting, half underground and without bunk beds. The women slept on some long boards on the floor, on which some hay was spread out. The ceiling of the room was so low that they were unable to sit up. At the same time, due to the steeply slanted roof, there was no more than 10 cm room for their feet. These were not barracks but dog kennels, and they were absolutely filthy. Nevertheless, the women managed to stay more or less clean and free of lice by trading their bread for soap from the men. This is why the men looked bedraggled and were full of lice. Here too the roll calls were conducted out in the open. Not all commandos were entitled to soup at noon, and unfortunately it was precisely those who had to work the hardest who were excluded from the rations. This occured in both the worse and better work commandos, at random and not for reasons of

punishment. The inmates owned neither shoes nor coats nor clothes. Thus they tried to protect themselves from the cold with rags from blankets. Anyone who was not assigned to a work commando received soup only a day. It was thanks to particularly favorable circumstances that some work commandos received soup twice a day: at noon and in the evening and, in addition, a slice of bread and marmelade or salami or something else.
From 'camp 2' the women were transferred to 'camp 8'. In order to get there they had to walk approximately twenty kilometers. When they arrived at the camp they found that it had been completely vacated, and for two days they had nothing to eat. The group consisted of approximately 800 newly arrived prisoners. The uniform stores were also absolutely empty, so that they could not even get blankets for the night. As of the third day in the camp everybody received half a liter of soup, and nobody had to work. They stayed there for 14 days, when they had to move to 'camp 7', where they stayed for approximately four months. It was the best place of all. Due to typhus the camp had been placed under quarantine and so they were spared the tortures of forced labor. Moreover, for the first time everybody in this camp received a full liter of soup.
After that they were taken to 'camp 11', a really terrible camp: they had to get up at four in the morning and march eighteen kilometers to Oberigling, where they had to clear away rubble. They received absolutely nothing to eat through the entire work-filled day. The bread ration (one eighth of a loaf of bread, or a quarter, if the bread showed signs of mold) with the usual margarine (as big as a small piece of chalk) or a little of the weird salami from the camp was distributed during work in the morning, at approximately ten or eleven o'clock.
All day long they received nothing else to eat, despite the fact that shoveling rubble was extremely hard work, especially for women. At night, when they returned, they were given soup. This 'starvation camp' was the most terrible of all, and the death toll was particularly high. Fortunately, they stayed for only ten days, because the American troops were approaching. For this reason the camp was vacated and set on fire. This was done in order to prevent evidence of the terrible events in these barracks from falling into the hand of the Americans.
The women, already ill, were transferred to 'camp 1', others were taken to a different place; no trace of them was left behind. In 'camp 1' they stayed for a total of three days. Then they were loaded onto open freight cars. During the night-trip it rained and sleeted. Suddenly it seemed as though the train was in the vicinity of the approaching American troops. The SS troops left the train and fled. The train, however, remained on the tracks next to a munitions transport. During the trip the train was bombed and shot at several times. In air raids five women were killed and many were injured. In the cars in which the men had been transported the number of deaths and injuries was considerably higher. When the train had stopped the hail continued, but

the women were so weak that they felt they were neither able to open the train car door nor climb over the car's side wall. But the men helped them. They told them that the train right next to theirs had been set on fire by fleeing SS personnel, both to prevent it from falling into the hands of the approaching troops, and to exterminate the deportees in this way. The women, who were terrified, threw themselves under the train cars and decided either to flee across the meadows to the woods or to hide in the nearby dairy. It was still night. While they fled they heard the noise of an explosion: the munitions train had blown up. They saw the brilliantly lit sky above Landsberg, which was on fire because of the air raids.

In order not to fall into the hands of the Germans again Sara Benatar suggested walking in the direction of the cannon fire. Judging from the noise of the explosion, the front could not be far away. But while they were heading towards the front they met Germans retreating on foot or in vehicles. The German soldiers began firing at the fugitives in order to push them back in the direction of the railroad. Many women and men who had followed Sara Benatar's advice, collapsed in the face of the Germans' firing.

The road was also covered with dead bodies. Some people had been killed during the air raids, others no longer had the strength to leave the train cars or to move away from the train. They were killed either in the explosion of the other train parked nearby or in the flames of the train cars. Others, who had thrown themselves under the train, died on the tracks. They were run over the moment the train began to move. Still others, who had been pushed back by the Germans, fell to the ground while attempting to climb back into the cars and no longer had the strength to stand up again.

Some of the stronger men managed to avoid recapture because they had been hiding in the woods behind trees and bushes.

When some of the deportees had just gotten back into the car, the train was set in motion and crushed those who had dropped to the ground, because they could not hold on tightly enough, and those who had been left lying on the tracks.

The few surviving women reached Dachau on 28 April 1945. They were the first deported women to set foot in this camp for men. The next day, 29 April 1945, at five o'clock in the evening, the camp was liberated by American troops.

Sara Benatar   Anne Cohen   Giovanna Hasson   Laura Hasson